DELINQUENT BEHAVIOR

fourth edition ————

DELINQUENT
BEHAVIOR

DON C. GIBBONS
Portland State University

MARVIN D. KROHN
State University of New York at Albany

Prentice-Hall, Inc., Englewood Cliffs, New Jersey 07632

Library of Congress Cataloging in Publication Data

Gibbons, Don C.
   Delinquent behavior.

   Includes bibilographies and index.
   1. Juvenile delinquency–United States.
2. Juvenile justice, Administration of–United States.
3. Rehabilitation of juvenile delinquents–United States.
I. Krohn, Marvin, D.   II. Title.
HV9104.G53   1986   364.3'6   85-12405
ISBN 0-13-197989-2

Editorial/production supervision and
   interior design: Barbara DeVries
Cover design: Ben Santora
Manufacturing buyer: John B. Hall

Printed in the United States of America

10 9 8 7 6 5 4 3 2 1

ISBN 0-13-197989-2 01

Prentice-Hall International (UK) Limited, *London*
Prentice-Hall of Australia Pty. Limited, *Sydney*
Prentice-Hall Canada Inc., *Toronto*
Prentice-Hall Hispanoamericana, S.A., *Mexico*
Prentice-Hall of India Private Limited, *New Delhi*
Prentice-Hall of Japan, Inc., *Tokyo*
Prentice-Hall of Southeast Asia Pte. Ltd., *Singapore*
Editora Prentice-Hall do Brasil, Ltda., *Rio de Janiero*
Whitehall Books Limited, *Wellington, New Zealand*

CONTENTS

PREFACE

The preface of earlier editions of this text described it as "a small book with a large cast of characters." That description drew attention to the fact that youngsters who engage in at least petty acts of lawbreaking during their adolescent years are extremely numerous. Then, too, the social audience that responds to youthful lawbreaking is a very large one, as is the collection of workers who run the juvenile justice machinery. Finally, the cast of characters is large in that about six hundred names of social scientists appear in the index. Theorizing about delinquency and research inquiry into this phenomenon has engaged that attention of a large number of scholars, particularly in the past two or three decades.

This edition differs from those which preceded it in that it has two authors rather than one. The expansion of the theoretical and research literature on delinquency has made it very difficult for a single author to master this material. And if the literature on delinquency poses a problem for professional sociologists, what about students who are confronted with it for the first time in a textbook? Some students are likely to feel overwhelmed by the details of the various theories and research studies considered in the pages of this book. Even so, it ought to be noted that only a sampling of contemporary theory and research on delinquency is presented here, for the social science literature continues to expand at a rapid rate.

This textbook endeavors to take stock of the knowledge accumulated to date. We have tried to provide a succinct, coherent picture of the major facets of youthful lawbreaking. Concerning the theoretical and research stockpile, we have also tried to address the question: "What does it all mean?" The reader will find about fifty major generalizations or propositions regarding the nature, causes, and control of delinquency distributed throughout the book and collated in the final chapter.

This is a sociological work in which social factors and influences in delinquent conduct are given heavy stress, although a good deal of commentary on psychological factors also appears. But an analysis of delinquency would be incomplete without some attention to social responses to youth behavior as well. Community attitudes have much to do with determining the rate at which youngsters will be apprehended by the police and turned over to the juvenile court. It may well be that many of the actions taken against offenders by courts, probation officers, training school employees, and so on, have the unintended effect of driving them further into careers in lawbreaking. Accordingly, we need to look closely at the social control side of the delinquency problem.

This edition has been revised and restructured considerably, with three new chapters on causation which are designed to clear up murky portions of the earlier editions and to provide the student with a more systematic understanding of causal thinking. This edition also contains a large quantity of new material on police responses to offenders, correctional treatment, and newer approaches to delinquency prevention and control.

We are indebted to a number of persons for help in the development of both the earlier versions and the present edition of this book. This edition and previous editions have benefited from the insights of Prentice-Hall reviewers including Richard Brede, Kansas State University, William E. Thompson, Emporia State University, Stephen Cernkovich, Bowling Green State University and Leonard Rosen, Temple University. We also wish to express our appreciation for the valuable secretarial assistance of Mary Smith and Fern Hudson, University of Iowa. As coauthors, we shared jointly in the revision and writing of the chapters of this edition. Finally, the defects that remain in the book are solely our own responsibility.

Don C. Gibbons
Marvin D. Krohn

DELINQUENT
BEHAVIOR

chapter 1

THE STUDY OF DELINQUENCY

INTRODUCTION

"Juvenile delinquency" is a social invention of relatively modern times. It grew out of the creation of the first American juvenile court in Cook County, Illinois in 1899, and involved legislation that separated youthful lawbreakers from adult ones, with differing court and correctional processes being employed with the two groups. At the same time, misbehavior on the part of children and adolescents has apparently been commonplace for a very long time, judging from the written records of earlier societies (Sanders, 1970). Indeed, some authorities have noted that the ancient Code of Hammurabi, written in 2270 B.C., contained passages that indicated a special concern for lawbreaking on the part of children (Cavan and Ferdinand, 1981: 6-9). Apparently over much of human history, the period of late childhood and adolescence has been marked by parent-child conflict, breaching of parental rules and limits by youngsters, and youthful misconduct, as young persons have gone about "testing their wings" and endeavoring to negotiate the social passage from childhood to adulthood.

"Juvenile delinquency" is often a normal or at least a common manifestation of the processes of maturation and development which children undergo. Moreover, as we shall see in subsequent pages of this book, it frequently consists of transitory, episodic, and relatively innocuous acts on the part of youngsters. However, the average citizen often holds very different views on delinquency and delinquents, believing the delinquency problem to be much more serious and threatening to social stability than is factually warranted. On this point, a national opinion poll in 1982 found that 87 percent of the citizens surveyed agreed that "there has been a steady and alarming increase in the rate of juvenile crime" (Galvin and Polk, 1983: 330). But the fact is that the arrest rates for juveniles actually *decreased* in the United States from 1971 to 1981, with the decline being most pronounced since 1974 (Krisberg and Schwartz, 1983: 333-64).

What is the nature of delinquency? What are the causes of juvenile misconduct? Public views of delinquents and various other persons who are judged to be deviants in American society are often wide of the mark. Not infrequently, lay persons exhibit a view of the world in which norm violators are viewed as a distinct breed of persons, sharply set off from conformists. As one sociologist has put it, lay citizens often regard nearly all those who are identified as deviants as "nuts, sluts, and preverts," that is, as persons who are markedly different from the rest of us (Liazos, 1972).

Regarding the causes of delinquency, citizens' beliefs often center around biological defects, inadequacies of family life, bad companions, or similar forces thought to be unique to delinquents. In other words, citizens usually attribute juvenile misconduct to a few bad influences—forces from which the public respondent is immune.

In the lay person's view of delinquency, the police, juvenile courts, probation departments, training schools, and other social control agencies merely *react* to youthful misconduct. Citizens often assume that there is a fixed occurrence of juvenile delinquency in the community over which the law enforcement and correctional organizations have little control. Rarely do citizens perceive that these agencies play a major role in determining the size of the group of juvenile delinquents through the policies they adopt and pursue. Concurrently, while training schools are sometimes denounced as "crime schools" that allegedly exacerbate youthful lawbreaking tendencies, most of the time citizens exhibit little appreciation of the possibility that the correctional machinery may play a significant role in pushing many youngsters toward persistent careers in criminality rather than away from these lines of conduct.

Parenthetically, these public notions about the delinquency problem also informed the delinquency textbooks and other writings of an earlier generation of sociologists. These books implied that youths come in two varieties, *delinquents* and *nondelinquents*. In turn, delinquency was viewed as something that certain juveniles "catch" or acquire due to adverse social circumstances, distortions in family life, and the like. Those who escaped those experiences were seen as relatively free from involvement in lawbreaking activities.

Beliefs of this kind continue to loom large in the public wisdom about "the delinquency problem." Consequently, many students in juvenile delinquency courses come into the classroom with preconceived opinions. They often approach courses in criminology and delinquency with considerable enthusiasm—for they apparently assume that a window will be opened for them through which they will be able to view the exotic, unusual activities of nuts, sluts, perverts, and delinquents.

However, as we shall discover in detail in the following pages, juvenile misconduct and responses to it are complex phenomena that require careful and detailed scrutiny if they are to be understood. Let us take a brief look at some of the major facets of the social reality of delinquency, that is, of juvenile lawbreaking and efforts to control it.

THE SOCIAL REALITY OF DELINQUENCY

The Invention of "Delinquency"

Although all societies apparently go about sorting some of their members out as wicked, sinful, or deviant, the kinds and numbers of persons who are the targets of social condemnation vary from one society to another and from one time period to another within a single society. Although it may not be true that yesterday's sinners are usually today's saints, a good deal of shifting does occur over time, so that social definitions of deviants and conformists undergo significant changes. Then, too, social responses to negatively regarded groups vary from one historical epoch to another. For example, criminals have suffered banishment from society at one time, while at others, persons guilty of identical crimes have been incarcerated in prison or workhouses, executed, or dealt with in some other way. Finally, these changes and fluctuations in socially devalued groups and social responses to them are not capricious or random, and do not occur by chance and happenstance. Instead, shifts in social definitions of right and wrong, normal and abnormal, and the like are related in important ways to major alterations in social, economic, and political conditions, as are these changing social practices.

In the past decade or two, historians and other social scientists have provided us with some richly textured accounts of changes that have occurred in societal standards of conduct and categories of socially devalued persons. A case in point is historian William Nelson's (1975) study of shifts in criminal law and procedures in the Massachusetts Puritan colony from 1760 to 1830. He rummaged through court records to uncover the nature of law and prosecution during that period and found drastic changes in the system. In the pre-Revolutionary period, juries were empowered to create laws as well as to determine matters of fact. The laws functioned to enforce the Puritan morality of a tightly knit religious community, and accordingly, blasphemy was a serious crime. Also, property and contract law restrained people from pursuit of wealth and financial speculation. However, that legal system became outmoded in post-Revolutionary America. The emerging economy required new laws that would reduce the strictures on economic activity and the pursuit of financial success. Property and contract laws were eventually revised to focus on the protection of private property. Nelson concluded that this transformation of the Massachusetts legal system both mirrored the changing nature of American society and helped to speed up the growth of an entrepreneurial society.

Another historical account of the twists and turns that have occurred in societal notions about "problem populations" such as paupers, criminals, vagrants, and the like can be found in Paul Boyer's (1978) study of public attitudes in the United States between 1820 and 1920 toward various persons who were at that time seen as "immoral" or in some other way tainted, flawed, or troublesome. Boyer indicated that the gradual but inexorable urbanization of American society over this period produced shifting moral judgments and also led to a variety of efforts to restore a moral order that was thought to be deteriorating. Historian David Rothman's (1971) penetrating historical examination of the growth and decline of incarceration of societal rejects and socially devalued persons in asylums, prisons, training schools, poor farms, and kindred places offers some parallel facts about historical alterations in societal responses to its members who are regarded as disreputable, immoral, or in some other way flawed.

Turning to youthful misconduct, if a group of citizens were asked to identify some of the major inventions of the twentieth century, they would probably nominate television, jet airplanes, space satellites, and other gadgetry. Few would declare that juvenile delinquency was a major social invention. Nonetheless, as a number of investigators have indicated, creation of the first juvenile court in 1899 and the accompanying legal category of juvenile delinquency, was the culmination of a longer historical drift beginning in the sixteenth and seventeenth centuries, in which the social concept of childhood slowly emerged (Platt, 1969; Schultz, 1973; Empey, 1982: 17–74; Schlossman, 1977). Before these two centuries, children were regarded as "adults in tiny bodies" and little or no special protection from harmful social conditions was provided for them (Aries, 1962). Slowly, over a period of several hundred years, *childhood* began to be defined as a distinct age period and *children* began to be singled out for special attention and protection. Finally, following the establishment of the first juvenile court, this new social apparatus quickly spread throughout the nation, as did the new social category of deviant— the *juvenile delinquent.*

The child-saving movement which led to the creation of the juvenile court and juvenile delinquency was part of a larger sweep of events in nineteenth-century America, often designated by historians as the Progressive Era (Gibbons, 1979: 18–37). The progressive movement centered around reformist concerns regarding the harsh concomitants of rapid industrialization and urbanization that were overtaking the country. Recruits to progressivism were appalled by the stark contrasts between the unbridled power and immense wealth of industrial plutocrats and the abject misery of the great mass of workers. Progressivism drew into its ranks a collection of middle-class farm owners, small businessmen, and myriad other individuals who supported programs for creating healthy work conditions, decent housing, public ownership of power, and scientific administration of cities, as well as efforts to deal positively with social problems.

There is little doubt that the child-saving movement, the invention of delinquency, and the creation of the juvenile court were responses to social changes that had been set in motion during this period of industrialization and rapid urbanization in the United States. However, when we return in Chapter 2 to a more detailed examination of the juvenile court, we shall see that some of these historical developments are murky, with the result that scholars are not in complete agreement concerning the origins of delinquency and the juvenile court. While most commentators agree that the newly created juvenile justice machinery was developed as a device through which unemployed youngsters and other troublesome juveniles could be controlled and made into malleable members of the working class, others see the juvenile court movement as an instrument of a powerful American ruling class, whereas still others argue that the sources of support were more diffuse.

The Production of Delinquency

Juvenile delinquency is a changing *social product,* with the size and nature of the population of juvenile delinquents being as much a matter of the level of concern in the community about youthful misconduct and policies of the police and courts as it is of the number of norm-violating juveniles. The boundaries of the category of delinquency are elastic, stretching and contracting with the changing winds of community opinion. The delinquency problem is a phenomenon involving interactions between juveniles, adult social audiences, and social control agencies.

Delinquency is a multidimensional problem. To understand it, we must consider the behavioral activities of youths, but we must also examine the ways in which the workings of the police, juvenile courts, and other segments of the social control machinery influence it. In addition, we need to understand various legislative dimensions of the problem and the state of public opinion and perspectives.

Legislators and citizens control the resources that can be allocated to delinquency control programs, specify other restraints upon rehabilitation and preventive endeavors, and constitute part of the problem in other ways as well. Furthermore, a truly adequate analysis of the delinquency problem would need to examine the ways in which it is related to basic features of the American economy, such as the enforced idleness assigned to youths by the system, and those deficiencies of the current social order which lead to pervasive alienation of the young.

The Nature and Extent of Delinquency

At the outset, we need to be clear about the basic ingredients of juvenile delinquency and the essential nature of juvenile delinquents. Juvenile delinquency consists of *acts* or *infractions* which are prohibited in the statutes of the individual states. Juvenile delinquents are youths who commit one or more of these infractions. When we identify someone as a delinquent, we ought to keep clearly in mind that this description usually refers to only a small portion of the total behavior of that youth. Most youngsters are "juvenile" most of the time, rather than delinquents; most of their activities center about going to school, leisure pursuits, sleeping, eating, working at part-time jobs, and other lines of activity that have little or nothing to do with misconduct. In short, juvenile delinquents do not constitute a special kind of person or social type. Delinquency is a sometime thing.

We also need to distinguish between juvenile delinquency, defined as behavioral infractions (illegal acts) that some youths engage in, and official *rates* of delinquency constructed from police statistics or juvenile court referrals. Although rates reflect violations occurring in the community, at least to some extent, they are sometimes only slightly correlated with the real incidence of infraction in the community. Thus a high delinquency rate in a neighborhood may reflect a high incidence of infraction, but it may also mirror police practices, the level of community concern about delinquency, or a combination of all these factors.

We shall see in Chapter 5 that individual police departments vary markedly in the ways they handle the misbehaving youths who come to their attention. Some law enforcement agencies refer nearly all juveniles they encounter to the court. Others handle almost all cases informally, giving tongue-lashings and verbal admonitions to youngsters rather than taking them to court. Then, too, a number of studies have shown that the police respond differently to black youths, males, and some other kinds of juveniles than they do to other offenders. Additionally, within a particular community the police often deal with youths from one neighborhood quite differently from youngsters from another area, sending those from the first to court while handling the other group informally. In all of this, it is apparent that police referral rates are an index to police practice as well as to youthful infractions.

A high volume of recorded lawbreaking or an increasing rate of delinquency does not necessarily mean that the community is experiencing a crime wave. Conversely, public concern about the delinquency problem is not solely a function of the true volume and seriousness of infractions, being influenced also by the degree of political and mass media attention devoted to the subject of crime in the streets. In the case of delinquency as well as in many other forms of deviant behavior, a wide gap often exists between the actual incidence of some form of conduct and citizen perceptions about that phenomenon. Citizens usually know very little about delinquency in their own communities or about the correctional system that is supposed to deal with the problem.

Another central point with respect to delinquent conduct is that the delinquent-nondelinquent dichotomy is highly misleading. The research evidence from self-report studies of "hidden offenders" and from inquiries into victimization that we shall examine in Chapter 3 suggests that persons who never violate the law are rarely encountered in modern societies. Some juveniles infrequently engage in law violations, while others break laws with greater frequency and in a predatory or aggressive manner. Finally, a very few become deeply enmeshed in misconduct and proceed on to a crime career as a way of life. The most important difference may be between those juveniles who commit some delinquent acts and those who commit many delinquent acts (Dunford and Elliott, 1984).

Delinquency Causation

By now, social science research has produced enough sound empirical evidence that it is possible to indicate a number of valid propositions about delinquency causation. One thing which is clear is that *juvenile delinquency exists in varying degrees and takes a variety of forms;* it is an omnibus term covering a wide spectrum of youthful infraction. Delinquent behavior varies in frequency, duration, and seriousness, and sometimes involves different forms of *specialization.* Some offenders engage in drug use, while others carry out sex offenses, predatory acts, or other patterns of conduct.

Whatever the particular acts of offenders, many of these youths are flirting with lawbreaking, rather than being deeply entangled in deviance. Most juvenile offenders engage in *episodic* acts of lawbreaking interspersed among longer periods of lawabiding conduct. Also, delinquency is most often a *transitory* phenomenon, and many youths grow out of this activity, whether anything is done to them or not. Finally, because most youthful offenders are psychologically normal and reasonably well-adjusted, their lawbreaking conduct cannot be attributed to psychological maladjustment.

Delinquency, like all other social behavior, has complex roots. One thing we have learned through a century of social science endeavors is that simple explanations of human behavior are usually inadequate. In the case of youthful lawbreaking, we should acknowledge that this activity usually is rooted in basic features of social organization and is no less normal or basic as behavior than is conforming conduct. Accordingly, we will need to discover and develop sociologically penetrating and complex theories if we are to provide an adequate characterization of the origins of delinquent conduct. Many of the pages in the chapters that follow center about that task.

In addition, given the many forms of delinquent conduct, it is unlikely that a single theoretical formulation can be developed to provide answers to causal or etiological questions. Rather, it is probably the case that female delinquency, for example, is to be explained by an etiological formulation different from the one that makes the most sense out of working-class, subcultural delinquency or some other pattern of misconduct (Shoemaker, 1984).

Traditional perspectives on causation have usually focused on some image of offenders that portrayed them as pushed or driven toward lawbreaking by a pattern of attitudes or motivation acquired through their particular life experiences. Thus male gang delinquents have often been viewed as alienated from lawabiding influences and groups as a result of their social position of economic precariousness or because of particular parental and peer influences in their community. In this view of things, these offenders acquire some kind of motivational motor that drives them toward nonconformity before they actually get involved in misconduct. For example, parallel arguments have been advanced regarding female delinquents who supposedly are motivated by hostility toward parental figures.

However, these motivational views are frequently wide of the mark. There is mounting evidence to indicate that many juveniles are not specifically motivated to engage in lawbreaking; rather, many of them drift into infractions by responding to situational pressures and inducements (Gibbons, 1971). Many youngsters engage in delinquent acts as spur-of-the-moment, hedonistic endeavors which constitute a form of risk-taking behavior.

Social Responses to Delinquency

From its origin in 1899 to the present, the juvenile court has usually been viewed as one of the finer inventions of the human mind. Traditional thoughtways have rarely paid much attention to the possibility that social responses toward delinquency, particularly those of the juvenile justice system, may propel many youths further into lawbreaking rather than out of it. Instead, the usual view has been that delinquency is a major social problem and that social control agencies ought to intervene when offenders come to their attention so as to rehabilitate those youngsters and rescue them from nonconformity. In all of this, it has usually been assumed that the juvenile control and correctional agencies are equal to the task of rehabilitation, and thus this is a realistic goal to pursue.

These assumptions have begun, however, to come under attack. The newer perspective on delinquency which stresses its episodic, transitory, and situational nature, along with the relatively innocuous and socially harmless character of much of it, leads to the conclusion that the best policy in many cases would be one of minimal intervention into the lives of juveniles.

Those of this persuasion argue that there is little evidence to indicate that court intervention in cases of petty or casual infraction is always useful; instead, it may often be harmful. In short, the fewer juveniles in court the better. Youngsters should not be placed in the quasi-official status of "delinquent" through such devices as informal probation, for there is no evidence that this practice has any effect upon them. Moreover, there are ethical and legal questions to be raised about such policies. This is the reasoning behind the establishment of diversion programs and other alternatives to the juvenile court, intended to keep juvenile offenders out of the official court machinery.

Our view is that delinquency is an important problem requiring attention, but we would assign it a relatively low position in a rank-ordering of social problems in need of control or amelioration. Who is to say that delinquency control ranks as high as smog reduction, alleviation of urban traffic congestion, or reversal of the general deterioration of the social, economic, and moral quality of life in American society? Youthful infraction often involves relatively less social cost than many other forms of deviance.

Then, too, we join with others who have argued fairly pessimistically about juvenile correctional endeavors. A basic fact of life which is of crucial import to efforts of this kind is that the causes of delinquency are not entirely understood, so that current treatment or prevention activities are a form of tinkering rather than skilled social engineering. Also, some serious ethical issues arise when we propose to intervene in the lives of many misbehaving youths; thus the best approach to delinquency would appear to be conservative, in at least one sense. There may be little warrant for efforts to expand the size of the target population for intervention efforts.

Programs of prevention and control are frequently poorly planned, uncoordinated, and operate at cross purposes. As one case in point, treatment and prevention efforts are often impeded by community agency policies in which certain youths are hoarded or locked out by admission policies of these agencies (Emerson, 1969). Delinquency control endeavors are frequently established and implemented not because of their proven value or demonstrated effectiveness, but rather because of political reasons. Funds for planning grants, demonstration projects, and so forth, are allocated largely on the basis of political expediency.

The sociological cynic would also point out that delinquency control agencies and officials have a stake in keeping the problem of juvenile lawbreaking alive, and in perpetuating current programs. The juvenile justice system, including the schools, police, juvenile courts, probation departments, correctional institutions, and other agencies, represents a substantial investment of the community's resources. A large variety of different individuals obtain much of their livelihood from "people-changing" activities of one kind or another. The group that profits from "the delinquency problem" includes correctional workers, but it also involves such diverse members as academic theorists and researchers who study the problem and who are paid to consult about it. Perhaps if the delinquency problem were to be markedly reduced, some other issue would have to be invented so that people-changers and "experts" could be put to work on it!

A Perspective on Delinquency

Our remarks on the social reality of delinquency can be reduced to a smaller collection of general propositions, or in other words, a guiding perspective on juvenile lawbreaking. As we shall demonstrate in detail in the chapters to follow, this perspective or set of basic assumptions has a considerable measure of support in the studies of juvenile misbehavior that have been conducted to date, and thus is more substantial than mere speculation.

1. Behavior which violates delinquency statutes is commonplace; nearly all youngsters engage in at least some delinquent behavior during their juvenile careers. At the same time, marked variations occur among offenders in the extent and seriousness of their involvement in lawbreaking. Some juvenile delinquents engage in repetitive, serious forms of misconduct, while others are implicated only in relatively innocuous kinds of misbehavior.
2. Those offenders who get into the hands of the police and are processed through the juvenile justice system tend to be the more career-oriented delinquents who are involved in serious misconduct. However, the factors which enter into police apprehension, court referral, and other decisions are several, therefore the offender's prospects of becoming identified as a juvenile delinquent are partially dependent upon characteristics of police officers, police departments, court personnel, and community influences.
3. Most juvenile offenders are relatively normal youths in terms of personality

structure in that they do not exhibit aberrant motives, deep-seated psychological tensions, or other marks of psychological disturbance. Officially processed delinquents often do show hostile attitudes, defiance of authority, and characteristics of that kind. However, these are not personality dimensions which are indicative of psychological maladjustment. In addition, some of these personality characteristics may be the product or result of correctional handling. At the same time, some youthful lawbreakers do show atypical personality patterns to which their delinquency may be a response.

4. Delinquency laws forbid a wide range of conduct, so that there are a number of behavioral patterns within the offender population.

5. The specific causal process that leads to one particular kind of delinquent behavior involves a number of etiological variables and may differ from that which produces another delinquent pattern. In this sense, delinquent behavior is the product of multiple causation. At the same time, it is possible to identify the different etiological processes which are involved in various forms of delinquency.

6. Delinquent behavior is learned behavior, acquired in the processes of socialization. Accordingly, the primary causes of juvenile misconduct are not to be found in biological factors (even though biological variables may play an indirect role in juvenile lawbreaking).

7. The learning of delinquent patterns is maximized in a criminalistic society such as the United States. Much delinquent behavior in the competitive, materialistic American society is societally generated and takes the form of direct and indirect assaults upon property.

8. Some delinquent patterns are mainly the consequence of social class variations in socialization and life experiences, along with other social-structural variables. In particular, situations in which legitimate avenues to the attainment of common American goals and values are blocked are importantly involved in certain forms of crime and delinquency. Those members of disadvantaged social groups and social strata may be relatively commonly involved in deviant behavior which is a response to their social and economic deprivation.

9. Some delinquent patterns are produced by familial and other socialization experiences which are not class-linked or class-specific. Among these are parental rejection and deviant sexual socialization. These kinds of experiences occur at all social class levels.

10. The defining agencies (police, probation services, courts, and so forth) play a part both in the definition of deviants and in the continuation of deviant activities. The result of apprehension and treatment may be quite contrary to the expected result. In other words, although one official function of correctional agencies and processes is the reformation of the offender, the actual outcome may often be the isolation of the person, reinforcement of deviant patterns, and rejection of society by the offender, the final result being nonreformation.

SOCIAL SCIENCE AND THE STUDY OF DELINQUENCY

The commentary to this point has emphasized the *sociological* study of delinquency. That emphasis is not misplaced, for the great mass of theorizing and empirical research on juvenile delinquency in the United States and elsewhere has been produced by sociologists (Finestone, 1976; Gibbons, 1979; Shoemaker, 1984).

Over the developmental period of American sociology from the turn of the century to the present, a great many specific explanations or perspectives on delinquency have enjoyed popularity, so that youthful offenders were first viewed as victims of social disorganization produced by rapid social change and later as driven to lawbreaking because of social strains arising from their disadvantaged position in the social order. More recently, official delinquents have been seen as the capriciously selected victims of the juvenile justice system, drawn from the ranks of American juveniles most of whom are thought to be involved in misbehavior. In this view of things, delinquency is a social label rather than a behavioral deviation characteristic of only a minority of youngsters. Other theorists have pointed to breakdown in the social bonds linking youths to conformity, and at the same time a small group of radical criminologists has located the sources of modern delinquency in the structural flaws of the political economy of corporate capitalism. We shall examine all of these arguments in the following chapters.

Sociological scholars have put forth a large variety of *sociogenic* arguments which assert that delinquency is the product of social processes and social factors. Some have been particularly attentive to social-structural influences which are related to delinquency rates and patterns, while others have exhibited more of a social-psychological bent, zeroing in upon interactional patterns among gang members, self-concept patterns among offenders, and related topics. But all this work has one feature in common, namely the assumption that *most juvenile offenders are psychologically normal youngsters whose deviance is a response to deleterious social circumstances and kindred influences.*

Although the emphasis in this volume is upon sociological perspectives on delinquency, it would be grossly misleading to imply that alternative points of view do not exist. For one thing, there has been a relatively long tradition of speculation and research by biological scientists, in which delinquency has been attributed to various biological imperatives or pressures that impel some youngsters into deviant activities (Hirschi and Rudisill, 1976; Cortés and Gatti, 1972; Shah and Roth, 1974).

Biogenic hypotheses holding that criminality is a response to biological forces of one kind or another have existed since the time of Cesare Lombroso (1836-1909), an Italian physician who argued that many criminals are atavists or biological throwbacks to an earlier type of human than *homo sapiens.* That now discredited work was followed by efforts to show that criminals and delinquents are biologically inferior, feeble-minded, and—more recently—differentially selected from among persons of mesomorphic or muscular somatotype or body build (Sheldon, Hartl, and McDermott, 1949; Glueck and Glueck, 1956; Cortés and Gatti, 1972).

The search for biological correlates of criminality has been flawed by low-level theorizing and claims that are inconsistent with modern knowledge in biology and genetics. Nearly all the biological research to date has been plagued with methodological deficiencies of such seriousness as to render the findings of these studies invalid. Even so, it would be a non sequitur to conclude that biological hypotheses can safely be ignored and bypassed in the search for etiological understanding. A careful reading of the evidence suggests, instead, that the last word may not have been heard on biological forces in human behavior and that this question remains open for further examination and study.

Other formulations on the causes of delinquency have been offered by psychiatrists and psychologists who contend in one way or another than delinquency is carried on by youths who are psychologically troubled or disturbed and that their lawbreaking is a response to these pressures emanating from "within the skin," so to speak.

It would be well to acknowledge the immense popularity of this line of explanation for social deviance of various kinds, which view concludes that "there must be something wrong with a person who would do that"—an interpretation offered for homosexuality, criminality, political radicalism, drug addiction, and a host of other forms of socially disapproved behavior. Concerning delinquency, many lay persons would doubtless agree with August Aichhorn (1955: 30), a pioneering figure in the development of psychiatric theories of delinquency, who asserted that "there must be something in the child himself which the environment brings out in the form of delinquency." In other words, delinquents behave as they do because they are in some way sick, maladjusted, or emotionally disturbed.

Contentions about the psychologically aberrant character of various kinds of deviants have been advanced with much enthusiasm by psychiatrists and psychologists and a large quantity of psychogenic theorizing and research evidence has been accumulated. Even so, the yield from psychogenic explorations has been neither impressive nor convincing, at least in the opinion of sociologically oriented students of delinquency. Many of the research studies of psychological problems among delinquents have been methodologically deficient, and thus any results in them favorable to the emotional problems argument are suspect. Many of these research investigations will be examined in Chapter 10.

Although convincing support for the thesis that delinquency is a response to psychological problems and pressures has not been produced by those who favor that view, it would be premature to conclude that this is a dead issue. For one thing, as we shall see later in this volume the hypothesis that many youngsters become engaged in delinquency because they lack the positive self-concepts which would insulate them from criminogenic influences in their social environment enjoys a measure of popularity among a number of sociological criminologists. Then, too, there may be a small but significant number of psychologically troubled youths mixed in among a much larger group of relatively normal delinquents. This issue is examined at length in Chapter 10. Finally, delinquency analysts need to heed the more fundamental point that has been made convincingly by Alex Inkeles (1970), namely that sociological accounts of human behavior will continue to be incomplete and inadequate until they provide some place for individual differences and psychological variations among human actors.

SUMMARY

This brief chapter has considered some of the erroneous notions about delinquency held by members of the general public—for example, that it consists solely of crime committed by some small segment of the youth population. Additionally, these opening remarks indicated that traditional views about delinquency offered by sociologists and other social scientists have borne a good deal of similarity to the perspectives of lay persons. The commentary moved on to argue that some new views and approaches to the phenomenon of delinquency are in order. In particular, the thesis was put forth that delinquency is best examined as a complex social product involving the activities of youths, the responses of social audiences to those behavioral infractions, the reactions of the law enforcement and criminal justice system to youthful misconduct, the state of public opinion about juvenile lawbreaking, and other influences all bound together to form the social reality of delinquency.

The first order of business in this endeavor to describe and analyze the multifaceted character of delinquency centers around providing a full account of infractions among juveniles. Chapter 2 discusses the nature and origins of laws which define juvenile delinquency, along with the major characteristics of the juvenile justice system which processes youthful offenders. Then, Chapter 3 turns to a more detailed picture of juvenile lawbreaking in American society, a picture constructed from various kinds of information.

REFERENCES

AICHHORN, AUGUST (1955). *Wayward Youth.* New York: Meridian Books.

ARIES, PHILIPPE (1962). *Centuries of Childhood.* tr. Robert Baldick. New York: Knopf.

BOYER, PAUL (1978). *Urban Masses and Moral Order in America, 1820–1920.* Cambridge: Harvard University Press.

CAVAN, RUTH SHONLE and FERDINAND, THEODORE N. (1981). *Juvenile Delinquency.* 4th edition. New York: Harper and Row.

CORTES, JUAN B. and GATTI, FLORENCE M. (1972). *Delinquency and Crime: A Biopsychosocial Approach.* New York: Seminar Press.

DUNFORD, FRANKLYN W. and ELLIOTT, DELBERT S. (1984). "Identifying Career Offenders Using Self-report Data." *Journal of Research in Crime and Delinquency* 21 (February) 57–86.

EMERSON, ROBERT M. (1969). *Judging Delinquents.* Chicago: Aldine.

EMPEY, LA MAR T. (1982). *American Delinquency.* Revised edition. Homewood, Ill.: Dorsey.

FINESTONE, HAROLD (1976). *Victims of Change.* Westport, Conn.: Greenwood.

GALVIN, JIM and POLK, KEN (1983). "Juvenile Justice: Time For a New Direction?" *Crime and Delinquency* 29 (July): 325–31.

GIBBONS, DON C. (1971). "Observations on the Study of Crime Causation." *American Journal of Sociology* 77 (September): 262–78.

GIBBONS, DON C. (1979). *The Criminological Enterprise.* Englewood Cliffs, N.J.: Prentice-Hall.

GLUECK, SHELDON and GLUECK, ELEANOR (1956). *Physique and Delinquency.* New York: Harper and Row.

HIRSCHI, TRAVIS and RUDISILL, DAVID (1976). "The Great American Search: Causes of Crime, 1876-1976." *Annals of the American Academy of Political and Social Science* 423 (January): 14-22.

INKELES, ALEX (1970). "Sociological Theory in Relation to Social Psychological Variables," pp. 403-31. In John C. McKinney and Edward A. Tiryakian, eds. *Theoretical Sociology.* New York: Appleton-Century-Crofts.

KRISBERG, BARRY and SCHWARTZ, IRA (1983). "Rethinking Juvenile Justice." *Crime and Delinquency* 29 (July): 333-64.

LIAZOS, ALEXANDER (1972). "The Poverty of the Sociology of Deviance: Nuts, Sluts, and Preverts." *Social Problems* 20 (Summer): 103-20.

NELSON, WILLIAM E. (1975). *Americanization of the Common Law: The Impact of Legal Change on Massachusetts Society, 1760-1830.* Cambridge: Harvard University Press.

PLATT, ANTHONY M. (1969). *The Child Savers.* Chicago: University of Chicago Press.

ROTHMAN, DAVID J. (1971). *The Discovery of the Asylum.* Boston: Little, Brown.

SANDERS, WILEY B. (1970). *Juvenile Offenders for a Thousand Years.* Chapel Hill, N.C.: University of North Carolina Press.

SCHLOSSMAN, STEVEN L. (1977). *Love and the American Delinquent.* Chicago: University of Chicago Press.

SCHULTZ, LAWRENCE J. (1973). "The Cycle of Juvenile Court History." *Crime and Delinquency* 19 (October): 457-76.

SHAH, SALEEM and ROTH, LOREN H. (1974). "Biological and Psychophysiological Factors in Criminality," pp. 101-73. In Daniel Glaser, ed. *Handbook of Criminology.* Chicago: Rand McNally.

SHELDON, WILLIAM H., HARTL, EMIL M., and McDERMOTT, EUGENE (1949). *Varieties of Delinquent Youth.* New York: Harper and Row.

SHOEMAKER, DONALD J. (1984). *Theories of Delinquency.* New York: Oxford University Press.

chapter 2

THE JUVENILE COURT
AND THE JUVENILE JUSTICE
"SYSTEM"

INTRODUCTION

Chapter 1 noted that "juvenile delinquency" is a modern social invention in that legal statutes which differentiate youthful lawbreakers from adult violators, and which provide for the processing of the former through a social control system separate from the one within which adult miscreants are handled, are of relatively recent origin. The American juvenile court system was first created in 1899, although that event was the culmination of a number of alterations in the legal processing of children as contrasted to adults that had occurred in preceding decades. Chapter 2 provides a review of the events leading up the the creation of the court, along with a discussion of the legal statutes under which courts operate and an analysis of the place of the court within the larger people-processing social machinery which is usually referred to as "the juvenile justice system."

ORIGINS AND DEVELOPMENT OF THE JUVENILE COURT

The Emergence of "Childhood" in Modern Societies

Juvenile tribunals were preceded by a long series of less sweeping changes in the handling of youthful offenders in the nineteenth century, which laid much of the groundwork for the creation of the juvenile court. However, it can also be argued that the juvenile court movement was the culmination of a much longer, gradual, but more fundamental set of social changes in the preceding three centuries in Europe and America, in which "childhood" emerged as a distinct social status (Empey, 1982: 17-74; Krisberg and Austin, 1978: 7-50; Teitelbaum and Harris, 1977: 1-44). The juvenile court reflects the view that children are more innocent, less guilty of criminal motives, and more in need of protection and kindly discipline than are adults. As a result, to understand the forces behind the juvenile court, the emergence of childhood as a social status distinct from "littlehood" must be examined.

LaMar Empey (1982: 17-74) has assembled a large share of the literature on the rise of childhood. As he indicated, throughout much of human history children were treated by adults with indifference, at best, and were often subjected to gross cruelty and abuse. Infanticide and child abandonment were common practices up to the eighteenth century in Europe. Children were regarded as adults in tiny bodies, rather than as immature, developing persons who require special attention and nurturance.

Although the factors that account for these earlier viewpoints concerning children are multiple and complex, most of them are related to such factors as the general meanness of life, harsh economic conditions, and social disorder that existed nearly everywhere in the world until the past several centuries. Life was cheap in societies characterized by poverty and wretchedness, high death rates, and other premodern conditions. According to Empey (1982: 34): "Under conditions like these, the cultural prescriptions we consider important today were lacking, especially those that make provisions for close ties between parent and child, that stress the importance of the nuclear family, that take delight in the innocence and beauty of children, and that provide long years of total economic support for a phase in the life cycle known as childhood."

The modern concept of childhood as a special age period occupied by dependent persons who need tender care and protection slowly began to take form in Europe in the sixteenth and seventeenth centuries. This development represents one part of a larger sweep of events designated by historians as the Renaissance period, the Protestant Reformation, colonization of the New World, and the Industrial Revolution. According to Empey, it was in the growing middle-class group within European societies that concern for the special needs of children was most emphasized, and it was also within this part of the population that nuclear family ideals and a stress upon formal education of children were most popular. Empey (1982: 44) has argued that the privacy provided by the nuclear family, and the intellectual and moral skills that were derived from schooling, were particularly attuned to special interests of a rising middle class wishing to distance itself from both the masses and the upper class.

The social concept of childhood had become well-developed in America by the nineteenth century. The protective posture of the citizenry toward its youngsters can be seen in a number of developments which mitigated the severity of punishment directed at juveniles, and which eventually led to the invention of the juvenile court.

Development of the Juvenile Court

The development of special laws and special procedures for juvenile offenders has been lengthy; some authorities have seen the beginnings of the juvenile court movement in the fifteenth-century English courts of chancery. Paul Tappan (1960: 388) observed that the development of a court of chancery jurisdiction provided special consideration to children. Equity was designed to provide aid to individuals and groups that could find no other remedy under the limitations of the rigid rules that had developed in the common law. Under chancery jurisdiction the court claimed a power of *parens patriae* over infants and their estates on the assumption that children, as wards of the state, were in need of special protection. However, chancery functioned primarily in the administration of the estates of well-to-do infants.

The harsh treatment of youthful offenders began to be mitigated in the United States in the early 1800s. The first juvenile reformatory was established in New York in 1825, followed shortly thereafter by similar institutions in Massachusetts and Pennsylvania. The movement to provide foster homes for neglected and destitute children originated in New York in 1853, while Chicago in 1861 provided a commission to hear cases of petty offenses by boys six to seventeen years of age. A Massachusetts law of 1869 provided that an agent of the state board of charities should attend trials of children to make recommendations for the disposition of these cases, and separate trials for juveniles were instituted in Boston in 1870. Between 1878 and 1898, Massachusetts began a system of statewide probation which included children, while New York created special hearings for juveniles below the age of 16 in 1892.

The gradual evolution of the juvenile court movement was also indicated in Robert Mennel's (1973) account of the development of juvenile procedures in the United States. He observed that prior to 1800, juvenile misbehavior was dealt with in the family rather than in special organizations and institutions. Less frequently, youthful offenders were severely dealt with as though they were adult criminals. However, nineteenth-century industrialization, urban migration, economic changes, and the population growth of the nation shifted responsibility for child misbehavior to bureaucratic institutions. Between 1825 and 1860, houses of refuge designed to control pauperism and thereby to strike at the roots of delinquency sprang up around the country. Houses of refuge were succeeded by reform schools, as well as by policies of "placing out" youths by sending them to live with a rural family in the Midwest.

The rise of custodial institutions of various kinds during the Jacksonian era from about 1820 onward, in which penitentiaries, asylums, almshouses, orphan asylums, and reformatories were created in great number across the land, has been examined in detail by historian David Rothman (1971) and by Steven Schlossman 1977: 7-17). Schlossman's account of the spread of the *parens patriae* doctrine in the nineteenth century indicates that the constitutional challenges it faced during the nineteenth and early twentieth century were unsuccessful. These concerns for the legal rights of juveniles ran counter to the prevailing social and legal thought of the period, which stressed such themes as universal education for children and the need to protect children, especially those of the poor, all benevolent motives which ignored children's legal rights and supported expansive intervention into their lives—"child-saving," in short.

What are the underlying historical factors that culminated in the creation of the first juvenile court in Cook County, Illinois in 1899? Schlossman (1983: 962) has provided one version of the interpretation favored by most criminologists:

> The campaign to establish juvenile courts was part of a broader social move-
> ment to accommodate urban institutions to an increasingly urban base and a
> predominantly immigrant population; to introduce control and planning into
> diverse aspects of city life heretofore monopolized by private enterprise; and
> to incorporate recent discoveries in the behavioral, social, and medical sci-
> ences into the education of children. The juvenile court also played a special
> symbolic role in the Progressive Era as the ultimate proving ground for the
> sturdy innovations reformers had urged—for example, kindergartens, child
> labor laws, school lunches, and vocational education—to enhance possibilities
> for optimal child development in the industrial city. Whenever a child was
> brought into court for reprimand or punishment, it was apparent either that
> these innovations were not reaching him (the most generous and typical
> explanation of the reformers) or that they were not having the predicted
> salutary effect.

The newly created juvenile court received a good deal of acclaim and was viewed by its supporters, both at the turn of the century and for several decades beyond, as a wise and humanitarian child-saving invention that represented a major break from earlier forms of handling of youthful lawbreakers (Rothman, 1980: 205-35). However, that interpretation has been challenged by Anthony Platt (1969), among others. Platt pointed out that the juvenile court movement had roots in the developments we have noted, and was not an entirely new social invention. Then, too, the philosophy that informed the juvenile court movement, accord-ing to Platt, was conservative in character. Advocates of the court argued that youths could be saved from a life of crime if they were removed from the evils of the urban community and placed in a training school or a healthful environment of the rural Midwest. The purpose of dealing with urban delinquents was to mold them in ways that would allow them to be assimilated into the mainstream of American life. The reformers who were most active and vocal in support of the juvenile court idea were interested in preserving traditional American values of parental authority and the autonomy of family units.

In a subsequent reinterpretation of his historical account of the rise of the juvenile court, Platt (1974) argued that although the "child-saving" movement was supported most directly by middle-class social reformers, its success in achieving significant reforms was due to support from wealthy and powerful members of a ruling class. Platt claimed that the juvenile court movement provided new proce-dures through which urban youths, particularly those from lower- and working-class groups could be subjected to social control and made into malleable members of the laboring population. The core function of the juvenile court, in this view, turns out to be the preservation of the power and influence of the ruling class.

Other scholars have disagreed with Platt's account of the rise of the court (Schultz, 1973; Schlossman, 1977; Hagan and Leon, 1977). In particular, John Hagan and Jeffrey Leon (1977) examined the development of juvenile legislation in Canada. They took issue with Platt's claims that the middle-class reformers who agitated for the development of the juvenile court worked in close partnership with the ruling class. They also argued against Platt's interpretation of the court as a social invention which was contrived as a ruling class instrument for the creation of a specialized labor market and industrial discipline. In the Canadian case, at least, the juvenile court and juvenile legislation appeared to be the last development in a longer historical movement from reformatories for juveniles, to training schools, and finally to the establishment of the court and community treatment ventures. Additionally, the major group that pushed for this legislation consisted of the organized probation movement, with little or no discernible influence being exerted by an industrial elite or ruling class.

However, there is little quarrel with the major thesis that the development of the juvenile court was the capstone event that followed a number of earlier alterations in the handling of youthful offenders in American society. Further, it is clear that these new responses to juvenile lawbreaking were not capricious or inexplicable events; instead, they were reflections of other, massive changes in the social and economic structure of American society.

Within ten years of the passage of the legislation which established the first juvenile court in 1899, twenty states and the District of Columbia had created juvenile court laws; by 1945, court legislation had been extended to all the states. At the present time, there is a juvenile court in every American jursidiction; approximately 2700 courts hear children's cases.

The juvenile court was assigned a broad mandate by its architects. As Empey (1982: 334) has indicated: "As envisioned by its inventors, the juvenile court would fulfill several important functions. It would (1) enforce the modern concept of childhood; (2) act as a surrogate for the family and the school: (3) prevent delinquency; (4) decriminalize children; and (5) rehabilitate juveniles." With the emergence of the court, emphasis shifted from the punishment of young criminals to their protection and treatment. The Illinois law specified that the treatment given the juvenile offender should "approximate as nearly as may be that which should be given by its parents." To secure these ends, juvenile court procedures evolved which differed markedly from those in criminal courts. In addition, a new category was identified in the laws: the juvenile delinquent.

The first juvenile court law in Illinois brought under one jurisdiction the cases of dependency, neglect, and delinquency (including incorrigibles and children thought to be threatened by immoral associations). This legislation also created a new vocabulary in which juvenile courts employed petitions instead of complaints, initial hearings instead of arraignment, adjudication of involvement in delinquency instead of conviction, and disposition rather than sentence. Courts were also supposed to be informal and solicitous of the juvenile's well-being. Lawyers, transcripts, and other trappings of adult courts were thought to be unnecessary or even harmful, for the court would protect the child. These tribunals were intended to operate in a clinical and therapeutic fashion; misbehaving youngsters were to be investigated, diagnosed, and treated, rather than punished, as in adult courts.

THE LAWS OF DELINQUENCY

The first delinquency statute in Illinois gave juvenile courts jurisdiction over dependent and neglected children as well as delinquents, and courts have retained this broad jurisdiction to this day. Although the specific language of the relevant statutes in the individual states varies somewhat, in every case the following four problems are identified as appropriate matters calling for court intervention: first, children who have committed an act which, if committed by an adult, would be a crime, and second, status offenders, that is, youngsters who appear to be beyond parental control or engaged in conduct thought to be harmful to themselves. Additionally, courts are expected to act in cases of neglected children, whose parents have failed in their responsibilities to care for them, and dependent children, youngsters whose parents are unable to provide them with proper care (Paulsen and Whitebread, 1974). It is lawbreakers and status offenders with which this book is concerned.

The statutes which define juvenile delinquency are similar in form throughout the United States (Sussman, 1959: 15–22; Rubin, 1958: 43–45). They first specify that the court has control over juveniles who have violated federal, state, or local laws or ordinances. In other words, they assert that delinquents are persons under some specified age who commit acts which would constitute crimes if carried out by adults. The laws vary from state to state in terms of the age limits of juvenile court jurisdiction, but the most common upper age limit is 17 years of age; persons over that age are held accountable as adult criminals and are dealt with in criminal courts (Levin and Sarri, 1974: 13). The maximum age limits of juvenile court jurisdiction by states are shown in Table 2-1.

There is an important fact that is disguised in Table 2-1, namely that not all misbehaving youngsters who fall into the hands of the police and who are processed further through the juvenile court remain within the juvenile justice system. Instead, the delinquency laws throughout the United States empower juvenile courts to remand youths under the maximum juvenile court age to criminal courts and thereby surrender jurisdiction over them. Additionally, a number of states have passed legislation which requires certain cases, such as homicides or youths above a certain age who are charged with serious offenses, to be transferred to criminal court (Levin and Sarri, 1974: 15–19). Juveniles who are remanded to criminal court and who are subsequently convicted of offenses thereby acquire the legal status of criminal. Certification of juveniles to criminal courts most frequently occurs in cases involving homicide or other serious offenses, but as in other areas of

TABLE 2-1 Maximum Age at Which the Juvenile Court Has Original Jurisdiction in Delinquency Cases, By State

STATE	AGE LIMIT	STATE	AGE LIMIT
Alabama	15	Montana	17
Alaska	17	Nebraska	17
Arizona	17	Nevada	17
Arkansas	17	New Hampshire	16
California	17	New Jersey	17
Colorado	17	New Mexico	17
Connecticut	15	New York	15
Delaware	17	North Carolina	15
District of Columbia	17	North Dakota	17
Florida	16	Ohio	17
Georgia	16	Oklahoma	15
Hawaii	17	Oregon	17
Idaho	17	Pennsylvania	17
Illinois	16	Rhode Island	17
Indiana	17	South Carolina	16
Iowa	17	South Dakota	17
Kansas	17	Tennessee	17
Kentucky	17	Texas	16
Louisiana	16	Utah	17
Maine	16	Vermont	15
Maryland	16	Virginia	17
Massachusetts	16	Washington	17
Michigan	16	West Virginia	17
Minnesota	17	Wisconsin	17
Mississippi	17	Wyoming	17
Missouri	16		

the legal system there are marked variations in these practices from state to state (Rubin, 1979b). In a few states, prosecuting attorneys are empowered by state law to send juveniles accused of certain offenses directly to the criminal court, bypassing entirely the juvenile court. In the majority of states, original jurisdiction of all juvenile offenses rests with the juvenile court, but remand or certification of selected youths to criminal courts is allowed by statute. Moreover, in some of these latter states, changes in state laws have recently occurred which permit juvenile courts to exercise this transfer option with relatively young court referrals, or which require the courts to hold transfer hearings for all youngsters accused of certain felony offenses.

American delinquency laws do not restrict jurisdiction of the courts to persons under a specified age who commit violations of the criminal codes. Instead, they all contain an additional omnibus clause or separate provision—often referred to as *status offenses*—awarding the court jurisdiction over youths who have behaved in ways not forbidden by criminal laws. The omnibus provisions differ somewhat from state to state, but the various state delinquency statutes collectively specify several dozen vaguely defined conditions for which a juvenile may be adjudicated a ward of the court.

The flavor of status offense provisions can be detected from a partial list of the conditions which are identified as comprising delinquency in these laws. For example, these statutes award juvenile courts the jurisdiction over children who engage in immoral or indecent behavior, exhibit immoral conduct around schools, engage in illegal occupations, knowingly associate with vicious or immoral persons, grow up in idleness or crime, patronize or visit policy shops or gaming houses, wander in the streets at night, habitually wander about railroad yards or tracks, are incorrigible, or deport themselves so as to injure themselves or others.

The extension of court jurisdiction to these forms of conduct has not been uniformly applauded (Rubin, 1979b: 34–55). Instead, critics have suggested that these categories of behavior are so vaguely defined that nearly all youngsters could be made the subject of court attention. What is a "vicious or immoral person"? What is "incorrigibility"? These are highly subjective characterizations of persons or situations. Further, considerable doubt has been expressed about whether these kinds of acts are predictive of serious antisocial conduct. Perhaps courts would be better off not to concern themselves with these relatively benign activities and conditions, and, at the very least, youngsters who have not been charged with criminal offenses should not be processed in the juvenile court with those who have engaged in criminal law violations.

This line of criticism of juvenile delinquency statutes resulted in the creation in 1961 of a separate section in the juvenile code in California (State of California, 1965: 35). The Welfare and Institutions Code of the State of California contains a tripartite jurisdiction section which awards the court control over dependent and neglected children (nondelinquents), youngsters who have violated the criminal law, and certain other juveniles who come under an omnibus provision. The sections of the code read as follows:

> *600.* Any person under the age of 21 years who comes within any of the following descriptions is within the jurisdiction of the juvenile court which may adjudge the person to be a dependent child of the court:
>
> a. Who is in need of proper and effective parental care or control and has no parent or guardian, or has no parent or guardian willing to exercise or capable of exercising such care or control, or has no parent actually exercising such care or control.
>
> b. Who is destitute, or who is not provided with the necessities of life, or who is not provided with a home or suitable place of abode, or whose home is an unfit place for him by reason of neglect, cruelty, or depravity of either of his parents, or of his guardian or other person in whose custody or care he is.
>
> c. Who is physically dangerous to the public because of a mental or physical deficiency, disorder, or abnormality.
>
> *601.* Any person under the age of 21 years who persistently or habitually refuses to obey the reasonable and proper orders or directions of his parents, guardian, custodian, or school authorities, or who is beyond the control of

such person, or any person who is a habitual truant from school within the meaning of any law of this State, or who from any cause is in danger of leading an idle, dissolute, lewd, or immoral life, is within the jurisdiction of the juvenile court which may adjudge such person to be a ward of the court.

602. Any person under the age of 21 who violates any law of this State or of the United States or any ordinance of any city or county of this State defining crime or who, after having been found by the juvenile court to be a person described by Section 601, fails to obey the lawful order of the juvenile court, is within the jurisdiction of the juvenile court, which may adjudge such person to be a ward of the court.[1]

This California model was followed in 1962 by New York State, which created a PINS (person in need of supervision) statute. Similarly, Illinois developed a MINS (minor otherwise in need of supervision) provision. Colorado enacted a CHINS (Children in need of supervision) statute, and the state of Georgia enacted an "unruly child" category in order to deal with noncriminal activities on the part of juveniles (Levin and Sarri, 1974: 12). By 1973, twenty-five states had created separate categories such as these within which to include status offenders.

Status offender statutes have come under heavy attack over the past decade or so, in considerable part as a manifestation of more general disenchantment with the juvenile court as a "child-saving" social agency. The President's Commission on Law Enforcement and the Administration of Justice (1967: 27) recommended in 1967 that "serious consideration should be given to complete elimination from the court's jurisdiction of conduct illegal only for a child." The same recommendation has been urged by the International Association of Chiefs of Police and by the National Council on Crime and Delinquency. Then, too, the federal government through the Juvenile Justice and Delinquency Prevention Act of 1974, as amended in 1977, required that practices of detaining status offenders mixed with other delinquents in closed institutions be discontinued. States that fail to comply with this mandate were to be cut off from federal funds. But despite these pressures, all fifty states and the District of Columbia continue to retain status offenders within the jurisdiction of the court.

Although status offender provisions remain in state delinquency laws, a few states have recently amended their laws to make status offenders subject to court jurisdiction only as dependent or neglected children. Additionally, the majority of states now prohibit preadjudicatory detention of status offenders and postadjudicatory commitment of such youngsters to training schools (Rubin, 1979a: 283).

Status offender provisions have been most fully developed and utilized in the United States and are nonexistent or much narrower in definition in most other countries around the world. However, omnibus delinquency statutes which encom-

---

[1] Table 2-1 indicates that the upper age limit of original jurisdiction for the juvenile court in California is 17 years of age. Original jurisdiction in cases of law violation on the part of persons 18 years old and above rests with the criminal court. However, in California, a special statutory provision allows criminal courts to transfer or remand persons between 18 and 21 years of age to the juvenile court, thus the Welfare and Institutions Code speaks of persons under the age of 21 years.

pass many of the kinds of status offenses included in American law do exist in India and certain other nations (Hartjen and Priyadarsini, 1984: 42–46).

How frequently are the status offense provisions of American delinquency laws employed? Some relevant data have been presented by Krisberg and Schwartz (1983: 339–42). They reported that 536,266 of the 1,624,310 juvenile arrests (33.1 percent) in 1971 were for status offenses, while the comparable figures for 1974 were 1,879,387, with 466,885 status offenses making up 24.5 percent of the total. While the total arrests of juveniles increased by 16.9 percent between 1971 and 1979, status offense arrests declined by 9.1 percent. Even so, a large share of the juvenile arrests made by the police in the United States continue to be for status offenses.

Krisberg and Schwartz presented parallel figures for juvenile court cases. They noted that the total number of juvenile court cases was 1,406,100 in 1975, declining to 1,307,000 in 1979. In 1975, status offense cases numbered 335,600, but they declined to 259,000 by 1979; thus status offense cases decreased by 21.1 percent. They also indicated that detention of status offenders has decreased markedly in recent years, due mostly to pressures exerted on local jurisdictions by the federal government. In 1975, 143,000 status offenders were detained, while the number decreased to 44,007 (68.0 percent) by 1979. This trend toward decreased numbers of youths charged with status offenses appearing in court should have its greatest impact upon juvenile females rather than males, for it is the former who have been most frequently brought to court for status offenses.

THE CONTEMPORARY JUVENILE COURT

The Court and the Juvenile Justice "System"

In Chapter 2 we have argued that delinquency, defined as youthful misbehavior that violates legal statutes, is extremely commonplace, so much so that most American youngsters engage in it at one time or another while making their way through childhood and adolescence. We will examine the supporting evidence for that claim in detail in Chapter 3. Relatively few members of this army of youthful lawbreakers become tagged as juvenile delinquents by the police or juvenile courts. In general, the social sorting processes occurring in local communities operate in a manner such that those youngsters who engage in serious and/or repetitive acts of misconduct run the greatest risk of coming to the attention of the juvenile justice "system."

The preceding comments have made repeated reference to the juvenile justice "system" in order to draw attention to two important facts. First, the term *system* is often a misnomer when applied to the juvenile processing apparatus, for that word is usually employed to designate an integrated collection of separate parts all working in relative harmony and producing some end product. In this usage, an automobile engine in good working order is a system in that its various parts operate in a synchronized fashion, producing energy to propel the automobile. In a similar way, we sometimes speak of a healthy human organism as a system, in order to draw attention to the functional interdependence of its various parts.

But what of the so-called juvenile justice system? Those who speak of a juvenile justice system often do so in a careless fashion, failing to inform the listener that this phrase slurs over the existence of organizational fractures, serious conflicts and disagreements between different component agencies within the juvenile justice machinery, and other evidence of the nonsystemic nature of that apparatus.

An equally important point about the so-called juvenile justice system is that what it delivers to youngsters often appears to be something other than justice. Documentation of that claim will be postponed to Chapter 5 and later chapters of this book, but let us note at this point that there is considerable evidence pointing to the operation of racism and sexism in decisions that are sometimes made by the police or juvenile courts.

What is meant by *the juvenile justice system*? This phrase is usually employed to designate all of the relatively formal agencies of social control that respond to youthful lawbreakers; thus it includes the police, the juvenile court, local and state correctional agencies for juveniles, and a varied array of private social agencies in local communities that also focus much of their attention on misbehaving youths. However, the police and the juvenile court are the most frequently mentioned components of the juvenile justice "system," principally because they deal with the largest numbers of alleged and/or adjudicated delinquents.

The juvenile justice "system" in the United States represents grand scale social machinery. Because this people-processing apparatus is manned by many individuals who are involved in making decisions about offenders, its nature cannot be fully captured in a few paragraphs. Figure 2-1 provides a graphic overview of many of the components and decision points in this "system" (Krisberg and Austin, 1978: 55. By permission of the publisher).

Police officers are most frequently involved in the initial decisions about reported juvenile lawbreakers, for they either observe these youths in acts of deviance, or more frequently, they learn about them from citizens. The police occupy a crucial position in the decision system; they control the initial sorting-out of youths, thus determining which are to be viewed as "bad" or "delinquent" and taken to court, and which do not need court intervention. The police take some youngsters directly to the juvenile court, while they give others citations to appear in court at some subsequent time. Although other persons—private citizens, school officials and others—report youngsters to juvenile court too, these cases are less frequent than are police referrals.

Those juveniles who end up at the juvenile hall or other court facility are submitted to a variety of decision makers. In larger courts, a probation officer serving in an intake capacity dismisses the referred children whom he or she concludes do not warrant court attention, or he or she determines the referrals as not delinquent enough to deserve formal court action but still needing some help. Many of these youngsters are persuaded to submit to informal probation, in which they report periodically to a probation officer even though they have not been formally adjudicated as delinquents. Petitions alleging delinquency are filed on a third group

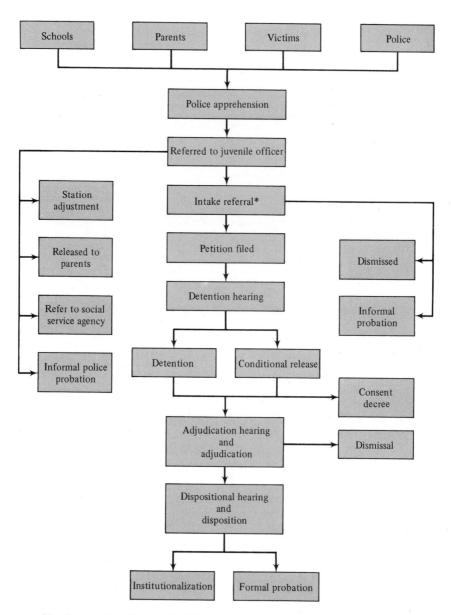

*In a few cases juveniles are referred directly to intake by schools, parents, or victims.

FIGURE 2-1 Juvenile Justice System Critical Decision Points

of offenders who are then scheduled for court hearing. Some of these juveniles are detained in juvenile hall while they await a hearing; others are released to their parents. Finally, when a court determines that youngsters are delinquents, this adjudication leads to still other decisions. Some wards are placed on probation, some are turned over to a private agency, and some are sent to custodial institutions for care and treatment.

The Juvenile Court and the Community

What is the place of the juvenile court in the larger community? Various publics or audiences hold differing views about the proper role of the court, in much the same way that citizens have conflicting expectations about the goals and functions that ought to be performed by other correctional and "people-changing" organizations and agencies. In short, some citizens expect correctional agencies to punish offenders while others would have them rehabilitate lawbreakers. Indeed, one of the major problems faced by correctional organizations in modern societies is that of divergent goals that are urged upon these structures by different interest groups in the community.

Detailed research evidence regarding citizens' views of the correctional machinery is not abundant (Gibbons and Jones, 1975: 68-70). However, a few studies have been conducted regarding public perceptions of the juvenile court. In one of these, William Lentz (1966) surveyed a sample of Wisconsin adults concerning their attitudes toward juvenile delinquents and the control of delinquency. Most of the citizens favored swift and impartial justice toward juveniles and probation in place of committing youths to training schools. Many asserted that youthful offenders are psychologically "sick" and in need of expert treatment.

A second investigation was carried out by Howard Parker (1970) and dealt with citizens' views of the juvenile court in four Washington State communities. Most of the respondents were ignorant of the workings of the court even though they lived in relatively small communities where they might be expected to be knowledgeable about local organizations. Most of the citizens asserted that the juvenile court did not punish offenders as severely as they would like. But when Parker then ascertained the dispositions that the citizens would have dealt out to selected real-life offenders, he discovered that most of them would have actually given the delinquents similar or less severe penalties than had been handed down by the court!

Juvenile Courts in Operation

Those courts dealing with youth problems are articulated with the other tribunals in specific sections of the country in a number of different ways. In some the juvenile court is a part of the circuit, district, superior, or municipal court, while in a few jurisdictions separate family courts have been established to deal with youngsters.

The majority of states provide for waiver or transfer of youths to adult courts if they are thought to be unsuitable subjects for juvenile handling. However, the conditions which govern the exercise of this option vary from state to state. Written criteria to guide the judges in deciding whether or not to waive a youth to the criminal court are rare. Most frequently, when criteria are stated they are in terms such as "not amenable to treatment in juvenile court." Until 1966, most states did not require a waiver hearing or legal protection for the accused youths. However, the 1966 Supreme Court decision in *Kent* v. *United States* held that juveniles are entitled to a hearing, assistance of counsel, access to records, and a statement of the reasons for the judge's decision to waive.

Many juvenile court statutes fail to provide detailed procedural directions for the operation of the court machinery. Many laws do state that when a complaint is received from the police, parents, social agencies, or some other source, a preliminary inquiry will be made to determine whether court action is required. In many larger metropolitan areas, this activity is conducted by a probation department intake division presided over by one or more probation officers who dispose of about half of the referrals at intake, without taking further formal action. The intake officer also determines whether juvenile referrals should be detained in the juvenile hall or other detention facility pending court action. Standards for detention vary from one location to another, as does the quality of the facilities for holding juveniles.

If a petition alleging delinquency is filed, the juvenile then appears before the judge for a hearing. Because the court is supposed to be informal and noncombative in nature, rules of evidence are often relaxed, and hearsay and unsworn testimony are introduced. Until the last decade or two, the standard of proof required in order to reach a finding of delinquency was markedly lower than the standard of proof required by the criminal court. Approximately two-thirds of the states had no statutory provision for the right of counsel and most accused juveniles were without legal representation. These informal proceedings usually took place privately and barred reporters and persons without specific interest in them.

In some jurisdictions a disposition hearing is conducted separately from the adjudication proceeding, but in many it is held at the same time as the hearing on the question of delinquency involvement. The social history document prepared by the probation officer to whom the case was assigned looms large in the disposition of the case. This report inquires into the social background of the juvenile and includes information and data, some of which is of indeterminate accuracy. The social history is supposed to be a guide to disposition of the case, but in many courts the report is given to the judge prior to the adjudication hearing.

Juvenile court judges usually have broad discretion regarding disposition of cases; they dismiss, warn, fine, or place the offender on probation, or send him or her to a private or public institution. Juvenile court judges often fall short of the ideal, for they are frequently both inadequately trained and overworked. A survey sponsored by the National Council of Juvenile Court Judges of 1560 juvenile court judges in the 1960s threw considerable light upon the characteristics and work styles of these persons (McCune and Skoler, 1965; Walther and McCune, 1965).

Almost all of them were males; their average age was 53; nearly all were married; and 71 percent had received law degrees. However, 49 percent of these judges had not received BA degrees, and 24 percent were without legal training. The legal experience prior to assuming a judgeship averaged nine years. Of the full-time judges in the group, 72 percent spent a quarter or less of their time on juvenile matters. Accordingly, the juvenile position was viewed as a minor part of the magistrate's responsibilities in most of the jurisdictions.

The judges in the study showed wide variations in salary, but most were underpaid. The average salary for full-time judges was less than that for judges of trial courts of general jurisdiction or lawyers in private practice. Not only were many of the judges underpaid, they were also undersupplied with resources. About one-third of them reported that they had no probation officers or social workers to assist them. But although these judges appeared to be undertrained in some cases and underpaid in others, a companion study of juvenile judges did indicate that, compared to police officers and nonjuvenile court judges, the juvenile judges were more social service–oriented and less punitive in posture.

This unflattering portrait of juvenile courts and juvenile court judges emerged in another national survey in 1973 (Smith, 1974), which found that only 12 percent of the judges devoted full time to juvenile court activities.

Another problem with the juvenile court concerns the probation officer staff. Juvenile probation is provided for by law in every state; thirty-one states have probation services in each county. But in the 164 counties in four states, no juvenile probation exists. Juvenile probation is administered under a variety of arrangements within the states, and many jurisdictions fail to provide merit or civil service coverage to employees. In the majority of probation services, salaries are inadequate and caseloads are too high.

Other court resources are also lacking. Juvenile court standards usually suggest that psychiatric services should be a part of the court, but these clinical services have rarely been provided. Foster homes and group homes rarely exist, and the dispositional alternatives available to the court fall short of the richness and relevance to individual needs envisioned by the court's founders.

The problems of the juvenile court run deeper than just personnel and resources. In the words of the 1967 President's Commission report (1967: 9):

> In theory the court's operations could justifiably be informal, its findings and decisions made without observing ordinary procedural safeguards, because it would act only in the best interest of the child. In fact it frequently does nothing more nor less than deprive a child of liberty without due process of law—knowing not what else to do and needing, whether admittedly or not, to act in the community's interest even more imperatively than the child's. In theory it was to exercise its protective powers to bring an errant child back into the fold. In fact there is increasing reason to believe that its intervention reinforces the juvenile's unlawful impulses. In theory it was to concentrate on each case the best of current social science learning. In fact it has often become a vested interest in its turn, loath to cooperate with innovative programs or avail itself of forward-looking methods.

This passage expresses the pessimism with the court that has been growing since the 1960s. The commission did not recommend the jettisoning of the court, but it did suggest that more juveniles be dealt with by prejudicial dispositions to keep them out of the court machinery. The commission also suggested that procedures designed to assure fair and reliable determinations should be infused into the court. In short, the commission came out forcefully for a return to a legalistic concern for due process and the rights of the child.

One study that documented this relatively dismal picture of the court was Robert Emerson's (1969) report on a juvenile court in a northern United States city, located in a metropolitan area with a population of about two million. The overriding conclusion of that inquiry was that the court failed to carry out its mandate to rehabilitate lawbreakers. Instead, it operated to bring about social control and, together with other organizations in the community, worked to maximize the satisfaction of the needs of those agencies, but with lesser concern for the wards being processed through the machinery.

Emerson's analysis showed that the court and the police shared a joint interest in dealing with "trouble" in the community; the court often handled youths in ways designed to assist the police in controlling "trouble" rather than endeavoring to individualize the rehabilitative treatment of lawbreakers. Also, the court and the child welfare department were bound together symbiotically, with the court providing emergency placement of welfare cases, as well as acting as a "dumping ground" for troublesome welfare cases. In turn, the welfare agency assisted the court in finding foster home placements and in related ways.

Emerson also indicated that court workers operated in terms of notions of trouble as they processed youths in the court. They differentiated between juveniles who were thought to be involved in socially disruptive trouble and others regarded as normal. Additionally, the court employees made judgments of moral character regarding the youths, sorting them into "normals," "hard-core delinquents," and "disturbed" youngsters. The central point about such characterological assessments in the court is that they may well have been invalid in many instances, with the subsequent handling of the juveniles being based on faulty prognoses. Emerson indicated that the court workers disposed of cases in terms of their judgments of moral character: they gave "normal" youths routine handling, sent "delinquents" to training schools, and referred "disturbed" youths for special care such as psychiatric treatment.

Some similar observations emerged from Michael Langley's (1972) inquiry into a juvenile court in a metropolitan area in Tennessee. He observed that decisions about whether to detain a juvenile before a court hearing had little to do with the treatment needs of the youth, that lawyers were rarely utilized in the court, and that dispositional decisions were infrequently based upon a diagnostic study and report by a probation officer. According to Langley (1972: 291): "This one metropolitan court is committed to a set of practices which emphasize the control and coercion of youths in a way that violates the rehabilitative objectives of individualized treatment. At the same time these practices violate the constitutional rights of these youths."

One of the most recent and detailed reports on American juvenile courts is a study by Stapleton, Aday, and Ito (1982), involving nearly 100 characteristics of a sample of 150 juvenile courts in metropolitan areas. The results of their complex factor analysis indicated that the courts varied along five major dimensions: inclusiveness, centralization, formalization, differentiation-task specificity, and intake discretion. Some courts were inclusive, and dealt with status offenders, while in some other courts status offenders were not subject to court intervention. Centralized courts were those which had control over detention, probation, and other adjunct operations, while courts scoring high on formalization were those in which bifurcated jurisdictional and dispositional hearings were held, lawyers took an active role in defending children, and so on. In courts that showed low task specification, the judge served as jury and prosecutor as well. In courts that scored higher on task specification, these functions were performed by a number of different court officials. Finally, intake discretion referred to the ability of intake officers to place children on informal probation or impose restitution upon them without an adjudication hearing being held. Variability among courts was observed by these investigators in that they found a number of courts in all of the possible combinations of these factors, that is, some courts were inclusive in scope but had low scores on the other dimensions, while other inclusive courts had high scores on some or all of the other factors. The central thrust of the study was that rather than courts all following a single organizational model, marked variability in juvenile court operations was revealed from one jurisdiction to another.

Procedural Justice for Juveniles

Much of the commentary and criticism of juvenile courts during the first several decades of their existence centered on their failure to become anything more than legalistic tribunals which were juvenile courts only in that they handled juveniles. In the initial flush of enthusiasm for the juvenile court idea, few voices were heard questioning the possible negative effects the court might have upon some of the persons who were processed by it. Little concern was expressed that its informal procedures might run roughshod over the rights of the individual. Those constitutional challenges which were raised concerning the court's inattention to due process were ignored. An opinion of the Pennsylvania Supreme Court of 1905 is a case in point, for it held that youths in juvenile courts have no rights of due process because they are not charged with crimes and the court is operating for their welfare and benefit. More recently, in the case *in re Holmes* in 1955, the Supreme Court ruled that since juvenile courts are not criminal courts, the constitutional rights accorded to accused adults do not apply to juveniles.

In the years since World War II there has been a growing reaction termed by one juvenile court judge as a "legal renaissance." A number of scholarly critics criticized the potential unfairness and arbitrariness of juvenile court procedures which failed to attend to the requirements of due process (Ketcham, 1961). Legislative studies in a variety of states came to the same conclusion, namely that juvenile court laws failed to provide sufficient legal safeguards for the accused juvenile. A number of states, including New York and California, revised or amended delinquency statutes in a legalistic direction, laying down guidelines for court proceedings and due process. The use of legally admissable evidence in adjudication stages of court appearance, bifurcation of adjudication and disposition portions of court hearings, and reforms in the areas of charges, detention, and confidentiality of court records were some of the changes urged by critics of the court (Siler, 1965; Rosenheim and Skoler, 1965).

These proposals have been implemented by a series of Supreme Court rulings, dating from 1966 in *Kent* v. *United States,* which held that juveniles are entitled to a hearing, legal representation, and other rights in the instance of waiver to a criminal court. The Supreme Court held in *in re Gault* in 1967 that juveniles are entitled to formal notice of the charges against them, the right of legal counsel, the right of confrontation and cross-examination of witnesses, and the privilege of protection against self-incrimination. The Gault case was far-reaching, for it extended to juveniles most of the protections of due process accorded to adults. Of equal significance was the decision rendered by the Supreme Court in 1970 in *in re Winship.* That decision held that the case against a juvenile charged with an act that would be a crime if committed by an adult must be proven "beyond a reasonable doubt," rather than by the less stringent standard of a preponderance of evidence. The Winship decision obliges juvenile courts to conform to the same evidential standard utilized in criminal court proceedings.

Parenthetically, it would be a mistake to assume that the Supreme Court will ultimately extend the full panoply of legal rights accorded to adults to juveniles as well. On this point, the court in 1971 in *McKeiver* v. *Pennsylvania* ruled that jury trials are not required in juvenile cases. Juvenile trials are allowed in only about a dozen states currently. It would also be a mistake to assume that court decisions or legislative changes will automatically and quickly bring about reforms in the procedures of individual juvenile courts. These changes may be slow and halting as due process is gradually extended throughout the nation. Indeed, a national survey of juvenile courts in 1976 concluded (Sosin and Sarri, 1976: 205-206): "The findings . . . clearly indicate that no revolution has occurred in the implementation of due process in the juvenile court. Most judges do concur that juvenile rights should be acknowledged and protected, but they agree far less about how and to what extent procedural safeguards must be implemented. . . . *Formal* compliance was supported more than *full,* substantive compliance."

Let us examine some of the bits and pieces of evidence on compliance with court rulings in specific courts. On the one hand, William Ralston (1971) reported that one juvenile court in Virginia moved with dispatch to conform to the requirements of the Gault decision. Similarly, Charles Reasons (1970) noted that lawyers were much more frequently in evidence at juvenile court hearings in Columbus, Ohio, after the Gault decision and that the number of court cases had been reduced through greater emphasis on legal fact-finding. Finally, Jerry Franklin and Don Gibbons (1973) conducted a study of juvenile court counselor opinions of due process standards that turned up evidence of considerable support among the workers for these standards.

The more pessimistic side of this matter is represented in observations by Edwin M. Lemert (1967, 1970), which centered around the implementation of legislative changes that were made in California's juvenile court laws in 1961. The revisions made mandatory the practice of bifurcated hearings, with adjudication separated from the disposition stage of court processing. Determination of delinquency was supposed to be on the basis of a "preponderance of evidence legally admissible in the trial of criminal cases." However, in a 1965 survey of California juvenile court judges Lemert found that a majority (67 percent) were still reading the dispositional (social) report prior to the jurisdictional or adjudicational portion of the hearing. The intent of the 1961 revisions was to prevent this practice because of the considerable amount of hearsay evidence contained in these reports.

The 1961 revisions also provided for legal counsel in juvenile cases. Lemert's research in California showed that while this legislation increased the use of counsel, wide variations continued to exist in the utilization of lawyers for accused juveniles. In some counties attorneys appeared in court in three-fourths or more of the cases; in some others lawyers were almost never found. Some further data on the failure of courts to implement Supreme Court rulings were found in a study by Norman Lefstein, Vaughn Stapleton, and Lee Teitelbaum (1969) of three juvenile courts in metropolitan areas of the eastern United States. Their research, conducted after the Gault ruling, was designed to determine the extent of compliance with that ruling in the three courts. They found that conformance with due process requirements was minimal or nonexistent. Judges and court workers circumvented the due process standards by misleading juveniles and their parents about these rights, delivering advice to youths in a slurred or wooden manner, and so on.

In a subsequent project in two of these same three courts, Stapleton and Teitelbaum (1972) conducted an experiment in which legal counsel was provided to randomly selected court cases and not offered to other youngsters. The lawyers had a significant impact in one court, obtaining dismissals for many juveniles and providing other protections to youngsters, while they were ineffective in the second court. Stapleton and Teitelbaum attributed these different results to the patterns of court structure in the two courts. In the traditional court, arraignment, adjudication, and disposition processes were merged in a single hearing, making it difficult for attorneys to intrude into the processing of youths. The second court operated more legalistically, allowing more opportunity for legal challenges and the like by legal counsel.

Another dismal report on implementation of due process was contained in a report by David Duffee and Larry Siegel (1971), dealing with an examination of court activities in a populous New York county. These researchers found that those juveniles who had been represented by lawyers received more severe dispositions in court than did comparable lawbreakers who had not been defended by attorneys!

Duffee and Siegel suggested that lawyers failed to serve as vigorous advocates of their youthful clients. Additionally, the court was more willing to send juveniles who had lawyers off to training schools, for it was able to argue that it had accorded due process to the youths.

We do not suggest that the concern for due process ought to be lessened because procedural safeguards are sometimes difficult to implement. Quite the contrary, as the findings reviewed here point to the need for continued scrutiny of courts and continued efforts at legislative modification of juvenile court law in the direction of ideal standards.[2]

SUMMARY

This chapter has examined the origins and development of the modern juvenile court. We have seen that while 1899 is the year of birth usually recorded for the American juvenile court, in actuality the court had a very long gestation period, involving a variety of historical events leading up to its appearance in Illinois at the turn of the century. The architects of the court viewed it as a child-saving organization rather than as a punitive court and were little concerned about providing due process protections to allegedly wayward youths. Also, through status offender provisions juvenile courts have been given broad powers to cast their nets widely in seeking out children to save. American delinquency statutes empower juvenile courts to intervene in cases in which youngsters are involved in violations of criminal statutes. But in addition juvenile court laws specify that youths can be made wards of the court and dealt with as delinquents if they are involved in various status offenses enumerated under omnibus clauses of these statutes. The behavioral categories identified in status provisions are extremely general and ambiguous ones, e.g., ungovernability, waywardness, or immorality. In effect, these laws put nearly all youths "at risk" of being dealt with as delinquents, for they could be interpreted broadly so as to sweep nearly all juveniles into the courts.

We have also seen that juvenile courts have often fallen considerably short of the mark as far as full implementation of the rehabilitative and preventive roles assigned to them are concerned. Disenchantment with the court has led to a variety of consequences, a major one being the provision of increased due process protec-

---

[2]The Supreme Court has continued to hand down rulings regarding due process for juveniles. For example, three rulings were made in 1978 and 1979. In *Fare* v. *Michael C.,* the court ruled that the police can interrogate juveniles when no attorney is present but a probation officer is on the scene. *Swisher* v. *Brady* held that judges may reverse a decision of a court referee without holding a new hearing, while *Smith* v. *Daily Mail Publishing Co.* ruled that newspapers may publish the name of a juvenile arrested for murder, along with an account of the case.

It appears clear from decisions such as these that expansion of due process protections for juveniles came to a halt after the *Winship* decision and that the current mood of the court, as in the case of the rights of accused adults as well, has shifted away from expansion of those rights.

tions to youngsters by the Supreme Court. Having identified the major contours of the juvenile justice "system," the stage has now been set for the study of delinquent behavior. It is to that task that we turn in Chapter 3.

REFERENCES

DUFFEE, DAVID and SIEGEL, LARRY (1971). "The Organizational Man: Legal Counsel in the Juvenile Court." *Criminal Law Bulletin* 7 (July-August): 544-53.

EMERSON, ROBERT M. (1969). *Judging Delinquents.* Chicago: Aldine.

EMPEY, LA MAR T. (1982). *American Delinquency.* Revised edition, Homewood, Ill.: Dorsey.

FRANKLIN, JERRY and GIBBONS, DON C. (1973). "New Directions for Juvenile Courts: Probation Officers' Views." *Crime and Delinquency* 19 (October): 508-18.

GIBBONS, DON C. and JONES, JOSEPH F. (1975). *The Study of Deviance.* Englewood Cliffs, N.J.: Prentice-Hall.

HAGAN, JOHN and LEON, JEFFREY (1977). "Rediscovering Delinquency: Social History, Political Ideology, and the Sociology of Law." *American Sociological Review* 42 (August): 587-98.

HARTJEN, CLAYTON A. and PRIYADARSINI, S. (1984). *Delinquency in India.* New Brunswick, N.J.: Princeton University Press.

KETCHAM, ORMAN W. (1961). "The Unfulfilled Promise of the Juvenile Court." *Crime and Delinquency* 7 (April): 97-110.

KRISBERG, BARRY and AUSTIN, JAMES (1978). *The Children of Ishmael.* Palo Alto: Mayfield.

KRISBERG, BARRY and SCHWARTZ, IRA (1983). "Rethinking Juvenile Justice." *Crime and Delinquency* 29 (July): 333-64.

LANGLEY, MICHAEL A. (1972). "The Juvenile Court: The Making of a Delinquent." *Law and Society Review* 7 (Winter): 273-98.

LEFSTEIN, NORMAN, STAPLETON, VAUGHN, and TEITELBAUM, LEE (1969). "In Search of Juvenile Justice: *Gault* and its Implementation." *Law and Soceity Review* 3 (May): 491-562.

LEMERT, EDWIN M. (1967). "The Juvenile Court—Quest and Realities," pp. 91-105. In The President's Commission on Law Enforcement and the Administration of Justice, *Task Force Report: Juvenile Delinquency and Youth Crime.* Washington, D.C.: U.S. Government Printing Office.

LEMERT, EDWIN M. (1970). *Social Action and Legal Change.* Chicago: Aldine.

LENTZ, WILLIAM P. (1966). "Social Status and Attitudes Toward Delinquency Control." *Journal of Research in Crime and Delinquency* 3 (July): 147-54.

LEVIN, MARK M. and SARRI, ROSEMARY C. (1974). *Juvenile Delinquency: A Comparative Analysis of Legal Codes in the United States.* Ann Arbor: National Assessment of Juvenile Corrections.

McCUNE, SHIRLEY D. and SKOLER, DANIEL L. (1965). "Juvenile Court Judges in the U.S. Part I: A National Profile." *Crime and Delinquency* 11 (April): 121-31.

MENNEL, ROBERT M. (1973). *Thorns and Thistles: Juvenile Delinquents in the United States.* Hanover, N.H.: The University Press of New England.

PARKER, HOWARD (1970). "Juvenile Court Actions and Public Response," pp. 252-65. In Peter G. Garabedian and Don C. Gibbons, eds. *Becoming Delinquent.* Chicago: Aldine.

PAULSEN, MONRAD G. and WHITEBREAD, CHARLES H. (1974). *Juvenile Law and Procedure.* Reno: National Council of Juvenile Court Judges.

PLATT, ANTHONY M. (1969). *The Child Savers.* Chicago: University of Chicago Press.

PLATT, ANTHONY M. (1974). "The Triumph of Benevolence: The Origins of the Juvenile Justice System in the United States," pp. 356-89. In Richard Quinney, ed. *Criminal Justice in America.* Boston: Little, Brown.

RALSTON, WILLIAM H. (1971). "Intake: Informal Disposition or Adversary Proceeding?" *Crime and Delinquency* 17 (April): 160-67.

REASONS, CHARLES E. (1970). *"Gault:* Procedural Change and Substantive Effect." *Crime and Delinquency* 6 (April): 163–71.

ROSENHEIM, MARGARET K. and SKOLER, DANIEL L. (1965). "The Lawyer's Role in Intake and Detention Stages of Juvenile Court Proceedings." *Crime and Delinquency* 11 (April): 167–74.

ROTHMAN, DAVID J. (1971). *The Discovery of the Asylum.* Boston: Little, Brown.

ROTHMAN, DAVID J. (1980). *Conscience and Convenience.* Boston: Little, Brown.

RUBIN, H. TED (1979a). "Retain the Juvenile Court? Legislative Developments, Reform Directions, and the Call for Abolition." *Crime and Delinquency* 25 (July): 285–86.

RUBIN, H. TED (1979b). *Juvenile Justice: Policy, Practice, and Law.* Santa Monica: Goodyear.

RUBIN, SOL (1958). *Crime and Juvenile Delinquency.* New York: Oceana.

SCHLOSSMAN, STEVEN L. (1977). *Love and the American Delinquent.* Chicago: University of Chicago Press.

SCHLOSSMAN, STEVEN L. (1983). "Juvenile Justice: History and Philosophy," pp. 961–69. In Sanford Kadish, ed. *Encyclopedia of Crime and Justice,* Vol. 3. New York: Free Press.

SCHULTZ, J. LAWRENCE (1973). "The Cycle of Juvenile Court History." *Crime and Delinquency* 19 (October): 457–76.

SILER, EUGENE E., JR. (1965). "The Need for Defense Counsel in the Juvenile Court." *Crime and Delinquency* 11 (January): 45–58.

SMITH, D. C. (1974). "A Profile of Juvenile Court Judges in the U.S." *Juvenile Justice* 25 (August): 27–38.

SOSIN, MICHAEL and SARRI, ROSEMARY (1976). "Due Process: Reality or Myth?" pp. 176–206. In Rosemary Sarri and Yeheskel Hasenfeld, eds. *Brought to Justice? Juveniles, the Court, and the Law.* Ann Arbor: National Assessment of Juvenile Corrections.

STAPLETON, VAUGHN, ADAY, DAVID P., JR., and ITO, JEANNE A. (1982). "An Empirical Typology of American Metropolitan Juvenile Courts." *American Journal of Sociology* 83 (November): 549–64.

STAPLETON, VAUGHN and TEITELBAUM, LEE (1972). *In Defense of Youth.* New York: Russell Sage.

STATE OF CALIFORNIA (1965). *Welfare and Institutions Code.* Sacramento: Department of General Services.

SUSSMAN, FREDERICK B. (1959). *Law of Delinquency.* New York: Oceana.

TAPPAN, PAUL W. (1960). *Crime, Justice and Correction.* New York: McGraw-Hill.

TEITELBAUM, LEE E. and HARRIS, LESLIE J. (1977). "Some Historical Perspectives on Government Regulation of Children," pp. 1–44. In Lee E. Teitelbaum and Aidan R. Gough, eds. *Beyond Control: Status Offenders in the Juvenile Court.* Cambridge: Ballinger.

THE PRESIDENT'S COMMISSION ON LAW ENFORCEMENT AND ADMINISTRATION OF JUSTICE (1967). *Task Force Report: Juvenile Delinquency and Youth Crime.* Washington, D.C.: U.S. Government Printing Office.

WALTHER, REGIS H. and McCUNE, SHIRLEY D. (1965). "Juvenile Court Judges in the U.S. Part II: Working Styles and Characteristics." *Crime and Delinquency* 11 (October): 384–93.

chapter 3

MEASURING ADOLESCENT MISBEHAVIOR AND "JUVENILE DELINQUENCY"

INTRODUCTION

How many delinquent youngsters are there in the United States? How common is juvenile lawbreaking in this country and elsewhere in the world? What proportion of all youthful lawbreakers are "official delinquents" who have fallen into the hands of the police and the courts? How many are hidden or undetected offenders who have managed to stay free of entanglement in the juvenile justice system? Even more important, what factors account for the fact that some youthful lawbreakers get dealt with by the police or courts while others manage to avoid those experiences? Are the juvenile offenders who get into the custody of law-enforcement or correctional agencies usually hard-core, career-oriented, persistent, serious delinquents? Do most hidden offenders engage only in relatively petty acts of misbehavior, or instead, are the hidden deviants similar to detected and officially processed ones in terms of misbehavior—only luckier? In short, does the juvenile justice machinery center its attention upon blacks and youngsters from inner-city, lower-income neighborhoods, many of whom have been engaged in relatively petty acts, while at the same time ignoring serious forms of lawbreaking by children from privileged backgrounds?

Before turning to explanations of delinquency, we need to assemble a detailed picture of delinquency which indicates the extent of lawbreaking conduct, to determine the extent of recognized or perceived delinquency, and to learn the size of the secret or hidden lawbreaker group. Finally, we need to examine the ways in which the recognized offenders resemble or differ from the hidden ones.

Chapter 3 focuses on the facts regarding the number and location of juvenile offenders in society, their social characteristics, and related topics. A central fact that will emerge concerns the ubiquity of lawbreaking by American juveniles. Nearly all youths engage in at least some petty acts of law violation during the adolescent period, and most of that misconduct never comes to the attention of the police. Chapter 3 will note that police arrests of juveniles far outnumber police referrals to courts, that many cases are handled informally by police officers, and that law enforcement agents often dispense on-the-street justice to juvenile offenders. Chapter 4 continues this mapping of the terrain of juvenile delinquency, examining "the many faces of delinquency," that is, various facets of youthful lawbreaking that are not so readily apparent from statistical data. Among other things, Chapter 4 examines sexual differences in delinquency, social class patterns in lawbreaking, the extent to which distinct types of delinquents can be observed, and a number of other dimensions of delinquency. Finally, in Chapter 5 our attention will turn to the social processes which lie behind the statistics in Chapters 3 and 4 and the details of the social behavior of police officers, probation officers, juvenile court judges, and others as they go about processing of misbehaving youths.

JUVENILE MISBEHAVIOR AND OFFICIAL DELINQUENCY

What *is* "Juvenile delinquency?" What is it that is being observed and measured as we go about the study of delinquency? While it initially may seem that these are simple and straightforward questions, the answers to which are obvious, in point of fact definition and observation is a good deal more complicated than first impressions indicate.

It seems clear enough that when citizens speak about or think about "juvenile delinquency," they entertain some picture of "hard-core delinquents," that is, male thugs in black leather jackets who band together in aggressive and predatory gangs in inner-city neighborhoods. Most citizens have few if any direct contacts with youthful offenders, so that their perceptions are heavily influenced by portrayals in the mass media which often center on this stereotypical picture of delinquents.

Although one can find a small number of juvenile offenders who match the characterization above, most criminologists would be quick to point out that the majority of youths who become entangled in the juvenile justice machinery and who become publicly identified as delinquents are not members of organized gangs nor even of peer groups made up of other offenders. Moreover, the largest share of officially identified delinquents are youngsters who have been involved in a relatively small number of relatively trivial illegal acts. Criminologists also frequently draw distinctions between official delinquency and law-violating behavior, or between *official delinquents* and *offenders,* in order to emphasize the fundamental fact that large numbers of individuals who engage in illegal acts manage to avoid being reported or apprehended for those acts. Moreover, criminologists often hasten to remind us that "official delinquents," that is, youths who have fallen into the hands of the police or the courts, may not be a representative sample of the larger group of offenders.

Over the past thirty years, criminologists have devoted a good deal of energy to the study of offenders-at-large, principally through the use of self-report questionnaires on which youngsters are asked to confess to a range of deviant or illegal acts they have committed but for which they have not been apprehended. Most of these self-report questionnaires have concentrated upon trivial acts of misbehavior, and not surprisingly investigators who have defined and measured "delinquency" in this fashion have discovered that most youngsters engage in it as they pass through childhood and adolescence.

The thrust of these remarks is that *delinquency* is not a term which has a single, patently obvious meaning. Instead, it sometimes refers to repetitive involvement in serious acts of criminality, while at other times it refers to relatively transitory, episodic, and petty acts. It would be well to keep this point clearly in focus as we make our way through this chapter. As we shall see, criminologists themselves have often acted as though police arrest records, juvenile court statistics, and self-report instruments all tap the same phenomenon. This blurring of important differences has led to a number of arguments, such as the controversy over whether delinquency is or is not related to social class position, that turn largely on how delinquency is defined. In other words, while lower-income youths are more likely to be involved in and apprehended for serious acts of lawbreaking than are youngsters from other social class backgrounds, involvement in more trivial forms of misconduct seems to be equally common across socioeconomic groups.

When we speak of *delinquency* in this book, the term refers to all juvenile lawbreaking, officially processed and otherwise. How can we begin to put together a reasonably detailed and accurate picture of juvenile misconduct, including both officially recognized delinquency and the activities of undetected offenders? A number of pieces of data are available to us which provide a multilayered description of delinquency. The innermost layers consist of official delinquents, including incarcerated offenders, court referrals, and youths arrested by the police, many of whom are not injected further into the juvenile justice system.

Reports from social agencies outside the juvenile court concerning juvenile lawbreakers handled by those organizations provide another source of information about the extent of juvenile misconduct. In addition, some of the contours of total delinquency are revealed by the numerous victimization surveys that have been carried out in the United States in the past two decades. Finally, a large number of self-report studies focusing on hidden delinquency have been conducted. These investigations provide us with details about "the dark figure of crime" as it is sometimes called, that is, the extent of unreported, undetected lawbreaking in the United States and other nations. This "dark figure of delinquency" is the large outer layer which makes up much of the delinquency problem.

TABLE 3-1   Numer of Children Held in Public and Private Juvenile Facilities on December 31, 1979

TYPE OF FACILITY	PUBLIC	PRIVATE	TOTAL
All facilities in the United States	43,234	28,688	71,922
Long-term facilities (Training schools, ranches, forest camps, farms, half-way houses, group homes)	31,049	27,955	59,004
Short-term facilities (Detention centers, shelters, reception or diagnostic centers)	12,185	733	12,918
Males	37,167	20,512	57,679
Females	6,067	8,176	14,243

OFFICIAL DELINQUENCY

The first thing that is apparent from statistics on officially handled cases of delinquency is that although officially processed juvenile lawbreakers constitute a sizable group within American society, they nonetheless are only a small part of the total youth population. For example, in 1979 youths 10 through 17 years of age numbered 28,276,000, while the number of delinquency referrals to juvenile courts was 1,306,700 (Flanagan and McCloud, 1983: 436). In the same year, over 71,000 youths were in custody in public and private juvenile facilities on any particular day, so that relatively few youngsters experienced institutionalization. Table 3-1 indicates the location of incarcerated juveniles in more detail. Parenthetically, the number of incarcerated youths has been declining in recent years, dropping from 76,671 in 1974 to 71,951 in 1979 (Flanagan and McCloud, 1983: 514-16).

Juvenile Court Cases

Beginning in 1940, the Children's Bureau of the Federal Department of Health, Education, and Welfare began publishing estimates of the number of delinquency, dependency, and neglect cases in juvenile courts each year. More recently, the Office of Youth Development of DHEW assumed that responsibility, collecting court statistics each year from a nationwide sample of approximately 2000 juvenile courts, then estimating the total cases. Juvenile court data collection is currently the responsibility of the National Center for Juvenile Justice.

Table 3-2 presents the estimated number of delinquency cases per year from 1965 to 1979 (Flanagan and McCloud, 1983: 436-37). Less than 5 percent of the youth population appeared in juvenile courts in 1979. Of course, a somewhat larger number of youngsters gets into court at some time during their juvenile years. Still, appearance in a juvenile court is an experience which occurs to relatively few juveniles. The seriousness of the delinquency problem would seem to be further minimized by the observation that in only about half of the 1,306,700 cases in

TABLE 3-2 Juvenile Court Cases and Child Population, United States, 1965-1979

YEAR	DELINQUENCY CASES	POPULATION (AGE 11-17)*	PERCENT
1965	697,000	29,479,000	2.4
1966	745,000	30,088,000	2.5
1967	811,000	31,000,000	2.3
1968	900,000	31,566,000	2.9
1969	989,000	32,157,000	3.1
1970	1,052,000	32,614,000	3.2
1971	1,125,000	32,969,000	3.4
1972	1,112,500	33,120,000	3.4
1973	1,143,700	33,370,000	3.4
1974	1,252,700	33,365,000	3.8
1975	1,406,100	30,720,000	4.6
1976	1,396,800	30,247,000	4.6
1977	1,355,500	29,551,000	4.6
1978	1,340,700	28,964,000	4.6
1979	1,306,700	28,276,000	4.6

* Child population for 1975-1979 consists of youths ages 10-17.

1979 were petitions alleging delinquency filed against the children. Nonjudicial or informal dispositions were made of 709,800, or 54.3 percent of these cases.

Juvenile courts process markedly larger numbers of males than females. Table 3-3 indicates the numbers of male and female referrals to courts from 1965 to 1979 (Flanagan and McCloud, 1983: 436). Female court referrals comprised 20 percent of the total in 1965, but the proportion of females increased somewhat in the period following 1965.

TABLE 3-3 Juvenile Court Cases by Sex, 1965-1979

	MALES		FEMALES	
	NUMBER	PERCENT	NUMBER	PERCENT
1965	555,000	80	142,000	20
1966	593,000	80	152,000	20
1967	640,000	79	171,000	21
1968	708,000	79	191,000	21
1969	760,000	77	228,000	23
1970	799,500	76	252,000	24
1971	845,500	75	279,500	25
1972	827,500	74	285,000	26
1973	845,300	74	298,400	26
1974	927,000	74	325,700	26
1975	1,071,400	76	334,600	24
1976	1,064,000	76	330,700	24
1977	1,036,900	77	315,600	23
1978	1,013,700	76	327,000	24
1979	1,018,900	78	287,800	22

How do juveniles get into juvenile court? Who refers youngsters to the court? And, what are the charges that bring youths to court attention? Data relative to these questions are presented in Tables 3-4 and 3-5 (Flanagan and McCloud, 1983: 437). These data indicate that it is police officers who do most of the business of court referral, for they were responsible for 84 percent of such referrals in 1979. Table 3-5 suggests that a large share of the work of juvenile courts is given over to the processing of relatively petty forms of delinquency.

What have the delinquency trends been in recent years as measured by court referrals? Table 3-2 indicates the estimated number of court cases in the United States from 1965 to 1979, in relation to the population of at-risk youths, that is, youngsters 10 through 17 years of age. If we take a long view first and dig back into juvenile court statistics to 1950, we would discover that court referrals numbered only 280,000 cases or 1.6 percent of the youth population in 1950, but have increased to over 1,300,000 referrals or 4.6 percent of the juvenile group in 1979. However, looking at shorter term trends, it can be seen that the delinquency rate has been stabilized at 4.6 percent of the youth population since 1975. Moreover, the numbers of youngsters who have been sent to juvenile courts have *decreased* since 1975, which is at variance with common public beliefs about delinquency (Krisberg and Schwartz, 1983: 342).

The usual interpretation of data such as those portrayed in Table 3-2 is that they are a direct indication of real changes in the rates of involvement of youths in lawbreaking. But there is another possibility behind these trends, namely that changes in delinquency are due, at least in part, to increased or decreased public concern about youthful misconduct. Moreover, the data presented in Table 3-2 may be misleading in another way. These trends deal only with the total population of youths 10 to 17 years of age, without consideration of shifts within that age

TABLE 3-4 Juvenile Court Cases, by Source of Referral to Court, United States, 1979

	ESTIMATED NUMBER OF DELINQUENCY CASES	PERCENT
Source of referral to court	1,306,700	100.0
Law enforcement	1,095,300	83.8
Parents, relatives	43,900	3.4
School	38,400	2.9
Probation officer	31,700	2.4
Social agency	13,800	1.1
Other court	28,600	2.2
Other	55,000	4.2
Manner of handling	1,306,700	100.0
Without petition	709,800	54.3
With petition	596,000	45.7

TABLE 3-5 Juvenile Court Cases, by Reason for Referral to Court, United States, 1979

REASON FOR REFERRAL TO COURT	ESTIMATED NUMBER OF DELINQUENCY CASES	PERCENT
Total	1,306,700	100.0
Part I offenses, total	554,300	42.4
Violent index offenses, total	60,600	5.0
Criminal homicide, total	1,800	0.1
Murder	700	0.0
Nonnegligent manslaughter	1,100	0.1
Forcible rape	2,600	0.2
Robbery	24,500	1.8
Aggravated assault	31,700	2.4
Property index offenses, total	493,700	38.0
Burglary	168,200	12.8
Larceny-theft	263,500	20.2
Motor vehicle theft	55,700	4.3
Arson	6,300	0.5
Part II offenses, total	752,500	57.6
Other assaults	74,900	5.7
Forgery, counterfeiting, fraud, and embezzlement	20,900	1.6
Stolen property; buying, receiving, possessing	29,800	2.3
Vandalism	73,400	5.6
Weapons violations	17,100	1.3
Prostitution, commercialized vice, sex offenses	11,000	0.8
Drug abuse violations	79,800	6.1
Liquor laws	73,500	5.6
Drunkenness	21,700	1.7
Disorderly conduct	39,400	3.0
Running away	69,600	5.3
Curfew violations	17,600	1.3
All other offenses	223,800	17.1
Miscellaneous offenses against persons	7,700	0.6
Contempt, escape, violation of probation and parole	33,300	2.5
Miscellaneous offenses against public order	57,900	4.4
Trespassing	26,600	2.0
Truancy	30,300	2.3
Ungovernable behavior	47,700	3.6
Miscellaneous status offenses	20,300	1.5

group that might account for changes in the volume of delinquency. For example, we should expect changes in court referrals over time if the juvenile group shifts in the direction of a greater proportion of older youths, for youngsters over 14 years of age are most frequently involved in official delinquency. This change in referrals would occur even if the older youngsters did not change in the direction of a higher rate of misconduct.

One indication of the effects of changes in age composition on court referrals is found in a study by Roland Chilton and Adele Spielberger (1970). These investigators reported that referrals to Florida juvenile courts rose sharply from 1958 to 1967 but that most of the increase was related to changes in the size of the delinquency-eligible population group. They computed 1967 delinquency rates that would have been expected, based on the 1958 age-specific delinquency rates. They concluded on the basis of these predicted rates that about 70 percent of the increase in referrals was due to alterations in the number of children in specific age groups, that is, much of the 1958-1967 increase in delinquency was attributable simply to the growth of the older juvenile portion of the youthful population.

Police Arrests

Since the police do not turn over to the juvenile court all of those children who fall into their hands, just how large is the group of juveniles they do contact? What portion of these youngsters end up in juvenile courts? Answers to these questions can be found in the reports of the Federal Bureau of Investigation, which collects nationwide arrest statistics, and in sociological investigations that have been carried out.

Although complete and accurate figures on the number of persons arrested each year are not available, due to the failure of many police agencies to report statistics to the FBI, and also to defects in the reporting procedures of some agencies that do report, estimates of the total volume of arrests are available. Table 3-6 indicates the total number of arrests estimated for the United States in 1983 by the FBI (Federal Bureau of Investigation, 1984: 179).

What is the contribution of juveniles to this large volume of arrests in the United States? Table 3-6 (Federal Bureau of Investigation, 1984: 179) shows that persons in the under-18 age group were responsible for 7.4 percent of the homicides, 14.5 percent of the forcible rapes, and 12.9 percent of the aggravated assault arrests in 1983. More important, this table indicates that juveniles are responsible for a relatively large share of property crimes, for they made up 38.3 percent of the arrests for burglary, 32.3 percent of the arrests for larceny, and over 33 percent of the motor vehicle theft arrests. Table 3-6 also indicates that juveniles make up a sizable share of the arrests for stolen property, vandalism, and liquor law violations.

As we saw in an earlier part of this chapter, juvenile court referrals have been decreasing in numbers in recent years. Accordingly, it should come as no surprise to also discover that juvenile arrests have decreased from earlier levels as well. On this point, Krisberg and Schwartz (1983: 340) have indicated that while the absolute numbers of juvenile arrests increased between 1971 and 1979, this increase occurred in the period from 1971 to 1974, with arrests declining during the last five years of this period. Rates of arrest of juveniles dropped as well; thus the decline was not solely a function of a decreased number of juveniles in the population. The total number of juvenile arrests was 1,624,310 in 1971, 1,879,387 in 1974, and 1,819,673 in 1979, with a 3.2 percent decrease in arrests between 1974 and 1979. The largest share of the decline in arrests was due to the decrease of status offense arrests, dropping from 536,266 in 1971 to 466,855 in 1979, a change of 9.1 percent. This shrinkage of status offense referrals reflects the policy effects of federal government efforts to get these cases out of juvenile courts, and the growth of diversion programs which we noted in Chapter 2.

The trends identified by Krisberg and Schwartz have continued, as is shown by Table 3-7 (Federal Bureau of Investigation, 1984: 173). This table indicates that while total arrest figures increased or decreased only slightly between 1974 and 1983, arrests of persons under 18 years of age decreased for most offenses in that same period.

The last set of arrest statistics to be considered are those for males and females. Table 3-8 (Federal Bureau of Investigation, 1984: 178) indicates the number of males and females under the age of 18 who were arrested in 1982 and 1983. Although Table 3-8 does not indicate the proportions of males versus females among arrested persons, it is readily apparent from this table that males are far more frequently arrested than are females. Females under 18 made up only 10.8 percent of the persons under 18 who were arrested for homicides in 1983, and they comprised 6.4 percent of the juvenile arrests for robbery, 16.1 percent of those for aggravated assault, 6.8 percent of those for burglary, 26.4 percent of those for larceny, and only 10.8 percent for motor vehicle theft.

The most revealing findings on police arrests and disposition of juvenile cases came from the massive study in Philadelphia by Marvin Wolfgang, Robert Figlio, and Thorsten Sellin (1972). Those researchers obtained information on the delinquency histories, as measured by police contacts, of the cohort of all boys born in 1945 who lived in Philadelphia at least between their tenth and their eighteenth birthdays, a total of 9945 boys. School records were searched for information on the social backgrounds and school records of the boys, while data on police contacts were obtained from the records of the Juvenile Aid Division of the Philadelphia Police Department.

The Philadelphia study contained a wealth of data on official delinquency as measured by police contacts. But some of the most central findings were the following. First, of the 9945 subjects, 3475 (35 percent) of them were involved with the police at least once to the extent that the contact had been officially recorded, while 65 percent had not experienced police apprehension. The proportions of white and black youths having contact with the police varied: 28.6 percent of the whites and 50.2 percent of the blacks were classified as offenders. Along the same line, lower socioeconomic class members were more frequently involved in police contact than were higher status boys; 44.8 percent of the former and 26.5 percent of the latter had been in the hands of the police.

Wolfgang, Figlio, and Sellin also examined offense patterns among those youths who had been apprehended by the police. Of the delinquents, 54 percent were repeaters, while 46 percent had been in the hands of the police only once. The recidivists were more frequently from lower socioeconomic backgrounds than were the one-time offenders. More white lower status boys were repeaters than one-time offenders, while upper status white youths were most often one-timers. Black delinquent boys from all economic levels were most commonly recidivists.

TABLE 3-6 Total Arrests, by Age, United States, 1983

OFFENSES	NUMBER OF PERSONS ARRESTED*			PERCENT	
	TOTAL ALL AGES	UNDER 15	UNDER 18	UNDER 15	UNDER 18
Total	10,287,309	564,983	1,725,746	5.5	16.8
Murder and nonnegligent manslaughter	18,064	157	1,345	.9	7.4
Forcible rape	30,183	1,332	4,388	4.4	14.5
Robbery	134,018	9,203	35,219	6.9	26.3
Aggravated assault	261,421	10,148	33,730	3.9	12.9
Burglary	415,651	59,400	159,192	14.3	38.3
Larceny-theft	1,169,066	168,095	377,435	14.4	32.3
Motor vehicle theft	105,514	8,628	36,497	8.2	34.6
Arson	17,203	4,113	6,457	23.9	37.5
Violent crime	443,686	20,840	74,682	4.7	16.8
Property crime	1,707,434	240,236	579,581	14.1	33.9
Crime Index total	2,151,120	261,076	654,263	12.1	30.4
Other assaults	481,615	29,817	78,487	6.2	16.3
Forgery and counterfeiting	74,508	1,191	6,738	1.6	9.0
Fraud	261,844	9,205	20,874	3.5	8.0
Embezzlement	7,604	78	459	1.0	6.0
Stolen property; buying, receiving, possessing	112,424	7,740	26,564	6.9	23.6
Vandalism	212,629	47,949	93,157	22.6	43.8

TABLE 3-6 (continued)

OFFENSES	NUMBER OF PERSONS ARRESTED*			PERCENT	
	TOTAL ALL AGES	UNDER 15	UNDER 18	UNDER 15	UNDER 18
Weapons; carrying, possessing, etc.	160,534	6,110	22,492	3.8	14.0
Prostitution and commercialized vice	119,262	270	2,837	.2	2.4
Sex offenses (except forcible rape and prostitution)	77,119	5,323	12,088	6.9	15.7
Drug abuse violations	616,936	11,819	72,687	1.9	11.8
Gambling	38,403	127	1,082	.3	2.8
Offenses against family and children	46,111	476	1,310	1.0	2.8
Driving under the influence	1,613,184	522	24,997	–	1.5
Liquor laws	427,230	8,990	114,159	2.1	26.7
Drunkenness	977,924	3,191	28,833	.3	2.9
Vagrancy	31,262	617	2,539	2.0	8.1
All other offenses (except traffic)	2,005,797	74,661	280,646	3.7	14.0
Suspicion (not included in totals)	12,262	1,004	2,828	8.2	23.1
Curfew and loitering law violations	68,148	18,721	68,148	27.5	100.0
Runaways	112,476	48,834	112,476	43.4	100.0

*Based on 10,827 agencies; 1983 estimated population 200,692,000. The reader should note that these arrest figures are somewhat lower than the total estimated arrests for the entire United States population, which for 1983 were set at 11,700,000 by the FBI. The age distribution of this larger group of arrests is not available.

TABLE 3-7 Total Arrest Trends, United States, 1974-1983*

	NUMBER OF PERSONS ARRESTED					
	TOTAL ALL AGES			UNDER 18 YEARS OF AGE		
OFFENSE CHARGED	1974	1983	PERCENT CHANGE	1974	1983	PERCENT CHANGE
Total	6,161,727	7,045,637	+14.3	1,634,667	1,253,728	-23.3
Murder and nonnegligent manslaughter	14,054	12,901	-8.2	1,384	1,015	-26.7
Forcible rape	17,402	20,850	+19.8	3,419	3,214	-6.0
Robbery	106,279	99,031	-6.8	35,726	27,668	-22.6
Aggravated assault	150,089	170,887	+13.9	24,814	23,560	-5.1
Burglary	330,363	279,529	-15.4	176,018	109,740	-37.7
Larceny-theft	706,277	827,878	+17.2	345,347	273,487	-20.8
Motor vehicle theft	102,418	76,238	-25.6	56,960	26,646	-53.2
Arson	10,335	11,506	+11.3	5,966	4,512	-24.4
Violent crime	287,824	303,669	+5.5	65,343	55,457	-15.1
Property crime	1,149,393	1,195,151	+4.0	584,291	414,385	-29.1
Crime Index total	1,437,217	1,498,820	+4.3	649,634	469,842	-27.7
Other assaults	274,749	348,990	+27.0	55,012	61,104	+11.1
Forgery and counterfeiting	39,879	49,645	+24.5	5,252	4,599	-12.4
Fraud	99,042	163,190	+64.8	4,665	19,390	+315.6
Embezzlement	5,994	4,434	-26.0	454	315	-30.6
Stolen property: buying, receiving, possessing	74,333	79,050	+6.3	25,282	19,710	-22.0
Vandalism	140,749	156,532	+11.2	96,107	68,782	-28.4

TABLE 3-7 (continued)

	NUMBER OF PERSONS ARRESTED					
	TOTAL ALL AGES			UNDER 18 YEARS OF AGE		
OFFENSE CHARGED	1974	1983	PERCENT CHANGE	1974	1983	PERCENT CHANGE
Weapons; carrying, possessing, etc.	114,794	112,925	-1.6	18,109	16,776	-7.4
Prostitution and commercialized vice	51,524	88,291	+71.4	2,223	2,246	+1.0
Sex offenses (except forcible rape and prostitution)	41,714	53,291	+27.8	9,298	8,508	-8.5
Drug abuse violations	456,449	432,319	-5.3	120,047	52,401	-56.3
Gambling	49,712	29,109	-41.4	2,184	933	-57.3
Offenses against family and children	40,584	24,940	-38.5	3,570	867	-75.7
Driving under the influence	671,210	998,127	+48.7	10,430	15,059	+44.4
Liquor laws	182,071	285,530	+56.8	75,984	81,208	+6.9
Drunkenness	952,626	631,857	-33.7	29,300	18,612	-36.5
Disorderly conduct	522,298	529,758	+1.4	101,884	79,965	-21.5
Vagrancy	33,726	25,061	-25.7	4,768	1,566	-67.2
All other traffic (except traffic)	758,444	1,421,672	+87.4	205,852	219,749	+6.8
Suspicion (not included in totals)	32,223	9,428	-70.7	10,228	2,075	-79.7
Curfew and loitering law violations	67,498	33,263	-50.7	67,498	33,263	-50.7
Runaways	147,114	78,833	-46.4	147,114	78,833	-46.4

* Based on 5,289 agencies; 1983 estimated population 135,616,000.

TABLE 3-8 Total Arrest Trends, by Sex, United States, 1982-1983*

OFFENSE CHARGED	MALES						FEMALES					
	TOTAL			UNDER 18			TOTAL			UNDER 18		
	1982	1983	PERCENT CHANGE	1982	1983	PERCENT CHANGE	1982	1983	PERCENT CHANGE	1982	1983	PERCENT CHANGE
TOTAL	7,987,961	7,723,276	− 3.3	1,363,178	1,226,188	−10.0	1,559,644	1,539,381	− 1.3	354,352	327,902	− 7.5
Murder and nonnegligent manslaughter	15,234	14,385	− 5.6	1,374	1,109	−19.3	2,349	2,229	− 5.1	124	135	+ 8.9
Forcible rape	26,637	27,030	+ 1.5	3,920	3,924	+ .1	250	232	− 7.2	61	37	−39.3
Robbery	122,656	116,127	− 5.3	32,769	31,023	− 5.3	9,618	9,226	− 4.1	2,347	2,181	− 7.1
Aggravated assault	212,267	203,714	− 4.0	27,319	25,826	− 5.5	31,639	31,955	+ 1.0	5,171	4,954	− 4.2
Burglary	386,487	348,896	− 9.7	153,623	133,748	−12.9	27,459	25,904	− 5.7	10,899	9,740	−10.6
Larceny-theft	770,295	736,442	− 4.4	261,140	246,616	− 5.6	321,113	309,362	− 3.7	92,830	88,553	− 4.6
Motor vehicle theft	94,300	87,180	− 7.6	33,258	29,272	−12.0	9,336	8,588	− 8.0	4,102	3,529	−14.0
Arson	13,944	13,200	− 5.3	5,277	5,215	− 1.2	2,043	1,790	−12.4	693	520	−25.0
Violent crime	376,794	361,256	− 4.1	65,382	61,882	− 5.4	43,856	43,642	− .5	7,703	7,307	− 5.1
Property crime	1,265,026	1,185,718	− 6.3	453,298	414,851	− 8.5	359,951	345,644	− 4.0	108,524	102,342	− 5.7
Crime Index total	1,641,820	1,546,974	− 5.8	518,680	476,733	− 8.1	403,807	389,286	− 3.6	116,227	109,649	− 5.7
Other assaults	365,173	370,935	+ 1.6	55,745	55,034	− 1.3	62,369	64,338	+ 3.2	15,222	15,276	+ .4
Forgery and counterfeiting	51,349	45,334	−11.7	5,016	4,135	−17.6	24,807	22,874	− 7.8	2,337	1,982	−15.2
Fraud	150,863	144,337	− 4.3	14,502	15,941	+ 9.9	101,924	96,847	− 5.0	3,967	4,550	+14.7
Embezzlement	4,845	4,655	− 3.9	402	314	−21.9	2,170	2,252	+ 3.8	151	120	−20.5
Stolen property; buying, receiving, possessing	96,104	91,004	− 5.3	24,543	21,981	−10.4	12,560	11,724	− 6.7	2,501	2,235	−10.6
Vandalism	172,423	168,671	− 2.2	77,551	74,899	− 3.4	17,831	18,194	+ 2.0	6,895	6,911	+ .2
Weapons; carrying, possessing, etc.	144,376	136,025	− 5.8	20,441	19,620	− 4.0	12,294	11,473	− 6.7	1,466	1,334	− 0.9

TABLE 3-8 (continued)

OFFENSE CHARGED	MALES TOTAL			MALES UNDER 18			FEMALES TOTAL			FEMALES UNDER 18		
	1982	1983	PERCENT CHANGE	1982	1983	PERCENT CHANGE	1982	1983	PERCENT CHANGE	1982	1983	PERCENT CHANGE
Prostitution and commercialized vice	31,032	33,481	+ 7.9	867	830	− 4.3	76,916	79,292	+ 3.1	1,989	1,815	− 8.7
Sex offenses (except forcible rape and prostitution)	58,544	64,802	+10.7	9,567	10,267	+ 7.3	4,762	5,314	+11.6	697	704	+ 1.0
Drug abuse violations	465,037	483,781	+ 4.0	60,943	55,710	− 8.6	73,550	79,207	+ 7.7	11,738	10,745	− 8.5
Gambling	31,314	31,322		1,184	967	−18.3	3,758	4,001	+ 6.5	46	50	+ 8.7
Offenses against family and children	36,389	36,722	+ .9	938	765	−18.4	4,826	4,587	− 5.0	545	430	−21.1
Driving under the influence	1,188,997	1,247,790	+ 4.9	21,380	18,679	−12.6	144,415	158,086	+ 9.5	2,799	2,710	− 3.2
Liquor laws	317,539	294,468	− 7.3	85,422	72,798	−14.8	57,343	57,141	− .4	25,910	24,121	− 6.9
Drunkenness	904,506	836,847	− 7.5	27,429	22,659	−17.4	83,131	79,949	− 3.8	4,608	4,110	−10.8
Disorderly conduct	626,274	514,094	−17.9	93,833	73,957	−21.1	107,049	98,668	− 7.8	17,661	15,318	−13.1
Vagrancy	27,264	26,888	− 1.4	2,862	2,009	−29.8	3,804	2,977	−21.7	582	354	−39.2
All other offenses (except traffic)	1,570,204	1,554,324	− 1.0	237,965	208,068	−12.6	282,567	280,372	− .8	59,250	52,689	−11.1
Suspicion (not included in totals)	7,295	6,739	− 7.6	1,983	2,018	+ 1.8	1,254	1,215	− 3.1	467	502	+ 7.5
Curfew and loitering law violations	58,082	48,270	−16.9	58,082	48,270	−16.9	16,101	14,462	−10.2	16,101	14,462	−10.2
Runaways	45,826	42,552	− 7.1	45,826	42,552	− 7.1	63,660	58,337	− 8.4	63,660	58,337	− 8.4

*Based on 8,792 agencies; 1983 estimated population 175,998,000

Nonwhite rates for offenses against both property and persons were higher than those of whites, and further, the more serious acts of bodily harm were committed by black youths.

These researchers also examined the activities of chronic offenders, defined as youngsters who had been involved in more than four violations. These delinquents comprised 18 percent of the total group of offenders but were responsible for over one-half of all offenses. They were also most frequently involved in serious offenses, with the nonchronic and one-time offenders having lower seriousness scores on a delinquency index. But the chronic offenders did not start out by committing petty offenses that eventually escalated into more serious ones; thus they did not show a career pattern of increasing seriousness of delinquency over time. Instead, they generally began their delinquent involvement by engaging in relatively serious offenses.

Regarding the police disposition or handling of these delinquency cases, Wolfgang, Figlio, and Sellin concluded (1972: 252):

> We have briefly analyzed the disposition of offenders taken into custody by the police. Some were given a remedial disposition, which means that the police recorded the delinquent behavior but did not further process the case for consideration by the juvenile court. Others were arrested formally and had their cases "adjusted" at an intake interview; still others were formally dealt with by means of a court penalty, such as probation or incarceration. Variables associated with a greater likelihood of a court penalty included being nonwhite, being of low SES level, committing an index offense, being a recidivist, and committing an offense with a relatively high seriousness score. However, in an effort to determine the relative effect of each of these variables, we had to conclude that the most significant factor related to a boy's not being remedialed by the police, but being processed to the full extent of the juvenile justice system, is his being nonwhite. That differential treatment based on race occurs is once again documented from this cohort study.

The thrust of these data is that juvenile courts receive the most serious cases dealt with by the police; they tend to process hard-core delinquents. Juvenile misconduct is a good deal more commonplace than suggested by the numbers of youths referred to juvenile courts, for as the Wolfgang, Figlio, and Sellin study indicated, about one-third of the youngsters in one large American city had at least one contact with the police during their juvenile age period.

VICTIMIZATION SURVEYS

Clearly, one major means of gauging the severity of the delinquency problem is through the statistics compiled by the police, juvenile courts, and related social agencies. As we have seen, these figures indicate that the juvenile justice machinery seems to operate in a manner similar to a series of nets of varying sized mesh, through which some fish are caught and others escape. The juvenile court net scoops up only part of the delinquent group that gets caught in the police net, while private agencies gain control of some offenders who are not known to the other agencies.

One indication that many juvenile lawbreakers avoid entanglement in any of these nets can be found in the victimization surveys that have been carried out in the United States in the 1960s and 1970s (Gibbons, 1982: 94-100; Empey, 1982: 129-48). These studies were inaugurated by a national survey conducted for the President's Commission on Law Enforcement and Administration of Justice, in which 10,000 citizens were asked whether they had been the victims of a crime in the previous year.

Most recent victimization studies have been carried out in a large number of American cities jointly by the Bureau of Justice Statistics of the U. S. Department of Justice and the U. S. Bureau of the Census. Although victimization surveys are not entirely without flaws and problems (Weis, 1983: 385-87), they do provide a valuable source of information additional to data on officially reported crimes. In general, these investigations show that acts of violence, common theft, and burglary occur four times or more frequently than is reported to the police. Males more frequently report victimization, as do blacks and lower-income persons. Most important for the discussion here, younger persons, particularly black youths, most often report having been the victim of rapes, robberies, aggravated assaults, thefts, and certain other offenses. Empey (1982: 144) has offered the following summary of these studies and their findings:

> Young people are more vulnerable than older people.
> Males are more vulnerable than females.
> Blacks are more vulnerable than whites.
> Poor people are more vulnerable than the affluent, at least to violent crimes.
> City dwellers are more vulnerable than country dwellers.
> In summary, when all of these factors interact, they indicate that the proto-typical victim, particularly of violent crimes, is the young, poor, black male who lives in an urban ghetto. The young, poor, white male is not far behind, followed closely by the young, poor, black female.

Although victimization studies focus upon the victims of criminality rather than the offenders who carry out these predatory or violent acts, the significance of these inquiries for the assessment of delinquency is still considerable. It is highly probable that in many cases victims and offenders closely resemble each other, so that young persons are the frequent victims of offenses by young persons. In short, the victim surveys provide supportive evidence pointing to the ubiquity of juvenile lawbreaking in American society. That contention is buttressed by the "hidden delinquency" research as well, to which our attention now turns.

"HIDDEN" DELINQUENCY

When all the misbehaving youngsters who have been observed by the courts, the police, or other agencies are added up, they still make up a minority of the youth population. But what of undetected or "hidden" delinquents? Are undetected law-breakers few or abundant? How do some delinquents remain "hidden" while others get caught up in the machinery of police arrest and court referral? Are hidden delinquents beneficiaries of discriminatory law enforcement in which their deviant acts are overlooked because they are from favored social class groups or because of other factors of that kind?

The importance of answers to these questions cannot be overemphasized. Research studies dealing with the causation of delinquency are based on assumptions about the true extent of misconduct. If these assumptions are faulty, causal research based upon them will be flawed. In the past, researchers have often assumed that most of the youngsters who have escaped the attention of the police, courts, or social agencies are free from involvement in lawbreaking, or at least from persistent and serious misbehavior. In turn, these "nondelinquents" have been compared to court cases or other recognized "delinquents." But suppose many "nondelinquents" are, in fact, frequently involved in undetected but serious and repetitive acts of law violation. If so, comparison of these persons with officially recognized delinquents would be highly misleading. Such comparisons might tell us a good deal about the factors that cause some delinquents to be officially tagged yet allow other youths to remain hidden and undetected, but little about causation.

How can we gauge "the dark figure of crime and delinquency"? How can we get evidence on the extent of unrecorded lawbreaking? During the past three decades, a technique frequently employed has been the self-report questionnaire, on which youngsters are asked to confess to those acts of lawbreaking in which they have been engaged.[1]

Early Work

The initial study of hidden delinquency was conducted by Austin Porterfield (1943) and involved a questionnaire which was administered to several hundred college students. All of these students reported that they had engaged in delinquency, but virtually none of them had been brought to police or court attention. Porterfield interpreted his findings as showing that children from poor economic areas or from situations of family or neighborhood disorganization are closely watched by the police; juveniles from comfortable backgrounds who commit similar acts are ignored by the police. But some respondents may have admitted petty and innocuous acts of thefts, mischief, and the like, which would account for their lenient handling.

---

[1] Self-report techniques have been the subject of a good deal of analysis, criticism, and commentary. For some of this material, see Nettler (1984); Reiss (1976); Hindelang, Hirschi, and Weis (1981).

TABLE 3-9 Behavioral Study of 101 Youths in Several Year Period

TYPE OF OFFENSE	UNOFFICIAL DELINQUENTS (NUMBER—61)	OFFICIAL DELINQUENTS (NUMBER—40)	BOTH GROUPS (NUMBER—101)
City ordinance offense	739	655	1394
Minor offense	1913	2493	4406
Serious offense	174	442	616
Total	2826	3590	6416

Another early study involved a quite different collection of youths, those who were involved in the Cambridge-Somerville Youth Study, a delinquency prevention project conducted in two communities near Boston, Massachusetts (Murphy, Shirley, and Witmer, 1946). A group of slum area boys regarded as predelinquents moving toward careers in serious lawbreaking were subjected to casework treatment. Caseworkers maintained detailed records of the delinquent acts of these boys over several years. The offense behavior of the 101 subjects of the study is shown in Table 3-9. Although 61 delinquents had not been reported to the juvenile court, while 40 delinquents had come to court attention, it is readily apparent from this table that all of the youths had been deeply enmeshed in misconduct. Only 95 (less than 1½ percent) of the 6416 offenses had been reported to the juvenile court. Those boys who had become known to the court were more frequently involved in serious delinquency than the unofficial delinquents; individuals in the officially known group had committed from 5 to 323 violations apiece and averaged 79 offenses, in contrast to the hidden group who showed a median of 30 offenses.

The major point on slum area hidden delinquency is the staggering amount of it turned up by this study. These data suggest that youthful misconduct may be a way of life for a large number of boys in urban working-class neighborhoods, an observation to be kept in mind when some of the more recent studies of hidden delinquents are examined. These show that youths from relatively comfortable social circumstances have often misbehaved, but it may well be that their midadventures are neither as serious nor as repetitive as those of slum-area boys (see also Reiss and Rhodes, 1961; Hardt and Peterson, 1968).

Short and Nye's Contributions

James Short and F. Ivan Nye have carried out a number of studies of hidden delinquency. One of the most important of these involved high school students in three Washington communities ranging from 10,000 to 30,000 residents, students in three midwestern towns, and delinquents in training schools in Washington state (Short and Nye, 1958). The subjects were asked to complete a questionnaire about the acts of misbehavior in which they had engaged as juveniles, and to indicate whether they had committed the acts more than once. An abridged version of the results is presented in Table 3-10, in which the delinquencies of the male subjects only are indicated (Short and Nye, 1958: 297).

TABLE 3-10 Extent of Delinquent Acts Admitted by Students and Training School Boys by Area

DELINQUENT ACTS	ADMIT ACT			ADMIT ACT MORE THAN ONCE OR TWICE		
	MIDWEST STUDENTS	WESTERN STUDENTS	TRAINING SCHOOL BOYS	MIDWEST STUDENTS	WESTERN STUDENTS	TRAINING SCHOOL BOYS
Driving a car without a license	81.1%	75.3%	91.1%	61.2%	49.0%	73.4%
Skipping school	54.4	53.0	95.3	24.4	23.8	85.9
Fist fighting	86.7	80.7	95.3	32.6	31.9	75.0
Running away	12.9	13.0	68.1	2.8	2.4	37.7
School probation or expulsion	15.3	11.3	67.8	2.1	2.9	31.3
Defying parents' Authority	22.2	33.1	52.4	1.4	6.3	23.6
Stealing items worth less than $2	62.7	60.6	91.8	18.5	12.9	65.1
Stealing items worth from $2 to $50	17.1	15.8	91.0	3.8	3.8	61.4
Stealing items worth more than $50	3.5	5.0	90.8	1.1	2.1	47.7
Gang fighting	24.3	22.5	67.4	6.7	5.2	47.4
Drinking Beer, wine, or liquor	67.7	57.2	89.7	35.8	29.5	79.4
Using narcotics	1.4	2.2	23.1	0.7	1.6	12.6
Having sex relations	38.8	40.4	87.5	20.3	19.9	73.4

The view that youths come only in two distinct types, "bad" delinquents and "good" nondelinquents, is most certainly not upheld by the results in Table 3-10. However, these findings do not lend much weight to the notion that juveniles get to the training school mainly as a result of discriminatory law enforcement based on social class factors or related criteria. "Nondelinquent" high school students engaged in many relatively petty acts of delinquency for which they could conceivably have been hauled into juvenile court, but the training school youths more frequently admitted to these same acts and, in addition, reported involvement in other, more serious forms of misconduct not common among the students. Finally, the training school boys declared that they had engaged in a large number of delinquencies with considerable frequency. The conclusion to be reached from the Short and Nye study is that *seriousness and frequency of delinquent conduct is one major determinant of the actions taken against juvenile lawbreakers.*

Nye and Short (1957) also developed a delinquency scale which allowed them to order youths in terms of degree of involvement in juvenile misconduct. This scale was based on seven items of behavior.

1. Driving a car without a driver's license or permit.
2. Skipping school without a legitimate excuse.
3. Defying parents' authority (to their face).
4. Taking little things (worth less than $2).
5. Buying or drinking beer, wine, or liquor.
6. Purposely damaging or destroying public or private property.
7. Having sex relations with the opposite sex.

The juveniles were sorted into fifteen categories on the basis of the number of these acts they acknowledged and the frequency with which they committed them. The results for high school and training school boys showed that some of the former had higher scores than the latter, that the high school boys were "more delinquent" as measured by the scale. Even so, 86 percent of the high school youths had scores of nine or less on the scale, while only 14 percent of the incarcerated juveniles had these low scores (Nye and Short, 1957: 299-300).

These results again point to the greater involvement in lawbreaking of official delinquents. Note too that the seven items in the scale centered upon relatively petty acts. In the development of this scale, several more serious delinquent acts which training school wards frequently admit had to be discarded, because few high school youngsters confessed to them. Thus this scale measured the degree of involvement in commonplace but relatively inconsequential forms of juvenile misconduct.

These results should be kept clearly in mind when the various self-report studies that followed those of Short and Nye are being considered. Juvenile delinquency is an umbrella term for acts as widely different as petty theft or teenager experimentation with alcohol, at the one extreme, and aggravated assault or homicide at the other. Researchers are likely to produce differing results when they employ measuring instruments that zero in on different collections of delinquent acts (Hindelang, Hirschi, and Weis, 1979). If a *truncated* delinquency scale such as the seven-item scale of Nye and Short is employed, the investigator may find that "delinquency" is ubiquitous and also that juveniles from different social class backgrounds are equally involved in it. On the other hand, if attention is focused upon more serious acts of lawbreaking, the researcher may discover that relatively few youngsters are "delinquent" by that measure and also that serious or chronic delinquency is related to the social class position of juveniles. We shall deal with this matter of social class and delinquency in more detail in Chapter 5.

National Surveys of Delinquency

We have an embarrassment of riches in the way of studies of hidden delinquency, most of which were carried out in single communities or other limited locales. Most of these studies produced results parallel to those of the investigations we have considered to this point, indicating that relatively petty delinquency is ubiquitous in American society. However, there are some national surveys of juvenile lawbreaking which ought to be given some attention.

In one nationwide survey of self-reported delinquency by Jay Williams and Martin Gold (1972), interviews were conducted with a probability sample of 847 boys and girls 13 to 16 years of age. Although 88 percent of the juveniles admitted committing at least one delinquent act in the previous three years, only 20 percent had any contact with the police, only 4 percent of them turned up in police records, only 16 youths had been sent to juvenile court, and finally, only 11 youngsters had been declared "delinquent" by the court. Although nearly all of the juveniles confessed to at least one delinquent act, relatively few of them reported that they had been involved in repetitive or serious misbehavior. White and black girls showed similar patterns of lawbreaking, while black males exceeded whites in seriousness of reported misconduct. In general, Williams and Gold found no marked socioeconomic relationship to reported delinquency.

One of the most recent and most enlightening reports on hidden delinquency comes from the findings of the National Youth Survey, a study of a national probability sample of 1726 youngsters 11 through 17 years of age (Ageton and Elliott, 1978; Elliott and Ageton, 1980). The authors of that report indicated that age and sex differences in delinquency involvement are usually less pronounced than those that are revealed in official statistics on youthful misconduct. More important, many of the self-report investigations conducted in the past have found little or no evidence of socioeconomic or racial differences in delinquency involvement, in contradistinction to patterns that have repeatedly turned up in official sources of data.

Elliott and Ageton argued that many self-report investigations have had methodological shortcomings. For one thing, many youngsters may either exaggerate or conceal their acts of misconduct. Then, too, the reliability of self-reports has been challenged, for many juveniles may fail to respond consistently to self-report questionnaires. Self-report questionnaires often exhibit a number of more specific defects as well. Many of these instruments are truncated, for they contain delinquent acts drawn principally from the lower or less serious end of the continuum of delinquent behavior. Also, many of them have included overlapping items, with the result that youngsters sometimes admit more than once to a single delinquent act. These questionnaires frequently involve ambiguous response categories such as *often* or *never*, making quantitative analysis of the findings difficult or impossible. Finally, self-report investigations have most often involved unrepresentative collections of juveniles rather than probability samples, with the consequence that the results cannot be generalized.

These problems identified by Elliott and Ageton should not be minimized. At the same time, we would reiterate some comments made earlier. The problems with the self-report technique are less severe than is sometimes argued (Hindelang, Hirschi, and Weis, 1981). On the whole, the self-report approach has been a useful one, particularly for tapping the behavioral domain of relatively petty misconduct (Hindelang, Hirschi, and Weis, 1979).

The National Youth Survey researchers endeavored to increase further the yield from self-report procedures, both by developing a more comprehensive set of behavioral items about which youths were quizzed and by administering the research instrument to a national probability sample of youths. First, a comprehensive set of offenses was employed, so that the full range of delinquent acts committed by juveniles was included in the survey. Overlapping items were screened out, precise response categories were developed, and youths were asked to report on delinquent acts carried on within the previous year. Finally, interviews rather than questionnaires were employed for data-gathering purposes.

The general findings regarding the frequency of reported delinquent acts that emerged from this national survey ran parallel to many of those results considered earlier in this chapter. Table 3-11 (Ageton and Elliott, 1978: 10) presents the percent of juveniles who reported committing specific acts of misbehavior during 1976. The most striking observation from that table is that while large numbers of youths admitted involvement in relatively petty acts of misconduct, relatively few of them confessed to more serious forms of lawbreaking, and similar to other investigations, fewer females than males in the National Youth Survey confessed to acts of delinquency.

Elliott and Ageton examined a number of patterns and relationships within the National Youth Survey sample. They reported that, overall, age was not related to involvement in delinquent acts. However, older boys more frequently confessed to certain offense groupings, including predatory acts directed at persons, the use of hard drugs, and public disorder offenses such as drunkenness and disorderly conduct. They also indicated that black youngsters reported more delinquencies, particularly involving predatory acts against property, than did white youths. Then, too, lower-status juveniles showed more frequent involvement both in delinquency generally and in predatory acts directed at persons than did youths from other socioeconomic backgrounds. Finally, self-reported delinquency was more common among juveniles from large metropolitan areas than among youths from smaller communities.

TABLE 3-11   Extent of Delinquent Acts in 1976 Admitted by National Youth Survey Sample

DELINQUENT ACT	TOTAL SAMPLE	MALE SAMPLE	FEMALE SAMPLE
Damaged family property	24%	29%	19%
Damaged school property	16	21	10
Damaged other property	18	24	10
Stole motor vehicle	1	1	—
Stole something worth over $50	2	4	—
Bought stolen goods	10	13	6
Thrown objects	47	57	35
Runaway	6	6	5
Lied about age	27	27	26
Carried hidden weapon	6	10	2
Stole something worth less than $5	18	22	13
Aggravated assault	6	9	3
Prostitution	1	1	1
Sexual intercourse	13	18	7
Gang fights	12	17	7
Sold marijuana	4	5	3
Cheated on school test	49	50	47
Hitchhiked	9	12	4
Stole from family	15	17	13
Hit teacher	8	10	5
Hit parents	6	6	6
Hit students	48	63	31
Disorderly conduct	32	35	29
Sold hard drugs	1	1	1
Joyriding	5	6	3
Got liquor for minors	5	6	3
Sexual assault	2	2	1
Strong-armed students	3	5	1
Strong-armed teachers	1	1	—
Strong-armed others	3	4	2
Evaded payment	21	26	15
Public drunkenness	14	16	11
Stole something worth $5–50	6	7	3
Stole at school	6	8	5
Broke into building or car	4	6	2
Panhandled	3	3	2
Skipped classes	31	34	29
Didn't return change	29	33	24
School suspension	10	13	7
Obscene calls	11	11	11
Use of:			
Alcohol	46	49	43
Marijuana	17	18	16
Hallucinogens	2	2	2
Amphetamines	3	3	3
Barbiturates	2	2	2
Heroin	—	—	—
Cocaine	1	2	1

SUMMARY

The conclusions about the extent of delinquency to be drawn from this mass of material should be self-evident. These conclusions, however, must be stated in terms such as *relatively large numbers* and *somewhat more,* for the available data do not lend themselves to precise statements about juvenile misconduct. A massive and complex research study would be required in order to be able to assert that some specific percentage of all offenders becomes known to the police, or that some specific proportion of lawbreakers receives a particular disposition from the police or courts. Such an investigation would have to be longitudinal in form, in which all of the children in a particular community would be followed over an extended period of time. Nonetheless, it is possible to state a group of conclusions about total delinquency in relatively definitive terms.

1. Less than 5 percent of the juveniles in this nation are actually referred to juvenile courts in any single year, although a larger portion of the youth population comes to court attention sometime during the adolescent years. Only about one-half of these referrals are regarded by court officials as serious enough to warrant the filing of a petition and a court hearing. The other half are dealt with informally.
2. Police agencies come into contact with almost twice the number of children known to the court. In general, they refer the serious cases to juvenile courts, while disposing of the less serious offenders informally, within the department, by admonitions and warnings.
3. A fairly large number of offenders is dealt with by public and private social agencies in the community, but many of the individuals they process are also known to the juvenile court. The majority of the cases known to agencies but which are unknown to the court are relatively petty ones.
4. Large numbers of youths at all social class levels and in all kinds of communities engage in acts of misconduct and lawbreaking which remain hidden or undetected. In this sense, nearly all juveniles are delinquent in some degree. However, many of the deviant acts of hidden delinquents are the kinds which would often be handled informally or ignored if reported to the juvenile court.
5. Not all of the hidden delinquency in the United States is petty and inconsequential. An indeterminate but important number of serious delinquencies is enacted by juveniles who manage to stay out of the hands of the police or courts.

Figure 3-1 shows another way of picturing the nature of delinquency in the United States. Different categories of offenders and nondelinquents are portrayed within a circle designating the total youth population. This diagram suggests that some portion of the total population of American youths is involved in conforming behavior, but it also implies that a large share of the juvenile group is involved in youthful lawbreaking. The latter is represented by the largest inner circle within the total group. Figure 3-1 also suggests that official delinquents are disproportionately involved in relatively serious acts of misbehavior, while hidden offenders are more frequently engaged in relatively petty offenses.

Figure 3-1 also hints at the sorting processes that go on in police agencies and

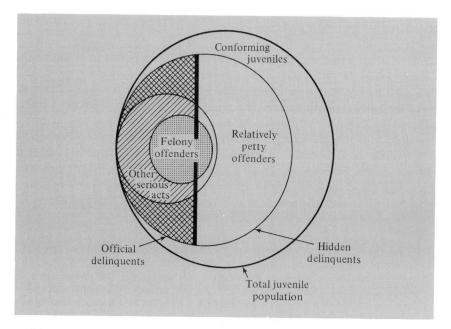

FIGURE 3-1 Delinquency and Nondelinquency in American Society

juvenile courts, in which more serious offenders get sifted into the official machinery of the juvenile justice system, while petty offenders get diverted out of that apparatus. These sifting and sorting processes will be examined in Chapter 5, but first, let us look at the various faces of delinquency, which is the concern of Chapter 4.

REFERENCES

AGETON, SUZANNE S. and ELLIOTT, DELBERT S. (1978). "The Incidence of Delinquent Behavior in a National Probability Sample of Adolescents." Boulder, Colo.: Behavioral Research Institute, mimeographed.

CHILTON, ROLAND and SPIELBERGER, ADELE (1971). "Is Delinquency Increasing? Age Structure and the Crime Rate." *Social Forces* 49 (March): 487-93.

ELLIOTT, DELBERT S. and AGETON, SUZANNE S. (1980). "Reconciling Race and Class Differences in Self-reported and Official Estimates of Delinquency." *American Sociological Review* 45 (February): 95-110.

EMPEY, LA MAR T. (1982). *American Delinquency*. Revised edition. Homewood, Ill.: Dorsey.

FEDERAL BUREAU OF INVESTIGATION (1984). *Crime in the United States, 1983*. Washington, D.C.: U.S. Government Printing Office.

FLANAGAN, TIMOTHY J. and McCLOUD, MAUREEN (1983). *Sourcebook of Criminal Justice Statistics, 1982*. Washington, D.C.: U.S. Department of Justice.

GIBBONS, DON C. (1982). *Society, Crime, and Criminal Behavior*. 4th edition. Englewood Cliffs, N.J.: Prentice-Hall.

HARDT, ROBERT H. and PETERSON, SANDRA J. (1968). "Neighborhood Status and Delinquency Activity as Indexed by Police Records and a Self-report Survey." *Criminologica* 6 (May): 37-47.

HINDELANG, MICHAEL J., HIRSCHI, TRAVIS and WEIS, JOSEPH G. (1979). "Correlates of Delinquency: The Illusion of Discrepancy Between Self-report and Official Measures." *American Sociological Review* 44 (December): 995–1014.

HINDELANG, MICHAEL J., HIRSCHI, TRAVIS, and WEIS, JOSEPH G. (1981). *Measuring Delinquency.* Beverly Hills, Cal.: Sage.

KRISBERG, BARRY and SCHWARTZ, IRA (1983). "Rethinking Juvenile Justice." *Crime and Delinquency* 29 (July): 333–64.

MURPHY, FRED J., SHIRLEY, MARY M., and WITMER, HELEN L. (1946). "The Incidence of Hidden Delinquency." *American Journal of Orthopsychiatry* 19 (October): 686–95.

NETTLER, GWYNN (1984). *Explaining Crime.* 3rd edition. New York: McGraw-Hill.

NYE, F. IVAN and SHORT, JAMES F., JR. (1957). "Scaling Delinquent Behavior." *American Sociological Review* 22 (June): 326–31.

PORTERFIELD, AUSTIN L. (1943). "Delinquency and Its Outcome in Court and College." *American Journal of Sociology* 49 (November): 199–208.

REISS, ALBERT J., Jr. (1976). "Settling the Frontiers of a Pioneer in American Criminology," pp. 64–88. In James F. Short, Jr., ed. *Delinquency, Crime, and Society.* Chicago: University of Chicago Press.

REISS, ALBERT J., JR., and RHODES, ALBERT LEWIS (1961). "The Distribution of Delinquency in the Social Class Structure." *American Sociological Review* 26 (October): 720–32.

SHORT, JAMES F., JR., and NYE, IVAN F. (1958). "Extent of Unrecorded Juvenile Delinquency: Tentative Conclusions." *Journal of Criminal Law, Criminology and Police Science* 49 (November–December): 296–302.

WEIS, JOSEPH G. (1983). "Crime Statistics: Reporting Systems and Methods," pp. 378–91. In Sanford H. Kadish, ed. *Encyclopedia of Crime and Justice,* Vol. 1. New York: Free Press.

WILLIAMS, JAY R., and GOLD, MARTIN (1972). "From Delinquent Behavior to Official Delinquency." *Social Problems* 20 (Fall): 209–29.

WOLFGANG, MARVIN E., FIGLIO, ROBERT M., and SELLIN, THORSTEN (1972). *Delinquency in a Birth Cohort.* Chicago: University of Chicago Press.

chapter 4

THE MANY FACES
OF DELINQUENCY

INTRODUCTION

Chapter 3 examined some of the features of juvenile lawbreaking in American society, but there are more faces of delinquency still to be considered. Some of these faces or dimensions to be explored focus on the demographic characteristics of juvenile offenders. For one, the issue of the social class distribution of delinquency was not settled in the previous chapter, nor was the question of racial differentials in lawbreaking discussed. Additionally, we ought to examine variations in delinquent involvement between males and females. The first portion of this chapter reports on these sociodemographic correlates of juvenile misconduct.

A second set of queries about faces of delinquency centers on delinquent acts and delinquent patterns. Some delinquency analysts have argued that there are types of delinquents exhibiting distinct behavior patterns and psychological characteristics that can be identified. Along this same line, we saw in Chapter 2 that the delinquency laws in the various states include a number of status offense provisions. Regarding these, we need to ask about the kinds of offenses that make up the status offense category, along with the question of whether the "status offender" is a distinct kind of delinquent. Finally, the issue of juvenile violence is one which captures the attention of many persons and is a particularly lively concern of lay persons. How frequently are "juvenile monsters" or excessively violent lawbreakers encountered? These are some of the faces of delinquency with which Chapter 4 is concerned.

SOCIAL CLASS, RACE, AND DELINQUENCY

When we look at the social backgrounds of collections of officially tagged delinquents such as juvenile court cases or youngsters from juvenile training schools, we quickly discover that the majority of them are from relatively deprived social backgrounds, that is, they are lower-class youngsters. Also, it is clearly the case that disproportionately large numbers of black youths turn up in collections of officially tagged delinquents. The latter might be said to be doubly deprived in that the black segment of the American population has been the target of social and economic discrimination over many decades. As a result of endemic and long-standing patterns of discrimination, the black population as a whole is comprised of a markedly larger portion of economically deprived persons than is the white majority. Moreover, those blacks who are economically disadvantaged are worse off than their white counterparts, for they earn lower incomes on the average, occupy less satisfactory housing, live in more deteriorated neighborhoods, and in other ways participate less fully in the rewards of American life than do whites.

The disproportionate involvement of blacks in crime in the United States is indicated in national arrest statistics. For example, blacks were involved in 48.9 percent of all rape arrests, 39.4 percent of aggravated assault arrests, and 62.5 percent of robbery arrests in the United States in 1983 (Federal Bureau of Investigation, 1984: 187). Black youngsters are also much more frequently involved in juvenile arrests than are white youths, relative to their numbers in the youth population. Table 4-1 indicates (Federal Bureau of Investigation, 1983: 188) that black juveniles were involved in 57.4 percent of the rape arrests, 69.3 percent of the robbery arrests, and 39.4 percent of the aggravated assaults attributable to persons under 18 years of age in 1983.

Even though these official statistics initially seem strikingly clear and appear to show that lawbreaking is much more frequent among blacks and lower-income youngsters than among other groups, there are a number of scholars who have argued that this racial and social class patterning is partially or completely an illusion. The moderate position on this issue revolves around the argument that while the official data reflect real differences in misconduct, that is, greater involvement in delinquency on the part of blacks and/or youths from lower-income groups, they also mirror differential enforcement of the law on the part of the police and the courts. We shall examine the evidence on differential and discriminatory handling of youths by the police and courts in Chapter 5. Our concern here is with the more extreme view which contends that blacks and/or lower-class youths are no more delinquent than their middle-class counterparts, only luckier.

Consider one example of these views. In his investigation of delinquency in Richmond, California, Travis Hirschi (1969: 66-81) gathered self-report data and

TABLE 4-1 Total Arrests, by Age and Race, United States, 1983

OFFENSE	ARRESTS UNDER 18*				PERCENT		
	TOTAL	WHITE	BLACK	OTHER	WHITE	BLACK	OTHER
Total	1,719,902	1,249,778	442,692	27,432	72.7	25.7	1.6
Murder and nonnegligent manslaughter	1,345	667	656	22	49.6	48.8	1.6
Forcible rape	4,373	1,815	2,509	49	41.5	57.4	1.1
Robbery	35,195	10,379	24,404	412	29.4	69.3	1.2
Aggravated assault	33,691	19,997	13,266	428	59.4	39.4	1.3
Burglary	158,842	114,492	42,101	2,249	72.1	26.5	1.4
Larceny-theft	376,152	256,033	112,349	7,770	68.1	29.9	2.1
Motor vehicle theft	36,403	25,824	9,808	771	70.9	26.9	2.1
Arson	6,447	5,341	1,028	78	82.8	15.9	1.2
Violent crime	74,604	32,858	40,835	911	44.0	54.7	1.2
Property crime	577,844	401,690	165,286	10,868	69.5	28.6	1.9
Crime Index Total	652,448	434,548	206,121	11,779	66.6	31.6	1.8
Other assaults	78,401	48,717	28,261	1,423	62.1	36.0	1.8
Forgery and counterfeiting	6,728	5,482	1,152	94	81.5	17.1	1.4
Fraud	20,859	10,163	10,486	210	48.7	50.3	1.0
Embezzlement	458	352	101	5	76.9	22.1	1.1
Stolen property; buying, receiving, possessing	26,488	17,672	8,513	303	66.7	32.1	1.2
Vandalism	92,964	77,418	14,560	986	83.3	15.7	1.0
Weapons; carrying, possessing, etc.	22,461	14,972	7,237	252	66.7	32.2	1.2
Prostitution and commercialized vice	2,837	1,336	1,466	35	47.1	51.7	1.2
Sex offenses (except forcible rape and prostitution)	12,065	8,700	3,236	129	72.1	26.8	1.0
Drug abuse violations	71,787	56,209	14,454	1,124	78.3	20.1	1.6
Gambling	1,082	276	745	61	25.5	68.9	5.7
Offenses against family and children	1,292	1,041	237	14	80.6	18.3	1.1
Driving under the influence	24,768	23,818	646	304	96.2	2.6	1.2
Liquor laws	113,573	107,820	3,723	2,030	94.9	3.3	1.8
Drunkenness	28,273	26,473	1,689	561	92.2	5.9	2.0
Disorderly conduct	97,915	66,513	30,625	777	67.9	31.3	0.8
Vagrancy	2,527	2,113	386	28	83.6	15.3	1.2
All other offenses (except traffic)	279,825	200,893	74,670	4,262	71.8	26.7	1.5
Suspicion	2,779	2,305	453	21	82.9	16.3	0.8
Curfew and loitering violations	67,784	47,303	19,600	881	69.8	28.9	1.3
Runaways	112,138	95,654	14,331	2,153	85.3	12.8	2.0

*Based on 10,756 agencies; 1984 estimated population 200,118,000

police arrest information on the boys in his sample. Examination of these data led him to conclude that there was no social class relationship to delinquency and only a slight relationship between race and delinquent involvement.

More generally, Charles Tittle, Wayne Villemez, and Douglas Smith (1978) have examined a number of reports on lawbreaking among adults and juveniles and have concluded that social class position is unrelated to criminal or delinquent involvement. However, others have taken issue with these investigators (Clelland and Carter, 1980; Braithwaite, 1981). Among other things, Braithwaite (1981) has argued that Tittle, Villemez, and Smith conducted an incomplete review of the literature and failed to take note of some important studies. In addition, Braithwaite contended that those who have reported no relationship between social class and lawbreaking have often failed to distinguish between subgroups within the working- or lower-class stratum, variously identified as the "stable working class" and the "hard living" or "unstable working class." It is the members of this latter subgroup, characterized by markedly precarious economic circumstances, who would be expected to produce the greatest number of delinquents. Failure to sample within this subgroup might then work against the researcher finding a social class link to delinquency even though such a pattern of differential involvement might exist. Still another criticism noted by Braithwaite had to do with the inclusion of predominately petty behavioral items in self-report instruments, with the result that the self-report method often fails to uncover class-related variations in more serious forms of misconduct.

Most of the studies on which Tittle, Villemez, and Smith drew in arriving at their conclusion of no relationship between class position and lawbreaking were self-report investigations, often of delinquents and including some of those we examined in Chapter 3. Perhaps we can get some purchase on this issue by reexamining some of the findings of those studies.

First, recall the conclusion arrived at in Chapter 3, namely that *relatively minor misbehavior is extremely commonplace and is not class-linked or restricted to lower-class youths,* at least in the United States. Parenthetically, at least one study in England (McDonald, 1969) *did* find a social class pattern in self-reported delinquency. In McDonald's self-report study of boys in an English suburb, a small city, a London middle-class area, and a London lower-class area, she found that working-class boys admitted more offenses of all kinds than did middle-class youths. Working-class youngsters also admitted committing individual offenses more repetitively than did the middle-class ones.

Let us also reexamine one self-report study in particular. Short and Nye's (1958) survey of high school students in three Washington communities, three midwestern towns, and delinquents in training schools found that the high school students reported many relatively petty acts of delinquency for which they could conceivably have been referred to the juvenile court. But, *the training school youths admitted these same acts and, in addition, they confessed to involvement in other, more serious forms of misconduct not common among the students.* The training school boys also declared that they had engaged in a large number of delinquent acts with considerable frequency.

Drawing on these same data, Nye and Short (1957) developed a delinquency scale based on seven items of misbehavior. As we saw in Chapter 3, the seven items centered on relatively petty acts. In constructing it, the more serious delinquent acts which training school wards frequently admit had to be discarded, because few high school youngsters confessed to them. Thus *this scale, which has been used in an identical or closely-similar form in a number of self-report studies, measures the degree of involvement in commonplace but relatively inconsequential forms of juvenile misconduct, rather than serious delinquency.* Even so, 86 percent of the high school youths in the Nye and Short study had scores of nine or less on the scale, while only 14 percent of the incarcerated juveniles had these low scores.

Short and Nye (1957-58) utilized their scale to examine the social backgrounds of training school and hidden delinquents and reported that nearly all of the institutionalized youths were from the lower half of the socioeconomic strata, in contrast to only 53 percent of a group of high school students. But when the high school youths alone were sorted into delinquency scale types, no relationship was found between delinquency and social class (Short, Nye, and Olsen, 1958). In other words, students with high or low delinquency scores were found in the four social classes in about the same proportions.

Can it be that both claims are correct, that there is and is not a social class relationship to delinquency? The answer should be apparent at this point—it depends on how "delinquency" is defined. *There is no important class patterning to petty misconduct* (cf. Hirschi, 1969), *at the same time that serious and repetitive delinquency is class-linked* (Hindelang, Hirschi, and Weis, 1979).

This is the conclusion of the National Youth Survey (Ageton and Elliott, 1978). That research found that while large numbers of youths admitted involvement in relatively petty acts of misconduct, relatively few of them confessed to more serious forms of lawbreaking. Unlike many self-report studies, the National Youth Survey involved a delinquency questionnaire that included a number of relatively serious acts of delinquency. In a later report on the data from this study, Elliott and Ageton (1980) examined the interaction between race, social class, forms of delinquency, and degree of involvement in these activities, in detail. Their findings have been summarized succinctly by Nettler (1984: 86):

1. Youthful admissions reveal significant race differences in criminal conduct. Blacks, compared with whites, admit to all offenses in the order of three to two and to predatory crimes against property in the order of more than two to one. Insignificant ethnic differences are reported for other crime categories.

2. "Lower-class" youths admit to more total criminality than "working- or middle-class" youths. They admit to nearly four times as many attacks on persons as "middle-class" youths and 1½ times as many as "working-class" youths. Other class differences by category of admitted crime are not significant.

3. Race and class differences are produced principally by relative differences in criminal conduct at the high end of the frequency continuum. In other words, when one compares kinds of people who *infrequently* commit crimes, differences in conduct by race and SES are minimal. But as one looks at *higher frequencies* of depredation, greater differences between groups become apparent.

Even more recently, Elliott and Huizinga (1983) have engaged in some detailed analyses of the National Youth Survey data, in which they probed further into the social class–delinquency question. Their major conclusion is consistent with the argument in this chapter, in that they asserted (Elliott and Huizinga, 1983: 149): "Class differences in both prevalence and incidence are found for serious offenses. For males, class differences are also found in the incidence of nonserious delinquency and global delinquency."

There is one final point that needs to be made before we leave the social class–delinquency issue. The National Youth Survey, as well as a number of other research investigations, examined self-reported delinquency involvement on the part of youths who have been assigned to social class groupings, based usually on the occupation of the principal wage earner in the juvenile's family. However, a number of these studies have given insufficient attention to the community contexts within which the youths are situated. Social class position is a characteristic of individuals, but it is also possible to sort neighborhoods and community areas along class lines, based on the economic position of the majority of residents within those areas. As some have argued, the meaning and impact of social class position on individuals may well vary depending upon the class or status area in which these individuals reside. Stated another way, the lower-class youngster who lives in a predominately middle-class area may encounter life experiences of a markedly different kind than those that are faced by lower-class youths who live in circumstances where they are surrounded by similarly disadvantaged persons. For one thing, schools located in middle-income areas usually provide a richer set of educational experiences to youths than do schools that serve mainly lower-income students. In other ways as well, pressures which impel juveniles into delinquency may be markedly more common in solidly lower-class areas than in middle-class ones. In short, there is good reason to examine variations in neighborhood social context as well as individual socioeconomic position when probing the social class-delinquency question.

The National Youth Survey researchers were not able to examine variations in the economic positions of communities in which juvenile respondents reside, because of the relatively small size of the national sample of 1726 youngsters. However, Braithwaite's (1981) review of a large number of studies of the social class position of areas in which juveniles live not only indicated that involvement in officially recorded delinquency is most frequent among persons who live in lower-class areas but also that self-reported lawbreaking is most commonly encountered in these areas as well.

SEX VARIATIONS IN DELINQUENCY

Until relatively recently, both popular wisdom as well as much scholarly thought has centered around a bundle of erroneous presuppositions about female lawbreaking, including the opinion that women are rarely involved in criminality. Lawbreaking was seen as a man's world. Sexual stereotypes holding that "boys will be boys" while girls are by nature delicate and submissive creatures were easily translated into the belief that criminal acts are rare among younger or older women. Additionally, the hypothesis that those females who engage in transgressions of the law were biologically flawed or psychologically aberrant was often offered as an explanation for the rare instances of female criminality that were noted by observers. Finally, lawbreaking among juvenile women was often assumed to be restricted largely to sexual misconduct which in turn was seen as a manifestation of parent-child tensions or flaws in "under-the-roof" culture.

Another feature of public conceptions of female lawbreaking has been that when females do infrequently get involved in criminality, they are usually accorded lenient treatment because of the protective attitudes toward women by males in American society. This notion has sometimes been referred to as the *chivalry hypothesis,* which alleges that females receive less severe correctional dispositions than men.

During the past decade or so, female criminality has been discovered by many laypersons and social scientists. Although juvenile and adult women have been involved in lawbreaking for many decades, it has only been within the past twenty years that much serious attention has been paid to their behavior. It is now apparent that females are actually involved in considerably more criminal and delinquent conduct than is reflected in official statistics. Also, studies have revealed that, contrary to the chivalry hypothesis, juvenile and adult females have often been the targets of more severe responses from justice system workers than have comparable male offenders. The chivalry hypothesis has often served to draw attention away from the harsh and inequitable sanctioning of female offenders (Gibbons, 1982: 389-92).

The recent surge of interest in female criminality and delinquency ought to be applauded. Doubtless it is true that on the whole this development has led to a more accurate portrayal of female lawbreaking than was true of earlier beliefs. However, it is also the case the some new misconceptions about juvenile and adult criminality have gained currency. In particular, Freda Adler's widely cited *Sisters in Crime* (1975) contains a number of dubious claims about women and crime, centering around the rise of "the new woman criminal." Adler's thesis is that the women's liberation movement has been a primary force moving men and women toward androgynous sex roles in which traditional sex-role distinctions are blurred. Women have become more competitive with males both in criminal and noncriminal activities, with the result that crime rates among women are rising more rapidly than crime rates among men. Finally, Adler claimed that women have begun to

✓

engage in "masculine," aggressive, collective forms of lawbreaking that were largely restricted to males in the past.

Investigators who have sorted out the existing crime data have failed to turn up convincing evidence in support of the new female criminal thesis (Simon, 1975; Steffensmeier, 1978).

One portion of Adler's analysis of the alleged explosion of crime among women centered on female juvenile offenders. She argued that while the ratio of male to female delinquents was about fifty to one in the early 1900s, it currently is about five to one, which indicates that female lawbreaking is increasing very rapidly. She also claimed that the women's rights movement is heavily implicated in the rise of female delinquency. Adler offered some tidbits of anecdotal evidence which appeared to show that much female lawbreaking has already become masculinized, in that many female delinquents have become involved in aggressive activities, in gang offenses, and in other kinds of conduct that formerly were the exclusive province of males. Finally, she asserted that as the movement toward sexual equality continues, the gap between male and female rates of criminality will continue to narrow. Adler (1975: 108) concluded that: "Female delinquency today is a serious problem not only because of its capacity for social disruption but because it often leads to future adult criminality. Although it is not a new problem, it is far more prevalent and has undergone ominous qualitative changes in recent years."

Table 3-9 in Chapter 3 presented arrest data for males and females in the United States in 1983, and it is with these figures that we might begin. That table indicated that there were 1,559,644 arrests of women (out of a total population of 176 million) in 1983, and of these, 327,902 were persons under 18 years of age. Arrests of juvenile females declined by 7.5 percent between 1982 and 1983. The juvenile arrests covered a wide range of offenses, but 109,649 of them were for "index offenses" or major crimes, thus it cannot be argued that female delinquency is uniformly of a minor nature. On the other hand, a substantial number of these arrests were for lesser offenses: 58,337 runaways, 24,121 liquor violations, and 52,689 other status offenses.

The argument that the women's movement has touched off a wave of female delinquency is less than persuasive in that the ratio of male to female delinquents in juvenile courts has changed relatively little since the early 1950s. It would be difficult to argue that the movement for sexual equality was underway in the 1950s. Also, the juvenile court data in Table 3-3 in Chapter 3 indicate that the percentage of female court referrals has hovered around 20-24 percent since 1965.

What are the facts regarding female delinquency? Are juvenile females becoming more involved in lawbreaking? Are female delinquents involved primarily in sexual misconduct? Is there any evidence that female offenses are becoming masculinized, with increasing numbers of young women engaging in violence and kindred activities?

Darrell Steffensmeier and Renee Steffensmeier (1980) have carried out a detailed analysis of trends in juvenile arrests for males and females from 1965 to 1977. They pointed out that comparisons of percentage changes in arrests of males and females are often quite misleading, for these do not take into account changes in the size or composition of the groups of males and females under 18 years of age. And even more important, where arrests are infrequent for one group, a small increase in the volume of arrests for that group may lead to a large percentage increase in arrests, even though the absolute differences in criminality for the two sexes remain large. Accordingly, some relatively complex rate computations are called for in order to draw meaningful conclusions about trends in arrest rates for juveniles.

These investigators indicated that refined arrest rate calculations showed that adolescent females have become involved in a larger share of arrests for larceny, particularly shoplifting, liquor law violations, and runaway activity, since 1965. The arrest rates for females for other assaults, embezzlement, forgery, driving under the influence of alcohol, and family offenses also came closer to those for males, but females still contribute so infrequently to these offenses that their absolute arrest gains were relatively insignificant. These researchers found little or no evidence supporting recent claims that female delinquency is changing in the direction of "masculinized" offenses. They found little indication of growing violence or involvement in gang activity on the part of female delinquents. Their conclusion was that juvenile females continue to be arrested principally for minor acts of deviance which are seen as a challenge to the authority of the family, the hold of the sexual double standard over women, and the maintenance of sexual inequality.

What about "the dark figure" of female delinquency? We have already touched upon some of the studies of unreported delinquency among juvenile females. One of these by James Short and Ivan Nye (1985) compared high school youths and training school wards in several parts of the United States. Their comparisons of self-reported delinquency among high school females and training school females in a western state showed that large numbers of the former admitted they had skipped school, defied parents, stolen items of small value, or engaged in similar acts once or twice. However, much larger numbers of training school wards said they had done these things, and many of them admitted involvement in more serious offenses as well. This contrast was even more marked when the subjects were asked to note those offenses they had committed more than once or twice. Few of the high school students acknowledged repetitive involvement in even the petty acts of misbehavior, while the incarcerated wards admitted frequent participation in both petty and serious acts.

Two other studies (Hindelang, 1971; Jensen and Eve, 1976) both carried out in the San Francisco Bay Area among youngsters who had not fallen into the hands of the authorities found that relatively large numbers of males and females admitted involvement in delinquent acts, particularly those that were relatively petty and innocuous. In general, boys reported more frequent participation in delinquent acts than did girls. At the same time, both groups were engaged in a relatively wide range of acts of lawbreaking rather than in specialized patterns of misconduct, so that these investigators concluded that versatility is more descriptive of male and female delinquency than is sex specialization. Chapter 3 also examined the findings of the National Youth Survey in which parallel results turned up (Canter, 1982) again showing that while juvenile females are less frequently engaged in lawbreaking, they are implicated in a wide range of forms of misconduct. Juvenile delinquency was less frequent among females, but the belief that it consists primarily of sexual misconduct, incorrigibility, and the like was not supported by any of this evidence.

Stephen Cernkovich and Peggy Giordano (1979) have provided still another set of findings dealing with unreported female delinquency. Their study, conducted in two Midwest high schools, also found that, with relatively few exceptions, boys admitted greater involvement in delinquency than did girls. More juvenile females than males did report disobeying parents, defying parents, and use of hard drugs. On the whole, both groups confessed to petty acts of misconduct most frequently. For both males and females, the most commonly reported acts were less serious, victimless, or status offenses. Finally, Cernkovich and Giordano indicated that males and females differed in frequency of delinquent involvement but not markedly in terms of the types of acts they committed. Again, the notion that female offenders are restricted to sexual misconduct, ungovernability, and the like was not borne out by these results.

The Cernkovich and Giordano study was revealing in some other ways. Contrary to much popular wisdom that views female delinquency as most commonly individualistic rather than group activity, these researchers reported that self-reported delinquent females most often engaged in lawbreaking in groups, particularly in mixed-sex peer groups. The stereotype of the female delinquent, who engages in solitary forms of lawbreaking or serves as a relatively passive accomplice of a romantic partner, was not confirmed by their data.

Finally, we ought to take note of Smith and Visher's (1980) review of a large number of studies of sex differences in deviance, criminality, and delinquency. In their view, these studies suggest that sex differences are smaller for self-reported than for officially recorded offenses and also for personal and juvenile offenses than for violent and property offenses. They also concluded that sex differences are greater in urban than rural areas and for minor rather than serious acts of lawbreaking. Finally, they asserted that the association between sex and lawbreaking has apparently been decreasing in recent decades.

DELINQUENT PATTERNS AND DELINQUENT CAREERS

Until relatively recently, there has been a good deal of interest on the part of criminologists in the notion that juvenile delinquents come in a variety of relatively distinct types. A corollary assumption has been that progress in the understanding of the causal origins of youthful lawbreaking may come from studying the different etiological processes behind each of these behavioral types or syndromes.

Such arguments have been popular among psychologists and psychiatrists as well. For example, many years ago, psychiatrist Richard Jenkins and sociologist Lester Hewitt (1944) advanced the argument that there are two common forms of youthful lawbreaking: adaptive and maladaptive delinquency. They claimed that delinquent behavior is not a form of neurotic behavior, for neuroticism involves a high level of inhibition, sense of duty, and introjected standards and strict superego control, while delinquency frequently manifests an opposite pattern. In addition, only the maladaptive or unsocialized offender has a disturbed personality. This is the aggressive lawbreaker who is poorly socialized, lacking in internalized controls, antagonistic toward his or her peers, and generally maladjusted. The more frequently encountered adaptive or pseudosocial offender is usually the product of lower-class slum areas and is reasonably well socialized and "normal" among his or her peers and parents. Although his or her hostile posture toward law enforcement and correctional agents is a source of concern to them, the adaptive delinquent is hardly a pathological person.

Although they employed a different set of labels than those by Jenkins and Hewitt, similar claims about the existence of normal and maladjusted delinquents have been made by a number of sociologists, including Albert Reiss (1952), Sethard Fisher (1958), and John Kinch (1962a, 1962b).

Contentions about psychologically maladjusted delinquents are no longer in vogue among sociologists, but this view that youthful offenders often are responding to psychological pressures and adjustment problems has continued to enjoy much popularity among psychologists, social workers, and a number of others. In particular, the Interpersonal Maturity Levels (I-Levels) perspective, developed in the California juvenile correctional system (Warren, 1976) has been an influential argument in this genre. The theory holds that there are a number of stages or levels of interpersonal maturity through which persons move as they become socialized. Not all individuals achieve the higher levels of interpersonal competence or maturity, remaining fixated at a lower level of development. Further, the I-Levels formulation strongly implies that delinquents are generally at lower or less developed levels of maturity than are nondelinquents. The I-Levels scheme classifies juvenile offenders into nine subtypes within three main interpersonal levels, such as "immature conformists," "neurotic, acting-out offenders," and "manipulators." Finally, for each diagnostic type, the scheme specifies different patterns of treatment, carried on by different kinds of treatment agents; thus it might be described as a "different-strokes-for-different-folks-by different-strokers" argument.

There are a number of questions to be asked about this categorization of patterns of delinquency. For one thing, the nine types are descriptions of kinds of youths encountered in correctional settings and may have little or no relevance to "hidden delinquents." And, as we shall see in Chapter 10 where more detailed attention is given to the I-Levels typology, real-life offenders, even in institutional settings, may be more difficult to sort out into distinct categories or types than is argued by the architects of the I-Levels argument.

As we have indicated, the typological view holding that the population of delinquents is made up of various distinct types of offenders enjoyed a good deal of popularity among criminologists until recently (cf. Ferdinand, 1966). Some representative cases-in-point would be Cohen and Short's (1958) and Cloward and Ohlin's (1959) descriptions of various delinquent subcultures, along with the claims by Don Gibbons (1965), arguing that nine delinquent types, distinguished from each other in terms of offense patterns and social-psychological characteristics (delinquency-related attitudes and self-concepts) can be identified. Additionally, criminologists have frequently singled out automobiles thieves ("joyriders"), middle-class delinquents, female delinquents, and other groupings as allegedly distinct types of offenders.

The extreme version of the typological position which posits the existence of distinct groupings of delinquents has been seriously undermined by self-report studies which suggest that (a) involvement in delinquent acts is ubiquitous, and (b) most delinquent conduct is petty in nature and episodic and transitory in form. In short, most youngsters flirt with deviant acts to some degree or another in the course of growing up.

Recent research on delinquent patterns has also challenged the view that those youngsters who are more heavily involved in lawbreaking—"hard-core" or apprehended delinquents—frequently specialize in particular kinds of delinquent acts or exhibit distinct attitudes and self-images in common (Klein, 1984). Instead, versatility or involvement in a diverse collection of offenses and crime switching have been more frequently observed among relatively serious delinquents. As a result, a good deal of skepticism has arisen concerning those typological schemes that would assign juvenile offenders to distinct offense-based classificatory pigeonholes.

However, the thrust of the argument here is *not* that juvenile lawbreaking is entirely random or unpatterned. Instead, there is a "soft" view of delinquent patterns and careers which is supported by a good deal of empirical evidence, much of which has been reviewed by Steven Lab (1984). As indicated by Lab, there have been a number of studies of the arrest records of groups of youths, including the Wolfgang, Figlio, and Sellin (1972) cohort study in Philadelphia, which we examined in Chapter 3. That study found that of 9943 members of the birth cohort, 3475, or 35 percent, had been apprehended by the police at least once. The official delinquents were divided by Wolfgang, Figlio, and Sellin into one-time offenders, recidivist nonchronic delinquents, and chronic offenders (more than 4 arrests), with the latter comprising 18 percent of the apprehended youths. The chronic offenders were more frequently involved in serious offenses than were the other lawbreakers. Also, most of them started their delinquent careers by committing relatively serious acts; thus they did not show a pattern of escalating seriousness. Although these groupings of offenders differed in the extent of delinquent activities in which they engaged, the researchers found little evidence of offense specialization on their part.

Other studies of offender careers, based on official arrest or juvenile court data, include those by Rojek and Erickson (1982), Bursik (1980), Lab (1984), and Shannon (1984). These are relatively complex pieces of research which differ from each other in methodological particulars as well as research findings, but in general they add up to much the same body of conclusions. First, many apprehended offenders are *one-timers* who desist from further lawbreaking, or at least manage to escape the attention of the authorities following their first apprehension. Second, many of the one-time offenders are involved in status offenses, while the remainder are most likely to have engaged in relatively minor criminal acts rather than felonies. Third, minor offenses are not often followed by increasingly more serious ones; hence escalation of delinquency careers is uncommon. Fourth, the population of apprehended offenders includes *repeaters* and *chronic* offenders, the latter being juveniles who have engaged in a relatively large number of delinquent acts. Fifth, a considerable number of repeaters and chronic offenders eventually desist from delinquency, such that much shrinkage in numbers occurs as we count those juveniles in a cohort who have committed five offenses as compared to those who have engaged in four, and so on.

What do we find when we expand our focus to include self-reports of lawbreaking, as contrasted to arrest records or court appearances? The recent analysis of the National Youth Survey by Franklyn Dunford and Delbert Elliott (1984) is worth examining. Dunford and Elliott opted for a straightforward conceptualization in which career offenders were defined as persons who commit delinquent or criminal acts at a high frequency over a prolonged period of time.

The seven birth cohorts of National Youth Survey subjects were examined by Dunford and Elliott. The juveniles were sorted out initially in terms of their self-reported involvement in various patterns of lawbreaking and the frequency with which they reported involvement in delinquency. The sorting process resulted in four delinquent types, including: nondelinquents, who were youths who had engaged in fewer than four relatively minor offenses in any given year, and exploratory delinquents, who were juveniles who had been involved in a larger number of offenses but in no more than a single serious violation in any single year. Nonserious patterned delinquents had engaged in a larger number of delinquent acts, no more than two of which were serious criminal violations, while serious patterned delinquents had reported committing at least three serious criminal acts in any single year.

Note that this classification only tells us about the delinquent conduct of individuals during a single year. Dunford and Elliott next sorted the youths into two groups, *career offenders* (those juveniles who persisted as either nonserious or serious patterned offenders for at least two years) and *noncareer offenders* (those who did not show patterned delinquency for two consecutive years). This scheme yielded four career types: *nonoffenders, noncareer delinquents, nonserious career offenders,* and *serious career offenders.* In subsequent portions of this research, Dunford and Elliott demonstrated that this typology is a valid one, for these types were also shown to differ significantly from each other in a number of ways. For one, the serious career delinquents were markedly more involved in lawbreaking than were the other types. Also, they were disproportionately male, urban, and older youths who showed the greatest exposure to delinquent peers, normlessness, and kindred characteristics.

STATUS OFFENSES AND STATUS OFFENDERS

Chapter 2 indicated that American delinquency laws contain one or more status offense provisions which empower juvenile courts to intervene in the case of youngsters who are "ungovernable," "beyond parental control," an "unruly child," and so on, but who have not violated any criminal law. Chapter 2 also noted that these omnibus or status offense provisions have come under a good deal of criticism in recent decades. Even so, Chapter 3 reported that these statutes are still being employed fairly frequently, so that although the trend in status offense referrals to courts has been downward in recent years, 259,000 youngsters or 19.8 percent of all court referrals in 1979 were there on status offense charges.

There is a variety of arguments that can be marshalled against status offense statutes (Thomas, 1976), many of which attack these laws on constitutional grounds. For one thing, it can be said that these statutes deprive juveniles of equal protection, in that adults cannot be charged with violating them. Also, these statutes are vulnerable to the criticism that they are lacking in specificity and are constitutionally vague. Then, too, these laws are defective insofar as they extend the reach of governmental interference and social control to activities in which governmental bodies have no legitimate interest. Still another complaint has been that, in operation, these statutes have been blatantly discriminatory because they have much more commonly been applied to females than males. Finally, status offender statutes are candidates for removal from juvenile court laws because of the well-known deficiencies of the juvenile court. Even if it could be argued that therapeutic intervention is needed in the case of runaways, disobedient children, and similar cases, it remains to be demonstrated that the juvenile court is capable of delivering rehabilitative assistance.

Charles Thomas (1976) has expressed agreement with these criticisms of status offense provisions but has also argued that many critics of these laws have invoked some other factual claims about status offenses and status offenders that are less convincing, or at the very least, that are not well supported by evidence. Specifically, some have argued that (Thomas, 1976: 441) "status offenders are a relatively homogeneous type of juvenile who are unlikely to have past or future records of involvement in other types of misconduct." This line of argument also implies that all of the acts that have been brought together under status offense rubrics are equally petty and inconsequential; thus they are behaviors and conditions that would be best dealt with through "benign neglect," "judicious intervention," or through help rendered by whatever voluntary agencies that exist outside the court and to which the juveniles in question would voluntarily go.

We agree that there has been considerable loose thinking and argumentation about status offenses and status offenders. It certainly is true that the proposition that status offenses of various kinds are all equally petty and unworthy of attention has yet to be demonstrated. Also, those who speak of status offenses and status offenders may be blurring an important fact, namely that there are relatively few offenders who engage solely in status offenses.

Thomas (1976) endeavored to collect data that would throw light upon these differing possibilities, by assembling court records on juveniles who appeared for the first time in two Virginia juvenile courts between 1970 and 1974. First referrals charged with misdemeanors made up 50.3 percent of the cases studied, along with 22.3 percent who were felony cases and 27.3 percent who were status offenders. Thomas also gathered data on recidivism on the part of these referrals, in order to assess the hypothesis that status offenders specialize in these offenses (and nonstatus offenders similarly specialize in violations of the criminal law).

The largest share of these first referrals were nonrecidivists, at least during the time period in question. But of the felony first referrals who got into difficulty for a second time, 12 percent were for status offenses, while the comparable figure for misdemeanor first referrals was 17 percent. Approximately 40 percent of the status offense first referrals who returned to court did so for status offense charges, but 60 percent of them came back charged with criminal activities!

These figures indicate that (a) substantial numbers of youngsters who first appear in court on status offense charges go on to engage in more serious acts of lawbreaking; and (b) a large number of youths who turn up in court on status offense charges have previously been charged with more serious types of lawbreaking. In general, much the same picture emerged in another study of status offenses (Kelley, 1983), conducted in Wayne County (Detroit), Michigan, although the proportion of first referral status offender recidivists who returned to court on other charges was somewhat smaller than in the Thomas investigation. In summary, these findings produced by Thomas and Kelley do not support the contention that the "status offender" is a distinct type of juvenile who is solely involved in petty misconduct.

VIOLENT OFFENDERS

The psychiatric literature dealing with delinquents contains a large number of accounts of youths who have been involved in "maladaptive delinquency" taking an extremely violent form (Jenkins and Hewitt, 1944; Topping, 1941; Redl and Wineman, 1957). There is little doubt that "unsocialized aggressive" youths do exist although they have not been given much attention by sociological students of delinquency. Quite probably, the number of youngsters who engage in extreme forms of violence which often seem unprovoked and "senseless" is quite small when compared to delinquents in general or even to those juvenile offenders who are involved in "garden-variety" aggression, that is, gang fighting, assaults carried out incidental to other crimes, forcible rape, and the like. At any rate, we shall take up the matter of unsocialized aggressive youths in Chapter 10, restricting our attention here to "garden-variety" aggression. This section is concerned in particular with the question of how common this kind of behavior is among the population of juvenile offenders. Does delinquency usually take a relatively violent form, or are most offenders involved in nonviolent offenses?

"Garden-variety" aggression was the subject of a study carried on by the Dangerous Offender Project at Ohio State University (Hamparian, Schuster, Dinitz, and Conrad, 1978). The research was similar to the cohort investigation of Wolfgang, Figlio, and Sellin, in that it examined a cohort of 1138 youths born in 1956 to 1960, who resided in Franklin County, Ohio, and who had been arrested in Columbus for at least one violent offense before reaching age 18. The cohort was not restricted to youngsters who had been arrested for violent offenses exclusively. The majority of arrests for violence were for homicides, rape, certain other sex offenses, armed or aggravated robbery, and aggravated assault.

The researchers examined five major, widely held beliefs about juvenile violence. The first of these hypotheses was that a large group of chronic offenders engages in much lawbreaking and is responsible for a large share of all known offenses in the community. A second claim was that the earlier the start of a delinquent career, the more offenses that will be accumulated by the youth, while a third was that there is a linear progression of delinquent careers with youngsters moving from petty offenses to increasingly more serious ones. The "young monster" hypothesis asserts that there is a growing number of depraved youths in the community who commit aggravated, horrifying crimes of violence. Finally, the extinction argument is that many delinquent careers are self-limiting, ending before youngsters enter adulthood.

Violent youths constituted only about 2 percent of the juveniles in Columbus. Blacks were heavily overrepresented in the arrest cohort, as were youths from deprived economic backgrounds. The members of the cohort averaged about four arrests per youth during the juvenile years, but few cases of repetitive violence were observed. About one-third of the juveniles were chronic offenders, who had been arrested five or more times. However, no evidence of a new mutant species of young monsters stalking the streets of Columbus showed up. At least in that city, this widely voiced claim about a new breed of extraordinarily violent youngsters appeared to be largely an invention of the mass media.

SUMMARY

This chapter has sifted through a variety of information on juvenile lawbreaking in an effort to get beyond the surface impressions conveyed by delinquency statistics. The central purpose of the chapter has been to examine some of the varied faces of delinquency. We began with the social class–delinquency issue which, as we have seen, turns largely upon how one chooses to define "delinquency." The most sensible conclusion to be reached concerning the role of social class position in delinquent conduct is the following one:

1. There is no significant social class patterning to petty misconduct; that is, juveniles at all social class levels are about equally involved in minor acts of lawbreaking. Additionally, involvement in petty delinquency is often limited to a few episodes of misconduct. However, those youths who engage in serious, repetitive forms of juvenile delinquency are most frequently from

lower-income backgrounds; thus serious delinquency is related to social class position.

The second portion of this chapter dealt with delinquency on the part of females. That section arrived at the following conclusions:

2. Juvenile misbehavior is more common among boys than among girls, but law-breaking is considerably more frequent among females than is indicated in police arrest data or juvenile court statistics. Involvement in delinquency on the part of juvenile females has apparently increased somewhat in the past decade or so. Although females are less often involved in misbehavior than boys, both groups tend to engage in a varied, diversified collection of delinquent acts, rather than in specialized forms of lawbreaking.

3. Females who become the subject of attention by the police or juvenile courts are often charged with sexual delinquency or with activities which adults in the community suspect are indicators of incipient sexual promiscuity. Police arrest data and juvenile court statistics both underestimate the extent of delinquent involvement among young females and apparently convey a distorted picture of the nature of female lawbreaking.

Another section of this chapter quarreled with the view that distinct types of delinquent offenders who specialize in particular offenses and who closely resemble each other in terms of self-image and the like can be identified, arguing instead that:

4. Juvenile misconduct is a phenomenon made up of a number of points along a behavioral continuum: one-time offenders, petty offense recidivists, serious offense recidivists, career offenders, and "ultra–hard-core offenders."

This chapter also examined the question of status offenses and status offenders. We saw that the status offense rubric is a broad one, so that acts of varying degrees of seriousness, in terms of posing dangers either to the general public or to the juveniles involved in them, are subsumed by status offense provisions in juvenile law. A related issue had to do with whether the "status offender" exists as an identifiable type of delinquent. The data considered in this section indicated that:

5. Although a considerable number of youthful offenders are individuals who get into the hands of the police or appear in juvenile courts solely on status offense charges, many of the persons who are at one time or another charged with status offenses also engage in acts of delinquency that involve violations of the criminal law.

Finally, this chapter took up the question of juvenile violence and arrived at the conclusion that:

6. Violent offenders are infrequently encountered, even among delinquents who have come to the attention of the police of the juvenile court. Also, juvenile violence often occurs in the course of another crime such as rob-

bery, rather than in the form of random outbursts of aggression by "young monsters."

Having come this far, we are now at the point where the parameters of the delinquency problem have been identified. Chapters 3 and 4 have provided a good deal of detail concerning the extent and characteristics of juvenile lawbreaking. In the next chapter, our attention turns to the activities of the police, juvenile courts, and other "people-processing" organizations that go about identifying, tagging, treating, and engaging in other actions with youthful lawbreakers.

REFERENCES

ADLER, FREDA (1975). *Sisters in Crime.* New York: McGraw-Hill.
AGETON, SUZANNE S. and ELLIOTT, DELBERT S. (1978). "The Incidence of Delinquent Behavior in a National Probability Sample of Adolescents." Boulder, Colo.: Behavioral Research Institute, mimeo.
BRAITHWAITE, JOHN (1981). *"The Myth of Social Class and Criminality* Reconsidered." *American Sociological Review* 46 (February): 36–57.
BURSIK, R. J., JR. (1980). "The Dynamics of Specialization in Juvenile Offenses." *Social Forces* 58 (March): 851–64.
CANTER, RACHELLE J. (1982). "Sex Differences in Self-report Delinquency." *Criminology* 20 (November): 373–93.
CERNKOVICH, STEPHEN A. and GIORDANO, PEGGY C. (1979). "A Comparative Analysis of Male and Female Delinquency." *Sociological Quarterly* 20 (Winter): 131–45.
CLELLAND, DONALD and CARTER, TIMOTHY J. (1980). "The New Myth of Class and Crime." *Criminology* 19 (November): 319–36.
CLOWARD, RICHARD A. and OHLIN, LLOYD E. (1960). *Delinquency and Opportunity.* New York: Free Press.
COHEN, ALBERT K. and SHORT, JAMES F., JR. (1958). "Research in Delinquent Subcultures." *Journal of Social Issues* 14 (No. 3): 20–37.
DUNFORD, FRANKLYN W. and ELLIOTT, DELBERT S. (1984). "Identifying Career Offenders Using Self-report Data." *Journal of Research in Crime and Delinquency* 21 (February): 57–86.
ELLIOTT, DELBERT S. and AGETON, SUZANNE S. (1980). "Reconciling Race and Class Differences in Self-reported and Official Estimates of Delinquency." *American Sociological Review* 45 (February): 95–110.
ELLIOTT, DELBERT S. and HUIZINGA, DAVID. (1983). "Social Class and Delinquent Behavior in a National Youth Panel, 1976-1980." *Criminology* 21 (May): 149–77.
FEDERAL BUREAU OF INVESTIGATION (1984). *Crime in the United States, 1983.* Washington, D.C.: U.S. Government Printing Office.
FERDINAND, THEODORE N. (1966). *Typologies of Delinquency.* New York: Random House.
FISHER, SETHARD (1962). "Varieties of Juvenile Delinquency." *British Journal of Criminology* 2 (January): 251–61.
GIBBONS, DON C. (1965). *Changing the Lawbreaker.* Englewood Cliffs, N.J.: Prentice-Hall.
GIBBONS, DON C. (1982). *Society, Crime, and Criminal Behavior.* 4th edition. Englewood Cliffs, N.J.: Prentice-Hall.
GIBBONS, DON C. (1985). "The Assumption of the Efficacy of Middle-Range Explanation: Typologies," pp. 151–74. In Robert F. Meier, ed. *Theoretical Methods in Criminology.* Beverly Hills, Cal.: Sage.
HAMPARIAN, DONNA MARTIN, SCHUSTER, RICHARD, DINITZ, SIMON, and CONRAD, JOHN P. (1978). *The Violent Few.* Lexington, Mass.: Lexington.
HINDELANG, MICHAEL J. (1971). "Age, Sex, and Versatility of Delinquent Involvements." *Social Problems* 18 (Spring): 522–35.

HINDELANG, MICHAEL J., HIRSCHI, TRAVIS, and WEIS, JOSEPH G. (1979). "Correlates of Delinquency: The Illusion of Discrepancy Between Self-report and Official Measures." *American Sociological Review* 44 (December): 995-1014.

HIRSCHI, TRAVIS (1969). *Causes of Delinquency*. Berkeley: University of California Press.

JENKINS, RICHARD L. and HEWITT, LESTER E. (1944). "Types of Personality Structure Encountered in Child Guidance Clinics." *American Journal of Orthopsychiatry* 14 (January): 84-94.

JENSEN, GARY F. and EVE, RAYMOND (1976). "Sex Differences in Delinquency: An Examination of Popular Sociological Explanations." *Criminology* 13 (February): 427-48.

KELLEY, THOMAS M. (1983). "Status Offenders Can Be Different: A Comparative Study of Delinquent Careers." *Crime and Delinquency* 29 (July): 365-80.

KINCH, JOHN W. (1962a) "Continuities in the Study of Delinquent Types." *Journal of Criminal Law, Criminology and Police Science* 53 (September): 323-38.

KINCH, JOHN W. (1962b) "Self-conceptions of Types of Delinquents." *Sociological Inquiry* 32 (Spring): 228-34.

KLEIN, MALCOLM W. (1984). "Offense Specialization and Versatility Among Juveniles." *British Journal of Criminology* 24 (April): 185-94.

LAB, STEVEN P. (1984). "Patterns in Juvenile Misbehavior." *Criminology* 30 (April): 293-308.

McDONALD, LYNN (1969). *Social Class and Delinquency*. London: Faber and Faber.

NETTLER, GWYNN (1984). *Explaining Crime*. 3rd edition. New York: McGraw-Hill.

NYE, F. IVAN and SHORT, JAMES F., JR. (1957). "Scaling Delinquent Behavior." *American Sociological Review* 22 (June): 326-31.

REDL, FRITZ and WINEMAN, DAVID (1957). *The Aggressive Child*. New York: McGraw-Hill.

REISS, ALBERT J., JR. (1952). "Social Correlates of Psychological Types of Delinquents." *American Sociological Review* 17 (December): 710-18.

ROJEK, DEAN G. and ERICKSON, MAYNARD L. (1982). "Delinquent Careers: A Test of the Career Escalation Model." *Criminology* 20 (May): 5-28.

SHANNON, LYLE W. (1984). *Assessing the Relationship of Adult Criminal Careers to Juvenile Careers*. Iowa City: Iowa Urban Community Research Center, University of Iowa.

SHORT, JAMES F., JR. and NYE, F. IVAN (1957-58). "Reported Behavior as a Criterion of Delinquent Behavior." *Social Problems* 5 (Winter): 207-13.

SHORT, JAMES F., JR. and NYE, F. IVAN (1958). "Extent of Unrecorded Juvenile Delinquency: Tentative Conclusions." *Journal of Criminal Law, Criminology and Police Science* 49 (November-December): 296-302.

SHORT, JAMES F., JR., NYE, F. IVAN, and OLSON, VIRGIL J. (1958). "Socioeconomic Status and Delinquent Behavior." *American Journal of Sociology* 63 (January): 381-89.

SIMON, RITA JAMES (1975). *Women and Crime*. Lexington, Mass.: Heath.

SMITH, DOUGLAS A. and VISHER, CHRISTY A. (1980). "Sex and Involvement in Deviance/ Crime: A Quantitative Review of the Empirical Literature." *American Sociological Review* 45 (August): 691-701.

STEFFENSMEIER, DARRELL J. (1978). "Crime and Contemporary Woman: An Analysis of Changing Levels of Female Property Crime, 1960-75." *Social Forces* 57 (December): 566-84.

STEFFENSMEIER, DARRELL J. and STEFFENSMEIER, RENEE HOFFMAN (1980). "Trends in Female Delinquency: An Examination of Arrest, Juvenile Court, Self-report, and Field Data." *Criminology* 18 (May): 62-85.

THOMAS, CHARLES W. (1976). "Are Status Offenders Really So Different? A Comparative and Longitudinal Assessment." *Crime and Delinquency* 22 (October): 438-55.

TITTLE, CHARLES R., VILLEMEZ, WAYNE J., and SMITH, DOUGLAS A. (1978). "The Myth of Social Class and Criminality." *American Sociological Review* 63 (December): 643-56.

TOPPING, RUTH (1941). "Case Studies of Aggressive Delinquents." *American Journal of Orthopsychiatry* 11 (July): 485-92.

WARREN, MARGUERITE Q. (1976). "Intervention with Juvenile Delinquents," pp. 176-204. In Margaret K. Rosenheim, ed. *Pursuing Justice for the Child*. Chicago: University of Chicago Press.

WOLFGANG, MARVIN E., FIGLIO, ROBERT M., and SELLIN, THORSTEN (1972). *Delinquency in a Birth Cohort*. Chicago: University of Chicago Press.

chapter 5

SOCIAL PROCESSING OF OFFENDERS

INTRODUCTION

Chapter 3 indicated that delinquency, defined as youthful misbehavior that violates legal statutes, is extremely commonplace, so much so that most American youngsters engage in it at one time or another while making their way through childhood and adolescence. But relatively few members of this army of youthful lawbreakers become tagged as juvenile delinquents by the police or juvenile court. And as we have seen in Chapter 4, social sorting processes occurring in local communities appear to operate in a manner such that those youngsters who engage in serious and/ or repetitive acts of misconduct run the greatest risk of falling into the hands of the police or being impelled into the juvenile court. However, the nature of these sorting processes and the operations of the juvenile justice system have yet to be explored in detail, which is the task of this chapter.

The juvenile justice system in the United States represents grand scale social machinery. Because this people-processing apparatus is staffed by many individuals who are involved in making decisions about offenders, its nature cannot be fully captured in a few paragraphs. But a brief summary of this system would note that the police are most frequently involved in the initial decisions about reported juvenile lawbreakers, for they either observe these youths in acts of deviance or, more frequently, they learn about them from citizens. The police occupy a crucial position in the decision system; they control the initial sorting-out of youths, thus determining which are to be viewed as "bad" or "delinquent" and taken to court, and which do not need court intervention. The police take some youngsters directly to the juvenile court, while they give others citations to appear in court at some subsequent time. Although other persons—private citizens, school officials, and others—report youngsters to juvenile court too, these cases are less frequent than are police referrals.

Those juveniles who end up at the juvenile hall or other court facility are submitted to a variety of decision makers. In larger courts, a probation officer serving in an intake capacity dismisses the referred children who he concludes do not warrant court attention, or he determines the referrals as not delinquent enough to deserve formal court action but still needing some help. Many of these youngsters are persuaded to submit to informal probation, in which they report periodically to a probation officer even though they have not been formally adjudicated as delinquents. Petitions alleging delinquency are filed on a third group of offenders who are then scheduled for court hearing. Some of these juveniles are detained in juvenile hall while they await a hearing; others are released to their parents. Chapter 3 indicated that about 71,000 juveniles were detained in public and private detention facilities on any particular day in 1979. Finally, when a court determines that youngsters are delinquents, this adjudication leads to still other decisions. Some wards are placed on probation, some are turned over to a private agency, and some are sent to custodial institutions for care and treatment. The nature of the juvenile justice apparatus and the decision points within it are illustrated in Figure 5-1 (Krisberg and Austin, 1978).

Sociological interest in the decision-making machinery which processes delinquents is twofold. In the first place, police agencies, juvenile courts, and other structures which deal with juveniles are social organizations. Sociology, which focuses on the study of social organizations, can learn much from an examination of these law enforcement and correctional systems. The people-work of these agencies cannot proceed without the development of rules, norms, and other social mechanisms. As in other large-scale organizations, the procedural standards which guide the functionaries of these systems are of several kinds and include both formal and informal rules. The unwritten or informal norms of police officers, juvenile court judges, and probation officers more often determine the ways in which offenders are processed than do the explicit, formal rules of procedure. A considerable number of sociologists have been interested in the study of the social workings of the juvenile justice system, quite apart from their specific concern about juvenile delinquency. For example, Aaron V. Cicourel (1968) dealt at length with the processes through which the police officers, probation agents, and others arrive at conclusions that juveniles exhibit "defiance of authority," "wrong attitudes," and the like. His analysis also cast considerable doubt upon the use of official records as accurate statements of what happened relative to juvenile incidents.

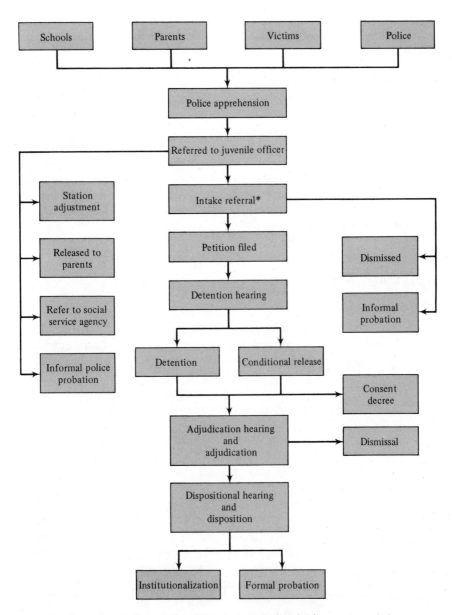

*In a few cases juveniles are referred directly to intake by schools, parents, or victims.

FIGURE 5-1   Juvenile Justice System Critical Decision Points*

*From Barry Krisberg and James Austin, *The Children of Ishmael* (Palo Alto: Mayfield Publishing Co., 1978), p. 55. By permission of the publisher.

The second reason for sociological interest in the social control machinery grows out of writings about labeling factors. Many commentators have suggested that the contact with control agencies and the acquisition of the delinquent or criminal label is a critical contingency which pushes a number of violators in the direction of repetitive involvement in misbehavior. Those deviants who become publicly identified as delinquents or hoods find that they are indelibly labeled and stigmatized. In turn, they find avoidance of further deviance to be extremely difficult because other persons continue to respond to them in terms of the stigmatizing label. Those who elude this labeling experience are thought to be less likely to become committed to chronic deviance. Although this hypothesis sounds plausible, hard evidence cannot be easily identified; a firm judgment about its validity must be held in abeyance (Gibbons and Jones, 1975). A first step in the assessment of the consequences of social labeling can, however, be made by investigation of agency handling of delinquents.

THE OFFENDER AND THE POLICE

Chapter 3 observed that the police have a great number of contacts with juveniles which do not result in court referral and that these episodes far outnumber the instances in which the police do decide to take a youth to the court. Some indication of the magnitude of police work with juveniles has been provided by David Bordua (1967) who reported that, in 1964, the Detroit police enumerated 106,000 "encounters" with youngsters. The Youth Bureau of that department conducted "interviews" with 23,645 suspected offenders and also talked to 10,157 other youths for the purpose of gathering evidence. The police termed 9445 of these contacts, involving only 5282 juveniles, as "official contacts." The discretionary role of the police is well captured by these statistics.

It would be well to note in passing that a good deal of confusion appears to exist among the police regarding their contacts with juveniles. In one study of this matter, Malcolm Klein, Susan Rosensweig, and Ronald Bates (1975) uncovered a wide variety of definitions of arrest among officers in forty-nine Los Angeles county police departments. Some persons regarded the booking of a youth as constituting an arrest, while others used the term to refer to detention at the police station, street interrogation of youths, interviews with youngsters, or any recorded police-juvenile contact. The persons actually charged with compiling official reports at police stations generally agreed that a juvenile arrest involved bringing a juvenile to the police station, but at the same time not all those who were brought to the station were recorded as arrests. Truancy cases, curfew violators, and certain other youngsters were not normally recorded as having been arrested.

Bordua (1967: 159-60) has argued that two approaches ought to be taken to the study of police decision making. He pointed out that police behavior should be examined microscopically in order to identify the characteristics of offenders to which the police attend in their actions. This kind of study would probe into the decision rendered by individual police officers as they decide whether to adjust a case informally or to deal with the juvenile more severely. But in addition, a comparative and historical perspective on police activities is also needed. Perhaps police departments vary as a whole in terms of policies for disposition of offenders. Particular police agencies may also exhibit changes in policies over time which influence their dispositional activities.

Offender Characteristics and Police Decisions

We have already seen in Chapter 3 that police agencies often sort out offenders in terms of seriousness of offense, sending those who have carried out more costly or aggressive actions further on in the justice machinery while adjusting informally many of the less serious cases. Also, a good deal of evidence indicates that the more serious, actionable offenses are more frequent among persons of lower socioeconomic status; hence referral rates are higher for those individuals.

One view of police activities is that the police are relatively evenhanded in their work; while they send more lower-income and black individuals further into the criminal justice system than they do whites or more affluent citizens, it is because the former are more involved in serious offenses. In this interpretation, race and economic status are held to be important only as they are *incidentally* related to offense seriousness (Black, 1970).

Another thesis is that law enforcement agents are *directly* influenced in their discretionary decisions by such factors as the social status of persons, and, in particular, that the police are biased in their actions toward blacks. In this view, the police act more harshly toward blacks who are involved in lawbreaking activities than they do toward whites who are engaged in comparable forms of conduct. This argument has been put forth by Barry Krisberg and James Austin (1978: 78-90) as well as by many others. Krisberg and Austin conceded that research evidence on police policies and practices toward juveniles is ambiguous, contradictory, and inclusive. Nonetheless, they argued that police decisions reflect community variations, socioeconomic and racial backgrounds of offenders, and variations in police department organizational structure.

Our task is one of ferreting out clues to the social dimensions which lie behind the statistical data on police decisions. On what basis do police officers decide to ignore cases of misbehavior? How do they decide that some juvenile offenders should be directed to juvenile court? What does the evidence show regarding factors additional to offense seriousness in police decisions?

This matter of discretionary decisions of police is complex. In the search for evidence on the factors that enter into police policies, we need to keep in mind that there are several decision points at which offense seriousness, race, economic status, demeanor of the offender, and other variables might be involved. First, these influences might be most crucial at the stage of initial contact with juveniles, when the police officer on the beat decides either to deal with a youngster informally or to refer him or her to the juvenile bureau of the department. Alternatively, discretionary behavior based on these characteristics might be most prominent at the point where juvenile officers consider whether to refer a case to juvenile court or to adjust it informally. Or finally, these factors might enter most heavily into decisions within the juvenile court.

These cautionary remarks should warn against premature conclusions of the sort that racial background, for example, is not a factor in police decisions, on the basis of research data showing that juvenile officers in a police department are not influenced in their decisions by racial factors. It might be that these considerations enter at an earlier point, when beat officers take harsher action against blacks than whites, referring more of the former to the juvenile bureau.

One early study on police dispositions was done by Nathan Goldman (1963), involving a small mill town, an industrial center, a trade center, and an upper-class residential area in Pennsylvania. The findings indicated that the police referred 65 percent of the black alleged offenders but only 34 percent of the white alleged delinquents to court. This differential handling of racial groups, however, was complex; in serious offenses the referral rate was about the same for both groups, but blacks apprehended for minor delinquencies were much more frequently taken to juvenile court than were their white counterparts.

Goldman reported, somewhat surprisingly, that the upper-class residential area had the highest arrest rate, but the communities with the lowest arrest rates, the trade center and the industrial center, had the highest proportion of serious offense arrests. The kinds of complaints leading to juvenile arrests in the upper-class area and the mill town were usually ignored by the police in "Trade City" and "Steel City." The police in the latter communities apparently had more serious lawbreaking activities to contend with than juvenile peccadilloes.

Several factors seemed to loom large in the police officers' decisions about juvenile offenders. They were strongly influenced by the seriousness of offenses. They were also affected by their views of the juvenile court; those who thought the court had harmful effects upon youths referred few of them to it. The officers also placed a good deal of emphasis on the demeanor of juveniles; those who were surly or defiant were more likely to be referred than those youngsters who were polite or contrite.

Other research regarding police decisions includes a study by Lyle Shannon (1963) in a Wisconsin community which suggested that the socieconomic status of offenders was not related to police decisions. Similarly, William Hohenstein (1969) examined the dispositions of juvenile cases by the Philadelphia police, concluding that the attitude of the victim was the main determinant of whether the case was referred to juvenile court, rather than offense seriousness or racial background. Norman Weiner and Charles Willie (1971) examined police decisions in Washington, D.C., and Syracuse, New York, and reported that rates of police contact with juveniles and referral of cases to juvenile court varied widely from area to area in these cities. The highest contact and referral rates were in low socioeconomic areas but the ratio of court referrals to police contacts did not vary markedly from area to area. Accordingly, they concluded that the police do not act differentially toward persons from poorer economic backgrounds.

Another study of police screening of juveniles was conducted by Robert Terry (1967) in Racine, Wisconsin, a community with a population of about 100,000. He found that the Racine police did not respond differentially to juveniles they encountered. Although they released different proportions of the boys and girls they contacted, this was because the males were involved in serious and repetitive misconduct more than were the females. Terry concluded that the relationships between economic status of offenders and the dispositions made of them by the police or court authorities were slight or nonexistent and also that the patterns which were noted were attributable to variations in the seriousness and repetitiveness of offenses. Fairly similar results were found in a study of police dispositions in Los Angeles by A. McEachern and Riva Bauzer (1967).

Let us examine one of the studies of police decision making in detail. The study in question was conducted during the summer of 1966 by Donald Black and Albert J. Reiss (1970).

These investigators placed thirty-six observers in police cars in Boston, Washington, D.C., and Chicago. The routine activities of patrol officers were recorded, with nearly 6000 incidents being observed, including 281 cases involving juveniles. Black and Reiss pointed out that most police encounters with juveniles were citizen-initiated, rather than being the product of police ferreting out cases of misbehavior. Over three-fourths of the juvenile cases, excluding traffic offenses, were the result of citizen reports to the police, leading Black and Reiss (1970: 66-67) to conclude: "Hence it would seem that the moral standards of the citizenry have more to do with the definition of juvenile deviance than do the standards of the policeman on patrol."

Another major finding from this study was that the majority of police contacts with juveniles were for acts of mischief and rowdiness, with only about 5 percent of them involving felony offenses. Only 15 percent of the youngsters were arrested, that is, taken to a police station.

Offense seriousness loomed large in police decisions to arrest youths. However, Black and Reiss found that the overall arrest rate was higher for blacks than for white youngsters, as were arrest rates of blacks for specific kinds of offenses. These observations seemed initially to point to the operation of discriminatory attitudes on the part of the police. However, Black and Reiss argued that these findings actually mirrored the more frequent direct participation of complainants in the interactions between police and black juveniles. The police had more contacts with black youngsters in which the complainant was also present and vigorously urged the police to arrest the juvenile. It is also worth noting that both the complainant and the accused youth were blacks in most of these encounters. Arrest rates for black and white juveniles were quite similar in cases where the complainants were not on the scene.

Some other ingredients of police-juvenile interactions emerged in this study, but they were of lesser significance than complainant involvement. Black and Reiss indicated that youngsters who were antagonistic toward officers were somewhat more likely to be arrested, but because the number of hostile youths was quite small, the demeanor of youths could not weigh heavily in police actions. Finally, juveniles were somewhat more likely to be arrested if evidence was found by the officer that directly linked the former to the offense.

Black and Reiss (1970: 68) identified eight propositions or generalizations to be derived from their findings:

1. Most police encounters with juveniles arise in direct response to citizens who take the initiative to mobilize the police to action.
2. The great bulk of police encounters with juveniles pertain to matters of minor legal significance.
3. The probability of sanction by arrest is very low for juveniles who have encounters with the police.
4. The probability of arrest increases with the legal seriousness of alleged juvenile offenses, as that legal seriousness is defined in criminal law for adults.
5. Police sanctioning of juveniles strongly reflects the manifest preferences of citizen complainants in field encounters.
6. The arrest rate for Negro juveniles is higher than that for white juveniles, but evidence that the police behaviorally orient themselves to race as such is absent.
7. The presence of situational evidence linking a juvenile to a deviant act is an important fact in the probability of arrest.
8. The probability of arrest is higher for juveniles who are unusually respectful toward the police and for those who are unusually disrespectful.

One might ask how widely these propositions might be generalized to other police departments. Regarding that question, Richard Lundman, R. E. Sykes, and John Clarke (1978) examined about 200 police-juvenile encounters which occurred in a large Midwest city in 1970–71. They found general support for the Black and Reiss propositions, although they added some clarifications and extensions of their own to them. For example, they argued that variations in proactive enforcement policies from one police department to another may increase or decrease the proportion of cases generated by police as opposed to citizen action. Then, too, they argued that blacks are more often involved in felony complaints than are whites, which is a major reason for greater numbers of them being reported to the court.

These studies add up to a picture of the police operating in a relatively legalistic fashion, rather than in terms of prejudices and biases. The police seem to be more impressed by the nature and seriousness of offenses than by any other factors. The major route to the juvenile court appears to be heavily traveled by those juveniles who are most persistently involved in lawbreaking.

Offense seriousness is not, however, the sole factor of importance. Several studies of police activity challenge the picture just sketched, at least to some degree. One of these was by Theodore Ferdinand and Elmer Luchterhand (1970) in a city of about 150,000 which they disguised as "Easton." They drew a sample of about 1500 teenagers from six inner-city neighborhoods in that community. When they checked police and juvenile court records, they found that 27 percent of the sample had been officially recorded as delinquents.

Ferdinand and Luchterhand found that proportionately more black than white youths had been referred to juvenile court by the police. After controlling for the influence of offense seriousness, recidivism, and type of offense, they found that blacks still were more frequently turned over to the court. In addition, attitudinal patterns of offenders were examined on the suspicion that the black referrals may have been more hostile and antisocial than the white youths. But, in fact, the researchers uncovered evidence to suggest that the black youths were *less* antisocial and aggressive than white offenders in these neighborhoods. Although the black youths were more frequently from broken homes, there appeared to be less family discord in those homes than in the case of white juveniles. Ferdinand and Luchterhand concluded that the police in "Easton" did discriminate against black male juveniles in particular. Higher rates of referral to the court were not simply due to greater seriousness of offenses, more hostile attitudes, or greater family discord among black teenagers.

Another investigation that turned up parallel results was conducted by Terence Thornberry (1973) in Philadelphia. He found that the police handled 67.9 percent of a sample of offenses by remedial arrest in which they disposed of the case informally and sent 13.9 percent of the cases to juvenile court; 11.4 percent of the offenders received probation, and 6.8 percent were incarcerated. The police sent more blacks to court than whites, but while larger numbers of black youths also were dealt with officially in court, fewer received probation, and more were sent to institutions. Thornberry (1973: 94): concluded that "the striking finding is that racial differences are quite apparent even when the influence of the seriousness of the offense is controlled."

What shall we make of the data examined to this point? The results we have scrutinized have been drawn from police records of various kinds. They seem to show that demographic characteristics of offenders are related to police dispositions, because seriousness of offense is correlated with background characteristics. Blacks and working-class youths commit the most harmful and costly acts of lawbreaking. At the same time, some investigations have indicated that the police behave differentially toward black youngsters, sending more of them to juvenile court than they do white youths involved in comparable offenses. *In all likelihood, what these discrepant findings reflect are real differences among communities and police departments with regard to the salience of race in police practices.* That is, it may well be that in some communities with a relatively small black population, for example, race is not an important factor in police behavior, while it appears more significant in other cities. In short, our research evidence may be mixed because law enforcement activities are lacking in uniformity.

On this point, consider the arguments of Dale Dannefer and Russell Schutt (1982), who have pointed out that the various studies of police and juvenile court bias have yielded contradictory results, in part because of methodological problems in the various studies, and in part because discrimination may be more important in one of these settings than in the other. In their study in an eastern state, they found that racial bias was more apparent on the part of the police than of court officials. Also, discriminatory decision making by the police was most pronounced in the largest of the two urban centers they studied, which also had the largest minority group population.

A Note on Institutional Racism

The studies considered above appear to indicate that in some communities the police are sensitive to social class and ethnic backgrounds of offenders, while in others these factors do not enter into police decisions concerning juvenile law-breakers. And even in those locales where racial considerations seem to be included in police actions, the police appear to attend first to offense seriousness and only to a lesser extent to racial or socioeconomic characteristics of offenders. In short, American police respond in a legalistic fashion to alleged lawbreakers. There is little evidence that individual police officers operate primarily in terms of blatant racist sentiments and that their actions are to be explained principally in those terms, but it could hardly be otherwise, for the police officer's mandate from the citizenry is to enforce the law, not to reinforce racial and other prejudices that exist within society.

However, Empey (1982: 323-24), Krisberg and Austin (1978: 78-90), and others have quite correctly argued that while individual police officers probably do not behave in an explicitly racist fashion, racism may nonetheless be reflected in the actions of the police. Long-standing patterns of racism that are endemic in American society operate as root causes of much delinquency that occurs in this country, particularly in inner-city neighborhoods in major urban centers. "Garden variety" crime and delinquency are social products that have developed out of the economic precariousness and social wretchedness that have been the lot of victims of "institutional racism," that is, socially pervasive patterns of racial discrimination in American society. More directly, police agencies and the juvenile court often define their tasks as centering around intervention in the lives of the poor and minority populations, for the members of these groups have been regarded as particularly prone to criminality. Empey (1982: 323) has put the matter well: ". . . it is clear that the tendency of the police to find and report higher rates of law-violating behavior, child abuse, and neglect among poor and minority children is not just the product of bigotry peculiar to them. Rather, it is a function of conditions for which the police are not solely responsible. Instead, the police are merely the front-line troops of conventional society who are expected to mop up ghetto communities after a long war of attrition in which racial and social segregation have taken a heavy toll."

The thrust of these observations is that societal forms of racism may be importantly involved in police responses to juveniles who are from different racial backgrounds. Racism may account in large part for higher rates of delinquency among lower-class black youths. Moreover, racism may be manifested in police responses in another, even more indirect but equally significant way, in which police patrol and surveillance activities are differentially concentrated in minority communities. It would not be surprising to find that the targets of excessive attention by the police would come to view that attention as harassment and would develop hostile attitudes toward the police, often viewing them as the agents of an oppressive social order. In turn, those youngsters who express hostility toward the police through various verbal or gestural means may run a heightened risk of being dealt with relatively harshly by the police. These more subtle factors in police decision making might be revealed if we were to examine particular instances of offender-officer interaction.

Offender-Police Interaction

As we have seen in the studies reviewed to this point, considerations additional to offense seriousness enter into police actions. The demeanor of the juvenile and the presence of complaining citizens are two of these factors. Let us examine this matter further. Bordua (1967) has reported on Detroit Police Youth Bureau officers who filled out a section on their report form entitled "Attitude Toward Officer." These officers filed petitions against juveniles in 67 percent of the cases of those identified as showing "honest" attitudes, in 70 percent of the "responsive" cases, in 78 percent of the "evasive" cases, and 80 percent of the "antisocial" attitude cases.

Sellin and Wolfgang (1964: 95-100) have also reported that a number of factors enter into police decisions. They asserted that the police they studied in Philadelphia based their dispositional decisions on (1) the prior record of the youth, (2) the type of offense and the role of the juvenile in it, (3) the attitude of the victim or complainant, and (4) the family situation of the offender. Other considerations included (5) the potential community resources which might be utilized for correction, (6) the general appearance of the offender and his or her attitude toward the police, (7) the possible overcrowding at the Youth Study Center, and (8) the police officer's anticipation of juvenile court action should an arrest be made.

Irving Piliavin and Scott Briar (1964) have contributed one of the most detailed studies of offender-police interaction. Their report was based on field notes of juvenile encounters with Juvenile Bureau officers over a nine-month period in a city with a population of 450,000. These officers dealt both with juveniles whom they observed near the scene of reported offenses and with youths whom they detected in acts of misbehavior. They had a number of dispositions available to them: They could release juveniles outright, reprimand them, cite them to the juvenile court, or arrest them and have them confined in the juvenile hall.

According to Piliavin and Briar, discretion in the handling of juveniles was widely used in this department for most offenses. Many of the officers felt that the juvenile court failed to rehabilitate offenders; thus they were reluctant to turn youths over to it. In addition, discretionary handling and the concept that justice for juveniles should be individualized were departmental policy.

The police dealt with various kinds of misbehavior. The 10 percent of it that was serious in nature was handled uniformly by referral to the court. The nature of the misbehavior was the sole determinant of police action in these cases, but in the remainder which involved minor delinquencies and a few serious ones, police decisions tended to be influenced by personal characteristics of the youths rather than by their offenses. Most of their contacts were with males, and in these cases the police arrived at characterological assessments, defining some as "good boys" and others as "bad ones," and their decisions followed these assessments. These characterological judgments were made on the spot and were based on scanty information; they usually emerged from the immediate interaction between the boy and the officer. Those youths who were identified as "bad guys" were often older boys, blacks, and youths with greasy hair, black jackets, and dirty Levis. The conclusion that a juvenile was a "bad boy" who deserved court attention was frequently based upon his failure to display the deference which the police officer felt to be his or her due.

Piliavin and Briar noted that black youths were frequently stopped by the police and given relatively severe dispositions because they often showed a hostile demeanor toward the police. But it was also noted that the police concentrated much of their attention in urban ghettoes, where they indiscriminately harassed citizens. This activity on the part of the police probably had much to do with the hostility demonstrated toward them by delinquent suspects. Thus the vicious circle continues: Police harassment of "suspicious" black youths led those youngsters to see police contacts as a routine, taken-for-granted aspect of their lives. In turn, they responded in a hostile or indifferent manner to the police, who then felt little compunction about referring them to court in large numbers. The high arrest and referral rate for black youths was then taken by the police as evidence in support of the stereotype of most blacks as potential criminals.

Additional light is thrown upon police-juvenile interaction in an essay by Carl Werthman and Irving Piliavin (1967). They presented a rich body of descriptive and analytical material on police–black gang member interaction. Their general premise was that the social perspectives of gang boys were very different from those of police. The delinquents viewed neighborhood streets as their "turf" or home, but the police did not honor this perception. The boys regarded the police as enemies who enforce laws produced and supported by the power structure of the community. These laws were seen as attempts to suppress minority group members and to perpetuate patterns of discrimination. The police regarded all residents of the black community as "suspicious" persons. The black targets of these police opinions were outraged by being perpetually viewed as criminals or incipient wrongdoers.

Delinquent boys in urban ghettoes employed a number of stratagems to avoid contact with the police; for example, they dispersed into smaller units when the police approached, positioned themselves near girls, wore their club jackets inside out to hide identifying marks, or wore wedding rings so that the police would assume they were married. However, these tactics often failed so that these youngsters were drawn into encounters with the police. When this happened, the juveniles were prone to display hostility and scorn toward the police, due to their perspectives on the role of law enforcement in the furtherance of discrimination. This interaction produced high rates of arrest and court referral.

Police Organization and Juvenile Dispositions

What about interorganizational variations among police departments? What can be said about changes in departmental policies relating to the handling of juvenile offenders? Several pieces of evidence at hand bear upon questions of this sort. For one, McEachern and Bauzer (1967) observed that the Santa Monica police referred to court about 20 percent of the delinquency cases they handled during the years 1940 to 1944; between 1955 and 1960, however, referrals made up over 40 percent of the youths known to the police. Similarly, Bordua (1967) noted that the Detroit police referral rate changed markedly between 1951 and 1964. He also presented FBI data for over 2000 police agencies in 1965, showing that 385 of them released less than 5 percent of the juveniles they contacted, 60 agencies turned loose more than 95 percent of the youngsters they encountered, and at least 50 police agencies were found in all of the 5 percent intervals between these extremes, proving that referral rates were extremely varied throughout the nation. Presumably, these rates were the product of variations in the seriousness of delinquency in communities, differences in police policies regarding disposition of cases, differences in the availability of community resources for the handling of youthful lawbreakers, and other factors of this sort.

James Wilson (1968) conducted the most detailed study of interorganizational variations among police agencies, dealing with "Eastern City" and "Western City," both of which had a population of substantially more than 300,000. Both communities were free from political machine domination. However, their police departments differed: Western City had a professionalized department, while Eastern City showed a fraternal law enforcement agency. The Western City professional department recruited impartially, practiced consistent enforcement of the law, was not frequented by graft, and was structured in a formal bureaucratic fashion. In short, it hewed closely to the model of the modern professional police force. Eastern City had a department which recruited entirely from among local residents, practiced differential law enforcement, showed considerable graft, and commonly had informal and fraternal relations in its operation.

The juvenile bureaus of these two police departments exhibited a number of points of difference. In Eastern City the police were moralistic in their outlook, holding that delinquents were the product of faulty personal or family morality. They verbalized restrictive and punitive attitudes toward offenders. In Western City, on the other hand, the officers were less moralistic and more therapeutic in their opinions. They tended to seek the causes of delinquency in conditions of general social pathology.

What effect did these perspectives have on the handling of delinquent referrals? The effect was the opposite of what one might suspect. The police department of Western City processed a larger proportion of its city's juvenile population than did Eastern City. Moreover, a larger share of those contacted were arrested in Western City than in the other community. These differences were not negligible either; the rate of juveniles contacted or arrested was several times higher in the western city than in the other community. These anomalous results seemed to indicate that the police who reacted most severely toward juveniles were the ones who verbalized nonpunitive and less moralistic views of offenders, while those who spoke harshly about lawbreakers were the ones who handled them informally outside the framework of the juvenile court.

Several factors explain these variations. There were structural and procedural differences in the two communities. In Eastern City the police officer who initially handled the juvenile was obliged to prepare the case and present it to the court; in Western City the case was turned over to a probation officer. The opportunity to avoid extra work was an incentive to dealing informally with offenders in Eastern City.

Wilson also argued that the professional orientation of the Western City department exerted pressure on officers to take formal action in juvenile cases, while in the fraternal department no such organizational ethos existed. Then, too, the western city had a centralized police department and juvenile bureau, while the eastern city's department and bureau were organized on a precinct station basis. The centralized and bureaucratic pattern of Western City led to uniform application of general rules of procedure, consistent enforcement of the law, and routine maintenance of formal records, all of which contributed to the juvenile policies of the department.

Police work in Eastern City was conducted quite differently. The use of personal judgment was stressed in the organization. Police officers had greater loyalties to the local neighborhood, for many of them had lived in the precinct in which they now worked. These officers engaged in personalized enforcement of the law, which, in the case of juveniles, meant that they turned few of them over to the court.

One final topic of Wilson's study concerned police dealings with blacks. The Eastern City officers had no particularized experience with blacks, so they tended to perceive them in a stereotyped manner. Most blacks were viewed as suspicious persons and as individuals from pathological families. Their dealings with blacks were conditioned by these perspectives. In contrast, the Western City officers tended to be more professional and impersonal in their interaction with blacks.

JUVENILE COURT DECISION MAKING

Our commentary in Chapter 2 touched upon decision-making processes in juvenile courts, and in particular, with implementation of due process decisions of the Supreme Court. But let us examine juvenile court decision processes in more detail.

In those small jurisdictions presided over by ill-trained judges and characterized by meager resources in the way of probation officer personnel and dispositional alternatives, the actions of judges are probably easily described. In all likelihood, one of two dispositions is made of cases. The juveniles are either dismissed by the court with an admonition or tonguelashing or are sent off to state custodial institutions. In larger jurisdictions, such as metropolitan areas or major counties, decision making is probably more complicated. In these courts probation officers are employed in some number. These individuals prepare social reports and make dispositional recommendations which the judges usually follow.

Unfortunately, an abundance of material dealing with decision making by probation officers and judges is not at hand. The studies of these persons and their activities that are available are relatively few in number and in some cases are only tangentially related to decision-making processes. Nonetheless, it is possible to assemble a sketch of some of the dimensions of decision behavior from research evidence.

Several time-and-motion studies of probation officers tell something about decision making. In one, Gertrude Hengerer (1954) found that the officers she studied in two California probation departments spent most of their time writing reports, driving from one place to another, and in similar operations. They had little time to devote to the delivery of therapy to juvenile offenders. Lewis Diana (1955) reported similar findings in an investigation in Allegheny County (Pittsburgh), Pennsylvania. His research showed that probation officers had few contacts with their cases and that these were, for the most part, quite superficial ones. It appeared that these harried probation officers dealt with relatively minor cases and disposed of the more serious delinquents by sending them to training schools.

Who gets referred to the juvenile court? What dispositions are made of those who are referred to court? On what basis are offenders sent off to probation or shunted off to training schools? Some broad answers to these questions appear in the report of the National Assessment of Juvenile Corrections study (Hasenfeld, 1976). This national survey of juvenile courts showed that approximately 60 percent of all court referrals involve youths charged with violations of criminal laws, while the rest are comprised of traffic, CHINS, dependency, and neglect cases. Police agencies refer 75 percent or more of the youths who are sent to courts. Male referrals are three or four times more frequent than female referrals. The following conclusion is of greatest significance to the discussion here (Hasenfeld, 1976: 71): "Nonwhite youths are three times more likely to be processed by the courts than white youths. This difference, it seems, cannot be accounted for by differences in the frequency of delinquent behavior. Rather, it may be attributed to differential handling of white and nonwhite youths by the agencies controlling the input of the cases to the courts."

Sociological investigators have not been in complete agreement regarding the extent to which their studies indicate the operation of socioeconomic or racial biases in court decision making. In one investigation of juvenile court dispositions, Frank Scarpitti and Richard Stephenson (1971) examined the flow of 1200 cases within a juvenile court in a large eastern county. Their data indicated that judicial sorting of delinquents into those who receive probation, institutional commitment, or some other disposition was not capricious. Most of these decisions revolved around assessments of delinquency risk; therefore the most socially disadvantaged, delinquent, and psychologically atypical boys were sent to training schools.

A parallel investigation by Arnold (1971) concerned court dispositions in Austin, Texas. He observed that probation officers did not discriminate against blacks and Mexican-American youths when they referred juveniles to a formal court hearing; instead, their decisions were based largely on the seriousness of delinquent offenses and kindred considerations. However, Arnold did report that judges sent more minority group members to the state correction agency than they did whites. He argued that the court was not excessively harsh with minority youngsters as much as it was inclined to let whites "get off easy."

Shannon's (1963) research in Madison, Wisconsin also appeared to indicate that economic status of delinquents was not a factor in the dispositions made of them. However, this city is smaller and quite different in structure from large, industrial, metropolitan communities, in which other patterns of juvenile handling might prevail. Terry (1967) reported that in Racine, probation dispositions were unrelated to ethnic status. He did find that probation decisions were influenced by the seriousness and repetitiveness of misconduct; thus males were more harshly dealt with because they were more deeply involved in delinquency. On the other hand, females who were retained for official handling by the court were more likely to be institutionalized than were males. A more recent inquiry conducted by Lawrence Cohen and James Kluegel (1978) in Denver and Memphis concluded that in these courts, which differed markedly in terms of court organization, present offense and prior delinquent record were the major determinants of juvenile court dispositions, while racial and economic backgrounds of court referrals played no part in court decisions.

On the other side of the coin, some researchers have found evidence pointing to the operation of racial and social biases in court decisions. An investigation by Edwin Lemert and Judy Rosberg (1948) in Los Angeles County indicated that court-adjudicated blacks and Mexican-Americans were less likely to be placed on probation than were whites, even when variables such as offense history were controlled. In another inquiry, Sidney Axelrad (1952) was concerned with the 300 boys who had been committed to the New York State Training School between 1933 and 1934. That study disclosed that black training school wards had been committed at a younger age, for less serious offenses, with fewer previous court appearances, and with less prior institutionalization than was true of whites. Axelrad attributed this differential to the greater incidence of unstable homes and other conditions of social disorganization characteristic of the black wards. In other words, the black boys got to the training school at an earlier age and for less serious delinquencies not because of ethnic status per se, but because of the social liabilities in their backgrounds.

A more recent study of discriminatory decision making has been conducted by Charles Thomas and Christopher Sieverdes (1975) in a juvenile court in a small city in the southeastern region of the nation. They found that offense seriousness interacted with other variables in court decisions in that serious offenders were most likely to receive harsh dispositions when they were also male, black, and from lower-income backgrounds. Also, serious offenders who had delinquent companions or were from unstable family backgrounds received more severe dispositions than did other youngsters who had committed serious offenses.

SEXUAL DISCRIMINATION IN THE JUVENILE JUSTICE SYSTEM

Discrimination against juvenile women by the justice system is not a phenomenon of recent origin. As Steven Schlossman and Stephanie Wallach (1978) have indicated in detail, the harsh punishment of young females for acts thought to mirror immorality arose during the Progressive Era at the beginning of the twentieth century. They amassed a large body of evidence pointing to the following conclusions (Schlossman and Wallach, 1978: 68):

> Although public response to female delinquency emerged in the Victorian era, not until the Progressive period was female delinquency widely perceived as a social problem requiring extensive governmental intervention. In the Progressive period the abundant literature on delinquency was riddled with stereotypical assumptions about women, and in particular, about immigrant women. These stereotypes laid a basis for more punitive treatment of delinquent girls than delinquent boys. Girls were prosecuted almost exclusively for "immoral" conduct, a very broad category that defined all sexual exploration as fundamentally perverse and predictive of future promiscuity, perhaps even prostitution. But while girls, unlike boys, were almost never accused of violating criminal statutes, they received stiffer legal penalties.

Schlossman and Wallach argued that differential responses to female offenders reflected chivalrous attitudes that viewed women as especially vulnerable to evil influences and temptations. But ironically, this protective viewpoint has led to female offenders being dealt with more harshly than men even though their offenses are less serious ones. For example, courts often place more boys on probation and send more females to training schools (Gibbons and Griswold, 1957; Eaton and Polk, 1961; but also see Staples, 1984).

Why did the citizenry become concerned with female delinquency during the Progressive Era and why were female offenders treated more punitively? According to Schlossman and Wallach, the explanation does not lie in increased female delinquency during this period. Instead, the heightened sensitivity to female delinquency and the development of correctional efforts were related to the eugenics movement which often viewed children of immigrants or from poverty backgrounds as innately inferior persons whose sexual activities needed to be curbed. Also, public concern about female offenders was influenced by theories of adolescence that grew up during this period. Finally, and most important, the Progressive Era movement for "social purity" had much to do with these developments. Schlossman and Wallach contended that intensified attention to female offenders was related to efforts by reform groups to revitalize Victorian morality and to punish women who violated its sexual standards.

Meda Chesney-Lind (1974) has argued that contemporary female delinquents are also the victims of sexist discrimination in the juvenile justice system. She points out that many states have allowed the incarceration of female delinquents for status offenses at the same time that they have provided that males can only be sent to training schools for offenses that constitute crimes when carried out by adults. Further, she noted that status offenses are disproportionately involved in the cases of females referred to juvenile court or sent to training schools, in that "hidden delinquency" studies have shown that females not infrequently also admit to theft and other nonstatus offenses. She concluded (Chesney-Lind, 1974: 45): "The findings of these studies indicate that official court statistics probably underestimate the volume of female delinquency while overestimating its sexual character." In short, the female screening processes ignore certain kinds of misbehavior, while at the same time they catch up many young women for relatively petty misconduct and for status offenses. Males who engage in these same activities are ignored by the police or other persons within the juvenile justice apparatus. An oversolicitous concern for the sexual morality of young women appears to underlie this heightened sensitivity to female status offenses. In short, the authorities are most likely to take actions against young females who are suspected of being involved in sexual misconduct or in danger of becoming entangled in sexual experimentation. Since the same close scrutiny is not maintained over males, it can be argued that the police and the juvenile court are involved in a form of sexual discrimination.

Chesney-Lind maintained that juvenile courts also discriminate against juvenile females by handing out harsher dispositions to females than to males, even though the latter are more frequently involved in serious violations of the personal or property rights of others. She presented findings from a study in Honolulu that indicated that juvenile detention was used quite frequently in relatively petty cases of female delinquency but not in similar male instances. She also observed that females are subjected to pelvic examinations and vaginal smears in many juvenile jurisdictions, even though such practices raise grave questions about infringement upon the civil rights of juvenile women. These practices grow out of the operating premises of court personnel holding that most delinquent females are involved in sexual misconduct, regardless of the specific charges that brought them to court attention. In turn, court workers apparently feel obliged to endeavor to confirm these suspicions by subjecting young women to interrogations, pelvic examinations, and vaginal smears.

Chesney-Lind reported sexual discrimination operating against female offenders at a variety of points in the juvenile enforcement and correctional systems. Her summary judgment held that (Chesney-Lind, 1974: 46):

If parents are unwilling or unable to control their daughter's behavior, our society believes, the court can and should. As a consequence, the labels of "incorrigible," "ungovernable," and "runaway" permit the same abuses that characterize the labels of "sick" or "insane." That is, saving or protecting girls often justifies treating them more severely than boys who break the law. Thus the courts' commitment to the sexual double standard and the subordinate status of women results in a clear violation of the civil rights of young women. Punishment in the name of protection is much like bombing a village to save it from the enemy.

Parallel observations about discriminatory handling of female offenders have been offered by Kristine Olson Rogers (1972). After examining institutional practices at a Connecticut state training school for juvenile females, she concluded that the institution was devoted to a correctional regimen designed to prepare young women to reeenter the community as nineteenth-century domestics. Little effort was expended by the staff of the institution on programs that would more adequately equip the young women released from it to deal with the variety of social adjustment problems they were likely to encounter in modern society.

Rogers also presented data indicating that nearly three-fourths of the female wards were in the institution for status offenses, while only 18 percent of male training school inmates in that state had been sentenced for those activities. Alarmingly, although the young women were involved in less serious offenses than were the males, they received longer sentences. According to Rogers (1972: 277), these differentials arise because the staff members of the boys' school are eager to return males to the community, while at the female training school, the "staff often insists that a girl finish an academic term even though her behavior would warrant release, or they may fear 'summer temptations' if a girl is released over the summer with nothing to 'keep her occupied,' or they may keep a girl through a pregnancy and for two months afterward until she is 'medically cleared.'"

Chesney-Lind and Rogers argued that juvenile courts discriminate against female offenders by imposing a sexual double standard upon them and by reacting in an overly harsh manner in cases where young women are suspected of sexual involvement. In turn, these court actions reflect broader societal concerns about the sexual activities of minor females and at the same time pay relatively slight heed to sexual misconduct on the part of juvenile males. Finally, young females are often sent to training school because no readily available and more desirable alternate placement is available for them in the community. It is frequently difficult to demonstrate that these correctional responses and actions are beneficial to the young women to whom they occur.

We should not rush too quickly to the conclusion that these negative observations by Chesney-Lind and Rogers apply uniformly to all juvenile courts across the nation. As is often the case, the real world turns out to be too complex to be described by a few unequivocal generalizations. Concerning juvenile courts, Katherine Teilmann and Pierre Landry (1981) have conducted a study of six different court jurisdictions across the country which indicated the existence of sex bias against females who were involved in certain offenses but bias against males involved in other delinquencies. They also indicated that status offenders, both male and female, receive harsher treatment from courts than do delinquent offenders. Although females are referred to court more often than boys for status offenses, they receive similar handling once they are drawn into the court system.

A study by Marvin Krohn, James Curry, and Shirley Nelson-Kilger (1983) is also germane. These investigators gathered police contact data on three birth cohorts (1942, 1949, 1955) in a north central city. The findings on juvenile arrests indicated that female status offenders were treated more harshly by the police in all of the time periods studied: 1948-1959, 1960-1966, and 1967-1972. In other words, they found no evidence for a decline in the paternalistic and discriminatory treatment of female status offenders. On the other hand, the researchers did report that female referral rates for misdemeanors were somewhat lower during the earlier two time periods than in 1967-1972, while sex variations in felony referrals were less apparent. These results led Krohn, Curry, and Nelson-Kilger to conclude (1983: 431): "We found rather consistent trends toward more egalitarian treatment of females and males for juvenile misdemeanors, adult misdemeanors, and adult felonies. However, we also found that sex differences in dispositions for the latter two types of police contacts had not completely disappeared by the 1970s."

SUMMARY

This chapter has been directed less at juvenile offenders than at the activities of those persons who are engaged in decision making within the juvenile justice system—police officers, probation officers, judges, and other workers in this collection of social control agencies. As we have seen, police-juvenile encounters are varied and complex, as are the interactions between youthful offenders and court workers, such that it is difficult to capture the richness of these behavioral configurations in a few pages. Nonetheless, the evidence considered in this chapter points to the following conclusions:

1. Police officers deal with large numbers of juveniles, most of whom they handle informally without court referral. The decision to take a youngster to the court is often in part a legalistic one. Those offenders who have been engaged in serious or repetitive acts of lawbreaking are most likely to be turned over to the court.
2. Police dispositions are related to demographic characteristics of offenders; thus males, blacks, lower-income youths, and older boys are most frequently dealt with formally by court referral. These demographic characteristics enter into dispositions in part because males, older boys, blacks, and lower-income youngsters appear to be disproportionately involved in serious, repetitive delinquencies. However, some studies have indicated that the police behave differentially toward blacks, sending more of them to juvenile court than they do whites involved in comparable offenses.
3. Police perspectives which hold that some groups, such as ghetto blacks or other lower-class minorities, are particularly criminalistic probably lead to

differential attention directed at them. Serious offenses by members of these groups then have a higher likelihood of being observed by the police and being acted upon. If so, the higher official crime and delinquency rates of these groups may be partially the product of police sentiments, rather than a reflection solely of basic differentials in involvement in crime.

4. In those instances of less serious delinquency, police officers often base their disposition decisions upon the demeanor of the offender. Youths who affect particular clothing styles or who are defiant and hostile tend to be referred more often than polite and contrite youngsters. It is probably also true that demeanor bears some relationship to seriousness of offense; those youths who have engaged in the most innocuous offenses also are most deferential toward policemen. This may explain why police dispositions show a general association with seriousness of misconduct.

5. Police departments show variations in organizational structure over time. Differences in organizational makeup between police agencies also exist. Accordingly, police dispositions of offenders, including juveniles, are far from uniform throughout the country.

6. Youths who have been involved in offenses which arouse members of the community, who commit law violations which result in sizable financial suffering to the victims, and who are repeaters, most often receive official and relatively punitive dispositions from the court, including being placed on the transmission belt to the training school. Ethnic characteristics, sex, age, and other demographic variables seem to be related to dispositions through their interconnection with offense variations, although there is also some indication that court decisions sometimes reflect discrimination against blacks and youths from lower socioeconomic backgrounds.

7. Other factors play a part in probation dispositions. In some agencies probation officers are attuned to the personality characteristics of wards and their decisions are based in part on this consideration. It also appears that ethnic factors are more directly involved in dispositions in some cases; therefore, on occasion minority group members are dealt with more severely than comparable white youths.

8. Contrary to fairly widely held beliefs that women of all ages receive preferential treatment in the juvenile and adult justice systems, the evidence points to discriminatory decision making against juvenile females, at least in a number of juvenile courts.

REFERENCES

ARNOLD, WILLIAM R. (1971). "Race and Ethnicity Relative to Other Factors in Juvenile Court Dispositions." *American Journal of Sociology* 77 (September): 211–27.

AXELRAD, SIDNEY (1952). "Negro and White Male Institutionalized Delinquents." *American Journal of Sociology* 57 (May): 569–74.

BLACK, DONALD J. (1970). "The Production of Crime Rates." *American Sociological Review* 35 (August): 733–48.

BLACK, DONALD J. and REISS, ALBERT J., JR. (1970). "Police Control of Juveniles." *American Sociological Review* 35 (February): 63–77.

BORDUA, DAVID J. (1967). "Recent Trends: Deviant Behavior and Social Control." *Annals of the American Academy of Political and Social Science* 359 (January): 149–63.

CHESNEY-LIND, MEDA (1974). "Juvenile Delinquency: The Sexualization of Female Crime." *Psychology Today* 8 (July): 43–46.

CICOUREL, AARON V. (1968). *The Social Organization of Juvenile Justice.* New York: Wiley.

COHEN, LAWRENCE E. and KLUGEL, JAMES (1978). "Determinants of Juvenile Court Dispositions: Ascriptive and Achieved Factors in Two Metropolitan Courts." *American Sociological Review* 43 (April): 162–76.

DANNEFER, DALE and SCHUTT, RUSSELL K. (1982). "Race and Juvenile Justice Processing in Court and Police Agencies." *American Journal of Sociology* 87 (March): 113–32.

DIANA, LEWIS (1955). "Is Casework in Probation Necessary?" *Focus* 34 (January): 1–8.

EATON, JOSEPH W. and POLK, KENNETH W. (1961). *Measuring Delinquency.* Pittsburgh: University of Pittsburgh Press.

EMPEY, LA MAR T. (1982). *American Delinquency.* Revised edition. Homewood, Ill.: Dorsey.

FERDINAND, THEODORE N. and LUCHTERHAND, ELMER G. (1970). "Inner-City Youths, The Police, the Juvenile Court, and Justice." *Social Problems* 17 (Spring): 510–27.

GIBBONS, DON C. and GRISWOLD, MANZER J. (1957). "Sex Differences Among Juvenile Court Referrals." *Sociology and Social Research* 42 (November–December): 106–10.

GIBBONS, DON C. and JONES, JOSEPH F. (1975). *The Study of Deviance.* Englewood Cliffs, N.J.: Prentice-Hall.

GOLDMAN, NATHAN (1963). *The Differential Selection of Juvenile Offenders for Court Appearance.* New York: National Council on Crime and Delinquency.

HASENFELD, YEHESKEL (1976). "Youth in the Juvenile Court: Input and Output Patterns," pp. 60–71. In Rosemary Sarri and Hasenfeld, eds. *Brought to Justice?* Ann Arbor: National Assessment of Juvenile Corrections, University of Michigan.

HENGERER, GERTRUDE M. (1954). "Organizing Probation Services," pp. 45–59 in *National Probation Association Yearbook,* New York: National Probation and Parole Association.

HOHENSTEIN, WILLIAM F. (1969). "Factors Influencing the Police Disposition of Juvenile Offenders," pp. 138–49. In Thorsten Sellin and Marvin E. Wolfgang, eds. *Delinquency: Selected Studies.* New York: Wiley.

KLEIN, MALCOLM W., ROSENSWEIG, SUSAN LABIN, and BATES, RONALD (1975). "The Ambiguous Juvenile Arrest." *Criminology* 13 (May): 78–89.

KRISBERG, BARRY and AUSTIN, JAMES (1978). *The Children of Ishmael.* Palo Alto: Mayfield.

KROHN, MARVIN D., CURRY, JAMES P., and NELSON-KILGER, SHIRLEY (1983). "Is Chivalry Dead? An Analysis of Police Dispositions of Males and Females." *Criminology* 21 (August): 417–37.

LEMERT, EDWIN M. and ROSBERG, JUDY (1948). "The Administration of Justice to Minority Groups in Los Angeles County." *University of California Publications in Culture and Society* 2: 1–28.

LUNDMAN, RICHARD J., SYKES, R. E., and CLARK, JOHN P. (1978). "Police Control of Juveniles: A Replication." *Journal of Research in Crime and Delinquency* 15 (January): 74–91.

McEACHERN, A. W. and BAUZER, RIVA (1967). "Factors Related to Disposition in Juvenile Police Contacts," pp. 148–60. In Malcolm W. Klein, ed. *Juvenile Gangs in Context.* Englewood Cliffs, N.J.: Prentice-Hall.

PILIAVIN, IRVING and BRIAR, SCOTT (1964). "Police Encounters with Juveniles." *American Journal of Sociology* 70 (September): 206–14.

ROGERS, KRISTINE OLSON (1972). "For Her Own Protection. . . Conditions of Incarceration for Female Juvenile Offenders in the State of Connecticut." *Law and Society Review* 7 (Winter): 223–46.

SCARPITTI, FRANK R. and STEPHENSON, RICHARD M. (1971). "Juvenile Court Dispositions: Factors in the Decision-Making Process." *Crime and Delinquency* 17 (April): 142–51.

SCHLOSSMAN, STEVEN and WALLACH, STEPHANIE (1978). "The Crime of Precocious Sexuality: Female Juvenile Delinquency in the Progressive Era." *Harvard Educational Review* 48 (February): 65–94.

SELLIN, THORSTEN and WOLFGANG, MARVIN (1964). *The Measurement of Delinquency.* New York: Wiley.

SHANNON, LYLE W. (1963). "Types and Patterns of Delinquency Referral in a Middle-sized City." *British Journal of Criminology* 3 (July): 24–36.

STAPLES, WILLIAM G. (1984). "Toward a Structural Perspective on Gender Bias in the Juvenile Court." *Sociological Perspectives* 27 (July): 349–67.

TEILMANN, KATHERINE S. and LANDRY, PIERRE H., JR. (1981). "Gender Bias in Juvenile Justice." *Journal of Research in Crime and Delinquency* 18 (January): 47-80.

TERRY, ROBERT M. (1967). "Discrimination in the Handling of Juvenile Offenders by Social Control Agencies." *Journal of Research in Crime and Delinquency* 4 (July): 218-30.

THOMAS, CHARLES W. and SIEVERDES, CHRISTOPHER M. (1975). "Juvenile Court Intake: An Analysis of Discretionary Decision Making." *Criminology* 12 (February): 413-32.

THORNBERRY, TERENCE P. (1973). "Race, Socioeconomic Status and Sentencing in the Juvenile Justice System." *Journal of Criminal Law and Criminology* 64 (March): 90-98.

WEINER, NORMAN L. and WILLIE, CHARLES V. (1971). "Decisions by Juvenile Officers." *American Journal of Sociology* 88 (September): 199-210.

WERTHMAN, CARL and PILIAVIN, IRVING (1967). "Gang Members and the Police," pp. 56-98. In David J. Bordua, ed. *The Police.* New York: Wiley.

WILSON, JAMES Q. (1968). "The Police and the Delinquent in Two Cities," pp. 9-30. In Stanton Wheeler, ed. *Controlling Delinquents.* New York: Wiley.

chapter 6 _____

DELINQUENCY CAUSATION: BASIC CONSIDERATIONS

INTRODUCTION

Chapter 6 takes up basic issues in causal explanation: succeeding chapters will pursue etiological matters in further detail. We need to begin the study of causation by examining the nature of explanation in behavioral science. What do we mean when we declare that we have discovered some of the causes of delinquency? What kinds of theories and hypotheses have been investigated so far in the search for elusive causes? How are valid theories and generalizations developed? These fundamental questions must be addressed preliminary to an examination of current research findings on delinquency.

CAUSATION AND EXPLANATION

Causal thinking is surely not foreign to the lay person. Few citizens are totally bewildered by the course of events and believe that "things just happen" by pure chance. Instead, most occurrences in the physical and social worlds are presumed to be caused by something—those events which preceded it and which somehow produced it. Consider the illustration of lung cancer. Many would agree on the cause (or one of the causes) of lung cancer—smoking. Cigarettes cause cancer because their ingredients lead to physical changes in lung tissue or, stated another way, cigarettes cause cancer because if people smoke them for an extended period of time, they will very likely end up with cancerous lungs.

Causal thinking in science bears some similarity to etiological reasoning on the part of lay persons. In both cases, relationships are identified; one phenomenon, event, or form of behavior is linked to another event which presumably led to it. In addition, a time sequence is usually implied such that the cause of something rests in a factor which preceded it at some point in time. In short, both the lay person and the scientist deal with causal statements taking an "if X occurs, then Y will probably follow" form. In the case of delinquency, an illustrative etiological claim would be: "If children are reared in family circumstances characterized by parental rejection, most of them will develop into aggressive and antisocial persons."

This example shows a third element that is common to the causal perspectives of citizens and scientists alike: probabilistic thinking. The example asserts that some event or factor usually or frequently leads to some other occurrence, but it does not contend that X always produces Y. Citizens and scientists both make some allowance for intervening variables, unanticipated events, or other factors which intrude into explanations and predictions. To put the matter another way, explanatory accounts are usually stated in terms of greater or lesser certainty because, at any point in time, our knowledge of all the factors and the interaction among them that enter into some phenomenon is less than complete. A major goal of scientific inquiry is to make explanations increasingly more precise and certain through a continuing process of theorizing and research activity, by which we move closer to complete causal accounts by successive increments.

Although scientific and lay notions of causation show some points of similarity, they are not by any means identical. The scientist must sort out spurious relationships from real ones. In the case of delinquency, a spurious relationship would be one in which some factor appears to be importantly involved in youthful misconduct when in actuality it is only incidentally related to the factors which lead to delinquency. An example of spuriousness may make this distinction clearer. Suppose that we were to discover that juvenile offenders more frequently read comic books and spend more hours per day watching television than do nonoffenders. One would be ill-advised to conclude that these are important causal influences. Rather, variations in the reading and television habits of youngsters are probably a reflection of more pervasive variations in parent-child relationships and influences. It is the latter that probably make up some of the real causes of delinquency. It is not likely that offenders would discontinue their lawbreaking simply by being deprived of their comic books or television programs, nor would nonoffenders suddenly engage in a burst of misconduct after increased exposure to these stimuli. But if the family interaction patterns that differentiate lawbreakers from nondelinquents were altered, we would predict that changes in the behavior of these youngsters would take place as well.

In the causal beliefs of lay persons, claims are usually made that some single factor or experience nearly always leads to delinquency. For example, inadequate parents are thought to invariably produce delinquent offspring. Also, citizens sometimes contend that poverty is not a cause of crime or delinquency because not all poor youngsters or adults steal, or that some other influence is not a cause because it does not always lead to the same result, crime or delinquency. By contrast, scientific explanations acknowledge that particular causal factors are not always linked to a single outcome, due to the operation of other, intervening factors. Consider the case of smoking and lung cancer and related ailments. Although smoking has been shown to be associated with lung cancer, not all persons who smoke experience cancer or emphysema. Further, some individuals develop lung cancer or respiratory ailments even though they have never engaged in smoking. The latter case indicates that respiratory problems and cancer may sometimes arise from more than one set of influences, including smog, industrial fumes, and kindred causes. The explanation for the less-than-perfect association between smoking and these physical ailments is that the effects of cigarette smoking are conditioned or mediated by other experiences which differentiate between individuals, such as variations in place of residence, physical vulnerability, and so on, as well as by the number of years that one has smoked, the number of cigarettes consumed each day, and so on.

Causal relationships in the case of social behavior can be likened to the example of lung cancer and smoking. For example, numerous criminological theorists and researchers have identified various patterns of parent-child tension and family disorganization as major influences in delinquency. At the same time, it is clear that some youthful offenders come from stable, warm family settings, while other youngsters who have encountered severely stressful family experiences nonetheless have been uninvolved in delinquency. But none of this is to be taken as evidence that family experiences can be dismissed as causally unimportant. Rather, these observations point to the complex nature of etiology, in which factors other than family patterns are also implicated, thus mediating or influencing the causal role of parent-child relationships. For example, the potentially harmful impact of parent-child tensions may sometimes be offset by warm relationships between certain youngsters and adult figures such as teachers and family friends. Also, some juveniles from stable family settings may be drawn into misconduct by their peers or by adult nonfamily members.

Tappan (1949: 64-65) expressed the orientation to causation which is followed in this book: "Cause is the exertion by multiple factors occurring in varied but specific configurations, of a determining influence upon the deviant behavior that ensues."

Explicit note should be taken of the terms *multiple factors* and *specific configurations* in Tappan's definition. Causation is the operation of some large but finite set of factors which bears an invariant relationship to delinquency. However, a more common kind of multiple-factor thinking which has had some supporters in the past holds that causal analysis must be eclectic, providing room for a vast multitude of factors of various kinds, all bearing some relationship to delinquency (Teeters and Reinemann, 1950). Exponents of this orientation have often congratulated themselves on their avoidance of dogmatism and rigidity and on their willingness to include myriad factors within some kind of explanatory porridge. Advocates of this version of multiple-factor thinking have suggested that the causes of delinquency vary from individual to individual, that it is therefore necessary to compile lengthy inventories of these causes in each instance of lawbreaking conduct. According to this line of reasoning, the best that can be accomplished in the way of explanation of juvenile delinquency is the accumulation of a very large set of variables or categoric risks all bearing some statistical association to delinquency. Proponents of this viewpoint contend that it is not possible to isolate any factor or group of factors which show an invariant relationship to delinquency.

This kind of causal nihilism should be rejected. If there are to be scientific explanations of delinquency, causal propositions will have to be developed which assert that some large but specific set of factors interact in particular ways to produce lawbreaking. Conventional forms of multiple-factor thinking contend as an operating principle that such statements are outside the realm of the discoverable. We agree with Cohen (1951) who has advanced an incisive critique of multiple-factor perspectives. He pointed out that the supporters of this framework usually confuse explanation by means of a single theory with explanation by means of a single factor. Few modern criminologists hold that delinquency is the product of one variable, although many would contend that some large but finite number of factors do combine to produce delinquency.

The task for the scientist is to discover the specific configurations of the multiple factors that influence delinquent behavior. In so doing it is often necessary to distinguish between variables that have a *direct* influence on delinquent behavior and those that have an *indirect* influence. An example from research conducted by Richard Johnson (1979) illustrates this distinction. It has often been observed that adolescents who do poorly in school are more likely to commit delinquent behavior than are those who do well in school. However, Johnson discovered that school performance did not have a direct effect on delinquent behavior, rather, it was directly related to the frequency with which adolescents associated with other adolescents who had committed delinquent acts. In turn, the greater the frequency of associating with delinquent others, the more likely adolescents were to commit delinquent behavior. Thus poor school performance was indirectly related to delinquent behavior in that it led adolescents to associate with misbehaving others which increased the probability of delinquent behavior among those adolescents.

Implicit in the above example is some notion of a time order. Adolescents who do poorly in school gravitate toward others who are engaging in delinquent behavior. Having come into contact with delinquent others, those adolescents then begin to engage in delinquent behavior. While the implicit time order may make intuitive sense, it is often very difficult to firmly establish the actual time order of events in the lives of adolescents. Most research on juvenile delinquency makes observations at only one point in time. It is therefore difficult to determine whether poor school performance led to delinquent associations or whether having delinquent associations was detrimental to an adolescent's performance in school. Even when a series of observations is made over time, it is not easy to identify which event actually preceded another event.

An additional consideration is that it is possible that two variables are reciprocally related. That is, poor school performance may sometimes produce a greater probability of association with delinquents at the same time that having delinquent associations increases the probability of poor school performance. The time order and causal direction is difficult to assess in such relationships. For example, Thornberry and Christenson (1984) found that while being unemployed increases the likelihood of committing a crime, committing a crime also increases the likelihood of being unemployed. Hence, it may not be accurate, and in many cases not possible to describe one variable as invariably causally prior to another.

Note that this discussion of scientific perspectives on causation makes no mention of the rigidly deterministic views that frequently turn up in lay persons' notions. Most social scientists, including criminologists, favor accounts of human behavior centered around what David Matza (1964) has termed *soft determinism.* This term draws attention to the possibility that while human actors are to a considerable degree constrained or influenced by social and environmental forces which surround them, they are at the same time *reactive* individuals who are able to exercise some degree of freedom or choice over their behavior. According to Matza (1964: 9) "... human actions are not deprived of freedom because they are causally determined."

The implications of soft determinism as a basic assumption behind causal theories are vast. If human behavior involves reactivity such that individuals are able to exert some independent influence over social-structural pressures, some degree of indeterminancy will probably always characterize causal accounts or explanations offered by social scientists. Some allowance will have to be made in those arguments for the operation of choice and freedom in human actions, with the result that perfect predictability of human behavior will never be achieved in scientific theories.

The search for causes concerns relationships that are relatively free from consideration of time, place, or other such limitations. Consider a report which declares: "During 1980, 71 percent of the delinquents in the juvenile court in Iowa City, Iowa were from broken homes, while only 32 percent of the nondelinquent high school youths in that city were from broken homes." This is a descriptive statement, not a causal one, for it makes no claims about delinquents at some other time or in other cities. A more satisfactory etiological contention would assert the existence of a strong and continued relationship between home factors and juvenile misconduct throughout the United States or across a number of nations of the world. Note that the preceding comments referred to causal associations that are relatively, rather than absolutely, unbounded by matters of space and time. In a young and immature field of inquiry, etiological propositions may have to be circumscribed and limited to refer to juvenile misconduct in the United States, in large cities, in rural areas, during the past twenty years, and so on.

Because of the complexities of real-world relationships which have been touched upon here, many social scientists prefer to speak of *relationships* or *associations*, rather than of causes. These terms capture the complexity of etiological factors and processes in human behavior better than does *causation*, in that it is difficult to disassociate the latter from oversimplified lay persons' connotations.[1]

EXPLANATIONS, THEORIES, AND RESEARCH

How should we go about discovering the factors which are implicated in delinquency and the combinations and permutations of them that operate in different forms of juvenile lawbreaking? Shall we engage in simple fact gathering? If we gather enough discrete observations, will the facts speak for themselves? If we make enough observations, will broad explanatory generalizations leap out at us from these findings? The answer to these questions is negative. In the first place, facts are unlimited in number; we can never exhaust the list of observations which could be made about delinquency. Some kind of theory is required which suggests what facts it is important to gather. In addition, facts never speak for themselves, so that their causal significance is never self-evident. The job of the delinquency analyst is to make sense of discrete empirical observations by linking them to other facets of the behavior under study. In short, the explanation of delinquency demands the development of theories, of guidelines which point our observational activities in particular directions.

A prominent example of the sterility of eclectic fact gathering is found in the massive investigation of offenders and nonoffenders by Sheldon and Eleanor Glueck (1950). These researchers utilized a large research staff and a great amount of money in an explicitly eclectic fact-gathering exploration of delinquent conduct, in which information on several hundred characteristics of lawbreakers and nondelinquents was collected. The Gluecks believed that the causes of delinquency would emerge from this mass of observations. Among these many variables were the educational attainment of the grandparents of the subjects, school subject

---

[1]The logic of scientific views of causation which stress multicausality, intervening variables, and associations or relationships is dealt with in Hirschi and Selvin (1966, 1967). Another reason for avoiding terms such as *causes* and *causation* is that this allows the theorist to escape becoming entangled in questions of ultimate or final causes. In the case of smoking and lung cancer, cigarette manufacturers and certain other persons frequently contend that smoking is not the real cause of lung ailments, in that no one has yet isolated the precise mechanism or chemical processes by which tobacco tar and other ingredients produce cancer and emphysema. In other words, some have argued that it is legitimate to speak of causes only when ultimate or final causes have been isolated. A parallel argument in the area of criminality would be that poverty or inadequate home conditions are not the real causes of criminality, rather, they are merely some relatively indirect indicators or correlates of the ultimate causes of lawbreaking. If we were to follow this line, it would be quite easy to become bogged down in a pattern of infinite regress, searching for the real causes of behavior. Scientific investigators usually define their task as one of uncovering associations, that is, strong correlates of the behavior to be explained, rather than searching for elusive final causes.

preferences and dislikes, frequency of movie attendance, dynamometric strength (handgrip), presence of genital pathology, and number of dental caries. As might be anticipated, the delinquents and nonoffenders did not differ on most of these variables; the Gluecks therefore found these factors to be unimportant in etiology. Had they begun with a coherent, persuasive theory, they might have expended their research funds more judiciously by not spending them on fact-gathering information on teeth, genitals, and hand-grip! Moreover, when the Gluecks concluded this enormous piece of research, they were compelled to introduce a theoretical perspective in order to make sense of the findings. They concluded that "under-the-roof" factors, centered around the family life of the subjects, were mainly responsible for their behavior. At the same time, other students of delinquency have interpreted the results differently, and contend that the facts point most dramatically to the role of peer group associations and subcultural influences in juvenile lawbreaking. Regardless of whether one finds the conclusions of the Gluecks or of their critics more persuasive, the major point being emphasized here remains the same, namely that the facts which they gathered only spoke after a theoretical interpretation was imposed upon them. The facts were mute up to that point!

George Homans (1967: 7) distinguished between the two main jobs of any science, discovery and explanation. Discovery is "the job of stating and testing more or less general relationships between properties in nature". When we predict and find an association between poor academic performance and delinquent behavior we have discovered a relationship. Only when we are able to demonstrate that the finding follows as a logical conclusion from more general propositions have we explained the phenomenon. There may be many alternative explanations for the relationship between academic performance and delinquency. By deriving the hypothesis from a set of more general propositions, we are able to identify additional hypotheses which we can examine in order to compare the viability of alternative explanations. Homans contended that we judge whether a discipline is a science by whether it attempts to discover relationships, while we evaluate how successful the science is by how well it explains those relationships. As we shall see, we have discovered many relationships regarding delinquent behavior but have not adequately explained many of them.

THEORETICAL PERSPECTIVES

In the period since about 1920, sociological criminology, which includes the analysis of juvenile delinquency, has flourished in the United States. The result is that we now have available a collection of diverse theories, along with a large supply of research findings that have come from specific studies carried on by sociologists.

How are we to come to grips with the voluminous theoretical and research literature on social factors in delinquency? How are we to cut through the discordant arguments and varied research findings so as to weigh and assess the importance of these theories and studies? Clearly, some kind of sorting scheme is needed which will identify common threads that bind some of these works together and which will distinguish groupings of theoretical-research perspectives from each other.

One method of distinguishing theoretical perspectives is to focus on two distinct but closely related problems or questions that must be confronted in our efforts to develop explanatory accounts of delinquency. The first deals with the development of explanations for the kinds and amounts of delinquency observed in a society or among different societies, while the second revolves around the discovery of the processes involved in the acquisition of delinquent behavior patterns by specific youths. Two questions are asked about delinquency: (1) What elements of social organization or social structure are responsible for the rates and patterns that are observed; and (2) what more specific processes existing within these social-structural settings result in delinquency on the part of some youngsters and non-delinquency on the part of others?

The first of these explanatory problems can also be termed the *rates question.* Suppose that a statistical study of lawbreaking patterns within a number of cities shows that certain forms of gang delinquency are heavily concentrated in inner-city neighborhoods, while auto theft and vandalism are frequent in other, more affluent city areas. The focus of attention in this case would be on such questions as: "Is there something about community social structure, such as social class patterns existing in different areas, which results in these observed patterns of misconduct?"

The second causal question takes the form: "Why do they do it?" The focus of interest in this case is upon the processes by which specific youths acquire delinquent attitudes and behavior patterns. To continue our illustrative case, suppose that we have noticed in our investigation that there are several patterns of behavior among juveniles in the high delinquency slum areas. Some boys have high occupational aspirations, are highly motivated in school, and are conformist in behavior. Others are not heavily caught up in patterns of misconduct, but are not given to mobility striving or achievement. They are unmotivated, conformist juveniles whose actions center about hedonistic fun seeking. A third group contains youths whose major social role is that of tough guy and delinquent. Presumably all of these youths are exposed to the broad, criminogenic influences of social structure within their neighborhoods; thus there must be additional variables accounting for their varied forms of conduct. If so, what socialization experiences lead these specific youngsters into different behavioral activities? Some candidate hypotheses would be that the lawbreakers are psychologically troubled, that they are from criminalistic family backgrounds, or that they are involved in peer associations with delinquency-prone youngsters. Whatever the hypothesis that might be offered, it would deal with a different explanatory issue than the question of rate variations.

While it is important to be cognizant of whether a theoretical perspective is primarily attending to the "rates question" or the "why do they do it?" issue, we must also recognize that many delinquency theorists have formulated arguments that are addressed to both issues. Moreover, the classification schemas that have sorted theories on the basis of what question they are trying to answer go on to distinguish the theories in terms of the *content* of the answers provided (Akers, 1985; Empey, 1982; Sykes, 1972; Orcutt, 1983). We therefore prefer to organize our discussion of theoretical perspectives around the similarities in the assumptions and concepts of different theories of delinquency. We need to interject a word of caution, however, since few theories are "pure" forms of any single perspective. Our basis for classification rests on the relative emphasis involved in the theories.

In distinguishing the major varieties of sociogenic theory on delinquency, we identify four major perspectives concerning lawbreaking and its causes: social control, strain, economic conflict, and cultural deviance. A brief summary of these perspectives will serve as an introduction to a more detailed discussion of specific theories and research findings presented in Chapters 7, 8, and 9.

The Social Control/Disorganization Perspective

The social control perspective begins with the assumption that we all would commit delinquent or deviant acts if we were not constrained from doing so. It is only when we are freed from constraints that we are in a position to misbehave. The theoretical and research challenge is to identify what it is that discourages some juveniles from committing delinquent behavior and why those factors do not operate effectively for certain individuals and/or groups.

The work done by sociologists at the University of Chicago in the early 1900s represents a social control theory that focused primarily on the social structural factors that result in the weakening of social constraints for groups of people residing in certain areas of the city (Park, Burgess, and McKenzie, 1967). The concept of *social disorganization* was used to describe the weak institutional structures within certain areas of the city populated by highly transitory, heterogeneous, and economically disadvantaged persons. Social disorganization precluded the formation of effective social controls, and hence these areas consistently had the highest rates of delinquency.

While the social disorganization approach focused primarily on the "rates question," more recent inquiries within the social control tradition provide answers to the "why do they do it?" question. These examine how well integrated juveniles are with conventional others and institutions. For example, Walter C. Reckless's (1973) containment theory suggests that a prosocial self-concept (the product of social integration) insulates juveniles from committing delinquent acts even if they are exposed to criminality in their social environment. While Reckless emphasized what he called inner containment, Travis Hirschi (1969) focused more upon outer containments. Juveniles are seen to form a *social bond* with society through their attachments, commitments, involvements, and beliefs in conventional people and institutions. Only when the social bond is weakened are juveniles free to commit delinquent acts.

It should be evident that the logic of the social control perspective can be used to account for both delinquency in the aggregate and for individual offenders. Delinquency rates will be higher in those areas where the social institutional structure is weak, thereby making it difficult to generate either inner or outer containments to prevent juveniles from committing delinquent behavior. Juveniles whose ties to conventional social institutions or people are weak or become attenuated are in a position where they may commit delinquent behavior.

Strain Theory

The strain perspective also was influenced by the work of the Chicago School. The observation that delinquency rates were higher in areas that housed a disproportionate number of lower-class residents has been interpreted by strain theorists as a response of juveniles to their lack of opportunities. Strain is conceived of as a *shared* problem of adjustment that derives from the social position occupied by a group of people. For example, one influential strain viewpoint, Robert K. Merton's (1938) theory of anomie, contends that various kinds of deviance, including criminality, stem from the unavailability of conventional or socially approved routes to material success. A corollary argument is that deviance is most common among lower-class persons because they experience the greatest disjunction between culturally approved goals and opportunities to achieve these goals.

Strain theories directed at juvenile delinquency have appeared in several varieties which can be differentiated by the source and the victim of strain. While Albert Cohen (1955) attributed gang or subcultural delinquency among working-class boys to their failure to attain social status within the middle-class institution of the school, Cloward and Ohlin (1960) focused on the perceptions among lower-class boys that they are deprived of or shut out from opportunities for material success. A version of strain theory has also been used to account for delinquency among middle-class boys: The strain for them has to do with gnawing doubts about their masculine identity and their status as tough, masculine figures. This strain is engendered by the peculiar structure of many middle-class families in which the father is frequently absent and relatively unavailable to his son so that he fails to provide an adequate role model for him.

The Radical/Economic Conflict Perspective

Radical-conflict theories are typically more concerned with the operation of the criminal or juvenile justice system than they are with providing an explanation for the behavior that is defined as criminal or delinquent. Radical theorists argue that criminal laws, including delinquency statutes, have been developed in order to serve the interests of a monolithic ruling class, made up principally of members who come from the top leadership of the major national and multinational corporations. Criminal laws are a statutory device employed by the ruling class in order to continue the domination, oppression, and repression of the masses which is fundamental to the survival of the political-economic system of corporate capitalism.

Various forms of criminal sanction, including processing by the juvenile court, constitute devices that the ruling class sometimes falls back on in order to maintain its political and economic domination.

According to radical theorists, the lower classes have higher crime rates in part because the legal system is structured to ensure this outcome. The economics of corporate capitalism are also seen as operating to generate unemployment and low wages, creating a strain toward criminal and delinquent behavior (Gordon, 1971; Greenberg, 1977; Spitzer, 1975). Greenberg (1977) has argued that this is particularly apparent for the juvenile population, resulting in high delinquency rates.

Since we have dealt with the operation of the juvenile justice system in Chapters 2 and 5, our subsequent treatment of radical-conflict theories will address how they account for juveniles behaving in ways that are defined as delinquent. Because the arguments of radical-conflict theorists center around social structural conditions which strain individuals and result in an adaptive illegal behavior and are in this way similar to strain theories, the radical-conflict perspective will also be discussed in Chapter 8.

The Cultural Transmission/Socialization Perspective

Cultural transmission theories view deviance, including crime and delinquency, as responses to behavioral norms, beliefs, and values that encourage deviance and lawbreaking and which are shared by members of certain segments of society, that is, deviant subcultures. The diversity of norms, beliefs, and values exists because of the coming together of different ethnic groups with different cultural backgrounds (Sellin, 1938); the emergence of values or focal concerns generated by the difficulties in dealing with the deprivations of lower-class life (Miller, 1958); or the ecological patterning in cities (Shaw and McKay, 1942; Sutherland and Cressey, 1978). These norms are transmitted from generation to generation, with younger persons being socialized to the norms, values, and beliefs supporting illegal activities as well as techniques of performing these behaviors.

One influential cultural transmission theory was formulated by Edwin Sutherland (Sutherland and Cressey, 1978: 100–10). Sutherland suggested that American communities are characterized by differential social organization; that is, within some areas of the city, definitions (e.g., norms, values, and beliefs) favorable to the violation of the law exist side-by-side with definitions unfavorable to the violation of the law. These are the areas in which high crime rates are to be expected. Individuals are more likely to commit criminal or delinquent acts if they are exposed to an excess of definitions favorable to the violation of the law. Thus, by positing the existence of subcultures fostering norms, values, and beliefs that encourage crime and delinquency, and by hypothesizing that these norms are learned through associating with people who embrace these favorable definitions, Sutherland used a cultural deviance approach to address both of the causal questions with which this section began.

SUMMARY

In this chapter, we have identified four perspectives into which sociogenic theories can be grouped. These perspectives differ in regard to their assumptions about what factors are more important in producing delinquency rates and/or individual delinquent behavior. These assumptions often reflect very basic differences in the way the proponents of the perspectives view the social order and the nature of human interaction.

Theoretical perspectives generate hypotheses which are then tested through research in order to determine how well the theoretical notions stand up as accurate accounts of the social world. Given the complexity of human behavior, it is a considerable challenge to develop theories that capture the richness of human phenomena and which explain those social facts.

In the next three chapters we will learn how sociologists have addressed this challenge and evaluate the relative success of their efforts. Chapter 7 will examine social control theories that share the assumption that we would all commit delinquent or deviant acts if we were not constrained from doing so, while strain and conflict perspectives will be discussed in Chapter 8. There are important differences between these two traditions but they do share a focus on the social structural conditions that generate illegal behavior. In Chapter 9, we deal with cultural transmission and socialization theories. The existence of deviant values and the process by which those values are learned are the shared emphases of the theories reviewed in Chapter 9.

Our examination of explanations of delinquent behavior will conclude with biogenic and psychogenic perspectives in Chapter 10. While sociologists typically view such viewpoints as incapable of accounting for the amount and ubiquitousness of delinquent behavior, these arguments may be useful in accounting for particular types of delinquent behavior. After examining the variety of biogenic and psychogenic approaches, we explore their possible applications in the explanation of "behavior problem" delinquency.

REFERENCES

AKERS, RONALD L. (1985). *Deviant Behavior: A Social Learning Approach.* 3rd edition. Belmont, Cal: Wadsworth.

CLOWARD, RICHARD A., and OHLIN, LLOYD E. (1960). *Delinquency and Opportunity.* New York: Free Press.

COHEN, ALBERT K. (1951). "Juvenile Delinquency and the Social Structure." Unpublished Ph.D. dissertation, Harvard University.

COHEN, ALBERT K. (1955). *Delinquent Boys.* New York: Free Press.

EMPEY, LA MAR T. (1982). *American Delinquency.* Revised edition. Homewood, Ill.: Dorsey.

GLUECK, SHELDON, and GLUECK, ELEANOR (1950). *Unraveling Juvenile Delinquency.* Cambridge: Harvard University Press.

GORDON, DAVID M. (1971). "Class and the Economics of Crime." *Review of Radical Political Economics* 3 (Summer): 51-75.

GREENBERG, DAVID F. (1977). "Delinquency and the Age Structure of Society." *Contemporary Crises* 1 (April):189-224.
HIRSCHI, TRAVIS (1969). *Causes of Delinquency.* Berkeley: University of California Press.
HIRSCHI, TRAVIS and SELVIN, HANAN C. (1966). "False Criteria of Causality in Delinquency Research." *Social Problems* 13 (Winter): 254-68.
HIRSCHI, TRAVIS and SELVIN, HANAN C. (1967). *Delinquency Research: An Appraisal of Analytic Methods.* New York: Free Press.
HOMANS, GEORGE C. (1967). *The Nature of Social Science.* New York: Harcourt Brace Jovanovich.
JOHNSON, RICHARD E. (1979). *Juvenile Delinquency and Its Origins.* Cambridge: Cambridge University Press.
MATZA, DAVID (1964). *Delinquency and Drift.* New York: Wiley.
MERTON, ROBERT K. (1938). "Social Structure and Anomie." *American Sociological Review* 3 (October): 672-82.
MILLER, WALTER B. (1958). "Lower-class Culture as a Generating Milieu of Gang Delinquency." *Journal of Social Issues* 14(3): 5-19.
ORCUTT, JAMES D. (1983). *Analyzing Deviance.* Homewood, Ill.: Dorsey.
PARK, ROBERT E., BURGESS, ERNEST W., and McKENZIE, RODERICK D. (1967). *The City.* 2nd edition. Chicago: University of Chicago Press.
RECKLESS, WALTER C. (1973). *The Crime Problem.* 5th edition. Santa Monica: Goodyear.
SELLIN, THORSTEN (1938). *Culture Conflict and Crime.* New York: Social Science Research Council.
SHAW, CLIFFORD R. and McKAY, HENRY D. (1942). *Juvenile Delinquency and Urban Areas.* Chicago: University of Chicago Press.
SPITZER, STEVEN (1975). "Toward a Marxian Theory of Deviances." *Social Problems* 22 (June): 638-51.
SUTHERLAND, EDWIN H. and CRESSEY, DONALD R. (1978). *Criminology.* 10th edition. Philadelphia: Lippincott.
SYKES, GRESHAM M. (1972). "The Future of Criminality." *American Behavioral Scientist* 15 (February): 409-19.
TAPPAN, PAUL W. (1949). *Juvenile Delinquency.* New York: McGraw-Hill.
TEETERS, NEGLEY K. and REINEMANN, JOHN OTTO (1950). *The Challenge of Delinquency.* Englewood Cliffs, N.J.: Prentice-Hall.
THORNBERRY, TERENCE P. and CHRISTENSON, R. L. (1984). "Unemployment and Criminal Involvement: An Investigation of Reciprocal Causal Structures." *American Sociological Review* 49 (June): 398-411.

chapter 7

SOCIAL DISORGANIZATION, SOCIAL CONTROL, AND DELINQUENCY

INTRODUCTION

Citizens are often fascinated by the activities of those who behave in ways that fall outside the boundaries of conventional behavior. Tales of the exploits of notorious criminals such as Jesse James and Bonnie and Clyde have been repeated many times, often glorifying the excitement of such behavior. Do we glorify even this heinous behavior because we are attracted to it? And if we are attracted to it, why do most of us refrain from such behavior?

The social control perspective assumes that we are, indeed, attracted to deviant behavior, either because it is exciting or rewarding, or because it is often the most direct or efficient way to achieve other ends. Theories sharing the social control orientation therefore do not concentrate on identifying the factors which cause delinquent behavior. Rather, they focus on identifying why most juveniles most of the time are constrained from deviating from societal norms. Theories flowing from this orientation can be distinguished from one another in terms of what they emphasize as constraining factors.

DURKHEIM'S CONCEPT OF SOCIAL INTEGRATION

The social control perspective has its intellectual roots in the work of the nineteenth-century sociologist Emile Durkheim. Responding to the social upheaval brought about by the French Revolution and by industrialization, he sought to identify the social forces that enabled social order to be established and maintained. Durkheim (1933, 1951) observed that societies usually regulate what he assumed to be people's insatiable desires, through cultural norms that place limits on goal seeking and define the proper means to achieve them. He also argued that changes in the social structure (e.g., industrialization, dramatic improvements or declines in the economy) or alterations in the social situation of individuals (e.g., becoming divorced) could render those norms ambiguous and/or ineffective. He called this cultural condition *anomie*. In an anomic society, individual variation in behavior in the pursuit of desires would increase, which might in turn result in a higher rate of crime (Webb, 1972).

The concept of regulation plays a definite role in social control theory as will be particularly evident in our discussion of social disorganization notions. In addition, Durkheim's analysis has been influential in generating the strain tradition. Recall that the common theme in strain perspectives is that the lack of opportunities provided by the social structure results in a shared problem (strain) to which delinquency is one form of adjustment. Durkheim's suggestion that social structural factors can result in an anomic culture leading to unfulfilled desires among the populace is the antecedent of the strain position. Kornhauser (1978), in recognizing the common intellectual heritage, and more importantly, the similarity in the underlying logic of the strain and social control positions, has characterized both as social disorganization perspectives.

Social control perspectives are more closely associated with Durkheim's concept of social integration. Durkheim did not formally define integration but it is clear that he had in mind the degree to which individuals and groups are attracted to and attached to society and its institutions. Social integration allows people to find meaning in social institutions or societal structure which, in turn, makes them more likely to conform to social norms. The degree of social integration was seen to be variable; less social integration would (for the individual) lead to egoism or a recognition of "no other rules of conduct than what is founded in his [*sic*] private interests" (Durkheim, 1951: 209).

Although Durkheim was not concerned with explaining juvenile delinquency nor even criminal behavior, his ideas have often been employed by American sociologists interested in crime and delinquency. In particular, the themes of deregulation and social disintegration were incorporated into the work of sociologists at the University of Chicago in the 1900s in the development of the social disorganization approach.

SOCIAL STRUCTURAL APPROACHES

The Chicago School and Social Disorganization

Chicago at the end of the nineteenth century was experiencing tremendous growth in its population and industry. Much of the population increase was the result of waves of immigrants coming to Chicago to seek the opportunities that only a rapidly developing city could provide. It was perhaps fortuitious that amid this dynamic social change, the first department of sociology was formed in 1892 at the University of Chicago.

The city provided the Chicago School (as the sociology department at the University of Chicago came to be known) with a field laboratory in which to study the processes and consequences of social change (Park, Burgess, and McKenzie, 1967). In their efforts to account for patterns of growth in the city, Robert Park and Ernest Burgess identified the ecological distributions of several social phenomena, including crime and delinquency. They found that rates of crime and delinquency were highest in inner city areas and declined with distance from the center of the city. In particular, the "zone of transition," a circular belt that surrounded the central business district, had the highest crime rates. Immigrants to the city were attracted to this zone since housing in it was inexpensive and close to opportunities for employment. Clifford Shaw and Henry McKay (1931, 1942) further observed that as successive waves of immigrants became financially established, they sought better housing outside this zone; hence the population of the zone of transition was ever-changing. But despite the turnover in residents, often consisting of the replacement of immigrants from one ethnic group with those from another, crime and delinquency rates remained high (Shaw and McKay, 1942).

Clearly, the persistence of high crime and delinquency rates was not due to the cultural characteristics which members of any ethnic group brought with them to Chicago; rather, it seemed to lie in the social dynamics of the zone of transition. The concept of *social disorganization* was used to describe the social nature of this part of the urban community. Social disorganization referred to a situation where residents were not integrated into the social institutions of their communities such as the church, school, and neighborhood groups, thereby rendering these institutions ineffective in controlling the behavior of the residents. Social disorganization was at first attributed to the rapid turnover of the population in these zones, the heterogeneity of local residents, and their lack of economic resources. When later research continued to find high levels of delinquency within certain areas of the city in spite of a more stable growth rate, Shaw and McKay shifted away from an emphasis on social disorganization to a focus on the lack of opportunities on the part of people living within these areas. In addition, they also argued that due to these conditions persisting over a period of time, values conducive to delinquent behavior had become part of the subcultural tradition that was being transmitted from one generation to another (Kornhauser, 1978). Thus Shaw and McKay's social disorganization approach overlaps with both strain and cultural transmission perspectives.

A pioneering study by Frederic Thrasher (1927) of 1,313 Chicago gangs has been characterized as a "pure" control theory (Kornhauser, 1978) and illustrates how delinquency has been explained from a social disorganization approach. Thrasher argued that in all neighborhoods children form play groups. What differentiates the play groups in socially disorganized areas from those in other areas is that social institutions in the former are not capable of controlling the type of behavior of these groups. Thrasher saw no need to explain why the behavior of play groups was often illegal, because in the absence of social controls, youths do not have to be motivated to engage in delinquent behavior since unconventional behavior offers a more exciting alternative than conventional activities. Participation in delinquency by these play groups did not make them into structured gangs. Rather it was only when there was a perceived threat from an external source, e.g., legal agents or competing youth groups, that structured gangs would emerge.

Thrasher's analysis clearly evidences the defining characteristics of a social control/social disorganization perspective. First, he assumed that delinquent behavior is an attractive alternative to conventional behavior. Second, he argued that some areas of the city have weak social institutions. Accordingly, when social institutions are weak, play groups are free to behave in a manner that is more exciting to them, in short, to be delinquent.

The Ecological Tradition

The ecological tradition begun by the Chicago School spawned a number of subsequent studies. In almost all of the ecological investigations, delinquency or crime rates have been found to be particularly high in inner city, deteriorated neighborhoods and very low in upper-income or suburban areas (Bates, 1962; Bordua, 1958; Chilton, 1964; Lander, 1954; Polk, 1957; Quinney, 1964). Consider the correlation coefficients in Table 7-1 in which the relationships between certain social and economic variables and delinquency in Baltimore, Detroit, and Indianapolis are shown.[1] These correlation coefficients are based on delinquency rates for census tracts in certain specific years in these cities. Table 7-1 reveals that six of the seven ecological variables were fairly strongly related to delinquency; the only exception was the proportion of foreign-born persons in census tracts. Taken together, the findings in Table 7-1 suggest that certain areas which have a monopoly

TABLE 7-1 Correlation Coefficients, Ecological Variables, and Delinquency, by City

VARIABLE	BALTIMORE	DETROIT	INDIANAPOLIS
Education	−.51	−.47	−.64
Rent	−.54	−.35	−.57
Owner-occupied dwellings	−.80	−.61	−.64
Foreign-born	−.16	−.44	−.11
Nonwhite	.70	.52	.41
Overcrowding	.73	.65	.85
Substandard housing	.69	.62	.81

[1] These zero order correlation coefficients were reported in Chilton (1964) for Indianapolis, in Bordua (1958) for Detroit, and in Lander for Baltimore (1954). These correlations and others in the chapter should be read as meaning that the closer they are to a value of 1.00, the greater the association of that factor with delinquency. Correlations which are negative involve associations in which values of the factor decrease as delinquency rates increase. Thus on the education item, delinquency rates for census tracts are highest in areas where mean educational level is lowest.

on conditions of social wretchedness are also the most ridden with delinquency and adult criminality.

These results can be interpreted from either a strain or social control perspective. A strain interpretation would suggest that the lack of opportunities for success through conventional means leads to delinquent and criminal adaptations. Thus, a concentration of people sharing lower-class status produces higher rates of delinquency and crime. A social control or disorganization interpretation would see the economic condition of the lower class as important only to the extent that it produces weakened social institutions. It is difficult, even with the most sophisticated analysis, to know which of these interpretations is more valid. Judith Wilks (1967: 149) has provided an excellent summary of this material:

> Interestingly enough, whether concentric zones, individual census tracts, or census tracts grouped into social areas are investigated, the most frequent finding is that offenses and offenders tend to be concentrated in areas characterized by low income, physical deterioration, mixed land usage, nontraditional family patterns (e.g. home broken in some manner and/or high percentages of single males, and/or women employed in the labor force), and racial-ethnic concentration which appear to produce low neighborhood cohesion and low integration of the neighborhood into the larger society. This statement is, of course, a gross oversimplification of the interrelationship of area attributes and crime and delinquency rates. As noted previously in order to predict and explain an area's crime rate, it is necessary to be aware of the existing social structure, ongoing social processes, and the population composition of the area, and the area's position within the larger urban and societal complex. It is only by taking such a perspective that we can:
>
> 1. gain an understandng of why the economic, family, and racial composition of an area is associated with offense and offender rates, and
> 2. understand why the nature of the association between these area characteristics and offense and offender rates varies over time and over different cities.

One indication of the nature of variations in neighborhood structure which probably influence delinquency patterns is found in a study by Eleanor Maccoby, Joseph Johnson, and Russell Church (1958). These investigators believed that in disorganized neighborhoods delinquency rates will be high due to the lack of community integration. In these areas adults will feel little responsiblity for the activities of the children of others, will ignore much of their deviant behavior, and will unwittingly encourage them to continue in misbehavior. The researchers selected two low-income neighborhoods in Cambridge, Massachusetts, one with a high delinquency rate and the other with a low rate. They hypothesized that the high delinquency area would show less social integration, that the values of citizens would be permissive toward delinquency, and that these persons would be reluctant to intervene in the behavior of others. The low delinquency area was hypothesized as showing greater willingness of adults to take action against lawbreakers, greater integration, and less permissive attitudes toward criminality. The results from interviews with citizens in the two areas confirmed the argument about neighborhood cohesiveness. In the high delinquency area, fewer people liked the neighborhood, fewer knew many neighbors by name, and fewer declared themselves to have interests compatible with those of their neighbors. However, the investigators did not find citizens in the high criminality area to have more tolerant or indifferent views of deviance than those in the low delinquency area. Finally, somewhat more of the respondents in the low delinquency area were willing to intervene in instances of lawbreaking not directly involving them, but in both neighborhoods the prevailing sentiment was one of reluctance to interfere in "other people's business."

While we cannot derive broad conclusions from the findings of one study, the Maccoby et al. research indicates that the social disorganization viewpoint may offer a more accurate explanation of why certain areas have high delinquency rates than do strain theories. As we shall see in Chapter 8, there are additional reasons to question strain perspectives.

SOCIAL PSYCHOLOGICAL APPROACHES

The notion of social disorganization was used by the Chicago sociologists primarily to account for patterns or rates of delinquency. While it was posited that social disorganization removes constraints on individuals, allowing them to engage in delinquency, the social psychological or "why do they do it?" question did not receive the same attention as the "rates question." However, a succeeding generation of theorists has identified and modified the social psychological arguments implicit in the writings of the Chicago School, in the form of theories that are generally known as social control theories.

Containment or Self-concept Theories

One version of social control theory is Walter C. Reckless's (1973) "containment" argument which he offered as an overarching explanation of criminality and delinquency. This notion consists largely of old wine in a new bottle, that is, a new set of terms to replace more conventional ones, strung together in causal propositions of relatively low sophistication and weak explanatory power.[2] The central thesis is that individuals are restrained from lawbreaking partly by outer containment such as social ties to others, consistency of valuations of the person made by others, and so on. Inner containment in the form of a prosocial self-concept is of major significance in keeping persons from wandering into lawbreaking. Reckless indicated that inner containment involves a grab bag of ingredients: "Inner containment consists mainly of self-components, such as self-control, good self-concept, ego strength, well-developed superego, high frustration tolerance, high resistance to diversions, high sense of responsibility, goal orientation, ability to find substitute satisfactions, tension-reducing rationalization, etc." (1973: 65).

---

[2] These notions are not much different from those of Carr (1950).

Containment theory grew in part out of a series of studies by Reckless and associates, in which samples of boys in Columbus, Ohio, nominated by teachers as "good" boys, unlikely to get into trouble with the law, and "bad" boys, thought to be headed for trouble, were followed over a four-year period in order to see which ones became involved in juvenile delinquency (Reckless et al., 1956, 1957a, 1957b; Dinitz et al., 1958, 1962; Simpson et al., 1960; Scarpitti et al., 1960; Reckless and Dinitz, 1967). The results indicated that the youngsters selected by teachers as "good" boys were also well-regarded by their mothers and showed positive self-concepts, while the "bad" boys were on poorer terms with their parents and had less positive self-images. Also, a much higher proportion of "bad" boys acquired official records with the police or juvenile court than did the "good" boys. Reckless and Dinitz (1967: 317) concluded that "a good self-concept, undoubtedly a product of favorable socialization, veers slum boys away from delinquency, while a poor self-concept, a product of unfavorable socialization, gives the slum boy no resistance to deviancy, delinquent companions, or delinquent subculture."

The hypothesis that the inner life of the individual, that is, personality dimensions, may relate to his or her overt behavior is a credible one that needs more scrutiny. On this point, the work of Reckless and associates was less conclusive than first appearances suggest. The critics of this research have noted a number of problems with it. Michael Schwartz and Sandra Tangri (1965) have presented evidence showing only moderate correlations between self-conceptions held by boys and their perceptions of the opinions of them held by others. They also noted a number of methodological problems with the research of Reckless and associates, including the use of court records as the measure of delinquent involvement (Tangri and Schwartz, 1967). They also pointed out that many of the questionnaire and test items used as self-concept measures appear to be invalid indicators. For example, questions that ask whether boys think of the police as corrupt are more properly regarded as dealing with factual matters than with self-evaluations. James Orcutt (1970) has offered some of these criticisms of this research, along with additional ones that compromise the results reported by Reckless and associates. For example, he commented that the sampling procedures were faulty; hence many of the boys may actually have been from areas where delinquency was uncommon and hence had little to be insulated against.

Mixed support for these self-concept and containment arguments has turned up in more recent research inquiries. In one tangential investigation by Schwartz and Stryker (1970) improved indicators of self-concept patterns were developed and employed in a study of deviant activities on the part of adolescents. T. F. Marshall (1973) carried out an inquiry among English youths which found a relationship between scores on a delinquency proneness scale designed to tap self-concept variations and involvement in delinquent activities. However, he also uncovered a number of cases in which youngsters with unfavorable delinquency proneness scores were uninvolved in lawbreaking and other instances in which law violators showed positive self-images.

McCarthy and Hoge (1984) have explored the impact of self-esteem, as measured at one point in time, on delinquency measured one and then two years later.

They found no substantial relationships between two different measures of self-esteem and subsequent delinquent behavior, concluding that scholars should look to concepts other than self-esteem to explain delinquent behavior.

In still another study utilizing data collected in a California city, Gary Jensen (1973) explored the containment argument, and in particular, Reckless's thesis that inner containment is a powerful factor which can insulate persons from external criminogenic pressures. According to Reckless, youths who exhibit positive self-concepts should be able to resist the pressures and temptations that arise even when they live in adverse social circumstances. Jensen utilized measures of self-esteem, sense of self-control, and acceptance of conventional moral beliefs as indicators of inner controls. He found that variations in inner control were only weakly related to delinquency involvement, with large numbers of offenders with strong inner controls and nonoffenders with weak insulation also turning up. But he also discovered that racially related factors were involved in lawbreaking, in that lower-class black youngsters were likely to be engaged in delinquency, even when they showed positive inner containment. In much the same way, boys with positive self-concepts, but who had delinquent companions, were more involved in delinquent misconduct than those without delinquent friends, while youngsters from deficient family backgrounds were also more often engaged in delinquency than were those from more supportive parental backgrounds. On the basis of these findings, Jensen (1973: 478) was moved to conclude that "it may very well be that some elements of inner containment are less important for delinquent involvement the greater the adversities of family, class and neighborhood."

Social Bonding Theory

Although Reckless identified both inner and outer containments as sources of constraint, he focused primarily on inner containments. In one sense, inner containments can be seen as the product of the individual's interaction with sources of outer containments. Social bonding theory focuses on that interaction in examining the juveniles' attitudes toward and interaction with conventional people and institutions. Positive attitudes toward and attachments to these sources integrate youth into the conventional order, increasing the probability of conforming behavior, while those who lack these feelings are more prone to deviant acts.

Institutions such as the school and the family have always loomed large in sociological explanations of delinquency. One major, early study of family patterns in delinquency was that of Sheldon and Eleanor Glueck (1950). In their comparison of 500 offenders and 500 nonoffenders, they reported that all the affectional patterns of a home—mother-child, father-child, child-parent, and child-child—bore a significant relationship to delinquency. The most important factor seemed to be the father's affection for the boy; 40.2 percent of the delinquents and 80.7 percent of the nondelinquents had affectionate fathers.

Whereas the Glueck's study was a fact-gathering one unguided by explicit theory, F. Ivan Nye (1958) explicitly used a control theory to examine the relationship between patterns of family interaction and delinquency. He reported that juvenile lawbreaking results from the failure of family controls.

Although Nye presented an early version of social control theory, Travis Hirschi (1969) has explicated a more detailed and formalized argument than any previous control perspective. Hirschi's formulation revolves around the concept of the *social bond* which refers to the ties individuals have to the social order. He identified four elements that constitute the social bond: attachment, commitment, involvement, and belief. Attachment refers to the strength of ties to others, such as parents or peers. For example, some youngsters are on markedly better terms with their parents than are others, and accordingly, the former exhibit greater attachment than do the latter. Commitment concerns the devotion of the person to conformist lines of conduct. Those juveniles who plan to go to college or who have high aspirations of some other kind would be said to show greater commitment than those who differ from them in these ways. Individuals also vary in the degree to which they are involved in activities that restrict the time they have available for deviant acts (involvement) and they differ in the strength of their attitudes toward conformity (belief). Regarding belief, Hirschi (1969: 26) contended that "there is *variation* in the extent to which people believe they should obey the rules of society, and, furthermore . . . the less a person believes he should obey the rules, the more likely he is to violate them." (Emphasis in the original).

This argument about social control formed the framework for Hirschi's study in Richmond, California, in which he obtained self-report data on delinquent conduct and on social control variables through questionnaires administered to a large sample of youths in that community. We have already noted in Chapter 3 that the delinquency index employed consisted of relatively petty acts of misbehavior for the most part, and also that Hirschi found that boys from all social class levels reported about the same degree of involvement in these acts. In short, his investigation dealt with a cross-section of relatively petty offenders in the community and it is to that group that his theory applies most directly.

The findings of this inquiry regarding the postulated elements of social control were consistent with the basic theory because the delinquent youths showed less attachment to parents, school and school teachers, peers, and conventional activities. The offenders also exhibited less positive attitudes toward conformity.

Hischi's results have been at least partially confirmed in other investigations. Much research has focused on affective relationships between parents and their children and their relationship to delinquent behavior. The findings indicate that juveniles who are on poor terms with their parents are more likely to have committed delinquent behavior (Nye, 1958; Reiss, 1951; Hindelang, 1973; Jensen and Eve, 1976; Linden and Fillmore, 1977; Conger, 1976; Hepburn, 1976). The school has also been identified as an important arena to which adolescents can be attached and committed and in which they are involved. Indicators of attachment to, commitment toward, and involvement in school such as grade point average, school aspirations, and time spent on homework have been consistently found to be related to delinquency (Hindelang, 1973; Polk, 1969; Polk et al., 1974; Elliott and Voss,

1974; Krohn and Massey, 1980; Wiatrowski et al., 1981; Johnson, 1979). In fact, in multivariate analyses, both Krohn and Massey (1980) and Wiatrowski et al. (1981) found that school-related variables were more strongly related to delinquency than were other indicators of elements of the social bond. Finally, those juveniles who believe in the legitimacy of conventional rules have been found to be less likely to commit delinquent acts (Jensen, 1969; Hindelang, 1973; Buffalo and Rogers, 1971; Cernkovich, 1978a, 1978b; Johnson, 1979).

While overall support for Hirschi's theory has been found, deficiencies in it have also been identified. Probably the most questionable claim is Hirschi's argument that attachment to peers constrains delinquency whether or not those peers commit delinquent acts. For Hirschi, it is the integrative effect of being attached to peers that is important, which he argued would be true even if one was attached to peers who were delinquent. However, he asserted that it was unlikely that attachments would form between delinquents and other adolescents because the latter would have little respect for those who commit lawbreaking acts. Hirschi found some support for an inverse relationship between attachment to peers and delinquent behavior but subsequent studies have not replicated this finding (Hindelang, 1973; Krohn and Massey, 1980). Moreover, Hirschi's own research indicated that having delinquent friends increased the probability of delinquent behavior. Accordingly, he revised his original theory by suggesting that both the weakening of the social bond and having delinquent friends are directly related to delinquent behavior.

Support for this modified version of social bonding theory has been found (Hepburn, 1976; Johnson, 1979; Huba and Bentler, 1982). John Hepburn conducted a study among 14- to 17-year-old males in a medium-sized midwestern city, which indicated that youngsters who came from families in which parent-child tensions or other forms of family disharmony existed were likely to engage in delinquent activity and to exhibit delinquent definitions or norms. Moreover, consistent with Hirschi's argument, parent-child problems occurred prior to the time that youths acquired delinquent peers or engaged in lawbreaking.

The consistency in the results from research which examines social bonding theory or aspects of it would suggest that Gibbons's (1979: 121) conclusion that "there are several signs that suggest Hirschi's theory is to be one of the more enduring contributions to criminology" may be correct. However, while the results are consistent, they are not particularly strong. In multivariate analyses, both Wiatrowski et al. (1981) and Krohn and Massey (1980) found that the social bonding variables did not explain a great deal of the variance in the frequency of delinquent behavior, that is, a number of adolescents who commit delinquent acts apparently are not accounted for by an attenuation of the social bond. Krohn and Massey also found that the theory is better able to account for less serious forms of delinquent behavior. To compensate for the theory's limited explanatory power and, in some cases, to provide for a better explanation of more serious forms of delinquent behavior, efforts have been made to integrate social bonding with causal arguments that provide motivating factors for committing delinquency. We will explore some of these in Chapter 9.

Role Theory

Paul Friday and Jerry Hage (1976) have endeavored to improve upon social control theory, arguing that Hirschi's argument focuses on one element of the social bond at a time rather than the interaction between these elements. More specifically, Friday argued that "integration is fostered when individuals interacting within a role set (such as the school) know individuals from another role set (such as community)" (Friday, 1981: 121). These shared and overlapping role relationships increase the constraint on individuals, making delinquency less likely. However, in modern society overlapping role relationships have become less common than formerly. For example, in highly urban societies, one's friends and neighbors are not necessarily the same persons (Fischer, 1984). Hence, the social control that either can exert is limited.

Unfortunately, Friday and Hage's ideas have received scant attention. There is no research that specifically examines hypotheses from this perspective; however, findings such as Maccoby et al.'s (1958) imply that role theory may hold some promise.

Delinquency and Drift

David Matza's (1964) drift argument regarding delinquency is not entirely unlike Hirschi's social control thesis. Matza maintained that motivational or deterministic characterizations of the offender do not ring true—they explain too much rather than too little and fail to account for maturational reform, that is, for the fact that large numbers of juvenile lawbreakers refrain from further misconduct near the end of the adolescent period without any sort of treatment intervention directed at them. If delinquents were truly driven into deviant acts, if personality defects or deep commitment to antisocial norms have produced their behavior, how could maturational reform be explained?

Matza's position on these matters was one of "soft determinism," in which drift plays a major role. In this argument, offenders are hypothesized to be in tune with and under the control of conventional anticriminal norms most of the time, so that in this regard they are little different from nondelinquents. Matza (1964: 28) declared: "The delinquent transiently exists in limbo between convention and crime, responding in turn to the demands of each, flirting now with one, now with the other, but postponing commitment, evading decision. Thus, he drifts between criminal and conventional action."

In Matza's view, many delinquents episodically engage in misconduct, not because they are driven into it, but because their usual attachment to prosocial conduct norms is temporarily broken by various neutralization techniques. These youths entertain various rationalizations which allow them to exculpate themselves from blame for their misdeeds. But for most offenders this release from moral restraint is temporary; they eventually drift back into law-abiding ways. In all of this process, the deviants exercise some degree of choice in their behavior, so that they are to some extent free to willfully violate the law or abide by it.

The major difference between the drift argument and Hirschi's control thesis is that the latter suggests that detachment from social controls is a relatively permanent state; thus offenders do not drift in and out of conventional attachments. If that is the case, techniques of neutralization or rationalizations would not be required to assuage guilt, for the potential offender already has attenuated or weakened ties to conformity.

EVALUATION OF THE SOCIAL CONTROL PERSPECTIVE

One of the attractive features of social control theories is that they are free from the contradictions between existing research findings and theoretical propositions that are contained in other theoretical statements (e.g., strain and cultural deviance). Social control theories are not class-based; thus they are equally applicable to middle-class delinquency and to lower-class misbehavior. Indeed, Karacki and Toby (1962) have used a social control perspective specifically to account for middle-class delinquency. They argued that the need for immediate gratification among middle-class boys resulted in a temporary lack of commitment to adult roles and values, resulting in delinquent behavior.

Note that Karacki and Toby characterized the lack of commitment as temporary. This points to another issue that social control perspectives handle well. Most juveniles who commit delinquent acts do not continue to engage in criminality throughout their lives; rather, they "mature out" of deviating. A social control perspective would hypothesize that maturation results from the establishment of ties to the conventional order which eventually occurs in most people's lives. For example, marriage and employment represent *stakes in conformity* that typically make it increasingly difficult to deviate. On this point, Henley and Adams (1973) found that the best predictor of cessation of smoking marijuana was getting married.

While social control perspectives account for phenomena which are difficult to reconcile with strain or cultural deviance perspectives, we must also recognize that, by themselves, control arguments provide an incomplete explanation of delinquency. Involvement with peers who commit delinquent behavior also appears to be an important causal influence. However, in that social control variables do predict the type of associates juveniles have, this modification can be incorporated into control arguments.

More problematic is the inattention of control arguments to sources of strain that may lead to the weakening of initially strong bonds (or the strengthening of weak ties). Positive or negative experiences within school settings, disruptions in family patterns, or other experiences may result in attenuated or strengthened social bonds. The early social disorganization theorists directed attention to influences which led to the weakening of community controls and which, in turn, lessened the constraints on individuals, but more recent social control arguments often ignore these factors. We will explore some integrated perspectives in subsequent chapters.

SUMMARY

This chapter has reviewed theories that fall within the social control framework. Following from their shared assumption that we are all attracted to deviant behavior, social control theories attempt to account for why many adolescents do not commit delinquent behavior. Their focus, therefore, is on the social institutions and people that influence adolescents not to deviate.

This approach informed efforts of the social disorganization theorists of the Chicago School who tried to account for the distribution of crime and delinquency throughout an urban area. While the social disorganization theorists concentrated on alleged defects in the social structure, Walter Reckless addressed processes occurring within the individual. He argued that individuals are often insulated from delinquent influences because they develop positive self-concepts.

The most popular current version of the social control perspective is Hirschi's social bonding theory. This theory takes a middle position between the macro-concerns of social disorganization views and the micro-emphasis of the containment argument. It is the integration of individuals to various social institutions and people that makes juveniles less likely to commit delinquent behavior.

Theories must be judged, in part, in comparison to alternative formulations. No single theory currently at hand has been able to account for all of the instances of delinquent conduct which have been examined by researchers. Therefore, we evaluate theories in terms of how well they account for delinquent behavior relative to competing formulations. Since we have not yet reviewed other theories, it is difficult to provide a final assessment of the social control perspective. However, we can identify some general conclusions from this chapter.

1. Rates of delinquent behavior across neighborhoods and communities reflect, in part, the degree to which the social institutions in them are effective in fostering social integration of residents into the fabric of community life. In turn, a lack of social integration or social disorganization often reflects the economic and social disadvantages faced by residents in low-income areas but it may also be a result of other social-structural factors such as residential mobility, ethnic or religious composition of the neighborhood, or the density of the population living in the community.

2. The social institutions that serve as the primary socializing agents in society, particularly the family and the school, are important influences in fostering bonds between individuals and conventional society and, thus, in reducing the probability of delinquent behavior. The role of the school is particularly crucial since this is the arena in which adolescents spend a good deal of their time.

3. Although the social bond and its constituent elements are related to the prob-

ability of delinquent behavior, other factors must also be taken into account to adequately explain delinquent conduct. For one, those youths who show low levels of social bonding are also more likely to associate with others who have committed delinquent acts. In turn, association with delinquent others is strongly related to delinquent behavior, with the result that elements of the social bond are related both directly and indirectly to delinquent behavior.

REFERENCES

BATES, WILLIAM (1962). "Caste, Class and Vandalism." *Social Problems* 9 (Spring): 349-58.

BORDUA, DAVID J. (1958). "Juvenile Delinquency and 'Anomie': An Attempt at Replication." *Social Problems* 6 (Winter): 230-38.

BUFFALO, M. D., and ROGERS, J. W. (1971). "Behavioral Norms, Moral Norms and Attachment: Problems of Deviance and Conformity." *Social Problems* 19 (Summer): 101-33.

CARR, LOWELL J. (1950). *Delinquency Control.* New York: Harper & Row.

CERNKOVICH, STEPHEN A. (1978a). "Evaluating Two Models of Delinquency Causation: Structural Theory and Control Theory." *Criminology* 16 (November): 355-62.

CERNKOVICH, STEPHEN A. (1978b). "Value Orientations and Delinquency Involvement." *Criminology* 15 (February): 443-48.

CHILTON, ROLAND J. (1964). "Continuity in Delinquency Area Research: A Comparison of Studies for Baltimore, Detroit, and Indianapolis." *American Sociological Review* 24 (February): 71-83.

CONGER, RAND (1976). "Social Control and Social Learning Models of Delinquency: A Synthesis." *Criminology* 14 (May): 17-40.

DINITZ, SIMON, KAY, BARBARA, and RECKLESS, WALTER C. (1958). "Group Gradients in Delinquency Potential and Achievement Scores of 6th Graders." *American Journal of Orthopsychiatry* 28 (July): 598-605.

DINITZ, SIMON, KAY, BARBARA, and RECKLESS, WALTER C. (1962). "Delinquency Vulnerability: A Cross Group and Longitudinal Analysis." *American Sociological Review* 27 (August): 515-17.

DURKHEIM, EMILE (1933). *The Division of Labor.* Translated by George Simpson. New York: Free Press.

DURKHEIM, EMILE (1951). *Suicide.* Translated by George Simpson. New York: Free Press.

ELLIOTT, DELBERT S. and VOSS, HARWIN (1974). *Delinquency and Dropout.* Lexington, Mass: Lexington.

FISCHER, CLAUDE S. (1984). *The Urban Experience.* 2nd edition. New York: Harcourt Brace Jovanovich.

FRIDAY, PAUL C. (1981). "Theoretical Issues in the Study of Deviance and Social Control," pp. 187-223. In Helmut Kury, ed. *Perspectiven und Probleme Kriminologisches Forschung.* Vol. 1. Bonn: Carl Hemann Verlag.

FRIDAY, PAUL C. and HAGE, JERALD (1976). "Youth Crime and Postindustrial Societies: An Integrated Perspective." *Criminology* 14 (November: 347-68.

GIBBONS, DON C. (1979). *The Criminological Enterprise.* Englewood Cliffs, N. J.: Prentice-Hall.

GLUECK, SHELDON and GLUECK, ELEANOR (1950). *Unraveling Juvenile Delinquency.* Cambridge: Harvard University Press.

HENLEY, JAMES R. and ADAMS, LARRY D. (1973). "Marijuana Use in Postcollegiate Cohorts: Correlates of Use, Prevalence Patterns and Factors Associated with Cessation." *Social Problems* 20 (Spring): 514-20.

HEPBURN, JOHN (1976). "Testing Alternative Models of Delinquency Causation." *Journal of Criminal Law and Criminology* 67 (December): 450-60.

HINDELANG, MICHAEL J. (1973). "Causes of Delinquency: A Partial Replication and Extension." *Social Problems* 20 (Spring): 471-87.

HIRSCHI, TRAVIS (1969). *Causes of Delinquency.* Berkeley: University of California Press.

HUBA, GEORGE J. and BENTLER, PETER M. (1982). "A Developmental Theory of Drug Use: Derivation and Assessment of a Causal Modeling Approach," pp. 147-203. In P. B.

Bates and O. G. Brim, Jr. eds. *Life-span Development and Behavior.* New York: Academic Press.

JENSEN, GARY F. (1969). "Crime Doesn't Pay: Correlates of Shared Misunderstanding." *Social Problems* 17 (Fall): 189–201.

JENSEN, GARY F. (1973). "Inner Containment and Delinquency." *Journal of Criminal Law and Criminology* 64 (December): 464–70.

JENSEN, GARY F. and EVE, RAYMOND (1976). "Sex Differences in Delinquency: An Examination of Popular Sociological Explanations." *Criminology* 13 (February): 427–48.

JOHNSON, RICHARD E. (1979). *Juvenile Delinquency and Its Origins.* Cambridge: Cambridge University Press.

KARACKI, LARRY and TOBY, JACKSON (1962). "The Uncommitted Adolescent: Candidate for Gang Socialization." *Sociological Inquiry* 32 (Spring): 203–15.

KORNHAUSER, RUTH ROSNER (1978). *Social Sources of Delinquency.* Chicago: University of Chicago Press.

KROHN, MARVIN D. and MASSEY, JAMES L. (1980). "Social Control and Delinquent Behavior: An Examination of the Elements of the Social Bond." *Sociological Quarterly* 21 (Autumn): 529–43.

LANDER, BERNARD (1954). *Toward an Understanding of Juvenile Delinquency.* New York: Columbia University Press.

LINDEN, RICHARD and FILLMORE, CATHY (1977). "Comparative Study of Delinquency Involvement." Presented at the annual meeting of the Canadian Sociology and Anthropology Association.

MACCOBY, ELEANOR E., JOHNSON, JOSEPH P., and CHURCH, RUSSELL M. (1958). "Community Integration and the Social Control of Juvenile Delinquency." *Journal of Social Issues* 14(3): 38–51.

MARSHALL, T. F. (1973). "An Investigation of the Delinquency Self-concept Theory of Reckless and Dinitz." *British Journal of Criminology* 13 (July): 227–36.

MATZA, DAVID (1964). *Delinquency and Drift.* New York: Wiley.

McCARTHY, JOHN D. and HOGE, DEAN R. (1984). "The Dynamics of Self-esteem and Delinquency." *American Journal of Sociology* 90 (September); 396–410.

NYE, F. IVAN (1958). *Family Relationships and Delinquent Behavior.* New York: Wiley.

ORCUTT, JAMES D. (1970). "Self-concept and Insulation Against Delinquency: Some Critical Notes." *Sociological Quarterly* 2 (Summer): 381–90.

PARK, ROBERT E., BURGESS, ERNEST W., and McKENZIE, RODERICK D. (1967). *The City.* Chicago: University of Chicago Press.

POLK, KENNETH (1957). "Juvenile Delinquency and Social Areas." *Social Problems* 14 (Winter): 320–25.

POLK, KENNETH (1969). "Class Strain and Rebellion Among Adolescents." *Social Problems* 17 (Fall): 214–24.

POLK, KENNETH, FREASE, DEANE and RICHMOND, F. LYNN (1974). "Social Class, School Experience and Delinquency." *Criminology* 12 (May): 84–96.

QUINNEY, RICHARD (1964). "Crime, Delinquency, and Social Areas." *Journal of Research in Crime and Delinquency* 1 (July): 149–54.

RECKLESS, WALTER C. (1973). *The Crime Problem.* 5th edition. Santa Monica: Goodyear.

RECKLESS, WALTER C. and DINITZ, SIMON (1967). "Pioneering with Self-concept as a Vulnerability Factor in Delinquency." *Journal of Criminal Law, Criminology and Police Science* 63 (December): 515–23.

RECKLESS, WALTER C., DINITZ, SIMON, and KAY, BARBARA (1957). "The Self-component in Potential Delinquency and Potential Nondelinquency." *American Sociological Review* 22 (October): 566–70.

RECKLESS, WALTER C., DINITZ, SIMON, and MURRAY, ELLEN (1956). "Self-concept as an Insulator Against Delinquency." *American Sociological Review* 21 (December): 744–56.

RECKLESS, WALTER C., DINITZ, SIMON, and MURRAY, ELLEN (1957b). "The 'Good Boy' in a High Delinquency Area." *Journal of Criminal Law, Criminology and Police Science* 68 (May): 18–25.

REISS, ALBERT J., JR. (1951). "Delinquency as the Failure of Personal and Social Controls." *American Sociological Review* 16 (April): 196–207.

SCARPITTI, FRANK R., MURRAY, ELLEN, DINITZ, SIMON, and RECKLESS, WALTER C.

(1960). "The 'Good Boy' in a High Delinquency Area: Four Years Later." *American Sociological Review* 25 (August): 555-58.

SCHWARTZ, MICHAEL and STRYKER, SHELDON (1970). *Deviance, Selves and Others.* Washington, D.C.: American Sociological Association.

SCHWARTZ, MICHAEL and TANGRI, SANDRA S. (1965). "A Note on Self-concept as an Insulator Against Delinquency." *American Sociological Review* 30 (December): 922-26.

SHAW, CLIFFORD R. and McKAY, HENRY D. (1931). *Social Factors in Juvenile Delinquency.* Vol. 2 of Report of the Causes of Crime. National Commission of Law Observance and Enforcement. Washington, D.C.: Government Printing Office.

SHAW, CLIFFORD, R. and McKAY, HENRY D. (1942). *Juvenile Delinquency and Urban Areas.* Chicago: University of Chicago Press.

SIMPSON, JON, DINITZ, SIMON, KAY, BARBARA, and RECKLESS, WALTER C. (1960). "Delinquency Potential of Preadolescents in a High Delinquency Area." *British Journal of Delinquency* 10 (January): 211-15.

TANGRI, SANDRA S. and SCHWARTZ, MICHAEL (1967). "Delinquency Research and the Self-concept Variable." *Journal of Criminal Law, Criminology and Police Science* 58 (June): 182-90.

THRASHER, FREDERIC M. (1927). *The Gang.* Chicago: University of Chicago Press.

WEBB, STEPHEN D. (1972). "Crime and the Division of Labor: Testing a Durkheimian Model." *American Journal of Sociology* 78 (November): 643-56.

WIATROWSKI, MICHAEL D., GRISWOLD, DAVID B., and ROBERTS, MARY K. (1981). "Social Control and Delinquency." *American Sociological Review* 46 (October): 525-41.

WILKS, JUDITH A. (1967). "Ecological Correlates of Crime and Delinquency." In The President's Commission on Law Enforcement and Administration of Justice, *Task Force Report: Crime and Its Impact—An Assessment.* Washington, D.C.: U.S. Government Printing Office.

chapter 8

SOCIAL STATUS, OPPORTUNITY, AND DELINQUENCY

INTRODUCTION

We have all heard or read accounts of delinquents or criminals which attributed their illegal acts to their inability to acquire desired goals through more acceptable means. Those goals may have been material (e.g., money, an automobile) or non-material (e.g., respect from their peers). For example, it is often argued that lower-class individuals commit a disproportionate amount of delinquency because they are at a disadvantage in competing for well-paying jobs. Similarly, the behavior of the class clown is sometimes explained by the fact that he or she does not do well academically.

The strain perspective reflects the essence of these accounts of delinquent behavior. Sociologists who favor a strain explanation view the social structure as differentially distributing opportunities to achieve desired ends. Some groups of people have greater opportunities to achieve their goals than do others. Those who perceive themselves to be in a disadvantageous position are under pressure to adapt their behavior in a manner that compensates for their limited opportunities. These perceptions and pressures to adapt are shared by those who face similar limitations. One way in which they may adapt is to commit illegal and/or unconventional acts.

This chapter will review a number of those theories that make up the strain perspective. As we might expect, these have been primarily used to explain lower-class delinquency, although some attempts have been made to apply the perspective more broadly. We will conclude the chapter with an examination of radical or economic conflict theories of delinquency. While strain and radical conflict theories differ in a number of ways, they both see the causes of delinquent behavior as lying in the social structural distribution of opportunities.

THE ORIGINS OF STRAIN THEORIES OF DELINQUENCY

Recall that the last chapter mentioned the work of Emile Durkheim as the basis on which social control perspectives were built. We also suggested that his work played a critical role in the generation of the strain perspective. Specifically, his concept of anomie was modified by Robert K. Merton and used to form an explanation for deviant behavior.

For Durkheim, anomie referred to the inability of the cultural system to effectively define the norms necessary to control man's [sic] insatiable desires. This condition was generated by social structural factors such as social dislocation resulting from the transition to an industrialized economy, marked and precipitous fluctuations of the economy, or an economic system placing inordinate stress upon the profit motive and acquisitiveness which rendered norms inapplicable and/or ineffective. Without normative regulation, widespread deviant behavior becomes probable.

Robert K. Merton (1938) adapted the concept of anomie to the specific conditions he saw existing in American society. He argued that American cultural goals emphasize material success-striving, with less concern given to norms that identify proper ways to achieve those goals. Stated another way, ends are more important than the means of achieving them. The social structure plays an important role in generating the cultural conditions of anomie. Specifically, the unequal distribution of opportunities in American society strains the culture toward anomie in that large numbers of persons are deprived of opportunities to achieve the success goals to which all citizens are encouraged to aspire.

If Merton had concluded his analysis at this point it would have been little different from Durkheim's and would fall in the social control tradition. Deviance would ensue because of the disjunction between emphases upon goals and means. However, he had more to say about the role of the social structure in the generation of deviant behavior, arguing that when an anomic culture is coupled with an unequal distribution of opportunities, economically and socially disadvantaged persons will be pressured toward deviant behavior in order to adapt to the *strain* created by goals that are unattainable through conventional activities.

Merton identified four types of deviant adaptations, two of which are relevant to delinquency. Those who continue to pursue conventional goals but through unconventional or deviant means are said to be engaged in innovation. Regarding the monetary success goal, some juveniles may pursue it by stealing cars rather than by seeking an education which will enable them to get a good job, particularly if their educational opportunities are circumscribed. Retreatism involves the rejection of both conventional goals and conventional means. For example, some juveniles who are blocked from conventional means to achieve success goals may give up those goals and take refuge in relatively passive, hedonistic pursuits such as drug use or drinking.

Although it has the ring of plausibility, there have been several criticisms of Merton's argument (Gibbons and Jones, 1975: 91-97). For one, the assumption that all Americans share similar goals and expectations revolving around monetary success has been questioned (Hyman, 1953). Also, Albert Cohen (1965) has criticized Merton for what he called the "assumption of discontinuity," that is, the assumption that strain leads almost inevitably to deviant or delinquent behavior. Cohen argued that additional factors intervene between perceived strain and behavioral outcomes, resulting in some individuals engaging in deviance while others are restrained from deviant pathways.

COHEN AND STATUS FRUSTRATION

The strain perspective has had a good deal of appeal to sociologists, largely because it appears to make sense of the frequent observation that rates of official delinquency are highest in low-income areas of the city. In fact, Shaw and McKay (1942: 438) observed that "among children and young people residing in low-income areas, interests in acquiring material goods and enhancing personal status are developed which are often difficult to realize by legitimate means because of limited access to the necessary facilities and opportunities." However, they never fully articulated a strain model, preferring to mix the strain explanation of delinquency with a social control and a cultural transmission perspective (Kornhauser, 1978).

One of the first and most influential strain theories of delinquency was developed by Albert Cohen (1955). Cohen suggested that a goal of most youths is social status. The problem for working-class boys is that they are at a disadvantage in obtaining high social status within middle-class institutions such as the school. They experience status threats when they are evaluated by a middle-class measuring rod, by a set of social expectations regarding the characteristics of "good boys." These expectations center about such traits as ambition, individual responsibility, talent, asceticism, rationality, courtesy, and control of physical aggression. The exemplary youth in the eyes of important members of the middle-class, such as school teachers, embodies most or all of these social characteristics. But the working-class boy has been inadequately socialized in these notions of proper behavior, so he finds himself at a competitive disadvantage in classrooms and other social arenas as he competes with middle-class peers for recognition by adults. According to Cohen (1955: 121): "The delinquent subculture, we suggest, is a way of dealing with the problems of adjustment we have described. These problems are chiefly status problems: certain children are denied status in the respectable society because they cannot meet the criteria of the respectable status system. The delinquent subculture deals with these problems by providing criteria of status which these children can meet."

These boys who withdraw from such situations of social hurt as the school find their way into the subculture of the gang, which provides them with a social setting in which to become insulated against assaults upon their self-esteem. Thus the delinquent gang represents a social movement among juvenile offenders. This subculture arose as a solution to *shared* problems of low status among working-class youths. In Cohen's words (1955: 59): *"The crucial condition for the emergence of new cultural forms is the existence, in effective interaction with one another, of a number of actors with similar problems of adjustment"* (emphasis in the original).

The delinquent gang, according to Cohen, encourages behavior that is opposite to the expectations of middle-class groups. Lower-class boys who are frustrated in achieving status by middle-class standards turn those criteria upside down, reject them, and behave in deliberate defiance of them, which is a phenomenon Cohen referred to as *reaction formation*. The behavior of delinquent gangs is *non-utilitarian, malicious* and *negativistic*. Cohen argued that much of the stealing and other misbehavior of gangs is motivated by interests other than rational utilitarian gain, that gang delinquents steal "for the hell of it." The malicious and negativistic character of gang behavior is revealed in a number of ways, most commonly in observations that gang members reap enjoyment from the discomfort they cause others and take pride in reputations they have acquired for meanness. Cohen also described subcultural deviance in terms of *short-run hedonism*, indicated by a lack of long-term goals or planning on the part of gang members. Finally, *group autonomy* is a hallmark of subcultural deviance, and delinquent gangs are said to be solidaristic collectivities.

Cohen drew his original portrayal of gang delinquency with broad strokes and joined relatively small areas of factual data with big swatches of speculation. No wonder a number of critics detected what they felt to be errors in the initial formulation! Gresham Sykes and David Matza (1959) advanced an early criticism in the form of some remarks about "techniques of neutralization." They argued that delinquents are at least partially committed to the dominant social order, experience guilt or shame when they engage in deviant acts, and contrive rationalizations or justifications for their acts of lawbreaking in order to assuage guilt feelings. Sykes and Matza then enumerated some of these techniques of neutralization, which include denial of responsibility for one's behavior, denial of injury, and condemnation of the condemners. These notions represent a useful contribution in their own right, in that they direct attention to some of the ways in which offenders define the situation so as to exculpate themselves from guilt regarding violations of norms they regard as valid in principle. However, a close reading of Cohen's theory indicates that he was not inattentive to the delinquent boy's sensitivity to middle-class ethical standards; the Sykes and Matza argument is compatible with that of Cohen.

One of the most systematic evaluations of Cohen's theory was produced by John Kitsuse and David Dietrick (1959) who noted several major problems. They charged that Cohen failed to make a compelling case for the argument that working-class boys care about middle-class persons' views of them. Kitsuse and Dietrick maintained that lower-class boys are not oriented to status in middle-class systems. Accordingly, in their view Cohen's notion of the delinquent subculture as a reaction formation is seriously undermined. These same critics also contended that Cohen's description of delinquent subcultures is faulty, in that real-life delinquents are more businesslike in action and less directly malicious toward respectable persons than the theory suggests. Finally, they claimed that the theory is flawed because it is ambiguous on the issue of how subcultures are maintained once they come into existence. Kitsuse and Dietrick proposed an alternative formulation to that of Cohen, arguing that the original motives of delinquent actors for participation in gangs are varied. Once they get involved in the subculture, hostile responses by respectable citizens, correctional agents, and others are directed at them. In turn, the offenders reject their rejectors through further deviant conduct. Thus, according to these authors (Kitsuse and Dietrick, 1959: 215): "The delinquent subculture persists because, once established, it creates for those who particpate in it, the very problems which were the bases for its emergence."

Bordua (1960; 1961; 1962) also raised a series of questions about theories of subcultural delinquency, including Cohen's. He noted that in most of these theories the image put forth of the delinquent is markedly different from that advanced by Thrasher (1927). While Thrasher's boys were caught up in the attractiveness of delinquent "fun," the delinquents of more recent theorists are driven by stresses and anxieties emanating from a prejudicial and harsh social environment. In addition, Bordua contended that Cohen's theory placed undue emphasis on the non-utilitarian character of gang misconduct. He also suggested that Cohen, as well as a number of other subcultural theorists, failed to accord sufficient weight to family, ethnic, and certain other social variables in delinquency causation. In particular, he pointed out that class-linked family patterns may be the source of much of the stress experienced by delinquent boys; the relatively loosely structured parent-child relationships, absentee fathers, and other common characteristics of many working-class families may have much to do with the development of problems and, subsequently, delinquency in lower-class boys.

Cohen responded to some of these criticisms of his work. In a paper with James F. Short (1958) rejoinders to a number of critical points were presented, including the assertion that there is more than one form of working-class gang delinquency. Cohen and Short agreed with this view and suggested that lower-class subcultures include the parent-male subculture oriented around semiprofessional theft. The characteristics of the parent-male subculture are enumerated in *Delinquent Boys*. Cohen and Short (1958:24) employed the label of *parent subculture* in order to suggest that other gang forms are specialized offshoots from it; thus "it is probably the most common variety in this country—indeed, it might be called the 'garden variety' of delinquent subculture."

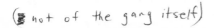 (not of the gang itself)

In endeavoring to account for the development of these different subcultural forms in individual neighborhoods, Cohen and Short laid much stress on an earlier paper by Solomon Kobrin (1951). Kobrin pointed out that areas vary in the extent to which conventional and criminal value systems are mutually integrated, so that in some communities criminality is meshed with the local social structure; adult criminals are prestigious citizens and are active in local businesses, fraternal organizations, politics, and so on. They serve as local heroes or role models for juvenile apprentice criminals. In other neighborhoods, criminality is individualistic, uncontrolled, and alien to the conventional social organization.

DELINQUENCY AND OPPORTUNITY STRUCTURES

The delinquency theory of Richard Cloward and Lloyd Ohlin (1960) represents a full scale alternative rather than a qualifying statement to Cohen's argument. Although Cloward and Ohlin also applied a strain perspective to explain gang delinquency, their boys are more concerned with monetary success than with middle-class status. They asserted (Cloward and Ohlin, 1960: 92): "It is our view that many discontented lower-class youth do not wish to adopt a middle-class way of life or to disrupt their present associations and negotiate passage into middle-class groups. The solution they seek entails the acquisition of higher position in terms of lower-class rather than middle-class criteria." Thus this argument is more similar to that of Merton's than it is to Cohen's.

Cloward and Ohlin argued that working-class gang delinquent subcultures are to be understood in the following terms: Lower-class boys share a common American value commitment to success, measured largely in material terms. But these youths are at a competitive disadvantage compared to their middle-class counterparts. Either they do not have access to legitimate or conventional means to reach these success goals, or, if they do have objective opportunities for achievement, they perceive their chances of success as circumscribed. Accordingly, for many working-class boys, a severe disjunction exists between aspiration levels and expectations, or between what they want out of life and what they anticipate they will receive. Pressures to engage in deviant behavior are generated by this goals-means discrepancy. If the boys blame others or the structure of society rather than their own inability for their limited access to legitimate means, they will be alienated and delinquent behavior will be a probable result.

Just as exposure to strain is influenced by their positions in the legitimate opportunity structure, the type of adaptation assumed by working-class youths is heavily influenced by their opportunities to engage in deviant behavior.

Borrowing from the insights of Kobrin, Cloward and Ohlin argued that some lower-class areas are characterized by integration of criminalistic and conformist patterns of social organization whereas others are lacking in stable criminalistic networks. In the organized, criminalistic neighborhood, criminalistic gang subcultures develop in which boys are involved in instrumental acts of theft and in careers which often lead them into adult criminal behavior. This community produces the budding gangster. In areas lacking in criminalistic traditions, gang delinquency tends to take the form of conflict subcultural behavior in which gang fighting ("bopping" and "rumbles") predominates. Finally, some boys who are failures in both the legitimate and illegitimate opportunity structures disengage themselves from the competitive struggle and withdraw into the retreatist subculture of the drug addict.

Initial reactions to the Cloward and Ohlin theory were extremely favorable; a number of action programs for the prevention and amelioration of juvenile crime were formulated on the basis of opportunity structure theory (Gibbons, 1965: 179–82). Still, a series of critical comments have been advanced on this theory (Bordua, 1961, 1962; Matza, 1961; Schrag, 1962). It has been noted that the definition of subcultures employed by Cloward and Ohlin limits applicability of their theory to a minority of all delinquents. Critics have contended that much gang delinquency in working-class areas is more spontaneous and unstructured than Cloward and Ohlin would have us believe. One authority has termed many of these deviant collectivities "near groups," in order to highlight their shifting membership, ambiguous role definitions, lack of group identifications, and other characteristics (Yablonsky, 1959). Regarding this objection, it would be possible to relax the definition of subcultures without abandoning the major ingredients of the theory.

Bordua and others who have assessed the opportunity structure formulation have also raised questions about its failure to deal systematically with variations in working-class family structures, racial factors, and other background variations among different working-class groups (Bordua, 1962). The major thrust of this body of commentary has been to suggest that real-life social structure in a society such as the United States is exceedingly complex because it is comprised of interwoven layers of social variables which are combined in varied ways and which produce behavioral outcomes such as delinquency. In short, existing theories of gang delinquency are not yet rich enough or elaborate enough to encompass the varieties of real-life experience.

RESEARCH ON DELINQUENT SUBCULTURES

There are two important questions we must ask in evaluating Cohen's and Cloward and Ohlin's theories of delinquent subcultures. The first relates to their respective descriptions of delinquent gangs. Do gangs engage in a diverse collection of nonutilitarian activities, as Cohen suggests, or do they exhibit specialization in particular types of criminality as Cloward and Ohlin argued? The second question asks whether the causal processes identified by the respective theories are restricted to gang formation and activity, or do they apply to delinquent behavior of various kinds? Both theories were originally put forth to account for gang formation and perpetuation; however, they have been used by other sociologists to explain other forms of delinquency as well.

Types of Delinquent Gangs and Gang Behavior

Support for the Cloward and Ohlin argument concerning specialization in certain deviant activities among delinquent gangs within specific neighborhoods has been reported by Irving Spergel (1961; 1963; 1964). His research in Chicago indicated that delinquency and crime tended toward a criminalistic form in a relatively stable black slum area, while in a more unstable neighborhood, juvenile criminality was untrammeled and violent in character (Spergel, 1963). In his New York City investigation, Spergel (1964) indicated that conflict behavior was most common in Slumtown, a disorganized area, while criminalistic delinquency was oriented around theft activities in one relatively integrated neighborhood and around racketeering in another community area. But this study was based upon very small samples of delinquents and nondelinquents. In addition, some of the research procedures utilized in it were not entirely clear; thus the results of the investigation must be treated cautiously.

While specialized criminalistic gangs may sometimes develop in association with adult organized criminal activity (Kobrin, 1951), most delinquent gangs display a much more versatile behavioral repertoire (Miller, 1975). The richest body of empirical evidence on gang delinquency and gang behavior is found in the Chicago studies of Short and others (Short and Strodtbeck, 1965). One investigation examined the delinquent and nondelinquent conduct of about 600 members of Chicago gangs. Street workers maintained detailed records of the day-to-day activities of these boys, and their findings showed that most of the offenders were involved in a wide range of deviant and nondeviant acts, rather than in the narrowly focused patterns suggested by Cloward and Ohlin. Short and his colleagues concurred with the earlier claim by Cohen and Short (1958) that an undifferentiated "parent delinquent subculture" exists from which more specialized deviant groups emerge. In other words, they suggested that the generic form of gang behavior involves behavioral versatility, and that, from this broad form, cliques and subgroups branch off into more specialized careers in deviant conduct (Short et al., 1965).

In a more recent study, Walter Miller (1975) found *behavioral versatility* to be the most appropriate term to describe delinquent gangs in Philadelphia and Boston. In Philadelphia most gangs engaged in theft, vandalism, drinking, drug use, and less violent forms of assault. The description of gangs in Boston was similar, with the most common offense being creating a disturbance.

The thrust of the research reviewed here is that the content of delinquent behavior among gang members is not much affected by differing levels of social integration found in a neighborhoods. Rather, Cohen and Short's (1958) description of a parent delinquent subculture typifies most gangs.

47 ?

Sounds like a compromise

see pg 151

While little support is found for Cloward and Ohlin's characterization of behavioral specialization by gangs, one should not conclude that Cohen was entirely correct in his description of their activities either. Although gangs do frequently engage in what appears from a middle-class perspective to be nonutilitarian behavior (Miller, 1975), they also engage in seemingly profitable activities. In an earlier study, Miller (1967) found that theft was the dominant form of criminal behavior in the gangs he observed. Acts of theft were two to three times more frequent than assaults. While not all theft can be attributed to utilitarian interests, certainly it cannot be said that gang behavior is exclusively nonutilitarian in nature.

Opportunity and Delinquent Behavior

What does the research evidence show about the different causal arguments put forth by Cohen and by Cloward and Ohlin? To begin with, it must be noted that although both Cohen and Cloward and Ohlin provided explanations for *gang* delinquency, most of the studies that have been guided by these perspectives have not specifically focused on the formation or maintenance of delinquent gangs. Rather, the research has typically examined whether strain can explain the frequency of delinquent behavior among a sample from the general population of juveniles.

The most extensive examination of strain as an explanation of gang delinquency was done by Short and others (Short, 1964; Rivera and Short, 1967; Short and Strodtbeck, 1965). Their findings showed that delinquents exhibited greater discrepancies between occupational aspirations and expectations than did nondelinquents. More delinquent boys viewed educational opportunities as closed to them than did nonoffenders. But these relationships were far from clear, for black youths who showed the greatest divergence between their aspirations and expectations, compared to the achievements of their fathers, were at the same time the least delinquent. Also, contrary to the hypotheses in the Cloward and Ohlin theory, those boys who had high educational aspirations but poor school adjustment or who perceived educational opportunities as relatively closed were less delinquent than those youths with low educational aspirations. Short and Strodtbeck (1965: 115) interpreted these results in the following way: "A possible explanation of findings reported in this paper lies in the hypothesis that for our boys, high aspirations are indicative of identification with conventional values and institutions. The stake in conformity thus indexed serves to protect the boys from delinquency involvement."

Short and his colleagues also examined the question of value commitments of delinquent boys. They found that contrary to theories which contend that subcultural delinquents are in rebellion against middle-class ideals, individual offenders verbalize allegiance to such middle-class values as cohesive family life, stable jobs, and conformist behavior (Short, 1964). However, the structure of gang life inhibits youngsters from expressing these sentiments openly, so that a state of "pluralistic ignorance" prevailed in which gang members saw each other in distorted terms.

Finally, and most important, Short (1964: 117-27) argued that although gang behavior is not a direct revolt against middle-class values or a protest against generalized invidious rankings of the boys by the wider society, status considerations are nevertheless of major importance in comprehending lower-class delinquency. He contended that delinquent activities are often a response to a host of real or imagined status threats experienced by boys and that most of these status threats emanate from the more immediate social world, including threats to the boys' status as males, gang members, and so on.

There have been several attempts to discover whether strain hypotheses apply to delinquent behavior in general rather than only to gang delinquency. Reiss and Rhodes (1963) studied a large number of boys in the Nashville metropolitan area. They measured strain in terms of status deprivation (Cohen), asking boys whether their peers had better clothes and lived in better houses. They found that a majority of delinquents do not experience status frustration. They also hypothesized that if Cohen was correct, juveniles living in areas of heterogeneous status should experience the greatest degree of status deprivation. However, they found that it was working-class youths living in areas populated largely by other lower-class persons who were most likely to engage in delinquency. These findings suggest that one requirement for the emergence of delinquent subcultures is the existence of similarly disadvantaged lower-class boys in effective interaction with one another.

In still another study, Erdman Palmore and Phillip Hammond (1964) investigated youngsters involved in the Aid to Dependent Children welfare program in Greater New Haven, Connecticut. The records of these youths, followed from age 6 to 19, showed that 34 percent had become known to the police or juvenile court. Palmore and Hammond argued that the Cloward and Ohlin theory implies that legitimate and illegitimate opportunities have a multiplicative effect upon youths. Deviance should be particularly frequent among persons who are cut off from legitimate opportunities and who live in circumstances in which illegal opportunities are numerous. The results agreed with this hypothesis; delinquency was most common among black youngsters who were school failures and who lived in situations of high family and neighborhood deviation. Delinquency rates were markedly lower among white youths who were school successes and who were from stable families and neighborhoods relatively free of criminalistic influences.

Much of the research on the strain perspective has attempted to measure the aspirations and expectations for success in attaining a good education or job. The logic of strain theory suggests that the larger the discrepancy between an adolescent's aspirations and expectations, the greater the likelihood of delinquent behavior. When aspirations and expectations have been measured in terms of long-term goals such as total education desired or type of career or occupation expected, the strain hypothesis has not been supported (Elliott and Voss, 1974; Johnson, 1979; Quicker, 1974; Gold, 1963). Delinquency is not the result of strain produced by the discrepancy between aspirations and expectations; rather, it is related to lack of commitment to conventional society reflected in the low aspirations and low expectations exhibited by delinquents (Hirschi, 1969; Kornhauser, 1978; Liska, 1971). Liska (1971) argues that the research evidence examining the strain perspective is, in fact, most consistent with a social control explanation.

What do we find if the measurement of discrepancy between aspirations and expectations is restricted to more immediate or short-run goals? For example, rather than asking juveniles about their future education, what if we ask them about their goals for the coming semester (e.g., grades, activities)? When strain is measured in this way, it does seem to have some relationship to delinquent behavior (Elliott et al., 1979; Elliott and Voss, 1974; Johnson, 1979; Quicker, 1974). However, school success is also an important variable in the social control perspective, thus making these results difficult to interpret. But whether disaffection with the school represents a strain or a lack of commitment (or both), there is no doubt that it plays a significant role in producing delinquent behavior.

School Performance and Delinquency

On the issue of blocked goal attainment, Schafer and Polk (1972) assembled a large body of data which showed that lower-class citizens place a high value upon educational success. At the same time, educational failure has repeatedly been shown to be disproportionately common among lower-income youths. The manner in which these experiences conjoin to produce delinquency was indicated by Schafer and Polk (1972: 230-31):

> These findings . . . clearly suggest that as a result of being negatively perceived and evaluated, students who fail tend to be progressively shunned and excluded by other achieving students, by individual teachers, and by the "system as a whole." Partly as a result of the internal frustrations generated by blocked goal attainment and partly as a result of the stigma which others tend to attach to educational failure, failing students' own assessments of themselves, their place in the world, and their future tend to progressively deteriorate and, understandably, the school experience becomes highly unsatisfying, frustrating, and bitter. . . The evidence suggests, then, that educational failure is one experience, especially when combined with a desire for success, that contributes to delinquency. While such failure has been shown to relate to delinquency regardless of family status there are at least two reasons why lower-income youth are especially susceptible to this influence toward illegitimate behavior. First, they fail more often, as noted earlier; and, second, students from higher-status backgrounds who fail are likely to be "held into" the legitimate system by greater pressures from parents and achieving peers and by less susceptibility to delinquent or criminal subcultures.

The role of the schools in the etiology of delinquency is complicated by the variety of unfavorable experiences that may play some part. Schafer and Polk enumerated a sizable list of these experiences; for example, working-class children begin school at a competitive disadvantage due to their social backgrounds. They

enter school less equipped in verbal skills and other learning characteristics. However, Schafer and Polk were most interested in the school conditions which exacerbate the educational problems of disadvantaged children. For one thing, school
teachers often assume that lower-class children have a limited potential for scholar-
ship, so that they give them short shrift in the classroom. Additionally, many
schools place disadvantaged youngsters in situations in which the academic instructions are irrelevant to the needs and interests of children, at the same time that
inappropriate teaching methods are used with them.

Schafer and Polk were also critical of those school programs of testing,
grouping, and "tracking," which usually assign disadvantaged children to low
ability groupings in which they receive little attention. Working-class youngsters
are commonly placed in vocational training programs of dubious merit. These same
disadvantaged youths receive little adequate academic and vocational counseling.
Schafer and Polk also pointed out that working-class youngsters infrequently receive adequate compensatory or remedial education and also are often taught by
inferior teachers in inadequate facilities in ghetto areas. However, more recent
research has failed to demonstrate that juveniles who were placed in low ability
tracks committed more delinquent behavior than those juveniles not placed in these
tracks (Wiatrowski et al., 1982).

One instructive report comes from an investigation in San Diego (Elliott,
1966; Elliott and Voss, 1974). Following Cohen's theory regarding working-class
boys and the status problems created for them by status frustration in the schools,
Elliott hypothesized that (1) the rate of delinquency will be greater for boys while
they are in school than when out of school, and (2) delinquents who drop out of
school will have a higher in-school delinquency rate than when out of school. He
reasoned that the status difficulties which are generated by school experiences will
be attenuated when the youngster extricates himself from the school situation.

In order to test these hypotheses, Elliott studied the 743 tenth-grade boys
who entered two San Diego high schools in 1959, following them through June
1962, when they had either graduated or dropped out of school. Of the 743 boys
in the study, 182 had dropped out and 561 graduated from high school. Delinquent
involvement was measured through official contact reports of the police, sheriff,
and other law enforcement agencies in the area.

The findings of this study showed that the overall delinquency rate (graduates
and future dropouts combined) of boys while in school was substantially higher
than the rate after they had left school. The highest delinquency involvement was
found among dropout youths from lower-income backgrounds prior to their
leaving school. However, delinquency rates were about the same for in-school
middle-class boys and for dropouts from this social stratum. Finally, delinquent
dropouts showed more offending behavior before they had left school than after
having departed from the school situation. In summary, Elliott's results, consistent
with his hypotheses, point to the role of school status problems in the creation of
delinquency.

MIDDLE-CLASS AND FEMALE DELINQUENCY

To this point, our concern has been principally with strain theories dealing with lower-class male delinquency. However, variations of the strain perspective have also been developed to account for delinquent behavior among middle-class boys and among females (Cohen, 1955; Parsons, 1947). Regarding middle-class boys, strain is alleged to be created by structural defects in modern middle-class families that deprive boys of opportunities for the gradual learning of the ways of male adulthood. Daring acts such as car theft, vandalism, drinking and smoking are presumed to serve as public pronouncements that the youth is a "real man." Cohen (1955: 164) has succinctly summarized this position:

> Because of the structure of the modern family and the nature of our occupational system, children of both sexes tend to form early feminine identifications. The boy, however, unlike the girl, comes later under strong social pressure to establish his masculinity, his difference from female figures. Because his mother is the object of the feminine identification which he feels is the threat to his status as a male, he tends to react negativistically to those conduct norms which have been associated with mother and therefore have acquired feminine significance. Since mother has been the principal agent of indoctrination of "good," respectable behavior, "goodness" comes to symbolize femininity, and engaging in "bad" behavior acquires the function of denying his femininity and therefore asserting his masculinity. This is the motivation to juvenile delinquency.

This line of theorizing may apply at best to only a small portion of middle-class delinquency (Silverman and Dinitz, 1974). England (1967) questioned why one should expect masculine identity anxiety to lead to delinquency rather than to redoubled efforts to achieve adult responsibility. Additionally, he argued that the difficulties experienced by middle-class boys in observing the occupational roles of their fathers or other adult males was overstated in this theory. Most white-collar fathers are not absent from the home often enough to affect their availability as role models. Finally, England asked why there has apparently been a dramatic upsurge in middle-class delinquency since the Second World War, given that the occupational and social structural conditions noted by Parsons were not radically altered in this period.

Our assessment of the masculine identity formulation is that it probably does not satisfactorily explain most delinquency, whether on the part of either lower- or middle-class boys. Quite probably, most middle-class boys, delinquent or otherwise, are not markedly troubled by these concerns.

Turning to female delinquency, Stephen Cernkovich and Peggy Giordano (1979) investigated whether perceptions of limited opportunities were implicated in female misconduct. They identified two dimensions along which youngsters may perceive blocked or limited opportunities: general opportunity and gender-based opportunity. The former refers to perceptions that one's life chances are limited because of socioeconomic position and the like, while the latter has to do with beliefs that one's opportunities are relatively closed due to one's gender. Their results indicated that delinquency was most common among youths from lower-income backgrounds and among those who perceived themselves as having limited general opportunities. Neither males nor females often perceived a lack of opportunity as being due to gender. Further, female offenders were no more likely than male ones to declare that they had gender-based liabilities.

RADICAL-CONFLICT THEORIES

For the most part, radical-conflict theories do not view criminals as persons who are behaviorally different from noncriminals; hence they do not search for the causes of crime or delinquent behavior. Rather, they have focused on how the distribution of power and resources creates delinquents and criminals among those who are disadvantaged. Beginning with a Marxian conception of classes, the law is seen as made and implemented for the owners of the means of production. The proletariat or workers are, therefore, most likely to have their behavior defined as illegal.

However, a few radical-conflict theorists have addressed the issue of why people engage in criminal or delinquent behavior. Their analysis is similar to the strain perspective in that illegal behavior is viewed as a rational response to an inequitable social structure, although radical-conflict theories place more emphasis on the capitalistic economic structure as generating inequalities in the social structure than do strain theories.

The key element in radical-conflict interpretations of crime and delinquent behavior is the need of a capitalist economic system to generate *profit* largely by keeping the costs of labor at a minimum, which is done by maintaining low wages and/or by increasing the efficiency of labor (industrialization). Increasing efficiency limits the role of the worker to an appendage of the machine that produces the product. The assembly line worker stands as an example. In advanced industrial systems, workers become alienated from the product of their labor; that is, they no longer feel that their work plays an integral role in the creation of the product. Increasing industrialization also is a constant threat to the worker's job. A more efficient means to perform tasks formerly done by human labor may be found, thus making that worker part of a surplus labor pool. The existence of this surplus labor pool provides a means by which employers maintain low wages. Workers must compete for jobs at the rate that employers are willing to pay or else they risk their jobs being taken by someone else.

Building upon this depiction of the plight of the worker in a capitalist economic system, David M. Gordon (1971, 1973) has argued that crime is a rational response to the structure of that system. He contended that (Gordon, 1973: 186): "Crimes of many different varieties constitute functionally similar responses to the organization of capitalist institutions, for those crimes help provide a means of survival in a society within which survival is never assured."

One of the few attempts to develop a radical-conflict perspective on the causes of juvenile delinquency has been presented by David Greenberg (1977). His general argument was that the disproportionate involvement of juveniles in major crimes is a product of the historically changing position of youth in industrial societies. His starting point was with the available evidence concerning age relationships in delinquency. He argued that subcultural theories cannot account for the fact that involvement in serious delinquency reaches a peak at about age 15 to 16 and declines in magnitude thereafter. If the thrust of the subcultural argument—that delinquent activities are valued positively by juveniles—is correct, then subcultural members ought to continue in those endeavors beyond age 16.

The formulation proposed by Greenberg emphasized the strains experienced by many youngsters in the transition period from childhood to adolescence. During this period, attachments to parents become weakened at the same time that youths become highly sensitive to peer judgments and standards. This peer group culture places pressures on adolescents to engage in a hedonistic social life, but increasing numbers of them are incapable of financing those activities because of the decline of teenage employment opportuntities in capitalist societies. According to Greenberg (1977: 197): "Adolescent theft then occurs as a response to the disjunction between the desire to participate in social activities with peers and the absence of legitimate sources of funds needed to finance this participation." However, as these adolescents get older they become less vulnerable to peer evaluations at the same time as legitimate opportunities to earn money increase, with the consequence that adolescent theft declines among older youths.

The status problems of many juveniles in modern societies are exacerbated by school experiences. Greenberg emphasized the restraints imposed on the autonomy of youngsters by modern schools as well as the stigmatizing and degrading experiences to which many adolescents are exposed while in school. Those who have a reduced stake in conformity rebel against these negative experiences by engaging in hostile acts directed at the schools and school personnel.

A related source of delinquent motivation identified by Greenberg results from the lack of employment for male adolescents, which creates anxiety about one's prospects for attaining masculine status in American society. In Greenberg's view, these three pressures on juveniles account for most of the delinquency in capitalistic societies. Exclusion from the world of work deprives adolescents of opportunities to finance the intensive leisure activities that are emphasized in peer norms. Stigmatizing school experiences directed particularly at low-status, unemployed males provoke hostile and aggressive responses from those juveniles. Finally, fear of failure to achieve adult male status positions, which is common among juveniles in the late adolescent period, results in violent, status-defining acts on their part.

Greenberg was not the first sociologist to point to exclusion of juveniles from the labor market as a major factor in delinquency, but contrary to most interpretations that regard this situation as a recent and short-range one created by the invasion of women into the labor market, teenage preferences for part-time work, and the like, he argued (Greenberg, 1977: 197) that it "may more plausibly be explained in terms of the failure of the oligopoly-capitalist economy to generate sufficient demand for labor, than to these recent developments." Greenberg's argument comes down to the view that juvenile delinquency in industrialized societies rests on the disadvantaged structural position of adolescents in advanced capitalist economies. If he is correct, juvenile delinquency is not likely to be reduced markedly by the kinds of remedies that have been proposed in the United States, such as job training for youths. Job training in a situation in which jobs for teenagers are limited or nonexistent is likely to be of little avail.

Mark Colvin and John Pauly (1983) have recently presented what they label a *structural-Marxist* theory of delinquency production. They argue that the power relationships to which most lower-class workers are subjected are coercive. The coercive social milieu in which the workers exist reduces their capacity as parents to deal with their children in anything other than a repressive fashion. In turn, this harsh, punitive environment hinders the bond that children form with their parents. In addition to the quality of affective relationships between children and the parents being poorer, children also become less interested in those activities deemed important by their parents, e.g., school. Hence the general social bond is weakened and delinquent behavior becomes a likely outcome.

Many of the specific delinquency-producing factors identified by Greenberg and by Colvin and Pauly have been noted in other theoretical perspectives as well. The weakening of attachments to parents and problems in the school are major components of Hirschi's social bonding theory, and strain perspectives also view the lack of legitimate opportunities as an important motivating factor. We have already reviewed much of the relevant empirical evidence on the hypotheses. Unfortunately, what has not been adequately researched is the argument that differentiates the radical-conflict position from other perspectives. Although comparative data are difficult to acquire, advanced capitalist economies have not been shown to have higher delinquency rates than countries with other economic systems. In fact, some capitalist societies such such as Japan have very low rates of delinquent behavior. Until research demonstrates that juvenile delinquency is a more widespread problem in capitalistic than in other societies, the radical-conflict position will remain a plausible but untested perspective.

SUMMARY

The notion that those who are economically disadvantaged and who perceive their opportunities as limited are thereby driven into lawbreaking is a popular explanation of delinquency among citizens. In the 1960s, when it was politically popular to focus on the plight of the poor, strain arguments provided the theoretical rationale for many delinquency prevention programs. These endeavors were designed to provide lower-class children with remedial aid to better prepare them to compete

probably right since those activities gave rise to the hindering of social bonds.

for rewards in schools and to gain entry into fulfilling, rewarding positions in the job market. While there may be many reasons why these programs were largely unsuccessful, one important factor is that the theoretical base on which they were built has not been supported by research.

Perhaps the biggest disappointment with the strain perspective has been its inability to adequately account for the formation and maintenance of delinquent gangs. Neither the causal processes identified by strain theories nor the descriptions of gang behavior have proven to be consistent with systematic observations of offenders in the real world.

To the extent that data consistent with strain hypotheses have been uncovered, the interpretation of these findings has been ambiguous. For example, a student's perception of his or her prospects for success in the immediate school environment may reflect a lack of integration into or commitment to the school rather than a perception of blocked opportunities.

Our review of strain theories and the research that has been generated by them has provided us with some general propositions.

1. Although delinquents are found throughout neighborhoods and communities in American society, organized group patterns of subcultural lawbreaking tend to be concentrated in urban working-class neighborhoods.
2. Neighborhoods in which gang delinquency is common share a number of ecological characteristics, including a high proportion of economically disadvantaged residents, but economic disadvantage alone does not appear to account for high rates of subcultural delinquency. Rather, poverty and low income are most likely to result in gang delinquency if those conditions are accompanied by low social integration ✻ see 142
3. Strain, as measured by perceptions that occupational and other long-term opportunities are limited, does not appear to be an important factor in producing delinquent conduct. However, the perception of limited opportunities relative to the more immediate concerns of adolescents is related to delinquent behavior.
4. The most common form of subcultural misconduct is the "parent subculture" pattern of delinquency characterized by behavioral versatility rather than specialization.

REFERENCES

BORDUA, DAVID J. (1960). *Sociological Theories and Their Implications for Juvenile Delinquency*. Facts and Facets, No. 2. Washington, D.C.: U.S. Government Printing Office.

BORDUA, DAVID J. (1961). "Delinquent Subcultures: Sociological Interpretations of Gang Delinquency." *Annals of the American Academy of Political and Social Science* 338 (November): 119–36.

BORDUA, DAVID J. (1962). "Some Comments on Theories of Group Delinquency." *Sociological Inquiry* 32 (Spring): 245–60.

CERNKOVICH, STEPHEN A. and GIORDANO, PEGGY (1979). "Delinquency, Opportunity and Gender." *Journal of Criminal Law and Criminology* 70 (Summer): 145–51.

CLOWARD, RICHARD A. and OHLIN, LLOYD E. (1960). *Delinquency and Opportunity*. New York: Free Press.

COHEN, ALBERT K. (1955). *Delinquent Boys.* New York: Free Press.
COHEN, ALBERT K. (1965). "The Sociology of the Deviant Act: Anomie Theory and Beyond." *American Sociological Review* 30 (February): 5-14.
COHEN, ALBERT K. and SHORT, JAMES F., JR. (1958). "Research on Delinquent Subcultures." *Journal of Social Issues* 14 (3): 20-37.
COLVIN, MARK and PAULY, JOHN (1983). "A Critique of Criminology: Toward an Integrated Structural-Marxist Theory of Delinquency Production." *American Journal of Sociology* 89 (November): 513-51.
ELLIOTT, DELBERT S. (1966). "Delinquency, School Attendance and Dropout." *Social Problems* 13 (Winter): 307-14.
ELLIOTT, DELBERT S., AGETON, SUZANNE S., and CANTER, RACHELLE J. (1979). "An Integrated Theoretical Perspective on Delinquent Behavior." *Journal of Research on Crime and Delinquency* 16 (January): 3-27.
ELLIOTT, DELBERT S. and VOSS, HARWIN L. (1974). *Delinquency and Dropout.* Lexington, Mass.: Heath.
ENGLAND, RALPH W. (1967). "A Theory of Middle-class Juvenile Delinquency," pp. 242-44. In Edmund W. Vaz, ed. *Middle-class Juvenile Delinquency.* New York: Harper & Row.
GIBBONS, DON C. (1965). *Changing the Lawbreaker.* Englewood Cliffs, N.J.: Prentice-Hall.
GIBBONS, DON C. and JONES, JOSEPH F. (1975). *The Study of Deviance.* Englewood Cliffs, N.J.: Prentice-Hall.
GOLD, MARTIN (1963). *Status Forces in Delinquent Boys.* Ann Arbor: Institute for Social Research, University of Michigan.
GORDON, DAVID M. (1971). "Class and the Economics of Crime." *Review of Radical Political Economics* 3 (Summer): 51-75.
GORDON, DAVID M. (1973). "Capitalism, Class and Crime in America." *Crime and Delinquency* 19 (April): 163-86.
GREENBERG, DAVID F. (1977). "Delinquency and the Age Structure of Society." *Contemporary Crises* 1 (April): 189-224.
HIRSCHI, TRAVIS (1969). *Causes of Delinquency.* Berkeley: University of California Press.
HYMAN, HERBERT H. (1953). "The Value Systems of Different Classes: A Social-Psychological Contribution to the Analysis of Stratification," pp. 426-42. In Reinhard Bendix and Seymour M. Lipset, eds. *Class, Status and Power.* New York: Free Press.
JOHNSON, RICHARD E. (1979). *Juvenile Delinquency and Its Origins.* Cambridge, Mass.: Cambridge University Press.
KITSUSE, JOHN I. and DIETRICK, DAVID C. (1959). "Delinquent Boys: A Critique." *American Sociological Review* 24 (April): 208-15.
KOBRIN, SOLOMON (1951). "The Conflict of Values in Delinquency Areas." *American Sociological Review* 16 (October): 653-61.
KORNHAUSER, RUTH ROSNER (1978). *Social Sources of Delinquency.* Chicago: University of Chicago Press.
LISKA, ALLEN E. (1971). "Aspirations, Expectations and Delinquency: Stress and Additive Models." *Sociological Quarterly* 12 (Winter): 99-107.
MATZA, DAVID (1961). "Review." *American Journal of Sociology* 60 (May): 631-33.
MERTON, ROBERT K. (1938). "Social Structure and Anomie." *American Sociological Review* 3 (October): 672-82.
MILLER, WALTER B. (1967). "Theft Behavior in City Gangs," pp. 25-38. In Malcolm W. Klein, ed. *Juvenile Gangs in Context.* Englewood Cliffs, N.J.: Prentice-Hall.
MILLER, WALTER B. (1975). *Violence by Youth Gangs and Youth Groups as a Crime Problem in Major American Cities.* Washington, D.C.: Law Enforcement Assistance Administration.
PALMORE, ERDMAN B. and HAMMOND, PHILLIP E. (1964). "Interacting Factors in Juvenile Delinquency." *American Sociological Review* 24 (December): 848-54.
PARSONS, TALCOTT (1947). "Certain Primary Sources and Patterns of Aggression in the Social Structure of the Western World." *Psychiatry* 10 (May): 167-81.
QUICKER, JOHN C. (1974). "The Effect of Goal Discrepancy on Delinquency." *Social Problems* 22 (October): 74-86.
REISS, ALBERT J., JR. and RHODES, ALBERT LEWIS (1963). "Status Deprivation and Delinquency." *Sociological Quarterly* 4 (Spring): 135-49.

RIVERA, RAMON and SHORT, JAMES F., JR. (1967). "Occupational Goals: A Comparative Analysis," pp. 70–90. In Malcolm W. Klein, ed. *Juvenile Gangs in Context.* Englewood Cliffs, N.J.: Prentice-Hall.

SCHAFER, WALTER E. and POLK, KENNETH (1972). "Delinquency and the Schools," pp. 222–77. In The President's Commission on Law Enforcement and Administration of Justice, *Task Force Report: Juvenile Delinquency and Youth Crime.* Washington, D.C.: U.S. Government Printing Office.

SCHRAG, CLARENCE C. (1962). "Delinquency and Opportunity: Analysis of a Theory." *Sociology and Social Research* 46 (January): 167–75.

SHAW, CLIFFORD R. and McKAY, HENRY D. (1942). *Juvenile Delinquency and Urban Areas.* Chicago: University of Chicago Press.

SHORT, JAMES F., JR. (1964). "Gang Delinquency and Anomie," pp. 98–127. In Marshall B. Clinard, ed. *Anomie and Deviant Behavior.* New York: Free Press.

SHORT, JAMES, F., JR. and STRODTBECK, FRED L. (1965). *Group Process and Gang Delinquency.* Chicago: University of Chicago Press.

SHORT, JAMES F., JR., TENNYSON, RAY A., and HOWARD, KENNETH I. (1965). "Behavior Dimensions of Gang Delinquency," pp. 77–101. In James F. Short, Jr. and Fred L. Strodtbeck *Group Process and Gang Delinquency.* Chicago: University of Chicago Press.

SILVERMAN, IRA J. and DINITZ, SIMON (1974). "Compulsive Masculinity and Delinquency: An Empirical Investigation." *Criminology* 11 (February): 498–515.

SPERGEL, IRVING (1961). "An Exploratory Research in Delinquent Subcultures." *Social Service Review* 35 (March): 33–47.

SPERGEL, IRVING (1963). "Male Young Adult Criminality, Deviant Values, and Differential Opportunities in Two Lower-class Negro Neighborhoods." *Social Problems* 10 (Winter): 237–50.

SPERGEL, IRVING (1964). *Racketville, Slumtown, Haulburg.* Chicago: University of Chicago Press.

SYKES, GRESHAM M. and MATZA, DAVID (1957). "Techniques of Neutralization: A Theory of Delinquency." *American Sociological Review* 22 (December): 664–70.

THRASHER, FREDERICK M. (1927). *The Gang.* Chicago: University of Chicago Press.

WIATROWSKI, MICHAEL D., HANSELL, STEPHEN, MASSEY, CHARLES R., and WILSON, DAVID L. (1982). "Curriculum Tracking and Delinquency." *American Sociological Review* 47 (February): 151–60.

YABLONSKY, LEWIS (1959). "The Delinquent Gang as Near Group." *Social Problems* 7 (Fall): 108–17.

chapter 9

CULTURAL VALUES, SOCIAL LEARNING, AND DELINQUENCY

INTRODUCTION

"Johnny is a really good boy; if only he hadn't started hanging out with the crowd." We often hear parents use similar expressions to explain why their son or daughter has gotten into trouble with the juvenile justice system. The implication of that argument is that Johnny learned from and/or was pressured into behaving in a delinquent manner by the people with whom he associated. The notion that delinquent behavior is learned from others with whom one interacts characterizes the theories that are included in cultural transmission/socialization perspectives.

In the previous chapter on strain perspectives, we noted that Cloward and Ohlin's (1960) differential opportunity theory suggested that the type of delinquent behavior exhibited by a gang is contingent on the illegitimate opportunities available in the neighborhood. Since they emphasized the importance of the existence of a culture that allowed for the learning of delinquent behavior, that part of their argument is similar to the theories we will review in this chapter. Indeed, Cloward and Ohlin attributed this idea to Edwin Sutherland, the most prominent socialization theorist. However, we distinguish their theory from cultural transmission/socialization perspectives because they identified the primary cause of delinquent behavior as located in blocked opportunities, or in other words, in socially generated strain. For cultural transmission/socialization theories, the primary cause is the norms, values, and behavior patterns characteristic of the group in which the juvenile interacts. Juvenile delinquency is not seen as a deviant adaptation to strain but rather as a conforming response within a culture or group that holds different norms and values than those represented in law.

CULTURAL CONFLICT THEORIES OF DELINQUENCY

Once again we begin our discussion of a theoretical perspective by referring to the seminal work of the Chicago School. David Matza (1969: 48) has stated: "Though the Chicagoans conceived disorganization, they described diversity and thus the possibility of choosing diversity became more readily available to subsequent students of social life." Matza was referring to the documentation by the Chicagoans of the mosaic of social worlds populated by different ethnic groups that comprised the urban scene. While the primary explanation offered by such observers as Clifford Shaw and Henry McKay to account for crime and delinquency in urban areas was framed in terms of social disorganization and the inability of conventional institutions to control behavior, much of the ethnographic work of the Chicago School actually suggested that socially organized groups existed within seemingly disorganized neighborhoods. Accordingly, delinquency may be the result of the ability of these groups to transmit norms and values contrary to the law, rather than their inability to transmit and enforce norms and values consistent with the law.

One interpretation of the impact of societal diversity on delinquency and crime holds that the latter results when cultures with differing norms and values come into close proximity. Thorsten Sellin (1938) is credited with the first detailed statement of the cultural conflict position. He suggested that the distinctive behavior of one group often becomes criminalized, that is declared deviant and illegal, by more powerful groups. Law making is the outcome of conflicts over whose norms and values will predominate. For example, Gusfield (1966) has described the passage of the Volstead Act, which established the prohibition of the sale of alcoholic beverages, as the result of a cultural, symbolic conflict between rural, Protestant Americans and the increasing urban non-Protestant immigrants. The cultural proscription of the drinking of alcoholic beverages characteristic of some fundamental Protestant groups was enacted into law to symbolically assert the dominance of rural over urban America. This dominance was being threatened and, indeed, soon disappeared; thus prohibition was a futile gesture.

Law violation might also occur if a person or group from one culture moves into another culture which has different norms. Much of the crime problem associated with immigrant groups was attributed to this form of cultural conflict.

Kornhauser (1978) has offered some trenchant criticisms of Sellin's cultural conflict position. She argued that he did not provide data to support his arguments; indeed, the data reported by Sellin which showed that foreign-born immigrants had lower rates of crime than first generation immigrants can be interpreted as contradicting his argument. Kornhauser (1978): 187) concluded that "when it comes to those things that lie at the core of the criminal law, there apparently is widespread agreement across and within cultures."

Lower-class Focal Concerns and Delinquency

A version of the cultural conflict perspective that was specifically designed to explain gang delinquency is Walter Miller's (1958) theory. According to Miller, it is not compliance with specific cultural norms contrary to the criminal law that generates delinquent behavior, but rather, it is adherence to broad themes or focal concerns that condition the specific acts of lower-class persons. Delinquency is the product of long-established, durable traditions of lower-class life, rather than the result of responses to conflicts with middle-class values.

Miller contended that lower-class culture is most strikingly embodied by those persons Michael Harrington (1962) described as populating "the other America," that is, the world of rural migrants to urban areas: American Indians, Puerto Ricans, and urban blacks. These persons are at the bottom of the social heap and have little prospect of ascending. The culture of this population segment can be described by a series of structural elements peculiar to it and by a complex pattern of "focal concerns."

One of the major structural patterns in lower-class society is what Miller termed the female-based household, in which the stability of the family unit is provided by one or more adult females. The mother and older daughters play multiple roles, providing economic support for the family unit as well as discharging the household and affectional duties. This kind of family structure results from the practice of serial monogamy, in which women find themselves involved in repetitive sequences of mate-finding, illegal or common-law marriage, and divorce or desertion by the male. Thus the household may be made up of a number of children, each of whom has the same mother but a different father.

For the boy who grows up in the female-dominated family, life is fraught with anxieties about sex-role identification. The young male is assaulted on all sides by verbal assertions that men are "no damn good" and feels he must become a "real man" as quickly as possible. The male adolescent peer group, territorially located on city streets, provides the training ground and milieu in which lower-class males seek a sense of maleness, status, and belonging.

These elements, along with the pervasive sense of material and social deprivation common to lower-class members, result in life patterns and experiences organized around what Miller called focal concerns. Focal concerns or values represent broad themes that condition the specific acts of lower-class persons. The focal concerns of lower-class society include trouble, toughness, smartness, excitement, fate, and autonomy. *Trouble* refers to a dominant concern about avoiding entanglements with the police, social welfare agencies, and similar bodies—encounters that are an ever-present possibility in this segment of society—while *toughness* denotes a concern for continued demonstrations of bravery, daring, and other traits which show that one is not feminine or soft. *Smartness* is a label for such things as the ability to dupe or outwit others, live by one's wits, and earn a livelihood through a "hustle" (such as pimping). Miller identified *excitement* as a generic concern to seek out weekend activities which disrupt the monotony of weekday routine jobs, and *fate* has to do with definitions by lower-class people that their lives are ruled by forces over which they have little control, that luck plays a major part in their life chances. Finally, *autonomy* refers to a profound avoidance of control or domination by others.

These structural elements and focal concerns combine in several ways to produce criminality. Those who respond to some of these focal concerns automatically violate the law through their behavior. When faced with a choice of lines of conduct, they select a deviant form of activity as the most attractive one. Miller's basic argument was that to be lower class in contemporary American society is to be in a social situation which contains a variety of direct influences toward deviant conduct, one form of which is juvenile delinquency.

David Bordua (1961) has presented a thorough critique of Miller's notions, noting among other things that Miller failed to acknowledge the detailed variations which can be observed in patterns of lower class culture. Miller's characterization seemed to many to be most applicable to certain urban slum area groups, particularly blacks, but hardly descriptive of such other lower-class groups as residents in Italian and Chinese enclaves. Specifically, the picture of serial monogamy and female-based households is accurate principally for blacks and does not hold for other low-income, disadvantaged groups. A third dispute centers around the danger of tautology in the focal concerns used to account for delinquent conduct. Miller was not always careful to distinguish between observations about these interests and evidence of the behavior they are designed to explain. Finally, Bordua observed that Miller did not effectively refute Cohen's (1955) contention that working-class boys are sensitive to middle-class standards. In Bordua's view, it is possible that both Cohen and Miller are partially correct. Perhaps many lower-class boys do not initially internalize middle-class norms as a part of their socialization, but when they get into schools and other competitive situations, these status-measuring standards are forced upon them. These experiences may then alienate lower-class boys, driving them into involvement in delinquent subcultures.

Miller also attributed delinquent behavior among the middle class to lower-class values (Kvaraceus and Miller, 1959). Kvaraceus and Miller argued that the deferred gratification pattern among middle-class citizens has been weakened by such developments as installment buying, mandatory school attendance, and changes in the economy. One of the results of these trends is that lower-class values have been diffused upward into middle-class society. These values tend in the direction of hedonistic pursuit of short-run pleasures, drawing middle-class youths who follow them into delinquency. Kvaraceus and Miller based their case in considerable part on an account of the spread of lower-class black jazz music, albeit in somewhat modified form, to middle-class groups. This argument is far from convincing; it remains to be shown that lower-class values are pursued by many middle-class persons. Even more important, it has not been definitively demonstrated that lower-class youngsters embrace a set of values markedly different from those of middle-class youths. While Short and Strodtbeck (1965) found that lower-class boys do hold allegiance to some lower-class values not endorsed by middle-class males, there was no difference among the classes in their support of middle-class values. Additionally, Short and Strodtbeck reported that gang members did not evaluate lower-class images higher than middle-class images. The concept of "value stretch" might better account for these findings than Miller's notion of focal concerns. Rodman (1963) coined this term to describe the situation in which lower-class persons share middle-class values but due to the problems created by their disadvantaged position, they "stretch" those values beyond conventionality as a means of adaptation.

In sum, while some lower-class boys may have a more varied set of values than middle-calss boys, these values are probably not reflective of focal concerns of the lower class. Rather they can be seen as one form of adaptive response to the disadvantages of lower-class life.

DIFFERENTIAL ASSOCIATION AND DELINQUENCY

The Theory of Differential Association

The most prominent cultural transmission theory, and possibly the most influential theory of delinquency, is Edwin Sutherland's theory of differential association (Sutherland and Cressey, 1978). Sutherland first formally stated his theory in 1937 but the seeds for the theory had appeared in earlier editions of his textbook (Sutherland, 1924, 1934).

Sutherland was influenced by the research taking place at the University of Chicago, along with the concept of cultural conflict as expressed by Sellin and the symbolic interactionism of Charles Horton Cooley and W. I. Thomas. Symbolic interactionism emphasizes the learning of attitudes and behavior through the process of interaction and communication. Moreover, this perspective does not treat persons as actors responding in uniform and unthinking ways to stimuli in their environment; rather, their conduct depends on how they define the situation (Thomas, 1923). That is, actors interpret information or perceptions from their surroundings, assigning meaning or structure to these perceptions.

Sutherland blended these intellectual strains into a concise statement that emphasized the similarity in the process by which both conventional and criminal behavior is learned. He was intent on rejecting the psychopathological and biological traditions that had dominated criminological thinking, and instead asserted that there is no inherent difference between the learning process that produces criminals or noncriminals; they simply learn different patterns of behavior.

The formal statement of differential association theory is comprised of the following nine propositions. (This theory can be converted into a theory of delinquency simply by substituting *delinquent* for *criminal* behavior and *delinquent acts* for *crime.*)

1. *Criminal behavior is learned.*
2. *Criminal behavior is learned in interaction with other persons in a process of communication.*
3. *The principal part of the learning of criminal behavior occurs within intimate personal groups.*
4. *When criminal behavior is learned, the learning includes (a) techniques of committing the crime, which are sometimes very complicated, sometimes very simple; (b) the specific direction of motives, drives, rationalizations, and attitudes.*
5. *The specific direction of motives and drives is learned from definitions of the legal codes as favorable or unfavorable.*
6. *A person becomes delinquent because of an excess of definitions favorable to violation of law over definitions unfavorable to violation of law.*
7. *Differential associations may vary in frequency, duration, priority, and intensity.*
8. *The process of learning criminal behavior by association with criminal and anticriminal patterns involves all of the mechanisms that are involved in any other learning.*
9. *While criminal behavior is an expression of general needs and values, it is not explained by these general needs and values, since noncriminal behavior is an expression of the same needs and values.* [Emphasis in the original] (Sutherland and Cressey, 1978: 80–82).

Sutherland's theory is relatively clear and straightforward, being markedly less prolix and murky than much sociological theorizing. Its central claims are that individuals learn some conduct definitions favorable to law violation and others that discourage them from lawbreaking. Persons who become involved in criminality have learned more pro-crime definitions than anti-crime ones. Conduct definitions are learned within primary groups, while group associations with carriers of criminal definitions vary in frequency, duration, priority, and intensity.

Although the formal statement of the theory addresses only the "why do they do it?" question, Sutherland did not neglect the "rates question." In fact in earlier versions of his theory, he included the statement (Sutherland, 1939: 7): "Cultural conflict is the underlying cause of differential association and therefore of systematic criminal behavior." He considered cultural conflict to be a specific aspect of social disorganization, with the latter term referring to societal conditions in which support for the social values expressed in the criminal law are absent. However, he eventually came to recognize that what he was actually describing was a situation of *differential social organization*, with society being organized in ways that both encourage and discourage crime and delinquency. Crime rates reflect differential social organization, that is, the degree to which a community is organized for or against crime. Individuals living in communities with more pro-crime influences will be more likely to come into association with definitions favorable to the violation of the law than will those who live in more conventional surroundings.

Donald Cressey, a student of Sutherland, has labeled the underlying theme in Sutherland's theory as the *principle of normative conflict* (Cressey, 1960). Normative conflict is manifested at the community level by the degree to which it is differentially organized for or against criminal values and at the individual level by the extent to which individuals differentially associate with definitions favorable or unfavorable to the legal codes.

Criticisms of Differential Association Theory

The differential association argument has been embraced by large numbers of criminologists, largely because it is a plausible account of etiology couched in sociological terms. At the same time, the theory contains some basic flaws. For one, the theoretical concepts are not defined with sufficient clarity and precision to allow for adequate empirical examinations. For example, Sutherland did not specifically identify the nature of definitions favorable to the violation of the law; nor did he adequately define intensity. Even if these terms had been defined and operationalized, there is some question as to whether one could measure the frequency, duration, intensity and priority of definitions favorable and unfavorable to the law. As we will see, research on differential association has typically been limited to assessing only associations and definitions conducive to the violation of the law.

The failure to measure both dimensions of the differential association ratio has, in part, led to another criticism of the theory. It has been suggested that the argument does not take into account the variability among individuals in susceptibility to definitions favorable to the violation of the law (Reckless, 1973), for example, individual personality factors that might increase or decrease susceptibility to criminal influences. Sutherland recognized that personality influences may be associated with some forms of criminality but asserted that differential association would still determine which individuals with these personality traits would become criminal.

A more problematic issue is the need to account for the experiences and associations with conventional definitions individuals have at different points throughout their lives. If a juvenile has been influenced earlier by those representing definitions unfavorable to the violation of the law, then we might expect that person to be more resistant to any criminalistic influences with whom he or she may be associating during the juvenile age period. This recognition led Reckless to generate containment theory (see Chapter 7). Voss (1964) has argued that Reckless's theory is simply the "flip" side of differential association; a good self-concept is the result of associating with definitions unfavorable to the violation of the law.

A final criticism of differential association theory is that even though it is a learning theory, Sutherland failed to spell out the nature of this learning process. Although Cressey (1960) has argued that Sutherland intended his theory to be

WHO
CARES

interpreted as a symbolic interaction perspective, it cannot be said that the differential association argument is a full-blown learning perspective in the symbolic interactionist genre.

Research on Differential Association Theory

As noted above, most of the research on differential association theory has focused on a juvenile's association with others who have been involved in delinquent behavior. Short (1957) provided one of the initial examinations of this aspect of the theory, in which he developed a scale tapping the dimensions of association that Sutherland had identified: frequency, intensity, duration, and priority. Short found that differential association was highly correlated with self-reported delinquent behavior.

There have been several more recent studies that have examined the relationship between some measure of association with delinquent others and either delinquent behavior (Voss, 1964; Matthews, 1968; Reiss and Rhodes, 1964; Stanfield, 1966; Johnson, 1979; Jensen, 1972; Hepburn, 1976) or adolescent alcohol and drug use (Krohn, 1974; Akers et al., 1979; Kandel, 1973; Jessor and Jessor, 1977; Orcutt, 1983). The findings from these studies have led Kornhauser (1979) to conclude that all inquiries have established that involvement in delinquency is related to the delinquency of companions and Kandel (1978) to assert that this relationship constitutes the strongest finding we have regarding adolescent misbehavior.

Establishing a strong and consistent relationship between delinquent associations and involvement in delinquency is only one step in the process of confirming Sutherland's theory. The logic of differential association theory suggests that associations are related to delinquent behavior because through such associations one learns more definitions favorable than unfavorable to the law. Favorable definitions should therefore intervene between associations and delinquent behavior. Jensen (1972) examined this issue and found that delinquent attitudes (definitions favorable to the violation of the law) do not mediate the relationship between association and delinquent behavior. He concluded that the effect on delinquent behavior of having delinquent peers is not solely a result of socialization to definitions favorable to the violation of law. Andrews and Kandel (1979) found similar results regarding adolescent drug use. However, in a reanalysis of the data used by Jensen, using a more sophisticated statistical technique, Matsueda (1982) found that his measure of the construct of definitions fully mediated the effect of association with delinquent others and measures of attachment to parents. Thus he concluded that Sutherland's argument was supported.

Another issue pertinent to the theory is the proper time order of the variables. Association with delinquent friends and favorable definitions should precede delinquent behavior. The investigation of time order necessitates collecting data at several time points but such research is difficult and costly, hence there have been few studies that have obtained such data. Some longitudinal research on adolescent marijuana use does confirm the time order implied in differential association theory

(Kandel, 1978; Ginsberg and Greenley, 1978; Andrews and Kandel, 1979). Huba and Bentler (1983) have found similar results regarding a variety of delinquent and substance-using behavior.

In sum, the research on differential association has been limited by the difficulty in measuring its concepts. Studies which have examined partial implications of the theory have been generally supportive. However, the findings also suggest that there may be alternative models that better explain the process of engaging in delinquent behavior.

SOCIAL LEARNING THEORY

Because of the problems encountered in attempts to measure the concepts incorporated in differential association theory and also because of its limitations as a learning theory, some sociologists have endeavored to revise and improve upon the theory (Glaser, 1956; DeFleur and Quinney, 1966; Jeffrey, 1965; Burgess and Akers, 1966). The most important of these endeavors have centered around reinforcement theory or social learning theory. C. R. Jeffrey (1965) first suggested introducing the concepts and processes that had been developed in operant conditioning research (Skinner, 1938) to explain criminal behavior. Burgess and Akers (1966) carried this suggestion further by revising Sutherland's differential association theory, systematically incorporating these principles in it. Akers has made it quite clear that their intention was to revise differential association theory, not compete with or supplant it (Akers et al., 1979; Lanza-Kaduce et al., 1982). The result was a theory composed of seven propositions:

1. Deviant behavior is learned according to the principles of operant conditioning.
2. Deviant behavior is learned both in nonsocial situations that are reinforcing or discriminating and through that social interaction in which the behavior of other persons is reinforcing or discriminating for such behavior.
3. The principle part of the learning of deviant behavior occurs in those groups which comprise or control the individual's major source of reinforcements.
4. The learning of deviant behavior, including specific techniques, attitudes, and avoidance procedures, is a function of the effective and available reinforcers and the existing reinforcement contingencies.
5. The specific class of behavior learned and its frequency of occurrence are a function of the effective and available reinforcers, and the deviant or nondeviant direction of the norms, rules, and definitions which in the past have accompanied the reinforcement.
6. The probability that a person will commit deviant behavior is increased in the presence of normative statemen⁺ˢ, definitions, and verbalizations which, in the process of differential reinforcement of such behavior over conforming behavior, have acquired discriminative value.
7. The strength of deviant behavior is a direct function of the amount, frequency, and probability of its reinforcement. The modalities of association with

deviant patterns are important insofar as they affect the source, amount, and scheduling of reinforcement. (Akers, 1985: 41)

Statements 2, 3, 5, and 6 of the theory deserve particular attention. Statements 2 and 3 taken together present the position that while some learning takes place in nonsocial situations, most of it occurs through social interaction with the groups which comprise the individual's major source of reinforcements. Akers (1979: 47) argued that the learning relevant to deviant behavior occurs in contexts wherein "other persons make reinforcers available." He also asserted (Akers, 1977: 48) that this is "the power and centrality of the direct and symbolic social rewards in society which lead to labeling this theory *social learning*." It is this emphasis which places Akers's theory in the realm of sociology rather than psychology (Akers, 1981).

It was also this social emphasis which led Akers to recognize the potential of imitation in the learning process. Individuals learn behavior from observing others who engage in a similar acts (Bandura, 1977; Staats, 1975). Imitation is seen as a result of vicarious reinforcement acquired when observing a model's behavior being rewarded. While imitation may operate at all times, its importance is in the acquisition of behavior.

Statements 5 and 6 incorporate Sutherland's emphasis on definitions. The definitions, verbalizations, and normative statements are discriminative stimuli for deviant behavior. That is, they derive their meaning from having been paired with a reinforcing stimulus in the past and serve as cues for the reinforcement. It is important to recognize that Akers saw these definitions as involving either overt or covert behavior. A person can apply these definitions to his own behavior through cognition. Akers (1977) argued that this conceptualization remains consistent with the symbolic interactionism implicit in Sutherland's original formulation while also being consistent with a "soft behaviorist" view of learning.

There are two classes of definitions which are important in the social learning process. Positive definitions are those which define behavior as desirable or permissible, while the second class of definitions are neutralizing definitions. Akers borrowed the latter notion from an earlier statement by Sykes and Matza (1957). Neutralizing definitions make disapproved behavior acceptable or at least tolerable in that stimulus situation. For example, while the car thief may recognize that it is not right to steal, he or she may neutralize (before the act) his or her behavior by arguing that the victim will not lose any money since the car is insured against theft.

Statement 6 also incorporates the notions of differential reinforcement. According to Akers et al. (1979: 638): "Behavior (whether deviant or conforming) results from greater reinforcement, on balance, over punishing contingencies for the same behavior and the reinforcing-punishing contingencies on alternative behavior." It is important to recognize that the likelihood of any behavior occurring is contingent on the relative probability of a reinforcing contingency compared with the probability of reinforcements elicited by possible alternative behaviors.

Akers et al. (1979) summarized the theory by describing a process whereby differential association with deviant groups provides the social environments within which definitions, imitation, and social reinforcement take place. The definitions, once learned, serve as discriminative stimuli for future behavior. After the initial acts, social and nonsocial reinforcers and punishers should become important as imitation becomes less important. From this statement, Akers et al. identified four main concepts—imitation, differential association, definitions, and differential reinforcement—that capture the learning process identified by the theory.

Akers's reformulation has been utilized, for the most part, as a post factum interpretation for making sense of the facts regarding a wide variety of forms of deviant conduct. However, Akers et al. (1979) have subjected this argument to research scrutiny, in which they investigated adolescent drinking and drug behavior. That study involved a self-report questionnaire administered to over 3000 male and female junior and senior high school students in seven communities in three midwestern states. Some of the questionnaire items solicited information on drug and alcohol use or abstention, while others were designed to get at imitation, differential association, conduct definitions, and differential reinforcement—key notions in reinforcement-learning theory. The results of this research indicated that each of these ingredients of social learning was to some extent involved in drug or alcohol use or abstention, but the single most important factor was differential association with peers who either engaged in alcohol and/or drug use or who refrained from these activities.

This research and, by implication, the social learning theory, have been criticized (Stafford and Ecklund-Olson, 1982; Strickland, 1982). Some have argued that because differential association and definitions explain almost as much of the variance in substance use as does the full model, there is no need to include concepts such as differential reinforcement. Stafford and Ecklund-Olson (1982) reanalyzed the Akers et al. data and discovered that differential reinforcement did not mediate the effects of differential association as social learning theory would predict. Lanza-Kaduce et al. (1982) responded by arguing that longitudinal data must be used to assess the causal ordering of the variables in the learning process. Subsequently, Krohn et al. (1983) reported on a longitudinal panel study of adolescent cigarette smoking in which Akers's hypothesized causal order was supported.

Criticisms of Social Learning Theory

As noted above, social learning theory is a restatement of Sutherland's differential association theory. Thus, while Akers recognized the potential reinforcing effect of nonsocial stimuli, he clearly identified social reinforcement emanating from groups with whom individuals interact as most important. This position has been criticized by Reed Adams (1973), who argued that nonsocial reinforcers are more potent than social ones. On the other hand, Taylor et al. (1973) suggested that by providing a role for nonsocial reinforcers, Burgess and Akers had performed a travesty upon Sutherland's theory.

The controversy over the relative importance of social and nonsocial reinforcers can only be addressed by research designed to compare the effectiveness of types of reinforcers. Taylor et al.'s complaint that the theory does not adequately reflect Sutherland's argument is an insignificant one if the purpose of any theory is to adequately explain a phenomenon. If by expanding Sutherland's argument, social learning is better able account for lawbreaking, it is of little importance whether Sutherland would approve of the modification.

The most problematic issue regarding social learning theory is whether it is tautological and hence incapable of being disproven. A positive reinforcement is defined as a stimulus which increases the probability of subsequent behavior of a specified kind. If a stimulus does not do so, it is not a positive reinforcer. In experimental situations researchers can often manipulate a subject's condition (e.g., deprive the person of food) to reasonably insure that some stimulus (food) will be a reinforcer. If the person is not conditioned by that stimulus the theory is questioned. However, in dealing with people in real-life social relationships, sociologists cannot be as familiar with the subjects' condition in regard to numerous potential social reinforcers. Hence it is difficult to identify a reinforcer independent of the behavior which follows it. Not being able to do so results in a circular argument. Akers (1977) suggested that social scientists must use their knowledge of culture and social structure in order to identify reinforcement contingencies; that is, he called for identification and measurement of values, at the group as well as the individual level, separate from observations about the strength of the behavior being explained by learning. This is not an entirely satisfactory solution to the tautology problem. However, as Liska (1969) pointed out, theories that are tautological can still be very useful in generating derived propositions that are testable.

Our final comment on social learning theory is that it may have failed to achieve one of its main objectives. That is, Burgess and Akers incorporated the concept of reinforcement into differential association theory to make it more testable. It has yet to be demonstrated that differential reinforcement is more amenable to operationalization than is differential association or the ratio of definitions. The minimal amount of research generated by the theory may be reflective of the difficulty in measuring these concepts in the social arena.

SUMMARY

Chapter 9 is the final one in a trio of chapters that have dealt with sociological explanations of juvenile delinquency. This chapter dealt with learning arguments and has generated the following conclusions:

1. Adolescents who have associated with peers who have committed delinquent acts are more likely to engage in delinquent behavior than those who have not had such associations. There is some evidence to suggest that the association

occurs prior to the delinquent behavior, although this relationship has not been firmly established.

2. Definitions favorable to the violation of law are related both to having delinquent associations and committing delinquent behavior. There is some uncertainty as to whether definitions favorable to the violation of law act as an intervening influence between delinquent associations and delinquent behavior.

3. The processes identified by social learning theory may explain how associating with delinquent others increases the probability of delinquent behavior among adolescents.

4. A model hypothesizing that social bonding variables increase the probability of associating with delinquent others, which in turn increases the probability of delinquent behavior, has been shown to be the most tenable explanation of delinquent conduct.

The last three chapters have dealt with a variety of theoretical approaches, along with a large share of the research that has evaluated these perspectives. Throughout our discussion we alluded to the possibilities for amalgamating theories into a model that would be better able to account for delinquent behavior than would any single theory by itself. It is now time to consider these possibilities in greater detail.

Several scholars have suggested models that would include concepts from social bonding theory and differential association theory (Conger, 1976; Jensen, 1972; Johnson, 1979; Elliott, Ageton, and Canter, 1979; Matsueda, 1982). Typically they treat the bonding variables as being causally prior to differential association and/or definitions favorable to the violation of the law. That is, bond levels develop first and then influence the associational ties established by individual youngsters. There is disagreement over whether the differential association variables totally mediate the effect of the bonding variables or whether the bonding variables sometimes have a direct effect on delinquent behavior. The research that has been conducted on these arguments indicates that the bonding elements often do influence the types of peers with whom one associates and that associating with delinquent others generates definitions favorable to delinquency. Figure 9-1 illustrates one form such a model might take. The combination of variables explains a substantial amount of the variance in delinquent behavior (Massey and Krohn, 1984: 10).

A number of questions about these arguments which integrate different causal hypotheses have yet to be adequately addressed. Most importantly, the time order or patterning of the independent or explanatory variables has not yet been clearly established. The need for longitudinal studies and data also is evident. However, it does appear that such a model would better account for the process by which individuals come to commit, and continue committing, delinquent behavior than would any single theory.

The explanation of the rates of delinquent behavior has not yet been fully integrated with the processual account delineated above. Some theorists have argued that variables reflecting economically or culturally disadvantaged social

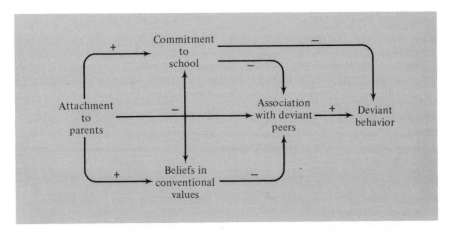

FIGURE 9-1   Hypothesized relationships between social bonding variables, differential peer association and deviant behavior. The "+" sign indicates a positive relationship between the variables while the "-" indicates an inverse relationship.

position—social status, race, and neighborhood influences, for example—are related to a lack of commitment to and poor performance in school and to lack of supervision of children by their parents. At the same time, these correlations are typically not large, which may be due to the fact that most research studies have focused on a wide range of juvenile misbehavior, including rather petty offenses. Relatively inconsequential and infrequent acts of delinquency are committed by large numbers of youths. These flirtations with misconduct probably arise out of myriad causal sources. At the same time, structural or strain influences may be importantly involved in cases of serious delinquency, but this fact is not revealed in studies that concentrate upon research samples heavily larded with petty offenders.

Although existing sociological theories do not provide a single comprehensive explanation of delinquent behavior, significant gains have been made in the past decade or so. We know considerably more about the forces that lead to juvenile lawbreaking than was true a dozen or so years ago. Contemporary criminologists have provided a sound foundation of theory and research on which future generations of theorists and researchers can build.

REFERENCES

ADAMS, REED (1973). "Differential Association and Learning Principles Revisited," *Social Problems* 20 (Spring): 447-58.

AKERS, RONALD L. (1977). *Deviant Behavior: A Social Learning Approach.* 2nd edition. Belmont, Ca.: Wadsworth.

AKERS, RONALD L. (1981). "Reflections of a Social Behaviorist on Behavioral Sociology." *American Sociologist* 16 (August): 177-180.

AKERS, RONALD L. (1985). *Deviant Behavior: A Social Learning Approach.* 3rd edition. Belmont, Ca.: Wadsworth.

AKERS, RONALD L., KROHN, MARVIN D., LANZA-KADUCE, LONN, and RADOSEVICH, MARCIA J. (1979). "Social Learning and Deviant Behavior: A Specific Test of a General Theory." *American Sociological Review* 44 (August): 636-655.

ANDREWS, KENNETH H. and KANDEL, DENISE B. (1979). "Attitude and Behavior: A Specification of the Contingent Consistency Hypothesis." *American Sociological Review* 44 (April): 298-310.

BANDURA, ALBERT (1977). *Social Learning Theory.* Englewood Cliffs, N.J.: Prentice-Hall.

BORDUA, DAVID J. (1961). "Delinquent Subcultures: Sociological Interpretations of Gang Delinquency." *Annals of the American Academy of Political and Social Science* 338 (November): 119-136.

BURGESS, ROBERT L. and AKERS, RONALD L. (1966). "A Differential Association-Reinforcement Theory of Criminal Behavior." *Social Problems* 14 (Fall): 128-47.

CLOWARD, RICHARD A. and OHLIN, LLOYD E. (1960). *Delinquency and Opportunity.* New York: Free Press.

COHEN, ALBERT K. (1955). *Delinquent Boys.* New York: Free Press.

CONGER, RAND (1976). "Social Control and Social Learning Models of Delinquency: A Synthesis." *Criminology* 14 (May): 17-40.

CRESSEY, DONALD R. (1960). "Epidemiology and Individual Conduct: A Case from Criminology." *Pacific Sociological Review* 3 (Fall): 47-58.

DeFLEUR, MELVIN L. and QUINNEY, RICHARD (1966). "A Reformulation of Sutherland's Differential Association Theory and a Strategy for Empirical Verification." *Journal of Research in Crime and Delinquency* 3 (January): 1-22.

ELLIOTT, DELBERT S., AGETON, SUZANNE S., and CANTER, RACHELLE J. (1979). "An Integrated Theoretical Perspective on Delinquent Behavior." *Journal of Research in Crime and Delinquency* 16 (January): 3-27.

GINSBERG, IRVING J. and GREENLEY, JAMES R. (1978). "Competing Theories of Marijuana Use: A Longitudinal Study." *Journal of Health and Social Behavior* 19 (March): 22-34.

GLASER, DANIEL (1956). "Criminality Theories and Behavioral Images." *American Journal of Sociology* 61 (March): 433-44.

GUSFIELD, JOSEPH R. (1963). *Symbolic Crusade: Status Politics and the American Temperance Movement.* Urbana: University of Illinois Press.

HARRINGTON, MICHAEL (1962). *The Other America.* New York: Macmillan.

HEPBURN, JOHN R. (1976). "Testing Alternative Models of Delinquency Causation." *Journal of Criminal Law and Criminology* 67 (December): 450-60.

HUBA, GEORGE J. and BENTLER, PETER M. (1983). "Causal Models of the Development of Law Abidance and Its Relationship to Psychosocial Factors and Drug Use," pp. 165-215. In William S. Laufer and James M. Day, eds. *Personality Theory, Moral Development and Criminal Behavior.* Lexington, Mass.: Heath.

JEFFREY, C. RAY (1965). "Criminal Behavior and Learning Theory." *Journal of Criminal Law, Criminology and Police Science* 56 (September): 299-300.

JENSEN, GARY F. (1972). "Parents, Peers and Delinquent Action: A Test of the Differential Association Perspective." *American Journal of Sociology* 78 (November): 63-72.

JESSOR, RICHARD and JESSOR, SHIRLEY L. (1977). *Problem Behavior and Psychological Development.* New York: Academic Press.

JOHNSON, RICHARD E. (1979). *Juvenile Delinquency and Its Origins.* Cambridge: Cambridge University Press.

KANDEL, DENISE (1973). "Adolescent Marijuana Use: Role of Parents and Peers." *Science* 1981 (September): 1067-70.

KANDEL, DENISE (1978). "Convergence in Prospective Longitudinal Surveys of Drug Use in Normal Populations," pp. 3-38. In D. B. Kandel, ed. *Longitudinal Research on Drug Use.* New York, N.Y.: Wiley.

KORNHAUSER, RUTH ROSNER (1978). *Social Sources of Delinquency.* Chicago: University of Chicago Press.

KROHN, MARVIN D. (1974). "An Investigation of the Effect of Parental and Peer Associations on Marijuana Use: Am Empirical Test of Differential Association Theory." pp. 75-89. In Marc Reidel and Terence Thornberry, eds. *Crime and Delinquency: Dimensions of Deviance.* New York: Praeger.

KROHN, MARVIN D., SKINNER, WILLIAM F., MASSEY, JAMES L., and AKERS, RONALD L. (1983). "A Longitudinal Examination of Social Learning Theory as Applied to Adolescent Cigarette Smoking." Presented at the annual meeting of the American Society of Criminology, Denver, Colorado.

KVARACEUS, WILLIAM and MILLER, WALTER B. (1959). *Delinquent Behavior: Culture and the Individual.* Washington, D.C.: National Education Association.

LANZA-KADUCE, LONN, AKERS, RONALD L., KROHN, MARVIN D., and RADOSEVICH, MARCIA J. (1982). "Conceptual and Analytical Models in Testing Social Learning Theory." *American Sociological Review* 47 (February): 169-73.

LISKA, ALAN E. (1969). "Uses and Misuses of Tautologies in Social Psychology." *Sociometry* 32 (December): 444-57.

MASSEY, JAMES L. and KROHN, MARVIN D. (1984). "A Longitudinal Examination of an Integrated Social Process Model of Deviant Behavior." Presented at the annual meeting of the American Society of Criminology, Cincinnati, Ohio.

MATSUEDA, ROSS L. (1982). "Testing Control Theory and Differential Association: A Causal Modeling Approach." *American Sociological Review* 47 (August): 489-504.

MATTHEWS, VICTOR M. (1968). "Differential Identification: An Empirical Note." *Social Problems* 15 (Winter): 376-83.

MATZA, DAVID (1969). *Becoming Deviant.* Englewood Cliffs, N.J.: Prentice-Hall.

MILLER, WALTER B. (1958). "Lower-class Culture as a Generating Milieu of Gang Delinquency." *Journal of Social Issues* 14 (3): 5-19.

ORCUTT, JAMES D. (1983). *Analyzing Deviance.* Homewood, Ill: Dorsey.

RECKLESS, WALTER C. (1973). *The Crime Problem.* 5th edition. Santa Monica: Goodyear.

REISS, ALBERT J., JR., and RHODES, ALBERT LEWIS (1964). "An Empirical Test of Differential Association Theory." *Journal of Research in Crime and Delinquency* 1 (January): 5-18.

RODMAN, HYMAN (1963). "The Lower-class Value Stretch." *Social Forces* 42 (December): 205-15.

SELLIN, THORSTEN (1938). *Culture Conflict and Crime.* New York: Social Science Research Council.

SHORT, JAMES F., JR. (1957). "Differential Association and Delinquency." *Social Problems* 4 (January): 233-39.

SHORT, JAMES F., JR. and STRODTBECK, FRED L. (1965). *Group Process and Gang Delinquency.* Chicago: University of Chicago Press.

SKINNER, B. F. (1938). *The Behavior of Organisms.* New York: Appleton-Century-Crofts.

STAATS, A. W. (1975). *Social Behaviorism.* Homewood, Ill: Dorsey.

STAFFORD, MARK C. and ECKLAND-OLSEN, SHELDON (1982). "On Social Learning and Deviant Behavior: A Reappraisal of the Findings." *American Sociological Review* 47 (February): 167-69.

STANFIELD, ROBERT E. (1966). "The Interaction of Family Variables and Gang Variables in the Etiology of Delinquency." *Social Problems* 13 (Spring): 411-17.

STRICKLAND, DONALD E. (1982). "Social Learning and Deviant Behavior: A Comment and a Critique." *American Sociological Review* 47 (February): 162–67.

SUTHERLAND, EDWIN H. (1924). *Principles of Criminology*. Philadelphia: Lippincott.

SUTHERLAND, EDWIN H. (1934). *Principles of Criminology*. 2nd edition. Philadelphia: Lippincott.

SUTHERLAND, EDWIN H. and CRESSEY, DONALD R. (1978). *Criminology*. 10th edition. Philadelphia: Lippincott.

SYKES, GRESHAM and MATZA, DAVID (1957). "Techniques of Neutralization: A Theory of Delinquency." *American Sociological Review* 24 (December): 97–114.

TAYLOR, IAN, WALTON, PAUL, and YOUNG, JOCK (1973). *The New Criminology*. New York: Harper and Row.

THOMAS, WILLIAM I. (1923). *The Unadjusted Girl*. Boston: Little, Brown.

VOSS, HARWIN (1964). "Differential Association and Reported Delinquent Behavior: A Replication." *Social Problems* 12 (Summer): 78–85.

chapter 10

BIOLOGICAL AND PSYCHOLOGICAL PERSPECTIVES ON DELINQUENCY

INTRODUCTION

This chapter deals with biological and psychological arguments regarding delinquency. Like other American sociologists, American criminologists have exhibited a general distaste for biological accounts of human behavior. But, even though sociologists generally find biogenic arguments about delinquency and criminality to be unpalatable, there is evidence at hand which suggests that biological hypotheses may have some merit (Shah and Roth, 1974). Accordingly, we cannot simply declare that biological explanations are invalid. Sociologists have also been unenthusiastic about explanations centering on alleged mental pathology on the part of juvenile and adult offenders. Even so, these are viewpoints which have many supporters and which need to be carefully examined.

BIOGENIC VIEWS OF DELINQUENCY

Biogenic accounts of criminality and delinquency can be traced back to the work of Lombroso, who claimed that many offenders are atavists or biological throwbacks that he termed *homo delinquens*. Later, efforts were made to show that lawbreakers are biologically inferior, feeble-minded, or, frequently, persons of mesomorphic or muscular somatotype or bodily build (Sheldon, Hartl, and McDermott, 1949; Glueck and Glueck, 1956; Cortés and Gatti, 1972).

The many years of biogenic exploration of delinquency have not produced valid generalizations about biological factors in deviance. Almost without exception, the biological theories that were advanced in the nineteenth and early twentieth centuries were scientifically naive, while the research was flawed in one way or another. For reasons of this kind, and equally because biogenic hypotheses run counter to the theoretical preferences of sociological criminologists, biological hypotheses have been out of popularity with those persons.

While most of the biogenic theorizing and research inquiry until recently has been markedly defective in one way or another, it would be a mistake to conclude, as some have done, that biological hypotheses can safely be ignored in the search for etiological understanding. A careful reading of the evidence suggests, instead, that the last word may not have been heard on biological forces in human behavior and that this question remains open for further examination.

Indeed, admonitions by sociologists regarding the need to "bring beasts back in" (Van den Berghe, 1974) have been followed by new efforts to uncover biosocial processes in human behavior (Wilson, 1975). It should be noted that modern work on biogenic factors stresses the *biosocial* nature of human behavior. Contemporary arguments on the question of biological factors in human behavior, including deviant conduct, are much more in tune with current thinking in such fields as biology and human genetics in which it is argued that human behavior is influenced by *interactions* between biological and genetic factors on the one hand, and social experiences on the other. The crude biological determinism claims of an earlier generation of criminologists have been supplanted by biosocial hypotheses which are addressed to the interplay of biological and environmental factors (Rowe and Osgood, 1984).

Consider the investigations of bodily structure among delinquents. The Gluecks (1956) found that mesomorphs (boys with athletic, muscular body type) were more frequent among the offenders they studied than among the nonoffenders. Mesomorphic structure characterized 60.1 percent of the lawbreakers, but only 30.7 percent of the nondelinquents. These findings were the result of careful measurement; thus there is little question about their accuracy. However, a process of social selection joined to biological differences rather than biological determinism explains the results. In other words, it is likely that recruits to delinquent conduct are drawn from the group of more agile, physically fit boys, just as Little League baseball or Pop Warner League football players tend toward mesomorphy. Fat delinquents and fat ballplayers are uncommon because social behavior involved in these cases puts fat, skinny, or sickly boys at a disadvantage. But while social selection is involved in these instances, we should not lose sight of the equally important fact that biological differences are the bases upon which this selection operates. Even though social selection can be invoked to account for mesomorphic delinquents and mesomorphic football players, the biological element in this sorting process does not vanish as a consequence. Stated another way, social scientists would be compelled to take cognizance of an important biological factor if a number of research efforts were to turn up consistent evidence of mesomorphy among law-breakers.

In another more recent essay, Hirschi and Hindelang (1977) have contributed to the renewed dialogue on biologically related factors in lawbreaking through their detailed review of the research evidence on delinquency and intelligence. They showed that intelligence is strongly related to delinquency, probably because of its effects on school performance. Youths with lower IQs who do poorly in school become engaged in juvenile misconduct. Scott Menard and Barbara Morse (1984) have conducted research on this issue which indicates that it is not IQ per se which operates causally to produce delinquency; rather, it is because in many school settings, measured intelligence is employed as a basis for differential treatment of youngsters. Those youths who become selected out for placement in vocational rather than academic educational tracks and who are negatively labeled in other ways due to their intelligence scores are pushed in the direction of involvement in misbehavior. The facts seem clear that intelligence is an extremely important variable that differentiates juvenile offenders, particularly officially processed youths, from nondelinquents, in spite of much "sociological wisdom" to the contrary. What is less clear regarding these findings is the extent to which measured intelligence is itself a social product arising from subcultural variations in learning environments and other social factors of that kind, rather than an index of innate intelligence.

There is other evidence indicating that we need to keep an open mind on the issue of biological factors in delinquency and criminality. In particular, Lee Ellis (1982) has examined the research findings on genetic influences in criminality, within a causal framework that assumes that genetic factors and social-environmental ones interact to affect central nervous system functioning, which in turn heavily influences behavior, both delinquent and nondelinquent. Ellis grouped a large number of studies into pedigree or family tree investigations, twin studies, karyotype or chromosomal inquiries, and adoption studies, and subjected them to detailed scrutiny.

According to Ellis, pedigree or family tree studies that trace the number of lawbreakers within a particular family are weak methodologically, and thus little can be concluded from them. On the other hand, investigations of identical and fraternal twins represent a stronger methodological approach. Ellis identified twelve twin studies that showed greater concordance or similarity of behavior among identical as opposed to fraternal twins, which is evidence in favor of genetic arguments in that identical twins share the same hereditary makeup whereas fraternal twins do not. However, as Ellis acknowledged, it may also be the case that identical twins are more often responded to more uniformly by others, which might be principally responsible for their similar behavior.

Karyotype studies explore variations in chromosomal patterns among persons, that is, variations in size, length, and number of chromosomes. According to Ellis, a number of investigations of males with the XYY or extra male chromosome pattern who have been compared with males with the more normal XY pattern have shown the former to be more often involved in criminality, apparently due to the lower IQs which are frequent among them. Finally, the logic of adoption studies is that if genetic influences operate in behavior, persons who have been adopted shortly after birth should resemble their genetic parents in behavior more closely than they do their adopted ones. Ellis noted that there is some supporting evidence for this line of argument as applied to criminality. His conclusion from this detailed and sophisticated review was that (Ellis, 1982: 43): "Among the fairly definitive types of studies, most of the evidence is extremely supportive of the proposition that human variation in tendencies to commit criminal behavior is significantly affected by some genetic factors."

PSYCHOGENIC THEORIES OF DELINQUENCY

Introduction

The central hypothesis guiding psychogenic investigation is that the critical causal factors in delinquency are personality problems to which juvenile misbehavior is presumed to be a response. August Aichhorn, a pioneering figure in the development of this argument, asserted (1955: 30): "There must be something in the child himself which the environment brings out in the form of delinquency." Delinquents behave as they do because they are in some way sick, maladjusted, or pathological. Aichhorn's statement also indicates a second assumption of psychogenic perspectives: That the environment may function as a precipitating force, but never as a primary force in causation. This assumption has led many psychologists and psychiatrists to pay little or no attention to delinquency rates and patterns within the areas or communities where they have carried out their research. But as we shall see in succeeding sections of this discussion, different psychogenic statements accord varying weight to the influence of environmental pressures and thus give more or less attention to social or environmental factors.

Nearly all psychogenic arguments have been mute on the matter of *rates* of deviance. They contend that personality problems account for delinquent conduct, but they fail to tell why juvenile misbehavior is common in some places or areas and less common in others. Such matters as social class patterning of juvenile law-breaking are ignored in psychogenic theories.

Although the voices of psychogenic commentators by no means speak in unison about delinquency, three general positions can be discerned in the writings of psychiatrists, psychologists, and others of the psychogenic persuasion. First, the *psychoanalytic* position, one of these variants, extends the psychoanalytic theory developed by Freud to crime and delinquency (Gibbons, 1982: 166-69). Second, there is a host of more *general arguments* regarding juvenile misbehavior and personality dynamics which do not stem directly from psychoanalytic thought. A third argument links delinquency to a particular form of personality structure, *psychopathy* or *sociopathy*.

We need not devote much space to psychoanalytic writings on delinquency. For one thing, psychoanalytic theories involve contentions about the workings of instinctual sources of psychic energy, and these are incapable of empirical verification. These instinctual mainsprings of lawbreaking are said to be unconscious ones that the offenders are unaware of. Only a trained psychoanalyst is qualified to investigate these motivational forces; therefore other observers are unable to see them in operation. Second, psychoanalytic arguments about lawbreaking are relatively unfashionable at present. Just as psychoanalytic perspectives on other forms of human behavior have been modified in the light of recent developments in cultural and behavioral science, so have psychogenic theories of delinquency. Relatively few persons now espouse orthodox versions of the psychoanalytic view of delinquency which are complete with instincts, unconscious motivation, and other theoretical baggage.

Emotional Problems and Delinquency

Since 1900, psychiatrists and others have written much about personality problems, emotional disturbances, and delinquency, independent of Freudian psychoanalytic theory (Quay, 1965): The emotional dynamics that have been identified have been of many kinds, and the origins of these problems have been alleged to involve a large variety of background experiences, with particular emphasis upon parent-child tensions and distorted primary group relations.

The thesis that delinquency is due to emotional problems must be taken seriously. Countless numbers of persons have put this view forward and it has frequently been urged as the basis on which treatment ventures ought to proceed. Numerous correctional rehabilitation programs have been based upon the argument that delinquents are emotionally troubled individuals. Accordingly, we need to ask whether this brand of causal theorizing has any factual base.

Early Studies

Cyril Burt's (1938) claim that 85 percent of the offenders he studied prior to 1938 were emotionally impaired stands as an early example of the general personality problem view. Probably the most influential of the early studies of delinquency and emotional problems was the research of William Healy and Augusta Bronner (1936) which compared 105 delinquents with 105 of their nondelinquent siblings in New Haven, Boston, and Detroit. After examining these youngsters, the investigators concluded that (Healy and Bronner, 1936: 122): "It finally appears that no less than 91 percent of the delinquents gave clear evidence of being or having been unhappy and discontented in their life circumstances or extremely emotionally disturbed because of emotion-provoking situations or experiences. In great contradistinction we found similar evidence of inner stresses at the most in only 13 percent of the controls."

Although these seem to be impressive findings, this investigation received critical attention as well as acclaim (Hakeem, 1958). The critics noted that the differences between the offenders and nondelinquents were probably exaggerated, because the staff members who reported on personality characteristics of the subjects were psychiatrists and psychiatric social workers predisposed to the opinion that the major etiological variable in delinquency is emotional disturbance. Also, the clinical judgments were obtained by subjective methods; no effort was made to disguise the identities of the subjects prior to the psychiatric examinations. The assessments may have been biased by the knowledge of the delinquent-nondelinquent status of the subjects. Additionally, the psychiatric workers were conducting a treatment program for the offenders and were in greater contact with them than with the nonoffenders. If they had spent an equal amount of time with the nonoffenders, would they have observed emotional problems which they originally overlooked? The critics have constructed such a damaging case against the Healy and Bronner study that its findings cannot be accepted as valid. Other research results give only partial support at best to these psychogenic contentions.

Proponents of psychogenic arguments must also contend with the findings of Karl Schuessler and Donald Cressey (1950), who reviewed many studies of personality characteristics of delinquents and criminals. They concluded that "of 113 such comparisons, 42 percent showed differences in favor of the noncriminal, while the remainder were indeterminate. The doubtful validity of many of the obtained differences, as well as the lack of consistency in the combined results, makes it impossible to conclude from these data that criminality and personality elements are associated." This survey of psychogenic studies was updated when Gordon Waldo and Simon Dinitz (1967) examined a large number of investigations conducted between 1950 and 1965. After carefully assessing the results of these inquiries, they concluded that no marked relationships between personality elements and delinquency were reflected in them. However, the research investigations examined by Schuessler and Cressey and by Waldo and Dinitz all concerned heterogeneous samples of offenders and nondelinquents. No effort was made to discover personality dimensions among offender types within the population of delinquents.

Some Other Studies

Michael Hakeem (1958) has reviewed findings from surveys of emotional disturbance among cases from an adolescents' court, a psychiatric clinic affiliated with a juvenile court, and a juvenile training school. The results show a diversity of diagnostic decisions in each of the investigations. One set of diagnostic labels categorized a number of offenders as suffering from psychoneurosis or neurotic character disturbances, while in the other two studies this category did not appear. Immaturity and mental conflict turned up in one report, but not in the others. Additionally, the three investigations, although handling comparable diagnostic groups, tabulated diverse proportions of delinquents. Hakeem therefore concluded that the results probably tell more about the biases of the psychiatrists than about characteristics of offenders. Also, some of the diagnostic categories in these three studies were of dubious validity. For instance, one study diagnosed about one-third of the cases as "conduct disorders." Were any identifiable characteristics of offenders apart from

Biological and Psychological Perspectives on Delinquency 177

the facts of involvement in misconduct used to recognize conduct disorders? It is quite likely that a tautological classification was involved, in which the delinquent activity of the juvenile was used to indicate the existence of a conduct disorder. If so, conduct disorder explains nothing.

One of the studies Hakeem discussed was the famous investigation of the Gluecks, *Unraveling Juvenile Delinquency* (1950). The offenders and controls in that study were given a psychiatric interview and Rorschach tests, a projective instrument designed to measure basic personality traits. The Gluecks reported that the delinquents were more socially assertive, defiant, and ambivalent to authority than were the nondelinquents. Also, they were more resentful of others, more hostile, more impulsive and vivacious, and more extroversive than the nonoffenders. A number of characteristics identified through the Rorschach tests as more common among delinquents were not clearly signs of maladjustment. Assertiveness, impulsiveness, and vivacity could indeed be argued as indicators that the delinquents were better adjusted than the nonoffenders.

Psychiatric diagnoses of the lawbreakers and the nondelinquent controls brought out several points. First, the differences between the two groups were not striking; about half of both groups showed no conspicuous mental pathology. Second, the delinquents classified as showing mental deviations exhibited a variety of disorders, while the disturbed nonoffenders were predominately neurotic or showing neurotic trends. This finding varies from many psychogenic arguments in the criminological literature which contend that delinquency is a form of neurotic, acting-out behavior.

Another body of research data involved studies using the Minnesota Multiphasic Personality Inventory (Hathaway and Monachesi, 1953). The MMPI includes eight scales in each of which certain responses to items are diagnostic of particular personality patterns. For example, persons with high scale points on the Pa, paranoia scale, give responses similar to those of individuals clinically diagnosed as suffering from paranoia.

One piece of research using this inventory involved its application to over 4000 Minneapolis ninth-grade students during 1948. In 1950, the same youngsters were traced through the Hennepin County Juvenile Court and the Minneapolis Police Department to determine which had acquired records of misconduct. Of the boys, 22.2 percent had become delinquent, while 7.6 percent of the girls had become known to the court or police. In examining the responses of delinquents and nonoffenders, the investigators found such results as these: 27.7 percent of the boys who had high Pd (psychopathic deviate) scale scores were delinquent, as were 25.4 percent of those with high Pa (paranoia) scale scores. Of the boys with "invalid" responses, indicating uncooperativeness, lying, and so on, 37.5 percent were offenders. Thus, delinquent boys tended to show disproportionate numbers in some of the scale areas of the MMPI, while substantially parallel results were noted with girls. More recent studies using the MMPI have turned up similar results (Rathus and Siegel, 1980).

Starke Hathaway and Elio Monachesi were modest in the claims they made on the basis of these data. In the main, they argued only that the inventory possesses some discriminatory power. Nonetheless, critics have noted the problems of inter-pretation involved in the variability of results, and have pointed out that a number of social factors correlate more highly with delinquency than do MMPI scores (Schrag, 1954; Waldo and Dinitz, 1967; Fisher, 1962).

John Conger and Wilbur Miller (1966) have engaged in an important inquiry into personality disturbances and delinquency. Their investigation involved samples from among the 2348 tenth-grade students in Denver in 1956. One sample involved all of the youngsters (271, or less than 15 percent of the total) who had become known to the juvenile court in that city. The other sample consisted of nondelin-quent youngsters who were matched with the offenders by age, socioeconomic status, IQ, school environment, and ethnic group.

Conger and Miller were able to conduct a longitudinal investigation of per-sonality dynamics and delinquency through the use of the youths' school records, which included teacher comments, ratings of personal-social development, and the like. The boys were also subjected to an eclectic assortment of personality tests at the end of ninth grade. These tests were designed to uncover personality variations which fall short of marked psychological pathology. They measured such things as impulsiveness, sociability, friendliness, closeness of interpersonal relationships, and dimensions of that kind.

In general, the researchers discovered that as early as the third grade, the fu-ture delinquents were seen by their teachers as less well-adjusted than their class-mates. The teachers regarded their social behavior as unacceptable and found the boys lacking in dependability, friendliness, fairness, and other such attributes. These differences persisted through the ninth grade, for the future lawbreakers con-tinued to be poorly regarded by their teachers.

The results of the psychological testing pointed in the same direction. The de-linquents, as a group, were more immature, egocentric, inconsiderate, impulsive, suspicious, and hostile than the nonoffenders. Interestingly, the offenders tended to view themselves in ways similar to the opinions held of them by their teachers.

These findings indicated first that the personality problems reported by teachers or in personality tests were of a relatively bland, less serious form than the psychological problems which are hypothesized in many psychogenic theories of delinquency. Second, the Conger and Miller data unquestionably showed that offi-cial delinquents were less well-adjusted than their nondeviant peers.

The consistency of teacher ratings of the boys over a period of time warrants special mention. The investigators assumed that these reports were accurate reflec-tions of the real behavior of the boys. However, many students of societal reaction experiences in deviant behavior would suggest that the processes through which cumulative biographies of boys are constructed by school teachers ought to be studied in detail. There is more than a slight possibility that once a boy gets pointed out as a "bad one," tough guy, or troublemaker in school records, subsequent reac-tions of teachers become heavily colored by this initial judgment. Then, too, the offender's own self-attitudes and views of others may be influenced by his perception of their opinion of him. If so, much of the hostility and defiance that later shows up in personality tests could be a product of these experiences.

The results of this study are not at odds with sociological theories. A number of theoretical statements by sociologists hold that delinquent conduct is a response to adjustment problems of various kinds which stem from school experiences, neighborhood influences, and other pressures. Sociologists have often pictured the delinquent as an individual with a relatively cynical and bleak outlook on life. The criticism of psychogenic formulations by sociologists has been pointed at those extremes which claim that most offenders are markedly maladjusted individuals, not at results such as those of the Conger and Miller study.

One more work on personality characteristics of delinquents comes from the Jesness Inventory (Jesness, 1963). This instrument, developed in the California correctional system, involves eight scales and a delinquency prediction score. The eight scales measure defensiveness, value orientation, neuroticism, authority attitude, family orientation, psychoticism, delinquency orientation, and emotional immaturity. Findings from the development and validation studies of this inventory indicated that offenders and nondelinquents did not differ significantly in defensiveness, value orientation, neuroticism, or family orientation. The two groups did vary on authority attitudes, delinquents exhibiting greater hostility toward authority figures. They also differed on psychoticism; the offenders were more suspicious and distrustful of other persons. Additionally, the offenders were differentiated from the nondelinquents on two empirical scales: delinquency orientation and emotional immaturity. Compared to nonoffenders, institutionalized delinquents were more concerned about being normal, showed more marked feelings of isolation, were less mature, lacked insight, and tended to deny that they had problems. The delinquency proneness prediction scales, built up from items in the separate scales, differentiated the two groups with some overlapping. Some nondelinquents had scores predictive of delinquency proneness, while some offenders had scores indicative of nondelinquency.

Two interpretations of these results are possible. Perhaps personality problems impelled the *institutionalized* delinquents toward deviance. But it is also possible that the attitudes discovered by Jesness were the *result* of involvement in misconduct. Perhaps the experiences of being tagged as a delinquent and being processed in the correctional machinery were the sources of the bleak and hostile outlooks of the lawbreakers. Surely it would be a surprise if we discovered that institutionalized delinquents have warm and friendly attitudes toward their jailers.

Interpersonal Maturity Levels Theory

The Interpersonal Maturity Levels (I-Levels) system developed in the juvenile correctional system in California is a case of psychogenic theorizing that merits special attention (Warren, 1976). Unlike most of the psychogenic work cited previously, this argument has actually been utilized as the theoretical foundation for correctional intervention endeavors. Treatment of juvenile offenders has been based on the contentions advanced in I-Levels theory.

The I-Levels socialization argument stresses that human development proceeds through a series of seven stages from neonatal dependence and nonhuman characteristics to adult maturity, interpersonal competence, and role-taking ability. At all seven stages there is a basic core structure of personality around which the individual's behavior revolves and which heavily influences his responses. Although there are seven stages or levels of interpersonal maturity through which persons move as they become socialized, not all individuals reach the highest levels of interpersonal competence or maturity; thus some remain fixated at a lower level of development. The architects of the I-Levels formulation implied that delinquents are generally at lower or less developed levels of maturity as contrasted to nondelinquents.[1] In this scheme, delinquents are assigned to maturity levels 2, 3, or 4, rather than to higher levels of personality development.

The I-Levels scheme further classifies juvenile lawbreakers into nine subtypes within the three main interpersonal maturity levels. For each diagnostic type, the scheme specifies different patterns of treatment, carried on by different kinds of treatment agents. In short, this is a highly clinical model of delinquency and treatment intervention.

A brief summary of the interpersonal maturity levels into which delinquents are alleged to fall, along with the subtypes within these levels, indicates[2] :

> *Maturity Level 2 (I_2)*. The individual whose interpersonal understanding and behavior are integrated at this level is primarily involved with demands that the world take care of him. He sees others primarily as givers or with-

[1] On this point, Warren has argued that the I-Levels theory is not a causal theory of delinquency and that it is not claimed that delinquents differ from nondelinquents in interpersonal maturity (personal communication). Also, Warren has noted (1976: 180): "No assumption is made that delinquents will fall at a particular stage; rather it is assumed that individual delinquents will be found at a number of points along the continuum, as would the individuals of any other population. The point is not that individuals are delinquent because they are immature, but rather that one would know something about the meaning of an individual's delinquency, as well as the nature of the intervention strategies required, if the individual's maturity level is identified."

Several comments are in order regarding I-Levels and causal theory. First, it seems highly likely that many persons interpret the argument as holding that delinquents are interpersonally less mature than nonoffenders and that lawbreaking is related to immaturity, in spite of the contrary contentions of Warren. Second, as a matter of fact, the I-Levels formulation assigns delinquents only to three low maturity classifications, which further implies that immaturity separates offenders from law-abiding juveniles. Finally, the remarks of Warren noted above would not seem to make sense unless it were assumed that delinquents are less mature than nondelinquents. If interpersonal maturity does not differentiate the two groups, how could knowledge of the delinquent's maturity level provide clues as to the nature or meaning of his or her delinquency or as to the type of treatment intervention needed?

[2] Some sense of the full theory of I-Levels can be gained from examination of the complete set of seven levels of development. These levels, identified in terms of the problem of interpersonal development that must be solved at each level, are: (1) the integration of separateness; (2) the integration of nonself differences; (3) the integration of rules; (4) the integration of conflict and response; (5) the integration of continuity; (6) the integration of self-consistency; and (7) the integration of relativity, movement, and change.

holders and has no conception of interpersonal refinement beyond this. He has poor capacity to explain, understand, or predict the behavior or reactions of others. He is not interested in things outside himself except as a source of supply. He behaves impulsively, unaware of anything except the grossest effect of his behavior on others.

Subtypes: (1) *Asocial, Aggressive* responds with active demands and open hostility when frustrated. (2) *Asocial, Passive* responds with whining, complaining, and withdrawal when frustrated.

Maturity Level 3 (I_3). The individual who is functioning at this level, although somewhat more differentiated than the I_2, still has social-perceptual deficiencies which lead to an underestimation of the differences among others and between himself and others. More than the I_2, he does understand that his own behavior has something to do with whether or not he gets what he wants. He makes an effort to manipulate his environment to bring about giving rather than denying responses. He does not operate from an internalized value system but rather seeks external structure in terms of rules and formulas for operation. His understanding of formulas is indiscriminate and oversimplified. He perceives the world and his part in it on a power dimension. Although he can learn to play a few stereotyped roles, he cannot understand many of the needs, feelings, and motives of another person who is different from himself. He is unmotivated to achieve in a long-range sense or to plan for his future. Many of these features contribute to his inability to accurately predict the response of others to him.

Subtypes: (3) *Immature Conformist* responds with immediate compliance to whoever seems to have the power at the moment. (4) *Cultural Conformist* responds with conformity to specific reference-group delinquent peers. (5) *Manipulator* operates by attempting to undermine the power of authority figures and/or to usurp the power role for himself.

Maturity Level 4 (I_4). An individual whose understanding and behavior are integrated at this level has internalized a set of standards by which he judges his and others' behavior. He can perceive a level of interpersonal interaction in which individuals have expectations of each other and can influence each other. He shows some ability to understand reasons for behavior, some ability to relate to people emotionally and on a long-term basis. He is concerned about status and respect, and is strongly influenced by people he admires.

Subtypes: (6) *Neurotic, Acting-out* responds to underlying guilt which attempts to outrun conscious anxiety and condemnation of self. (7) *Neurotic, Anxious* responds with symptoms of emotional disturbance to conflict produced by feelings of inadequacy and guilt. (8) *Situational Emotional Reaction* responds to immediate family or personal crisis by acting-out. (9) *Cultural Identifier* responds to identification with a deviant value system by living out his delinquent beliefs.

The basic argument that individuals progress through stages of interpersonal development is not at issue. That claim is consistent with a mass of social-psychological evidence indicating that socialization is a process of cumulative growth of interpersonal competence. However, critics have singled out a number of other problems with this argument (Gibbons, 1970; Beker and Heyman, 1972). What is at issue is that portion of the I-Levels formulation that contends that juvenile lawbreakers are less mature than youthful conformists (see fn. 1). This is an untested assumption, for no one has subjected the argument to research in order to discover whether delinquents truly are more immature than nondelinquents. No research efforts have been made to determine the distribution of maturity levels among non-offenders. However, the research data on personality characteristics of offenders already examined in this chapter are tangentially related to this core proposition of I-Levels theory. Those data do not provide much support for the view that delinquents are markedly immature.

The diagnostic procedures through which youths are assigned to I-Levels are relatively subjective, so that the accuracy of the diagnostic assignments is questionable. At least two efforts have been made to verify, through the use of objective measuring instruments, the interpersonal maturity level categorizations in which juvenile wards have been placed. In the case of the Butler and Adams (1966) study, the researchers did not find that personality inventory scores of delinquent girls correlated with their I-Levels diagnoses. Similarly, Austin (1975) reported that boys in a California state training school who had been sorted into I-Levels categories through clinical interviews did not turn out to vary in interpersonal maturity as measured by personality tests. Instead, those who had been diagnosed as least mature were younger and less sophisticated about moral issues than were boys who had been classified as more mature.

Psychopathy and Delinquency

One popular psychogenic hypothesis argues that many delinquents (and criminals) exhibit a particular form of mental pathology: psychopathic personality (or sociopathic personality). The term *psychopath* is usually employed to designate a pattern of pathology characterized by egocentricity, asocial behavior, insensitivity to others, and hostility. Actually, the designation is only one of a number of synonymous terms employed, including *psychopathic personality, constitutional psychopathic inferior, moral imbecile, semantic dementia, sociopathy,* and *moral mania.*

If such a personality pattern exists, it might bear more than a slight relationship to delinquency, for persons showing these traits might be less governed by the demands of society because they are lacking in inner controls and are insensitive to contemporary conduct norms. But if we are to make any use of the concept of psychopathy, we must first develop some means by which to recognize psychopaths. Here is where the trouble begins—the concept has not been defined in a satisfactory manner. Most of the definitions indicate a rather general and unspecific form of behavior.

Even though the notion of psychopathy is extremely ambiguous, a number of authorities have asserted that sociopaths exist and that they appear in the population of delinquents in inordinate numbers. But in none of these cases is any indication given of the presence of such personality problems in the population at large or in the population of offenders.

However, there is one important study of the psychopathy question which deserves attention. Lee Robins (1966) traced the adult adjustments of 524 child guidance clinic patients in St. Louis 30 years after they had been treated at the clinic. A comparison group of 100 normal school children were similarly subjected to a follow-up study. Most of the guidance clinic juveniles had been sent to the clinic by the juvenile court; over 70 percent had been referred for "antisocial conduct," i.e., runaway behavior, truancy, and theft. The investigators managed to obtain interviews concerning 82 percent of those individuals who had lived to the age of 25, either with the subjects or with their relatives.

The clinic patients who had been referred for antisocial conduct showed adult careers filled with frequent arrests for criminality and drunkenness, numerous divorces, occupational instability, psychiatric problems, and dependency on social agencies. For example, 44 percent of the antisocial male patients had been arrested for a major crime, while only 3 percent of the control group had serious criminal records. In short, the clinic subjects generally exhibited ruined adult lives.

A major part of Robin's research concerned the detailed study of sociopathic personality among the subjects. Sociopaths were defined as persons who exhibited *"a gross, repetitive failure to conform to societal norms in many areas of life, in the absence of thought disturbance suggesting psychosis"* (Robins, 1966: 79, emphasis in the original). The diagnosis of sociopathic personality was made in terms of adult behavior patterns. To be judged a sociopath, an individual had to exhibit symptoms of maladjustment within at least five of nineteen life areas; that is, he had to show some combination of poor work history, financial dependency, use of drugs, sexual misconduct, and so on. The final determination that a subject was a sociopath rested with two psychiatrists who made clinical judgments from interview material. In all, 22 percent of the clinic subjects and 2 percent of the controls were designated as sociopaths. The clinic cases that were diagnosed as sociopaths had been referred almost exclusively for antisocial behavior, particularly theft.

Robins asserted that there is some kind of disease or personality entity behind the symptoms which produces sociopaths, but no convincing evidence of this elusive disease appeared in this report. Instead, the argument looks tautological in form. While the report showed that many youngsters who got into juvenile courts and guidance clinics lived fairly disordered lives as adults, making a career of failure, there was little evidence that these individuals were pathological personalities. Indeed, some of the findings tended to undermine the sociopath concept. For example, the data suggested that those antisocial children who avoided the juvenile court or training school were less likely to become sociopaths than those who had been through these organizations. Is it perhaps the crude machinery of these agencies, rather than psychopathy, which contributes to adult misfortune and wrecked lives? About a third of the sociopaths were judged to have given up much of their deviant activity by the time of the follow-up investigation. Since sociopaths are supposed to be especially intractable, how did these people escape from deviance?

We regard any attempt to proceed further with the psychopathy-delinquency line of inquiry, as presently framed, a futile business. We cannot now answer questions about the relationship of delinquency and sociopathy in the terms in which they are bound.

An Evaluation of Psychogenic Hypotheses

What are we to make of all this material on psychogenic factors in delinquency? Our analysis has rejected psychoanalytic claims and notions about psychopathy as untestable. Viewpoints which are incapable of empirical verification have no place in theories of delinquency causation. We have also seen that those contentions that delinquents are characterized by gross psychological pathology do not square with the facts. The mass of studies which have searched for these severe emotional disturbances have failed to find them. In short, it appears that delinquents are no more or less ridden with personality pathology than are nonoffenders.

Consider those findings which indicate that institutionalized delinquents or court referrals are more hostile or defiant than nondelinquents. We have suggested that one plausible interpretation of these results is that they may reflect the effects of court appearance or institutionalization. These attitudes may not have preceded involvement in misconduct. A frequent outcome of experience with correctional agencies may be some deterioration of the actor's self-image as he or she takes on some of the invidious identity imputed to him or her by correctional agents and society. Studies usually argue that emotional factors produce deviance, and do not as frequently entertain the reverse possibility. There is, however, a case to be made for the hypothesis that contacts with the "defining agencies"—the social control organizations—contribute to the development of deviant personalities or role-conceptions (Foster, Dinitz, and Reckless, 1972; Mahoney, 1974).

However, it may be the case that personality factors of a nonpathological form do operate in delinquency in a more directly causal fashion. Some of the studies examined previously, such as the Conger and Miller research, compel us to acknowledge the possibility that youngsters who get involved in delinquency commonly feel powerless in their social surroundings, alienated, hostile, bored with school, or have other feelings of personal inadequacy. Moreover we have already observed that such a line of argument is compatible with sociological formulations which stress the adverse effects of social circumstances upon juveniles.

This line of thinking suggests that careful theorizing is in order regarding the operation of psychological pressures in delinquency. We need to discontinue the fact-gathering sorties that have been all too common, and turn to research which is designed to test explicit hypotheses concerning postulated relationships between particular psychological patterns, social influences, and delinquent behavior.

One model of the sort of theory and research that needs to be developed is found in the pioneering work done by Richard L. Jenkins and Lester Hewitt (1944). They advanced the argument that there are two common forms of misbehavior: adaptive and maladaptive delinquency. They suggested that only the maladaptive or unsocialized offender has a disturbed personality. This is the aggressive lawbreaker who is poorly socialized, lacking in internalized controls, antagonistic toward his peers, and generally maladjusted. By contrast, the more frequently encountered adaptive or pseudosocial offender, who is usually the product of lower-class slum areas, is reasonably well socialized and psychologically normal. And, as we shall see shortly, the research conducted by these two investigators supported this argument.

"BEHAVIOR PROBLEM" DELINQUENCY

To this point, this chapter has examined the broad proposition that juvenile offenders are commonly plagued by emotional problems and other psychological difficulties to which their deviant acts are a response. But the conclusion seems warranted that even when attention is restricted to juvenile offenders who have become the subjects of official handling, little support for this argument is evident. Juvenile court referrals, probationers, or training school wards do not appear to differ much in psychological well-being from nonoffenders. When psychogenic claims are examined against broader samples of offenders which include hidden delinquents, these assertions are weakened further. The self-report studies show that many of the youths who are usually included as nondelinquents in the customary comparisons with official delinquents have actually been involved in misconduct. If these youngsters were counted as delinquents, their numbers would further inflate the group of normal, psychologically healthy offenders.

Taken en masse, it is clear that while juvenile lawbreakers are sometimes hostile, defiant, and suspicious individuals, they are not markedly different from nonoffenders in terms of psychological adjustment. The psychiatrist's claim that most delinquents are motivated by aberrant urges is unequivocally erroneous. Yet, at the same time, most of us are unwilling to completely reject the possibility that the population of youthful offenders does contain some psychologically disturbed individuals. Even though the broad psychogenic position that most juvenile lawbreakers are psychologically disturbed must be rejected, this does not necessarily mean that there are no atypical, emotionally troubled youths who become involved in misconduct.

One currently popular thesis about psychological maladjustment and delinquency centers about hyperactivity (Conrad and Schneider, 1980: 155-61). Hyperactive youngsters are defined as persons who show excessive activity levels, aggressiveness, poor control over their behavior, and the like. One currently fashionable argument is a biopsychological one, linking hyperactivity to food additives, principally salicylates and food coloring. However, the supporting evidence for this contention is slight, at best (Conners, 1980). Some research has also been conducted on hyperactive and normal youngsters which appears to show that the former engage in more substance abuse and antisocial behavior than do the normal youths (Hechtman, Weiss, and Perlman, 1984). Finally, other research efforts have been made to isolate the predispositional factors that lead to hyperactivity, additional to the studies of alleged dietary influences (Lambert and Hartsough, 1984).

It is also the case the youthful arsonists sometimes make their way into juvenile courts, even though firesetting is an uncommon form of delinquency. The observers who have examined groups of these youngsters tend to agree that they are atypical children (Macht and Mack, 1968). For example, Alan Gruber, Edward Heck, and Ellen Mintzer (1981) studied 90 youths with firesetting records whom they located in residential treatment centers. These researchers concluded that most of the arsonists were from families characterized by substantial social chaos, instability, and lower-income socioeconomic position.

These instances of delinquency involving apparently atypical children are infrequently encountered among juvenile court referrals for at least two reasons. The first and most important one is that "garden variety" thefts, vandalism, joyriding, and the like are exceedingly common among juveniles, and for that reason they make up the bulk of court complaints. But forms of misconduct such as firesetting and deviant sexual behavior are quite likely to be seen by citizens, police officers, court officials, and other adults as symptomatic of serious psychological maladjustment. Those individuals who are implicated in these activities are likely to be absorbed by child guidance clinics or to be placed into private psychiatric care. Those disturbed offenders who are from lower-class backgrounds or who live in communities lacking in clinical facilities tend to end up in juvenile courts tagged as delinquents.

Juvenile aggression is the most commonly encountered pattern of delinquency involving psychologically deviant youngsters turning up in juvenile courts. This behavior problem form of lawbreaking has been carefully examined by a number of skilled researchers so that, unlike the other kinds of conduct, there is a considerable research literature dealing with youthful aggression.

Unsocialized Aggression

"Garden variety" aggression, including violent acts carried on by relatively normal youths, often in the course of committing some other crime, has already been examined in Chapter 4. However, there is another form of aggression—individualistic aggression. This behavior, sometimes called *unsocialized aggression*, involves acts of violence, physical assault, and extreme cruelty directed at persons, animals, and other objects, carried on by persons acting alone. Aggression of this form is viewed as deviant by all except the actor (Hersov, Berger, and Shaffer, 1971).

This behavior can be arranged on a continuum, with one end of the scale involving persons of exceedingly meek disposition, some of whom are probably regarded as deviant by others because of their timidity. Most "normal" persons would be placed further along on the scale of aggression, since they are occasionally hostile and assertive. However, at some point, combativeness exceeds the tolerance of others, so that the actor's behavior arouses the concern of others. Youths who are quick to engage in fist fights with peers or who periodically assault others might be placed at that point on the continuum. Finally, there are some unsocialized aggressive individuals who engage in markedly violent and dangerous acts, who exhibit gross cruelty to animals, and who show aggression in other ways.

One early and well-known piece of research on aggressive offenders, by Jenkins and Hewitt (1944), concerned 500 children who had been referred to a child-guidance clinic in Michigan. They discovered three basic patterns of child maladjustment among the clinic referrals: pseudosocial offenders (gang delinquents), unsocialized aggressive youths, and overinhibited children (nondelinquents). About two-fifths of the youngsters fell into one of these three categories, with the remainder being unclassified.

The unsocialized aggressive children had been involved in an assortment of violent and cruel acts directed at children, adults, and animals. In turn, the major background experience which turned up in the cases of these children was early and severe parental rejection. Many were illegitimate, while others had experienced psychological rejection by their parents. The unsocialized aggressives were markedly different from the pseudosocial youngsters who were relatively normal children from low-income backgrounds and situations of parental neglect. Parental neglect in this instance was measured by large family size, loose supervision by the parents, and the like, in short, parental indifference.

The work of Fritz Redl and David Wineman (1957) with aggressive youngsters provided a rich body of observations of these children. They studied a group of hostile youngsters who were undergoing treatment in Pioneer House, a small group home in Detroit. The subjects were between 8 and 11 years of age, had normal IQs, and apparently exhibited relatively mild patterns of aggression. In order to be accepted for treatment, the subjects had to be manageable in the residential center and able to attend school.

Redl and Wineman made it abundantly clear that aggressive children are the product of atypical and deficient family backgrounds. They argued (Redl and Wineman, 1957: 50): "Aside from continuity, the quality of the tie between child and adult world was marred by rejection ranging from open brutality, cruelty, and neglect to affect barrenness on the part of some parents and narcissistic absorption in their own interests which exiled the child emotionally from them." Redl and Wineman indicated that in addition to parental rejection, open, naked sibling rivalry was found in the backgrounds of many of the children. They also exhibited poor school and community adjustment, and most of them had also been exposed to some traumatic experience, such as the death of a parent. Indeed, these youngsters were from inadequate family and social situations, for Redl and Wineman enumerated some other "missing links" in their lives: Many of them were deprived of gratifying recreational outlets, opportunities for adequate peer relationships, satisfactory community ties, and other personal resources.

In the opinion of Redl and Wineman, the aggressive subjects showed deficient ego controls and had low frustration tolerance, an inability to cope with insecurity, anxiety, and fear, and other shortcomings in the area of impulse control. Redl and Wineman also presented a rich description of the ego mechanisms of aggressive children. These mechanisms are defense techniques through which the actor endeavors to follow out his or her antisocial impulses in the face of threats and persuasion from others. These defense techniques include assertions like, "We were all in on it," "He had it coming to him," and other rationalizations by which the person tried to exculpate himself or herself from blame.

Another investigation of aggressive children has been reported by Albert Bandura and Richard Walters (1959). This study was a careful, painstaking, empirical inquiry structured by a clear, explicit, theoretical framework. The investigation involved 26 aggressive boys and their parents, who were compared with 26 control group youngsters and their parents. Most of the aggressive youths were from a probation department in the San Francisco Bay area. The delinquent and control subjects were of average or above average IQ, from intact homes, and from relatively comfortable backgrounds. Most of the fathers of the boys were skilled laborers or minor white-collar workers. Apparently, the aggressive children in this study were near the mild end of the hostility scale, in that most of them had been involved in truancy and disruptive school behavior. The benign character of this aggression was also revealed in interview material which indicated that some of the boys had exhibited verbal hostility toward their parents but none of them had physically assaulted them. In fact, the parents were horrified by the suggestion that their child might have struck them. The aggressive boys also showed hostility toward teachers and peers, but incidents of physical attack upon these persons were relatively uncommon. Interestingly, the boys' parents often appeared to have encouraged their aggressive activities outside the home.

The Bandura and Walters investigation was structured around a detailed socialization theory that adequate socialization which produces normal, well-adjusted children requires the development of a dependency motive whereby the child learns to want the interest, attention, and approval of others. Once a dependency need has been established, socialization demands and restrictions must be imposed upon the child so that he learns the pattern of deferred gratification. The youth who is allowed to avoid socialization pressures in the form of demands and restrictions tends to seek immediate and unconditional impulse gratification and to behave in other socially unacceptable ways. Finally, the Bandura and Walters formulation contended that consistent discipline is a prerequisite of adequate socialization. Applied to aggressive delinquency, the theory holds that this pattern of deviance arises out of the disruption of a child's dependency relationship to his parents.

Bandura and Walters hypothesized that the aggressive boys and the normal control youths would both show satisfactory early life experiences with parents, in which both groups acquired dependency needs through the nurturing experiences of infancy. But they expected to find that the aggressive boys had subsequently been subjected to some degree of rejection and had been frustrated in their dependency strivings. Then, too, it was hypothesized that the aggressive delinquents had been inconsistently or insufficiently disciplined by their parents.

These hypotheses were tested through lengthy, focused interviews with the boys and their parents; rating scales were compiled from the interviews; and thematic personality tests were given to the boys. On the whole, most of the findings were consistent with the guiding hypotheses of the research.

The interview materials showed that all of the boys, whether aggressives or controls, had received a good deal of parental affection and warm interaction in infancy. However, as they grew older, the control group boys experienced closer and warmer relationships with their fathers than did the aggressive youths. Both the aggressives and controls were on relatively warm terms with their mothers. The aggressive boys showed less emotional dependency on their parents than did the controls, while they also had more anxiety about relating to their parents in a dependent manner. A number of the aggressive youths had been rebuffed and sometimes punished when they had endeavored to secure dependency gratification from their parents. They had been admonished to stop being a "baby" or had been encouraged to "stand on their own two feet." The interviews with the aggressive youths also showed them to be less dependent upon teachers and peers than the control boys. For example, the aggressive youngsters were less likely to seek help with their school work from parents, teachers, or peers than were the controls. Finally, the aggressive boys felt more rejected by their parents than did the controls, although the degree of perceived rejection was quite mild.

In the area of sexual socialization and sexual behavior, the findings indicated that the early sexual training of the two groups was quite similar. However, the parents of the aggressive boys were more permissive regarding adolescent sexual experimentation with members of the other sex than were the parents of the control youths, that is, the parents of the aggressive boys tended to assume that their sons would become involved in sexual intercourse with teenage girls. Not surprisingly, the aggressive boys had actually experienced more sexual activity than the control youngsters. But in all these cases the differences between the aggressives and the control subjects were relatively slight.

Consistent with the hypotheses of the study, the aggressive boys had been subjected to fewer disciplinary pressures by their parents than had the control youngsters. Fewer behavioral limits had been placed upon them, and their parents had lower expectations regarding their school performance than was true of the controls. Although fewer restrictions were imposed upon the aggressive boys by their parents, the aggressives were more inclined to resist and resent these parental controls than were the nonaggressive boys. The social-psychological concomitants of these parent-child patterns were that the aggressive boys showed less identification with their fathers than did the control group youths. In addition, the aggressive children exhibited weaker guilt feelings about violations of conduct standards than was true of the normal youths.

The overall flavor of the Bandura and Walters findings is captured in their summary (Bandura and Walters, 1959: 354-55).

> The fathers of the aggressive boys were typically hostile to, and rejecting of their sons, expressed little warmth for them, and had spent little time in effective interaction with them during the boys' childhood. Although the

mothers' greater warmth had apparently sufficed to establish dependency needs during the boys' infancy, their tendency to punish and discourage dependency behavior reduced the boys' striving for secondary rewards in the form of dependency gratification, thus reducing the effectiveness of important sources of control. Because of the fathers' rejection and the mothers' inconsistent handling of dependency behavior, the boys became anxious and conflicted in dependency situations. This dependency conflict generalized to other authority figures and even to peers, so reducing their effectiveness as possible socializing agents. The parents' use of punitive methods of discipline not only further alienated their sons but fostered the hostility and aggression with which the boys had responded to emotional deprivations. The absence of consistent socialization demands, and the failure of the parents to follow through on the demands that they made, provided some reinforcement of defiance and resistance and left the boys without any clear guides for controlling and directing their behavior.

Although there was no evidence that any of the parents in this study had displayed consistently blatant antisocial behavior, many of the fathers of the aggressive boys undoubtedly provided hostile and aggressive models for imitation. There was also evidence that many of the parents had subtly, if not openly, instigated and encouraged their sons' aggressive behavior outside the home and in some cases even toward the other parent.

Research evidence on aggressive youths continues to accumulate. In a relatively recent study, Gloria Faretra (1981) conducted a long-term follow-up of 66 youngsters who had been placed in a New York City mental hospital for aggressive conduct. She reported that these aggressive youths showed a marked amount of antisocial and criminal behavior persisting into adulthood, although their involvement in psychiatric services lessened over the follow-up period.

We should not leave this matter of aggressive behavior and its roots without pointing out the parallels between the causal argument here and social control and bonding theories, examined in Chapter 7. There is considerable similarity among these formulations, indicating that sociologists do not always march to a different drummer than the one which leads psychologists and psychiatrists.

SUMMARY

It is not uncommon to find sociologist-criminologists heaping scorn upon the assertions of psychiatrists and psychologists which hold that criminalistic persons are also characterized by personality maladjustment. Harsh judgements about psychogenic claims have been based upon several grounds. It has often been argued, not without merit, that many of the writings of psychiatrists are hopelessly ambiguous, tautological, and in other ways so vague as to be unamenable to research test. Then, too, much of the empirical work of psychogenic students of deviance has been flawed; fuzzy, intuitive, subjective procedures have been employed, exceedingly small numbers of cases have been examined, and other critical defects have marred much of this work.

However, the theorizing and research on aggressive delinquents cannot be easily dismissed as faulty or worthless. In particular, the studies of Jenkins and Hewitt and of Bandura and Walters were examples of careful, thoughtful scientific investigation. We venture to claim that these investigators have established the existence of aggressive offenders and have demonstrated that parental rejection is a factor of major importance in this behavior. If we were to judge most of the research of sociologists in the area of delinquency against the methodological standard set by these inquiries on aggression, many of the former would have to be evaluated as inadequate. In short, scientific candor compels us to conclude that the link between parental rejection and aggressive conduct is one of the more firmly established generalizations concerning delinquency.

The major conclusions of this chapter can be stated in the following generalizations:

1. Offenders who are engaged in bizarre forms of misconduct and/or exhibit pathological patterns of personality structure are relatively uncommon among the total population of juvenile offenders and are even relatively infrequently encountered within the group of officially handled lawbreakers. "Behavior problem" kinds of delinquency include firesetting and deviant sex behavior, but the most common form of behavior problem lawbreaking is individualistic aggression. In turn, aggressive behavior comes in various gradations, so that unsocialized aggressive offenders are markedly deviant individuals, while other delinquents exhibit aggression and personality problems of a milder form.

2. Overly aggressive offenders are the product of situations of parental rejection, with the most severe forms of aggression stemming from conditions of early and marked rejection and the milder patterns from less marked instances of parental rejection.

This chapter and the nine others which preceded it have been concerned primarily with American delinquency. Our attention has been directed at various patterns of juvenile lawbreaking which are common in this nation. However, juvenile misconduct is not restricted to the United States. We might well ask whether any of the patterns identified in preceding chapters have counterparts in other lands. Accordingly, in Chapter 11 our interest shifts to the question of international patterns of juvenile delinquency.

REFERENCES

AICHHORN, AUGUST (1955). *Wayward Youth.* New York: Meridian Books.
AUSTIN, ROY L. (1975). "Construct Validity of I-Level Classification." *Criminal Justice and Behavior* 2 (June): 113-29.
BANDURA, ALBERT and WALTERS, RICHARD H. (1959). *Adolescent Aggression.* New York: Ronald.
BEKER, JEROME and HEYMAN, DORIS S. (1972). "A Critical Appraisal of the California

Differential Treatment Typology of Adolescent Offenders." *Criminology* 10 (May): 3-59.

BURT, CYRIL (1938). *The Young Delinquent.* London: University of London Press.

BUTLER, EDGAR W. and ADAMS, STUART N. (1966). "Typologies of Delinquent Girls: Some Alternative Approaches." *Social Forces* 44 (March): 401-407.

CONGER, JOHN JANEWAY and MILLER, WILBUR C. (1966). *Personality, Social Class, and Delinquency.* New York: Wiley.

CONNERS, C. KEITH (1980). *Food Additives and Hyperactive Children.* New York: Plenum Press.

CONRAD, PETER and SCHNEIDER, JOSEPH W. (1980). *Deviance and Medicalization: From Badness to Sickness.* St Louis: C. V. Mosby.

CORTES, JUAN B. and GATTI, FLORENCE M. (1972). *Delinquency and Crime: A Biopsychosocial Approach.* New York: Seminar Press.

ELLIS, LEE (1984). "Genetics and Criminal Behavior: Evidence Through the End of the 1970s." *Criminology* 20 (May): 43-66.

FARETRA, GLORIA (1981). "A Profile of Aggression from Adolescence to Adulthood: An 18-Year Follow-up of Psychiatrically Disturbed and Violent Adolescents." *American Journal of Orthopsychiatry* 51 (July): 439-53.

FISHER, SETHARD (1962). "Assessing a Famous Personality Test." *American Behavioral Scientist* 6 (October): 21-22.

FOSTER, JACK DONALD, DINITZ, SIMON, and RECKLESS, WALTER C. (1972). "Perceptions of Stigma Following Public Intervention for Delinquent Behavior." *Social Problems* 20 (Fall): 202-209.

GIBBONS, DON C. (1970). "Differential Treatment of Delinquents and Interpersonal Maturity Levels Theory: A Critique." *Social Service Review* 44 (March): 22-33.

GIBBONS, DON C. (1982). *Society, Crime, and Criminal Behavior.* 4th edition, Englewood Cliffs, N.J.: Prentice-Hall.

GLUECK, SHELDON and GLUECK, ELEANOR (1950). *Unraveling Juvenile Delinquency.* Cambridge: Harvard University Press.

GLUECK, SHELDON and GLUECK, ELEANOR (1956). *Physique and Delinquency.* New York: Harper and Row.

GRUBER, ALAN R., HECK, EDWARD T., and MINTZER, ELLEN (1981). "Children Who Set Fires: Some Background and Behavioral Characteristics." *American Journal of Orthopsychiatry* 51 (July): 484-88.

HAKEEM, MICHAEL (1958). "A Critique of the Psychiatric Approach," pp. 89-95. In Joseph S. Roucek, ed. *Juvenile Delinquency.* New York: Philosophical Library.

HATHAWAY, STARKE and MONACHESI, ELIO D., eds. (1953). *Analyzing and Predicting Juvenile Delinquency with the Minnesota Multiphasic Personality Inventory.* Minneapolis: University of Minnesota Press.

HEALY, WILLIAM and BRONNER, AUGUSTA F. (1936). *New Light on Delinquency and Its Treatment.* New Haven: Yale University Press.

HECHTMAN, LILY, WEISS, GABRIELLE, and PERLMAN, TERRYE (1984). "Hyperactives as Young Adults: Past and Current Substance Abuse and Antisocial Behavior." *American Journal of Orthopsychiatry* 54 (July): 415-25.

HERSOV, L. A., BERGER, M., and SHAFFER, D. (1977). *Aggression and Antisocial Behavior in Childhood and Adolescence.* New York: Pergamon Press.

HIRSCHI, TRAVIS and HINDELANG, MICHAEL J. (1977). "Intelligence and Delinquency: A Revisionist Review." *American Sociological Review* 42 (August): 571-87.

JENKINS, RICHARD L. and HEWITT, LESTER E. (1944). "Types of Personality Structure Encountered in Child Guidance Clinics." *American Journal of Orthopsychiatry* 14 (January): 84-94.

JESNESS, CARL F. (1963). *Redevelopment and Revalidation of the Jesness Inventory.* Sacramento: Department of the Youth Authority.

LAMBERT, NADINE M. and HARTSOUGH, CAROLYN S. (1984). "Contribution of Predispositional Factors to the Diagnosis of Hyperactivity." *American Journal of Orthopsychiatry* 54 (January): 97-109.

MACHT, LEE B. and MACK, JOHN E. (1968). "The Firesetter Syndrome." *Psychiatry* 30 (August): 277-88.

MAHONEY, ANN RANKIN (1974). "The Effect of Labeling Upon Youths in the Juvenile Justice System: A Review of the Evidence." *Law and Society Review* 8 (Summer): 583-614.

MENARD, SCOTT and MORSE, BARBARA J. (1984). "Structuralist Critique of the IQ-Delinquency Hypothesis: Theory and Evidence." *American Journal of Sociology* 89 (May): 1347-78.

QUAY, HERBERT C. (1965). *Juvenile Delinquency*. Princeton, N.J.: Van Nostrand.

RATHUS, SPENCER A. and SIEGEL, LARRY J. (1980). "Crime and Personality Revisited: Effects of MMPI Response Sets in Self-report Studies." *Criminology* 16 (August): 245-51.

REDL, FRITZ and WINEMAN, DAVID (1957). *The Aggressive Child*. New York: Free Press.

ROBINS, LEE N. (1966). *Deviant Children Grown Up*. Baltimore: Williams and Wilkins.

ROWE, DAVID C. and OSGOOD, D. WAYNE (1984). "Heredity and Sociological Theories of Delinquency: A Reconsideration." *American Sociological Review* 49 (August): 526-40.

SCHRAG, CLARENCE C. (1954). "Review." *American Sociological Review* 19 (August): 490-91.

SCHUESSLER, KARL F. and CRESSEY, DONALD R. (1950). "Personality Characteristics of Criminals." *American Journal of Sociology* 55 (March): 476-84.

SHAH, SALEEM and ROTH, LOREN (1974). "Biological and Psychophysiological Factors in Criminality," pp. 101-73. In Daniel Glaser, ed. *Handbook of Criminology*. Chicago: Rand McNally.

SHELDON, WILLIAM H., HARTL, EMIL M., and McDERMOTT, EUGENE (1984). *Varities of Delinquent Youth*. New York: Harper and Row.

VAN DEN BERGHE, PIERRE L. (1974). "Bringing Beasts Back In: Toward a Biosocial Theory of Aggression." *American Sociological Review* 39 (December): 777-88.

WALDO, GORDON and DINITZ, SIMON (1967). "Personality Attributes of the Criminal: An Analysis of Research Studies, 1950-1965." *Journal of Research in Crime and Delinquency* 4 (July): 185-202.

WARREN, MARGUERITE Q. (1976). "Intervention with Juvenile Delinquents," pp. 176-204. In Margaret K. Rosenheim, ed. *Pursuing Justice for the Child*. Chicago: University of Chicago Press.

WILSON, EDWARD C. (1975). *Sociobiology*. Cambridge: Harvard University Press.

chapter 11 _____

INTERNATIONAL PERSPECTIVES ON DELINQUENCY

INTRODUCTION

The suspicion that juvenile delinquency is largely an American phenomenon is widely shared among lay persons. The common view is that those features of American society which produce juvenile misconduct and adult criminality are relatively lacking in other nations. Thus the assumed higher level of lawbreaking in the United States is supposedly due to the disrespect for law and order, widespread social disorganization, and other characteristics of this country.

Whatever the true level of juvenile delinquency in various nations, theorizing and research studies concerning youthful misconduct have been largely restricted to the United States until relatively recently. In short, most of our knowledge of youthful lawbreaking has been confined to *American* delinquency. Generalizations about youthful misconduct have been based upon American juvenile deviance. However, the past several decades have witnessed a growth of interest and attention directed at crosscultural aspects of delinquency and criminality (Clinard and Abbott, 1973). We will examine those general formulations which identify such factors as societal complexity and affluence as the major ones which lie behind the delinquency rates which vary from one nation to another. Then we will turn our interest to a series of studies of juvenile misconduct in various parts of the world.

DELINQUENCY, SOCIAL CHANGE, AND AFFLUENCE

According to various authorities, delinquency increased markedly in many countries throughout the world in the period since World War II. For example, T. C. N. Gibbens and R. H. Ahrenfeldt (1966) contended that youthful lawbreaking became more common in Belgium, Canada, Japan, Russia, and a number of other nations. One major proposition relative to this worldwide upsurge in delinquency claims as its cause the growing complexity of these nations and the breakdown of traditional patterns of social organization in them. In brief, the greater degree of industrialization, modernization, urbanization, and the like, the higher the rates of delinquency and criminality.

Ruth and Jordan Cavan (1968) collected a mass of material bearing upon the social complexity thesis. They assembled data on delinquency among Eskimos, as well as on youthful lawbreaking in Mexico, India, Russia, England, and eight other European countries. Their report on juvenile misconduct among Eskimos is indicative of the cultural complexity view. Cavan and Cavan asserted that delinquency was nonexistent among Eskimos until recently, due to the social control exerted by their extended family pattern, harmonious folk culture, lack of social class differences, and other factors of that sort. However, with the increase of social contacts with non-Eskimos, movement to towns, and breakdown of traditional social structure, delinquency and crime among Eskimos have become prominent. Much of this behavior takes the form of loitering, drunkenness, and sexual deviance. In the same way, Cavan and Cavan indicated that juvenile and adult lawbreaking are least frequent in Mexican villages and increase as we move from villages to small towns to Mexico City. In India, delinquency and crime are most common in the cities (although less often encountered than in Western societies). Also, lawbreaking is apparently on the increase in India. According to Cavan and Cavan (1968: 100-101): "At present, city delinquency, like much of city life itself, is in a rudimentary stage of development. It grows out of poverty, dire need, and lack of social organization in the slums."

One of the most incisive discussions of the ingredients of social change which produce an upsurge of delinquency is found in the writings of Toby (1967; 1979). He asserted that in industrialized (and industrializing) societies, the sociocultural gulf between adolescents and adults tends to increase due to changes in the economic order and certain other factors. Then, too, the traditional agencies of socialization and social control which contain the behavior of juveniles within socially approved limits tend to break down under the influence of modernization. Finally, the sting of economic deprivation increases with the rise of affluence, so that the "have-nots" grow more resentful of their place at the bottom of the economic heap. Their sense of being unjustly deprived grows as they compare themselves to others who are not so unfortunate. In Toby's words (1967: 132): "People steal, not because they are starving, but because they are envious, and they are more likely to be envious of the possessions of others in countries with rising standards of living."

Toby (1979) has commented at length about "the revolution of rising expectations" in developing nations and the sting of relative deprivation as major factors in delinquency. Toby's thesis bears considerable similarity to Durkheim's (1951) theory of anomie, which holds that deviant behavior becomes most marked during periods of rapid social change. It can also be said to be a broad version of the control or social bond perspective. Drawing upon a body of statistical evidence and also upon a number of case histories, he argued that the upsurge of delinquency outside the United States in recent decades has been most pronounced in developing countries, in which persons have only recently come to entertain rising expectations and the hope that their precarious economic situation will be remedied by industrialization and other manifestations of economic development. Further, he argued that (Toby, 1979: 117) in these nations undergoing economic changes, "when affluence not only arouses predatory motives but offers the potential predator some prospect for 'getting away with it,' the probability increases that the motives will find expression in action. The reason why economic development tends to increase the rate of property crime is that economic development not only increases affluence; it also stimulates urbanization which loosens social control and provides the *opportunity* for delinquency and crime."

Economic development results in a number of more specific consequences which contribute to delinquency, according to Toby. For one, it often produces overurbanization, bringing to cities large numbers of rural migrants who lack opportunities for employment. Many of them are pushed into crime and delinquency because of their economic problems. An even more significant concomitant of economic development centers around the loosening of extended family bonds which in rural societies usually exert much control over the behavior of individuals. Toby's view was that economic development leads to urbanization, which in turn leads to greater individualism and anonymity. Social bonds become attenuated and persons are thus freer to commit crimes.

Diminished family control is particularly significant for adolescents in developing nations. Toby claimed that unlike traditional societies where youths are members of large, extended kinship groups, in urbanizing and developing countries parents lose much of their control and influence over their offspring during adolescence. As a consequence, large numbers of juveniles drift into youthful lawbreaking. Of course, not all families or juveniles are equally vulnerable to criminogenic influences. Toby argued that the breakdown of adult controls most often leads to delinquency in such circumstances as slum neighborhoods or broken homes.

Toby also directed attention to the important role played by adolescent gangs and peer groups in delinquency, arguing that gangs form in contemporary societies in considerable part because of alterations in the institutional structure characteristic of rural, agrarian societies. Juveniles in developing or modernizing societies are rarely tied closely to groups of older adults. Finally, he contended that those youngsters who experience educational failure are likely to show a reduced "stake in conformity" and are thereby prone to gravitate to delinquent activities. Those juveniles who see themselves as relatively deprived, but who also view their future as bleak and unpromising, have relatively little to lose by lawbreaking.

We might profitably examine Toby's (1979: 148) conclusions concerning economic development and delinquency. He argued that:

> Widespread poverty is nothing new. It is widespread affluence that is new. But the relationship between subjective dissatisfaction and objective deprivation is more complicated than was at first thought. Poverty does not cause crime but resentment of poverty does, and resentment of poverty is at least as likely to develop among the *relatively* deprived of a rich society as among the *objectively* deprived in a poor society. Industrial societies are also urbanized societies; and urbanized societies offer greater opportunities to steal and get away with it. Social control of adolescents is especially weak, thus explaining the world epidemic of adolescent crime.
>
> Formal education is not new, either. But *mass* education, extending to the late teens, has new implications that go beyond its direct goal of transmitting the content of the cultural tradition. One implication is that segregating youngsters in schools and adults in the occupational system increases the differentiation between the teenage and the overall culture. Another is that the gap has widened between those youngsters who successfully upgrade their verbal and quantitative skills in the schools and those who develop serious educational disabilities. For academically successful adolescents, school is a bridge between the world of childhood and that of adulthood. For children unwilling or unable to learn, school is a place where the battle against society is likely to begin.

Much of this theorizing should have a familiar ring. These themes have loomed large in the explanation of American delinquency. As an interpretation of youthful lawbreaking outside the United States, this perspective suggests that as countries around the world come to resemble American society in terms of social and economic structure, they are likely to experience pronounced increases in delinquency parallel to those that appear to have occurred in this country.

Toby (1967: 132) found evidence for the relationship between affluence and delinquency in the case of post–World War II Japan. He indicated that the crime rate rose most rapidly from 1955 to 1964 among persons under 18 years of age, while it did not change markedly for persons over 18 years of age. These trends were also revealed by Hideo Fujiki (1972). The total number of persons arrested for crimes in Japan did not increase in the years 1948 to 1958, but the subgroup of arrested juveniles did increase in size, particularly from 1953 to 1958. The increment in juvenile arrests was out of proportion to the growth of the youthful population segment. According to Fujiki, this upsurge of adolescent lawbreaking took place in a period of growing prosperity and rapid economic growth.

Toby (1967: 137-40) found further evidence of the upturn in delinquency in Swedish statistics which showed that the most pronounced increases in rates of criminality were for individuals under the age of 20. Some parallel material for Europe was contained in E. Jackson Baur's (1964) report on juvenile offenses in the

Netherlands. According to Baur, juvenile court cases increased by 108 percent in that nation between 1954 and 1961, and parallel increases occurred in Belgium, Norway, and Denmark in this same period. Interestingly, nearly all of the change in delinquency in the Netherlands was due to an increase in traffic cases centering around offenses having to do with motorbikes. From 1949 to 1961, motorbikes grew in number from under 5000 to over 1 million. Traffic offenses made up 67 percent of all juvenile offenses in 1954 and 81 percent of all youthful violations in 1960.

Baur's interpretation of the changes in juvenile misconduct in Holland centered around the hypothesis of growing affluence. In both the United States and the Netherlands, the gross national product, the level of wages and salaries, and the value of personal consumption expenditures increased significantly between 1954 and 1960. Baur maintained that affluence makes its impact upon juvenile behavior in several ways. It works directly by leading persons to entertain new desires for property, leisure pursuits, and the like, and it operates indirectly through the deterioration of family solidarity which accompanies modernization. He echoed Toby's hypothesis about affluence when he concluded (Baur, 1964: 369): "Spreading prosperity may increase delinquency both among those whose money enables them to do things that bring them into conflict with the law, and among those who resort to stealing to satisfy wants raised above their means by the affluence of others."

Our remarks to this point have been general, and have paid relatively little concern to variations in juvenile misconduct in specific countries. Indeed, relatively diffuse remarks are in part a reflection of the delinquency literature which shows a paucity of good evidence concerning youthful lawbreaking in particular nations. Yet there is some excellent evidence about juvenile crime in certain countries. In particular, delinquency has been studied by a number of investigators in England (Downes, 1966: 100–36). As a result, it is possible to examine the question of differences and similarities between juvenile lawbreaking in England and the United States.

DELINQUENCY IN ENGLAND

The gross outlines of delinquency in Great Britain have been presented by the Cavans. Among other things they noted that, as in the United States, rates of juvenile misconduct increased markedly during both the first and second world wars. In addition, they reported that delinquency continued to grow in the period since World War II. Delinquency is most common among older youths and the most serious acts of lawbreaking are accomplished by these juveniles. Boys outnumber girls by an even greater ratio than in the United States. Finally, clear-cut delinquent gangs are relatively uncommon in England, although loosely structured antisocial groups are to be found in London and other large cities (Scott, 1966). The Cavans also enumerated theories which were put forth in the 1960s regarding British delinquency, mostly centered around the alleged pernicious effects of social-structural factors. These arguments represent English variants upon strain theories which have been produced regarding American delinquency.

One indication that British delinquency is relatively similar to the American brand is found in an ecological study by C. P. Wallis and R. Maliphant (1967). These researchers studied 914 London boys who were incarcerated in detention centers, juvenile institutions, and prisons. In general, they found that these youths were predominantly from low income slum areas which ranked high on various measures of social breakdown. In other words, they were from the same sections of urban communities which produced large numbers of juvenile offenders in the United States.

John Barron Mays (1954, 1959, 1965) has also contributed material which bears out the parallels between British and American delinquency. Mays, as superintendent of a settlement house in a Liverpool slum area, studied a group of 80 neighborhood boys and concluded that they were the products of the widespread criminogenic influences of the area. His interpretation closely paralleled the "delinquency tradition" argument which was favored by Thrasher, Shaw and McKay, and a number of other American students of juvenile lawbreaking. Regarding English delinquency Mays asserted (1954: 82): "Delinquency (in underprivileged neighborhoods) has become almost a social tradition and it is only a very few youngsters who are able to grow up in these areas without at some time or another committing illegal acts."

T. R. Fyvel (1962) discussed postwar delinquency in Great Britain, in particular, the "teddy boy" phenomenon among working-class youths in the late 1950s. "Teddy boys" affected Edwardian clothing styles and other exaggerated mannerisms and were also involved in lawbreaking. Fyvel also reviewed evidence suggesting that trouble-making and "hooliganism" among the young were common in other European nations as well. Thus while England had its "teddy boys" in the period of the late 1950s, West Germany and Austria were plagued with the *halbstarken* ("half-strong"), Sweden by the *skinnknute* ("leather jackets"), and France by the rise of *blousons noirs* ("black jackets").

Fyvel put forth a multidimensional causal argument which is somewhat similar to the multifactor perspective sketched in Chapter 9. His general thesis was that postwar affluence in England and other European nations was responsible for the increase of juvenile lawbreaking. In particular, affluence was singled out as being heavily involved in the rise of "teddy boys" in England and their counterparts in other European countries.

The essence of Fyvel's argument was that "teddy boys" (and girls) were working-class youths who were drawn to the "teddy boy" subculture because they felt themselves to be outcasts from the mainstream of contemporary English society. The alienation of these youngsters was exacerbated by the educational patterns of postwar Britain, centered around a system of "tracking." The most able lower-class youths were skimmed off and placed in an educational path leading to a middle-class lifestyle. However, those who were judged to be average or unexceptional in ability were diverted into an uninspiring school experience designed to prepare them for mundane jobs. These "also-rans" were the candidates for the "teddy boy" subculture. Fyvel (1962: 122) suggested that the "teddy boy" phenomenon was a minority movement among working-class boys, drawing members from "a concentration of the insecure, of unstable adolescents, those with weak family ties and the fewest special interests, who are drawn to the nightly café life like as to a drug, to hold back their anxieties."

David Downes's (1966) essay and research report concerning subcultural delinquency in England is one of the most significant contributions to an understanding of British delinquency. His contentions have a good deal in common with those of Fyvel. Downes began with a detailed and incisive critique of the gang subcultural theories put forth by Cohen, Cloward and Ohlin, and others, all of which center around variables such as feelings of social or economic status deprivation which are presumed to impel working-class youths toward organized group misconduct. In Downes's view, these formulations do not apply to working-class lawbreaking in England. He suggested that British delinquent youths are not motivated by feelings of economic deprivation or failure in the economic world, nor are they concerned about attaining middle-class social status. They are not ambitious and do not aspire to middle-class social positions. Instead, they are interested in achieving the leisure goals of enjoyment and excitement.

Downes suggested that the English school system has much to do with the creation of uncommitted, alienated working-class youngsters, some of whom fall into delinquency. This system early in life begins to prepare the less advantaged persons for routine jobs in semiskilled and unskilled occupations. The majority of working-class boys have restricted social horizons, so that they are reconciled to a lifetime of dull unrewarding unemployment. But instead of being deeply resentful of their place in the social scheme, most of them become relatively fatalistic; they place a low value on work and turn to hedonistic pleasure-seeking for relief from the monotony of employment. The similarity of all this to Miller's (1958) characterization of lower-class culture in the United States is obvious. Downes's (1966: 110–11) views are nicely indicated in the following passage:

> The gradual erosion of 'working-class culture,' especially those standards relating to the socialization of the child, is throwing into increasingly sharp relief the unplanned, squalid and violent version of it which persists among the unskilled, slum dwelling or slum-clearance sector of the working class. The encouragement of spontaneity and autonomy from an early age leads the working-class boy to resist the assertion of middle-class authority he is bound to encounter via school and the law. Working-class culture is at once rigorously defined and sufficiently at odds with the controlling middle-class culture to make a head-on clash almost inevitable.

Downes drew this image of the alienated but apathetic working-class individual from a study in two dockside working-class areas in London, the Stepney and Poplar districts. Adult criminality was much more frequent in Stepney than in Poplar. However, in neither district was it organized and career-oriented. The delinquency which developed in these areas consisted of informal gangs involved in nonutilitarian acts characterized by versatility and short-run hedonism. The juvenile offenders apparently did not graduate into careers in adult lawbreaking, so adult crime was not an alternative avenue for the materially oriented, upwardly mobile youngsters there. Instead, most of the delinquents drifted out of lawbreaking in early adulthood.

Downes's observations about London working-class delinquency were paralleled by Peter Willmott (1966). In his investigation of youths in East London, he found that the probability of a boy getting into court before the age of 21 was about one in three. Willmott found a delinquency cycle among boys similar to that reported by Downes, in which most began with petty thievery which reached a peak at about age 14, followed by "hooliganism" which reached a peak at about 17 years of age. Most of the boys studied by Willmott showed no marked sense of resentment or frustration concerning their position in the social or economic order.

The lines of argument concerning British delinquents offered by Fyvel, Downes, and others have been continued in a more recent discussion by Julian Tanner (1978) of the "mod" and "skinhead" subcultures among English youths in the 1960s. At the outset, it should be noted that many of the members of these working-class youth culture groups are *not* involved in juvenile misconduct. The central thrust of Tanner's essay was that these two youth subcultures recruited members from different parts of the English working-class and they offered solutions to status problems that differentiated the two groups.

The mod subculture arose in the early part of the 1960s. According to Tanner, it was a response to the contradictory situation facing working-class juveniles. On the one hand, they were bombarded by the ideology of the much-heralded "affluent society," but on the other, they were confronted with their own deteriorating economic prospects. Stated differently, members of the mod group were lower-class boys who had come to develop heightened economic aspirations because of general affluence in the nation, but who were frustrated in their mobility striving. As a result, they retreated into the exaggerated leisure styles, inordinate concern with clothing styles, and other aspects of conspicuous consumerism that were at the heart of mod behavior. These were youngsters who felt the "sting of relative deprivation" generated by postwar affluence and who responded by parodying the values of a consumer-oriented society.

By contrast, the more recent "skinhead" subculture involved juveniles who rejected hippie or mod styles of dress or behavior and who endeavored instead to reaffirm traditional working-class values through their behavior. Tanner viewed their behavior as a symbolic protest against changes wrought in traditional working-class culture by the economic and social shifts in England in the 1960s. Skinheads were unskilled lower-class boys who aspired to "good working-class jobs," but who were also witnessing the drying up of many of these jobs and the destruction of traditional working-class slum communities by urban renewal and redevelopment programs in England.

Some of the recent theorizing about delinquency and youth problems in England has taken a more critical or radical turn, in which some criminologists have zeroed in upon the alleged crisis of advanced capitalism said to now characterize British society (Hall, Critcher, Jefferson, Clarke, and Roberts, 1978; Cohen, 1972). In the view of these persons, English society has fallen into a state of permanent economic malaise which has exacerbated both the conditions that lead to delinquency and the responses of the authorities to those conditions. The British economic and political system is unable to deal in ameliorative ways with the criminogenic conditions that produce juvenile lawbreaking; thus repressive policies directed at wayward youths have become commonplace. In short, as social life has deteriorated in Britain, some of the theories of delinquency have become more pessimistic as well.

This commentary on delinquency in England would not be complete without mention of the Cambridge University longitudinal study of British youths (West, 1969; West and Farrington, 1973, 1977; West, 1982). Over a two-decade period these investigators followed the development of 411 working-class London boys born between 1951 and 1953. They collected data on teacher judgments of the boys when they were between eight and ten years old, finding that some were identified by teachers as particularly difficult and aggressive boys. Social workers visited the homes of the boys in 1961 and collected information on the attitudes of parents toward the youths, disciplinary techniques employed by the parents, and certain other matters. In 1974, as the boys moved into adulthood, each was classified according to whether he had become involved in criminality. According to Farrington and West, the families that most commonly produced criminals were quarrelsome ones in which little parental supervision had been provided, and further, they often included a parent with a criminal record.

In a summary report on this research (West, 1982), the findings were said to indicate that delinquency and criminality are most likely to develop in large, low-income families characterized by "dissatisfactory" child-rearing practices. Also, the parents of offenders are often persons of below-average intelligence, may of them with criminal records.

All of this material points consistently in the same direction. English delinquency and criminality have a good deal in common with American lawbreaking in that property offenses and group forms of law violation are the mode in both nations. In both countries, "garden variety" offenders often come from working-class backgrounds. But British delinquency differs in some ways from the American version. In particular, the latter more often is the training ground for careers in adult criminality. Conversely, British society lacks opportunity structures in organized crime, gangsterism, and the like. As a consequence, English delinquency seems more benign in form and less frequently culminates in adult deviance.

DELINQUENCY IN OTHER COUNTRIES

We have already observed that delinquency has been more heavily studied in England than in any other nation except the United States. Reliable information about youthful misconduct is relatively scarce for most other areas and is of varying quality; thus it must be regarded with some skepticism and caution.

Other European Nations

Cavan and Cavan (1968) pulled together a variety of reports on juvenile delinquency in eight European nations. They claimed that this information showed group delinquency to have become quite common in these eight countries since the second World War. This same contention has been advanced by Toby, as we have already seen. Then, too, the study by Baur in the Netherlands claimed that juvenile lawbreaking increased markedly in that country in the postwar period.

Other reports on European delinquency include those by Mark Field (1955), Walter Connor (1970), and Paul Hollander (1969), dealing with the Soviet Union. Field, after culling through mass media comments on criminality in Russia, claimed that these showed that juvenile delinquency has become a problem of major proportions in that country, particularly in the form of drunkenness and the occasional formation of juvenile gangs. He also asserted that juvenile lawbreaking is often encouraged by the indifference shown toward it by Russian adults. Field also discussed the emergence of the *jeunesse dorée* group of offenders, consisting principally of the children of powerful officials and successful intellectuals. These youngsters were said to engage in debauchery, crime, and dissipation.

The observations of Connor and Hollander paralleled those of Field. Drawing upon a variety of information, Connor (1970) contended that juvenile misconduct in the Soviet Union is primarily a problem involving urban, lower-class males with low educational attainment and poor prospects for economic and social mobility. The most common form of youthful lawbreaking appears to be property offenses, as is also the case in the United States. Hollander (1969) indicated that delinquency became common in the U.S.S.R. in the period since World War II. He attributed the rise in juvenile lawbreaking to the blandness and uniformity of life in that socialist nation, as well as to economic disjunction caused by the gap between rising expectations of youth and the inability of the Soviet system to meet the demands for consumer goods and economic mobility. Although Soviet officials and criminologists tend to locate the causes of delinquency in factors outside the social structure, such as contamination of youth by foreign influences and the like, Hollander contended that delinquency is actually quite closely related to such factors as broken homes, truancy, and low socioeconomic status.

The Cavans (1968: 104–31) also provided information on Russian delinquency. They claimed that since World War II, juvenile lawbreaking has become frequent in all the strata of Soviet society. Working-class youths from slum areas sometimes become *stilyagi*, or "hooligans," dressing in American-style clothing, listening to popular music, and engaging in antisocial conduct in the form of public drunkenness and rebelliousness. Among the children of the socially elite, some become "gilded youths" and get caught up in drinking and wild parties. A general cause which runs throughout these forms of juvenile deviance, according to the Cavans, is a desire on the part of youths to escape from the boring and repressive features of Soviet life.

Gang delinquents in Paris have been studied by Vaz (1962), who found them to be similar to British offenders in many respects. His investigation involved several weeks of interviewing social scientists, educators, and correctional authorities in Paris. Vaz found that gang boys in Paris engage in a variety of offenses, including sex violations, assaults, robbery, drinking, and vandalism. However, many of the delinquent acts center around property violations; fighting gangs and drug addiction are nonexistent among Parisian gangs. In addition, no recognized community of adolescent gangs was observed; rather, the Paris gangs were loosely organized and small. Finally, the absence of large criminal or gambling syndicates in Paris meant that the American form of structural connections between juvenile and adult criminal groups was not found in Paris. As a consequence, most Parisian delinquents do not aspire to careers as adult offenders.

As in the United States and England, gang delinquency in Paris occurs mainly in areas characterized by economic deprivation, inadequate housing, family disorganization, lack of recreational facilities, and the like. In both the United States and Paris, gangs flourish in older deteriorated slums and in newly developed, low-rent housing blocks where traditional patterns of social organization have been disrupted. Juvenile offenders are often from multiproblem families within these neighborhoods.

Another bit of evidence on European delinquency can be found in a report by Carl-Gunnar Janson (1970) dealing with juvenile lawbreaking in Sweden. He maintained that there has been a large increase in youthful criminality in that country since the end of World War II. Janson contended that many theories of causation that have been in vogue in the United States do not apply to Sweden, that Swedish delinquency cannot be explained as a result of immigration, urban slums, or social class strains revolving around economic deprivation. Instead he argued that the rise in Swedish delinquency is due to the decline of *expressive patience*, which was his term for what American scholars have identified as the deferred gratification pattern. Janson claimed that the spread of general economic stability in Sweden has led many youths to abandon expressive patience, postponement of gratification, and success striving in favor of hedonistic pleasure seeking. Janson's thesis bears a good deal of similarity to arguments about American youth culture.

Other Countries

Our knowledge about delinquency in the world becomes very skimpy once we dispose of American and European studies. Reports on juvenile lawbreaking in Asia, Africa, and elsewhere are few and scattered. Moreover, these bits and pieces are impressionistic and sketchy in many instances. A case in point is the essay on youthful offenders in Taiwan (Formosa) by Tsung-Yi Lin (1964). Although the author titled his report as a statement on Chinese society, it does not deal with mainland Communist China.

According to Lin, there are two kinds of juvenile offenders in Taiwan, the *tai-pau* and *liu-mang*. The latter term is an old one which, roughly translated, means "vagrant" or "lawbreaker," while *tai-pau* designates a form of delinquency which has recently arisen.

A number of contrasts exist between the old-style offenders and the newer *tai-pau*. The *tai-pau* are concentrated in large cities, while the *liu-mang* are found in the older sections of cities and towns. The *tai-pau* are noted for their Western dress, conspicuous appearance, and attention-getting mannerisms, and they hang around theaters, cafés, ping-pong houses, and parks. The *liu-mang* dress in native costume, live mainly with their parents, and much of their social activity takes place in their homes, the marketplace, or the temple. The *tai-pau* are middle- or upper-class youngsters who are involved in hedonistic activities, who engage in truancy, and who steal in order to support their fun seeking. The *liu-mang*, on the other hand, are lower-class youths who are involved in drug trafficking, prostitution, and other racketeering. They are the closest approximation to American-style delinquents. According to Lin, these two patterns reflect the two subcultures which now coexist in Taiwanese society. The *liu-mang* are the delinquent representatives of the illiterate, tradition-oriented part of Chinese society, while the *tai-pau* are the products of recent social changes in Taiwan. They are one manifestation of westernization of this society and they derive from the literate, affluent, cosmopolitan subculture of Taiwan.

Lois DeFleur (1970) has provided a description of delinquency in Cordoba, Argentina, a large, rapidly industrializing city of over 500,000 population. She contrasted a sample of juvenile court cases in that city with findings on American delinquents contained in governmental reports. In general, she found many points of similarity between offenders in the two countries.

In both Argentina and the United States, court referrals averaged about 15 or 16 years of age. In both places boys outnumbered girls in a ratio of about five to one. Offense patterns were roughly comparable in both countries; very few serious offenses such as murder or manslaughter occurred. Crimes of theft were numerically most common in both sets of data.

However, cultural differences between the United States and Argentina do have some effect upon youthful misconduct. For one thing, female sexual offenders were rare in Argentina and this reflects a tolerant view of sexual experimentation in that nation. Most of the sex delinquencies were the work of boys and centered around child molesting.

Although theft was common among delinquents in both countries, it apparently takes a more violent form in the United States than in Argentina. Also, female theft in the United States involves shoplifting, while girls in Cordoba were more often charged with stealing from an employer. Vandalism and auto theft were infrequent or virtually absent in Cordoba, as was drug use. Finally, the assaultive acts reported to the Cordoba court were of a relatively petty form which tends to be handled informally in this country.

A second report on delinquency in Argentina is a study by Pedro R. David and Joseph W. Scott (1973), dealing with juvenile court cases in Toledo, Ohio, and Rosario, Argentina. Both of these communities are metropolitan areas of over a half-million population. David and Scott noted that Argentinian definitions of delinquency differ from those in the United States in that juvenile court laws do not contain prohibitions against status offenses in the former. David and Scott also observed that juvenile lawbreaking that comes to court attention is heavily concentrated in areas of low socioeconomic status in both cities, although delinquency rates appear to be considerably higher in Toledo than in Rosario. One finding in this investigation differed from DeFleur's results, namely that in Rosario, assaultive acts predominate as the reason for court referral. David and Scott argued that the differences in offense patterns among court referrals in Toledo and Rosario are to be explained in terms of differences in opportunity structures for youthful lawbreaking. Thus delinquents in Argentina rarely steal cars due to the scarcity of automobiles, and they are infrequently engaged in drinking offenses because they learn habits of moderation in drinking early in their childhood socialization.

Another bit of crosscultural data on delinquency is to be found in S. Kirson Weinberg's (1964) investigation in Ghana. He studied male offenders incarcerated in an institution in Accra, Ghana, and training school female wards in the same city. These youths were then compared with a collection of nondelinquent high school students.

Weinberg's evidence showed that the offenders were from disrupted homes more frequently than were the nondelinquents. More delinquents resided with guardians or distant kin, more had been shifted from one home to another, more had been runaways, and more had been traumatized by these breaches in family life. In addition, the offenders were alienated from school, having completed fewer grades and being more truant than the nonoffenders. The offenders were also more involved with deviant peers than were the nondelinquents. Weinberg concluded (1964: 481) that delinquents in Ghana have a number of experiences in common with American lawbreakers:

> These indicators point to the transcultural influences of the family, school, and peers in both Ghanaian and American societies. In both societies, delinquents seemingly experienced more frustrating, less controlling, and less secure relationships with their parents than did the nondelinquents. In both societies, delinquents seemed relatively less able than nondelinquents to adapt and to discipline themselves to the norms of the school. And in both societies, the delinquents were thrust into marginal social roles and were predisposed or coerced to accept the deviant norms and practices of their delinquent peers amidst the rapidly changing context of the urban community.

We should also note in passing that a closely related inquiry by Olufunmilayo Oloruntimehin (1973) in Lagos, Nigeria turned up parallel evidence pointing to the importance of family factors or "under-the-roof" culture in the etiology of delinquency in that country. Two-thirds of the offenders he studied in juvenile institutions were from disordered family situations, as contrasted to less than 5 percent of the control group cases of nondelinquents.

Some final investigations in this relatively meager catalogue of crosscultural inquiries have to do with delinquency in the Near East. Shlomo Shoham and Leon Shaskolsky (1969) conducted a study of 100 referrals to the Tel Aviv, Israel, juvenile court along with the same number of nondelinquents. They found that the offenders did not differ from the nonoffenders on a variety of scales and measures dealing with personality characteristics, feelings of powerlessness or normlessness, family cohesiveness, and social background characteristics. Although they were somewhat perplexed by the failure of these research instruments to differentiate lawbreakers from nondelinquents, such a result might not be surprising. Most of the court referrals had been turned over to the juvenile authorities for relatively petty acts of misbehavior and probably were, in fact, not much different from youngsters that had not been referred to court. In short, these results would probably be duplicated in comparisons of first referrals to court and nondelinquents in the United States as well.

Some other information on delinquency in the Near East can be found in a report by Carl Chambers and Gordon Barker (1971) on youthful misconduct in Iraq. Their discussion included statistical facts on court referrals in that country, showing that most of them are males, about 16 years of age, predominantly from urban areas, and mainly involved in acts of violence or property crime. However, most of the observations of Chambers and Barker center around the handling of offenders in the juvenile justice system, rather than upon causal factors.

One of the most recent ventures into the cross-cultural study of delinquency was by Hartjen and Priyadarsini (1984), in which they conducted a comprehensive investigation of lawbreaking in Tamil Nadu state in India. These researchers gathered data on the forms and quantity of delinquency in a major city and a village in that Indian state, along with information on citizens' perceptions of laws, delinquents, and the handling of offenders, as well as data on the juvenile justice system processing of youthful lawbreakers.

The first portion of this study having to do with the extent of delinquency involved a self-report questionnaire administered to high school boys and approved school (training school) inmates, along with official statistics that were gathered by the researchers. The findings indicated that rates of recorded or official juvenile misbehavior are considerably lower among Indian youths than would be encountered in the United States, although both Indian and American delinquents appear to concentrate their illegal activities upon property violations. Official rates of delinquency were higher in the urban center than in the rural community. Additionally, Hartjen and Priyadarsini indicated that contrary to the pattern in the United States juvenile offenders are responsible for a relatively small portion of all recorded crime. The self-report instruments employed by these researchers yielded findings indicating that undetected as well as detected lawbreaking is relatively uncommon among Indian juveniles.

Hartjen and Priyadarsini concluded that low rates of delinquency are found in India largely because of the high level of social integration of youths into Indian society. Finally, they also noted (Hartjen and Priyadarsini, 1984: 121) that "not only is delinquent behavior in India infrequent and mild, but official reaction to such behavior is also infrequent and lacking in severity . . . there does appear to be a distinct tendency in India not to treat youthful misconduct as a matter for formal social control."

SUMMARY

The international aspect of juvenile delinquency is unsatisfactory because of the thinness of the theoretical and research literature available. The indications seem to be that what "everybody already knows" is true, namely that delinquency is more widespread, more organized, and more serious in form in the United States than anywhere else in the world. Gangsters and juvenile delinquents are not found very often elsewhere. But at the same time a fair amount of evidence seems to indicate that the spread of modernization, industrialization, and affluence in other countries has begun to generate juvenile misconduct on a sizable scale. In particular, England and certain other European countries are well on the road toward patterns of youthful lawbreaking which duplicate those of the United States.

The major generalizations from the material in this chapter are these:

1. Although the United States apparently has the highest delinquency rate of nations of the world, juvenile misconduct has increased markedly in many other nations since World War II. The most pronounced increases in delinquency rates have been in European countries. Although the reasons for the upsurge of juvenile lawbreaking are numerous and complex, they center around recent industrialization, the growing complexity of societies and the breakdown of the old social order, and the increasing affluence of European countries.

2. In a number of ways, delinquency in England is similar to juvenile lawbreaking in the United States: Males are much more frequently involved in misconduct than are females, juvenile lawbreaking occurs in loosely structured gangs, and it is most common in deteriorated, working-class neighborhoods similar to American "delinquency areas." Juvenile delinquency has apparently increased markedly in England since World War II. Juvenile offenders in that country are frequently drawn from the group of alienated, uncommitted, working-class youths who are involved in the pursuit in short-run, hedonistic pleasures. Most of them do not show a marked sense of status frustration.

One thing is clear: More research concerning youthful offenders around the world is needed. For example, very little research has been carried out on hidden delinquency outside the United States. Other lines of empirical inquiry need to be pursued. We can safely predict that an increased amount of this sort of research will probably be conducted in the decade to come.

Chapters 1 to 11 have dealt with questions of delinquency causation. However, one major facet of the etiological issue still remains. What are the causal consequences of putting offenders into probation supervision, training schools, or some other kind of "treatment"? Do these experiences actually divert them from criminal careers? Perhaps the correctional actions directed at juvenile offenders have a benign effect on them, so that their subsequent deviant careers are unaffected by such experiences. Still another possibility which has received all too little attention is that youthful lawbreakers may be pushed further into criminal careers by the stigmatizing effects of correctional handling. Quite probably, various treatment efforts affect different juvenile offenders in different ways, so that no single result is produced. This matter is complex and demands detailed attention.

REFERENCES

BAUR, E. JACKSON (1964). "The Trend of Juvenile Offenses in the Netherlands and the United States." *Journal of Criminal Law, Criminology and Police Science* 55 (September): 359-69.

CAVAN, RUTH SHONLE and CAVAN, JORDAN T. (1968). *Delinquency and Crime: Cross-cultural Perspectives.* Philadelphia: Lippincott.

CHAMBERS, CARL D. and BARKER, GORDON H. (1971). "Juvenile Delinquency in Iraq." *British Journal of Criminology* 11 (April): 176-82.

CLINARD, MARSHALL B. and ABBOTT, DANIEL J. (1973). *Crime in Developing Countries.* New York: Wiley.

COHEN, STAN (1972). *Folk Devils and Moral Panic: The Creation of the Mods and Rockers.* London: MacGibbon and Kee.

CONNOR, WALTER D. (1970). "Juvenile Delinquency in the U.S.S.R.: Some Quantitative and Qualitative Indicators." *American Sociological Review* 35 (April): 288-97.

DAVID, PEDRO R. and SCOTT, JOSEPH W. (1973). "A Cross-cultural Comparison of Juvenile Offenders, Offenses, Due Process, and Societies: The Cases of Toledo, Ohio, and Rosario, Argentina." *Criminology* 11 (August): 185-203.

DE FLEUR, LOIS B. (1970). *Delinquency in Argentina—A Study of Cordoba's Youth.* Pullman: Washington State University Press.

DOWNES, DAVID M. (1966). *The Delinquent Solution.* New York: Free Press.

DURKHEIM, EMILE (1951). *Suicide,* trans. J. A. Spaulding and George Simpson. New York: Free Press.

FIELD, MARK G. (1955). "Alcoholism, Crime, and Delinquency in Soviet Society." *Social Problems* 3 (October): 100-109.

FUJIKI, HIDEO (1972). "Recent Trends of Juvenile Crime in Japan." *Journal of Criminal Law, Criminology and Police Science* 53 (June): 219-21.

FYVEL, T. R. (1962). *Troublemakers.* New York: Schocken.

GIBBENS, T. C. N. and AHRENFELDT, R. H. (1966). *Cultural Factors in Delinquency.* Philadelphia: Lippincott.

HALL, STUART, CRITCHER, CHARLES, JEFFERSON, TONY, CLARKE, JOHN, and ROBERTS, BRIAN (1978). *Policing the Crisis: Mugging, the State, and Law and Order.* London: Macmillan.

HARTJEN, CLAYTON A. and PRIYADARSINI, S. (1984). *Delinquency in India.* New Brunswick, N.J.: Rutgers University Press.

HOLLANDER, PAUL (1969). "A Converging Social Problem: Juvenile Delinquency in the Soviet Union and the United States." *British Journal of Criminology* 9 (April): 148-66.

JANSON, CARL-GUNNAR (1970). "Juvenile Delinquency in Sweden." *Youth and Society* 2 (December): 207-31.

LIN, TSUNG-YI (1964). "Two Types of Delinquent Youth in Chinese Society," pp. 169-76. In S. N. Eisenstadt, ed. *Comparative Social Problems.* New York: Free Press.

MAYS, JOHN BARRON (1954). *Growing Up in the City.* Liverpool: University of Liverpool.

MAYS, JOHN BARRON (1959). *On the Threshold of Delinquency.* Liverpool: University of Liverpool.

MAYS, JOHN BARRON (1965). *The Young Pretenders.* New York: Schocken.

MILLER, WALTER B. (1958). "Lower-class Culture as a Generating Milieu of Gang Delinquency." *Journal of Social Issues* 14 (3): 5-19.

OLORUNTIMEHIN, OLUFUNMILAYO (1973). "A Study of Juvenile Delinquency in a Nigerian City." *British Journal of Criminology* 13 (April): 157-69.

SCOTT, PETER (1966). "Gangs and Delinquent Groups in London," pp. 319-34. In Rose Giallombardo, ed. *Juvenile Delinquency.* New York: Wiley.

SHOHAM, SHLOMO and SHASKOLSKY, LEON (1969). "An Analysis of Delinquents and Nondelinquents in Israel: A Cross-cultural Perspective." *Sociology and Social Research* 53 (April): 333-43.

TANNER, JULIAN (1978). "New Directions for Subcultural Theory: An Analysis of British Working-class Youth Culture." *Youth and Society* 9 (June): 343-72.

TOBY, JACKSON (1967). "Affluence and Adolescent Crime," pp. 132-44. In The President's Commission on Law Enforcement and Administration of Justice, *Task Force Report: Juvenile Delinquency and Youth Crime.* Washington, D.C.: U.S. Government Printing Office.

TOBY, JACKSON (1979). "Delinquency in Cross-cultural Perspective," pp. 105-49. In La Mar T. Empey, ed. *Juvenile Justice: The Progressive Legacy and Current Reforms.* Charlottesville, Va.: University Press of Virginia.

VAZ, EDMUND W. (1962). "Juvenile Gang Delinquency in Paris." *Social Problems* 10 (Summer): 23-31.

WALLIS, C. P. and MALIPHANT, R. (1967). "Delinquent Areas in the County of London: Ecological Factors." *British Journal of Criminology* 7 (July): 250-84.

WEINBERG, S. KIRSON (1964). "Juvenile Delinquency in Ghana: A Comparative Analysis of Delinquents and Nondelinquents." *Journal of Criminal Law, Criminology and Police Science* 55 (December): 471-81.

WEST, DONALD J. (1969). *Present Conduct and Future Delinquency.* London: Heinemann.

WEST, DONALD J. (1982). *Delinquency: Its Roots, Careers and Prospects.* London: Heinemann.

WEST, DONALD J. and FARRINGTON, DAVID P. (1973). *Who Becomes Delinquent?* London: Heinemann.

WEST, DONALD J. and FARRINGTON, DAVID P. (1977). *The Delinquent Way of Life.* London: Heinemann.

WILLMOTT, PETER (1966). *Adolescent Boys in East London.* London: Routledge and Kegan Paul.

chapter 12

CORRECTIONAL PROCESSES AND DELINQUENT CAREERS

INTRODUCTION

There are myriad experiences that happen to youngsters who get caught up in the juvenile justice machinery. Some are apprehended by the police but are released after having received nothing more than a warning or tongue lashing. Others are taken to a juvenile detention center and held for juvenile court action. Still others are less fortunate, for they are carted off to a jail to be detained pending court action. Many of these detained juveniles are subsequently released by court officials and are not processed through a formal court hearing. Juveniles who are given formal court hearings receive a number of dispositions. Some are placed on probation where they are subjected to supervision in the community. On occasion, a few are sent off to private agencies, such as psychiatric facilities, while others are placed in youth care facilities or other short-term institutional settings. Those offenders who are regarded by the court as the most difficult, least tractable cases end up in the agency of last resort—the state training school. Those juveniles ultimately are released from training schools and usually reappear in the community, under supervision, on parole. The outlines of this juvenile processing machinery are depicted in Figure 12-1. (Also see Figure 2-1, p. 26).

What about the correctional handling of offenders in agencies such as probation services, training schools, and parole organizations? Many lay persons see these

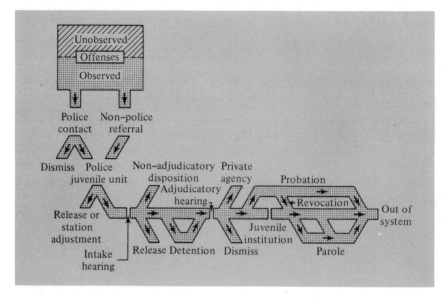

FIGURE 12-1

activities and experiences as sharply marked off from the processes of causation, for correctional events are seen as things which happen *after* delinquent behavior has been caused. In short, correctional actions are undertaken to correct or reverse the effects of causal factors and to change the offender back to a nondeviant.

However, the events of the real world may not be as simple as the citizen thinks. For one thing, many persons, ordinary citizens and criminologists alike, question the therapeutic efficacy of correctional processes. As a case in point, although training schools are supposed to turn out wards who refrain from further deviance upon release, many training school graduates continue in criminality, eventually ending up in adult penal institutions. In these instances, the correctional institution has failed. The usual interpretation of these failures is that the offenders are so enmeshed in lawbreaking and antisocial perspectives by the time they get to the institution that little can be done with them there. In this view, although the training school failed to rehabilitate, it cannot be held directly accountable for the offender's reinvolvement in delinquency. The training school is presumed to have neither a positive nor a negative effect upon the deviant. In short, the institution is said to "have done the best it could" with the intractable raw material with which it must work.

But another complication in the real world is that correctional organizations may sometimes have direct effects upon deviant careers. In particular, the experience of being placed on probation or in an institution may have identifiable negative consequences upon the deviant career of the offender. This possibility is captured in the common sense contention that training schools are "crime schools." According to this hypothesis, youths who are processed through these places come out with hardened attitudes, the resolve to go forth and commit more delinquent acts, and the intention to avoid getting caught. This argument suggests that correctional institutions (and other correctional activities) are not simply benign in character, having no important impact upon offenders; instead, these organizations function in ways which are at cross purposes with their official aims. These agencies may involve delinquents and criminals in experiences which stigmatize them as "bad guys" or which operate in other ways to foreclose upon their possibilities to extricate themselves from long-term careers in deviance.

We shall begin with statistical source material regarding the size of the juvenile correctional workload in the United States. We will also examine some data concerning correctional outcomes in that section, particularly regarding the rates of parole violation from institutions.

We must devote some detailed attention to sociological theorizing concerning deviant behavior which identifies various social reactions or labeling experiences as critical in the development of deviant careers. This point of view hypothesizes that correctional experiences may have harmful social-psychological effects upon persons who are subjected to them. One important part of this task centers around the study of training school social organization. There is a growing body of sociological evidence on the social structure of juvenile institutions which we need to inspect in order to get some sense of what these places are like and how they may be perceived by those youths who live a part of their lives in them. What are the effects of training schools upon persons who are incarcerated in them? Although statistics dealing with parole success or failure are not too hard to come by, relatively little evidence identifies the particular social-psychological effects of the training school experience upon wards. Finally, how can correctional experiences be redesigned to have greater positive impact upon offenders?

THE FLOW OF CASES IN
THE CORRECTIONAL MACHINERY

Delinquent conduct of at least a mild form is characteristic of nearly all youths as they pass through the adolescent years. A wealth of evidence on hidden delinquency makes it clear that the correctional nets snare only a fraction of the law-breaking youths in the nation. Law enforcement and correctional agents sift through the cases the come to their attention in order to screen out from official processing many of the youngsters who have been observed in misconduct. The police deal with many contacts by admonishing the youngsters or by some other informal action, while probation agencies dismiss or place on unofficial probation some of the cases brought to them by the police. Doubtless some of these children who have been informally disposed of by correctional agents commit further acts of law-breaking. In turn, some of these juveniles ultimately get officially processed and appear in correctional caseloads. At the same time, many of the youths who have been dealt with in an unofficial fashion refrain from further involvement in misconduct.

The filtering, sifting, and sorting operations which characterize the juvenile justice machinery are highlighted in Figure 12-2. That figure indicates that approximately 1,306,700 cases were referred to juvenile courts in 1979. The dispositions made of these referrals are shown in Figure 12-2, with only 59,000 of the original group of referrals being retained in custody following adjudication.

There are a number of observations to be made about Figure 12-2. For one, it is apparent that large numbers of youngsters who are held in detention centers or jails are not subsequently held for court hearings. Rather, over one-half of the cases referred to courts are dismissed or handled informally. These figures raise disturbing questions about the extent to which some court officials may be using detention as a punitive device, contrary to the philosophy of detention which holds that only those youngsters who represent a clear danger to themselves or others should be detained.

Figure 12-2 also indicates that not all youngsters who are adjudicated by courts are sent further on into the juvenile justice apparatus, for about one-fourth of all adjudicated cases are ultimately dismissed. Figure 12-2 notes that the majority of the adjudicated cases in 1979 were sufficiently minor ones that they resulted in probation supervision in the community rather than in incarceration in a custodial institution.

In the United States in 1979, a daily average of 71,922 youths were found in custodial institutions for delinquents, including both short-term facilities such as detention centers and long-term facilities such as training schools (Flanagan and McCloud, 1983: 514-16). Institutionalization is used as a last resort for youthful

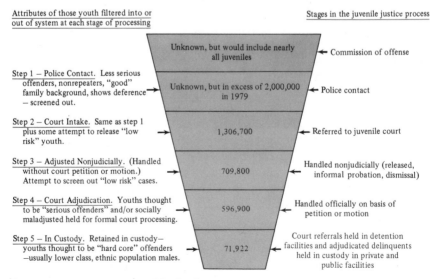

FIGURE 12-2 The Delinquency Filtering Process

offenders; only a small fraction of all known delinquents end up in these places. The data regarding incarceration of juveniles in various facilities within the juvenile justice system indicate that in 1979, of the 71,922 youngsters held in juvenile facilities on any particular day, 12,918 were in detention centers or reception or diagnostic centers, while 59,004 were in training schools and other long-term facilities. Concerning incarceration of juveniles, Krisberg and Schwartz (1983: 347–55) have reported that between 1974 and 1979, the 50 states were evenly split between those 25 which reported declining rates of training school admissions and the 25 that had increased rates of admissions. Vermont, New Mexico, New York, Texas, and North Carolina led the states which experienced admission declines, while Kentucky, Oregon, Washington, Delaware, and Indiana showed the greatest increases in admissions.

LABELING THEORY AND DELINQUENCY

What consequences flow from the decision to put offenders through one part or another of the correctional machinery? The possibility that the effects may be harmful to the lawbreaker, pushing him or her further into deviance, was noted many years ago by Frank Tannenbaum (1938), although his insights were generally ignored until recently. He contended that the effects of official dealings with deviants, ostensibly therapeutic in nature, instead constitute a process of "dramatization of evil." He argued that the result of official handling in the courts, training schools, and related places was frequently the reverse of the announced purposes of such actions. Instead of diverting the person from a deviant career, such experiences alert citizens in the community to the presence of an "evil" person in their midst. Once an individual becomes singled out as "bad," he or she is likely to be consistently thought of as "evil" in the future, quite apart from how he or she actually behaves. A lack of deportment change confirms the original diagnosis in the eyes of the community, and a behavior modification appears to be a clever attempt to hide his or her true nature. Either way, the offender cannot win, so his or her possibilities for action become narrowly circumscribed. In many instances, sentiments of being unjustly dealt with develop and these operate as rationalizations for misconduct. As a result, the end product of treatment is to reinforce the very behavior which the correctional agents are attempting to reduce.

During the past several decades, the perspective which holds that reactions to deviants represent an important area for study has become prominent in sociology (Gibbons and Jones, 1975). This point of view is often designated as the *labeling* orientation to deviance, for it places great emphasis upon the reaction and labeling processes directed at deviants of one kind or another. As a case in point, Howard Becker (1963: 34–35) said about the drug addict career:

> When the deviant is caught, he is treated in accordance with the popular diagnosis of why he is that way, and the treatment itself may likewise pro-

duce increased deviance. The drug addict, popularly considered to be a weak-willed individual who cannot forego the indecent pleasures afforded him by opiates, is treated repressively. He is forbidden to use drugs. Since he cannot get drugs legally, he must get them illegally. This forces the market underground and pushes the price of drugs up far beyond the current legitimate market price into a bracket that few can afford on an ordinary salary. Hence the treatment of the addict's deviance places him in a position where it will be necessary to resort to deceit and crime in order to support his habit. The behavior is a consequence of the public reaction to the deviance rather than a consequence of the inherent qualities of the deviant act.

The labeling orientation applied to delinquency and criminality results in a number of hypotheses. Perhaps the initial contacts offenders have with the police and courts have stigmatizing effects upon them; they become identified as "bad" persons, and their opportunities for disengaging themselves from deviance become constricted. By contrast, lawbreakers who remain hidden more easily drift out of misconduct. Additionally, the experience of being on probation may be harmful to some offenders, so that they encounter difficulties in holding a job, remaining in good standing in school, and so forth. Finally, incarceration in an institution may be a criminogenic influence which produces antisocial attitudes. Most of the stress in labeling formulations has been upon alleged harmful influences of these experiences, although they could conceivably work in a different fashion to drive persons out of deviance.

There is merit to the labeling and social reaction orientation to deviance and criminality. At the same time, this view is not yet a coherent theory supported by an abundance of research evidence. Instead, it is a general orientation, largely speculative in form, with little data in support of it. The various ways in which different social reactions and correctional processes might affect delinquents and adult lawbreakers have not been spelled out, nor has much empirical investigation been devoted to these processes (Gibbons, 1979, 152-56; Wellford, 1975; Mahoney, 1974).

A number of variables have to be considered in a full-blown exposition of the effects of correctional experiences upon offenders. To begin with, these experiences conceivably could have any one of three effects: *positive,* in which they propel persons out of deviance; *neutral* or *benign,* in which they have no effect upon offenders; and *negative,* in which they contribute to the reinvolvement of the actor in additional lawbreaking. Quite possibly, some correctional encounters have more positive or negative repercussions upon deviant careers than do others. For example, the first appearance of delinquents in the juvenile court may have a markedly traumatic impact upon them, but later occurrences, such as being placed in a forestry camp, may contribute little to their subsequent behavior. In short, to acknowledge that correctional agencies have deleterious effects does not mean that all such organizations are equally criminogenic.

We ought not to lump all training schools, all probation agencies, or other correctional structures together when we look at the question of labeling processes. Quite probably those wards who are processed through a state training school in a progressive correctional system are influenced by institutionalization in quite different ways from those that play upon wards in a punitive, harsh training school. The same point holds for probation agencies and parole services; some are staffed by professional correctional workers and others are simply quasi-police agencies.

Neither should offenders be lumped together as though correctional organizations have the same impact upon all of them. Instead, incarceration in a training school might have very different meanings for first offenders as opposed to urban gang delinquents who are wise in the ways of institutions.

TRAINING SCHOOL SOCIAL ORGANIZATION

Training Schools: An Overview

Most training schools are relatively small compared with adult prisons; in many states, the boys' schools handle a few hundred boys or less, and the girls' schools handle even fewer. A national survey of juvenile corrections in 1974 indicated that the number of youths in state institutions, including training schools, camps, and ranches varied across the states from a low of fifty-six to a high of 2,858, with a mean of 560 for all states (Vinter, Downs, and Hall, 1975). In thirty of the fifty states, the average daily population of incarcerated juveniles was under 500 youngsters. This survey also indicated that incarceration rates vary widely from state to state; for example, 41.3 juveniles per 100,000 total population incarcerated in Wyoming to only 2.2 youths per 100,000 in Massachusetts and 2.1 youngsters in New York.

Training schools usually involve a relatively open architecture; they are unwalled institutions made up of a number of dormitory buildings euphemistically called *cottages.* Groups of several dozen juveniles, or *wards,* as they are often called, inhabit these dormitories, and much of the social life of the institutions goes on within these structures. Training schools also include an assortment of other buildings, such as a school, trade training shops, and barns and other farm buildings. Juvenile institutions often resemble residential academies or schools, although many of them are more deteriorated. Escapes, or "rambles," are frequent from training schools, partly because of the ease of escape from such places.

Until the past few decades, the superintendent of the training school was often the product of the political "spoils" system—an ex-county sheriff or similar person to whom a political debt is owed. It goes without saying that he was often a singularly unimpressive figure, ill-trained for the job of maintaining and managing a custodial institution. However, training schools have more recently become managed by professional administrators, many of whom have had training in social work or other "helping professions." The rest of the staff tends to be divided into two general groups. The first includes work supervisors, teachers, and sometimes social caseworkers, who deal with the inmates in one capacity or another during the day. Also included in this group are the kitchen personnel, clerks, and similar workers. The second general group of employees in the school is made up of cottage supervisors or cottage parents who have the major responsibility of managing the wards at night and during those times of the day when they are not involved in some formal program. The cottage workers have the greatest amount of interaction with the wards and the most difficult experiences with them. Prevention of runaways and other disturbances of the institutional routine is usually their responsibility.

Training schools in the past have usually operated a minimal treatment program. Most inmates have been placed in a school program or some kind of vocational or other work experience. Occasionally they receive some kind of individual therapy from a social caseworker, but this tends to be a relatively infrequent event.

The overriding concern in juvenile institutions has revolved around prevention of escapes and large-scale disturbances. Staff members regard runaway behavior as serious indeed, for even though most fugitives are quickly apprehended and normally do not create any incidents in the surrounding community, the community reacts negatively to escapes. Consequently, the juvenile institution which acquires a reputation for frequent escapes usually receives hostile and highly vocal criticism. In turn, runaways come to be defined as extremely serious by the employees.

Juvenile facilities share certain structural shortcomings with their adult counterparts, the prisons. In both places, uncooperative individuals must be restrained in some way, but a number of potentially effective control techniques are not available to the authorities. Wards cannot be controlled by constant physical beatings or by starvation. Although the training school personnel can keep their charges "in line" by occasional beatings and other kinds of physical coercion, they must be circumspect in the use of force. This is not to say that corporal punishment is never used. Coercion which transcends the official rules is employed, but tends to be relatively mild in form and used as a supplement to other control devices (Fisher, 1961). There is a very real danger that the word will get out to the community if beatings become a regular part of the disciplinary program of the school. Cottage parents who utilize physical aggression as a main technique of control are also in some danger of reprisals. The worker may be physically able to intimidate any individual ward but may not emerge the victor in a fight with a half-dozen or more inmates.

The stratagem commonly employed to deal with uncooperative boys parallels the arrangements in adult prisons. The institutional staff enters into tacit bargains with certain inmate leaders in the dormitories. These older, physically mature, sophisticated juveniles operate "kangaroo courts" in which they coerce other weaker youths into docile behavior. In addition to keeping order and preventing "rambles," these toughs use their power to force other inmates into homosexual practices, obtain money from them, and victimize them in other ways.

As these remarks suggest, there is a prisoner system in juvenile institutions; a kind of inmate code characterizes training schools, a juvenile parallel of that found in prisons, centering around the same kinds of antisocial norms as the adult counterpart, and antiadministration and antitreatment in content. It prescribes "playing it cool" as model behavior for wards; they are expected to do their time as pleasantly as possible, without entering into meaningful relationships with staff members.

A pattern of role-types or social roles also exists in juvenile institutions. The system tends to be relatively simple, based on differences in physical prowess and criminal sophistication. Two major role-types emerge in training schools, "toughs" or "dukes," and "punks." The former are juveniles who have been in the institution for a relatively long time, have extensive delinquency records, and are physically superior to other inmates. The second group is made up of boys who are physically immature and are often less sophisticated offenders.

Research on Training School Organization

Many years ago Albert Deutsch presented a body of impressions of state training schools (1949). He traveled around the country looking at a large sample of these institutions, then reported that ten "deadly sins" characterize most of them—regimentation; institutional monotony in the form of unvaried diets and the like; mass handling of inmates without regard to individual needs; partisan political domination; and other such faults. Additionally, he listed public penury, isolation, complacency, excessive physical and mental punishment, Babelism, and enforced idleness as other deficiencies. *Babelism* was his term for various semantic reforms that have been common in corrections, in which "the hole" is renamed the "adjustment center" but the character of the punishment program is not changed; the recreation program is retitled "mass treatment"; or the name of the institution is changed from Boys' Industrial School to Brown Mountain School for Boys.

Unfortunately, this dismal description of juvenile correctional programs has remained relatively accurate since the survey by Deutsch. The National Assessment of Juvenile Corrections project, carried out under Law Enforcement Assistance Administration funding, collected data on forty-two juvenile correctional programs in sixteen states throughout the country (Vinter, Newcomb, and Kish, 1976). Three types of programs—institutions, group homes, and day treatment endeavors—were studied. A rich body of information was obtained through a youth questionnaire, staff questionnaire, and a program questionnaire, providing the most comprehensive collection of information on juvenile correctional programs ever compiled.

The study report indicated that a very rough process exists through which more serious offenders generally are assigned to relatively close supervision and restrictive settings. However, this sorting process is far from entirely rational. In particular, while females generally have been involved in less serious offenses than males, they fare badly at the hands of juvenile justice decision makers, for they receive relatively harsh dispositions for minor offenses. On the other hand, black youngsters appear not to receive discriminatory dispositions, although they are uncommonly encountered in group homes.

More to the point, although various employee groups across all three program types generally agreed that treatment ought to receive the highest priority, in fact the findings pointed to an excessive use of restrictive measures and controls, even in day treatment centers and group homes. Also, the data confirmed a suspicion long held by criminologists, namely that there is a "critical mass" of tougher, recidivist offenders gathered up in large institutions who reinforce each others' negative views of the justice system and who set the social-emotional tone for the entire institution. The report also emphasized the marked variations that occur in juvenile corrections from one jurisdiction to another. The report provided a wealth of ammunition for critics of an expanded juvenile justice apparatus which would reach out to draw increasing numbers of youngsters into it.

Lloyd Ohlin and William Lawrence (1959) have discussed the treatment problems which arise in training schools where interaction occurs among hostile "clients," and group norms define the model inmate as one who is "playing it cool," that is, who is refraining from significant involvement with therapeutic agents. Their remarks paralleled the earlier ones of Topping (1943), who noted that treatment of "pseudosocial" delinquents (gang offenders) is complicated by the group interaction which develops among these offenders in institutions. She reported that many of them exhibited a classical "crime-punishment" orientation in which they saw themselves as serving time to pay their societal debt. Many of these same youngsters disavowed any conceptions of themselves as having problems or need of therapy. In both of these investigations, procedural tactics which might circumvent some of these difficulties were suggested, including development of treatment efforts centered within cottage units in order to utilize the inmate social organization in therapy.

The social structure of a boys' training school in Colorado has been described by Gordon Barker and W. Thomas Adams (1959). Rigid interaction and communication barriers between inmates and staff members were reported, along with a pervasive spirit of authoritarianism in which the offenders did not identify with the values and goals of the staff. The authors also noted the existence of a status order among the inmates, heavily centered around displays of physical toughness and victimization of peers. They speculated that this system may be the result, at least in part, of widespread insecurities among delinquent boys regarding masculinity.

Howard Polsky (1962) has provided a detailed description of the social structure among inmates through a study of the boys residing in a cottage within a private correctional institution. He reported a diamond-shaped status system in which a few boys had very high or low rank among their peers, with the largest group falling into a middle range. Polsky claimed that this system was independent of the particular youths who filled it at any particular period; it persisted relatively unaltered over time even though cottage residents entered and left the system. Departure of a leader, for example, produced competition, conflict, and jockeying among inmate aspirants for the position, followed by reestablishment of equilibrium. According to Polsky, the status types in the cottage included "toughs" and "con artists" at the apex of the order, "quiet types" in the middle range, and "bushboys" and "scapegoats" at the bottom of the system. The latter were subjected to unrelenting physical and psychological attacks by those higher in the pecking order. Probably the most significant of Polsky's observations was that the inmate system was abetted by the institutional staff. He noted (Polsky, 1962: 133): "Thus, the theme of aggression with all of its authoritarian overtones is structurally configured in the cottage. Under the roof the cottage parents join the older boys in scapegoating the defenseless low-status boys—the sneaks, punks, and the sick. The latter 'deserve' the beatings because of *their* provocativeness and 'unfitness.' The unwritten compact of cottage parents and toughs makes it unbearable for the 'deviants' because they are blamed for everything."

In an examination of a training school in California, Fisher (1961) observed the social structure among inmates. He found that both the wards and supervisors rank and victimize certain boys and, moreover, the low-ranked boys in the eyes of the officials were also the low-status inmates in the ward hierarchy. Staff workers often interpreted disruptive behavior by low-status boys as evidence of psychological maladjustment rather than as a result of the social structure and interactional patterns among offenders. Low-ranked victimized inmates were defined as "mess-ups," implying that they willfully engaged in disapproved behavior out of psychological tensions. Instead of attempting to undermine the inmate system, the authorities reacted to boys in its terms, so that institutional rewards were differentially accorded to boys who had high status among their peers.

George Weber (1957) also identified a number of areas in which conflict arises between professional and nonprofessional personnel in institutions where treatment is emphasized. One major problem which he identified and which was also noted by Ohlin (1958) centers around the role difficulties of cottage workers. Their authority position is often reduced or undermined in treatment-centered institutions. They are likely to feel that their prestige has been lowered with the entry of professional personnel into the program. Redefinition of the role of the cottage workers also occurs, and they are expected to run a quiet and well-disciplined dormitory and to contribute to therapy. But because they are not given clear instructions on how to accomplish these ends, they experience much the same role dilemma as prison guards. Weber and others (Weber, 1961; Zald, 1962) have suggested that a number of negative consequences develop from introduction of "rehabilitation" into previously custodial institutions. Staff cooperation is reduced and replaced by conflicts between professional and custodial personnel, defensive reactions develop among cottage workers, and other difficulties arise. Inmates manipulate these conflicts to their own ends by playing competing groups against each other.

Another ambitious research study on training schools compared six juvenile institutions (Street, Vinter, and Perrow, 1966). These training schools varied in size; several were very small institutions while others had inmate populations of well over 100 boys. Some of the schools were private institutions, others were state schools. These facilities also varied in terms of program, ranging from institutions favoring obedience and strict conformity by boys to treatment-oriented milieu operations. The researchers supposed that variations in size might influence the social structure of the schools, as would the different auspices under which these places operated. State facilities should be under greater pressure from the general public. Finally, the investigators hypothesized that the treatment-oriented schools would be more conflict-ridden than the strictly custodial plants.

In general, the findings supported these contentions. Among other things, the institutions varied in terms of the leadership "styles" of their executives. The staff members exhibited different perspectives on delinquents; the workers in custodial institutions viewed boys as more willful than did employees in treatment schools. Rather marked variations in the level of staff conflict existed from school to school, with greatest staff conflict in the rehabilitation-oriented institution in which a high degree of staff *interdependence* existed; in the milieu treatment school, staff members representing different segments of the school program were in frequent communication with each other and were involved in much joint decision making.

TRAINING SCHOOL LIFE AND FEMALE DELINQUENTS

Our remarks to this point have dealt principally with male delinquents and correctional institutions for male lawbreakers. In part, this concentration of attention reflects the fact that males far outnumber females who are incarcerated. In addition, institutions for female juvenile offenders have been less often studied than those for male delinquents. We examined one of these relatively rare inquiries in Chapter 5, Kristine Rogers's (1972) report on Connecticut institutions for boys and girls. Some criminologists who have studied female institutions have indicated that many of the wards in these places participate in pseudo-family relations with their peers. For example, Seymour Halleck and Marvin Hersko (1962) noted that participation in "girl stuff" was admitted by two-thirds of the girls in the institution they studied. "Girl stuff" was the inmate argot label for such activities as "going together," dancing, or other physical contact between the girls. Although these dating and interactional patterns are often presumed by the staff members to be homosexual liaisons, only 11 percent of the wards said that they had engaged in fondling other girls, and only 5 percent admitted genital stimulation of another girl.

Halleck and Hersko maintained that almost all of the girls they studied had been involved sexually with males prior to incarceration, but hardly any had achieved a mature sexual adjustment. These investigators concluded that sexual intercourse was employed by the young women to obtain an affectional relationship. The unsatisfactory feminine identification on the part of these females grew out of deprived family backgrounds which included alcoholic, mentally disordered, or inadequate parents. Halleck and Hersko argued that these youngsters were attempting to obtain gratification of dependency needs through involvement in "girl stuff," in much the same way that they had made parallel attempts with boys and men outside the institution.

The social relationships among wards reported by Halleck and Hersko are not peculiar to the training school they studied. Barbara Carter (1973) has described similar patterns in another state training school. Most of the young women in that institution played either "butch" or "femme" roles, with femmes being much more numerous than butches. (The latter were young women who played male roles, affecting mannerisms and dress styles of young men.) Butches were most commonly black inmates, while femmes were usually drawn from the group of white wards. Carter maintained that most of these simulated dating relationships among training school inmates were emotional and symbolic rather than physical. She argued that these dating-courtship patterns are properly to be interpreted as institutional adaptations and strategems used by the wards to attempt to maintain continuity with their lives outside the training school. The social meaning of these simulated heterosexual dating patterns is that "it is the world of the adolescent girl on the outside, imported into the institution and appropriately modified to fit the formally structured world of the institution" (Carter, 1973: 36, also see Giallombardo, 1974).

MEASURING CORRECTIONAL OUTCOMES

Two problems confront us as we attempt to identify the effects of correctional experiences upon lawbreakers. The first of these is that the full range of possible consequences of different forms of correctional treatment and handling upon the various kinds of offenders who are subjected to these processes has not yet been identified in a theoretical structure. The second problem revolves around the research problems which lie in the path of anyone who would accumulate evidence on these matters.

To begin with, there is a paucity of data of any kind on correctional outcomes. Correctional agencies have infrequently engaged in even the most routine forms of statistical record keeping; they have rarely been equipped with funds for this sort of activity. But, in addition, many correctional services have a stake in *not* knowing about their impact upon their charges. In a great many instances, existing agencies have a low success rate with the wards they handle, often for reasons over which they have little control, such as inadequate financing. But if they were to publicize systematically gathered statistics showing their inefficiency, they might find their financial resources further reduced by the political figures who control economic resources.

However, there are other obstacles to the development of adequate data on correctional outcomes. Consider first the broad problem of measuring the effects of defining processes on deviants. Research investigations on an heroic scale would be called for in order to examine fully the kinds of hypotheses advanced by the labeling school of thought. For example, in order to determine whether the process of being identified by the police as an offender has career consequences for deviants, the ideal research design would be one in which samples of criminal deviants were somehow randomly subjected to either police apprehension or nonapprehension. In this way, we might be able to discover whether police contact per se has identifiable effects on lawbreaker careers. Carrying this program a step further, apprehended offenders might be randomly indicted and placed through a trial or dismissed by the authorities in order to study the stigmatizing effects of court handling. In the same way, randomly assigned groups of adjudicated offenders might be placed on probation or turned loose, while other samples might be sent off to institutions or ignored. In addition, some way would have to be found to control the effects of other experiences which occur to deviants additional to the labeling ones under study. This kind of investigation has a strange sound to it, for it is obvious that experimentation on this scale is not likely to be encouraged by the general public. In addition, if we were somehow able to obtain a mandate to pursue this sort of inquiry, such research would be exceedingly difficult to prosecute.

Research obstacles and pitfalls are also common in instances of correctional outcome research on a more modest scale, such as investigations concerning the *relative* effectiveness of two or more training schools. It is possible to examine several institutions and to find that one produces fewer parole violators than the other without being able to separate out from the influences of other variables the precise contribution which these places make to parole success or failure.

Paul Lerman (1968) has indicated a number of cases in which correctional outcome studies of this kind have been flawed by logical or methodological deficiencies. To take one instance, Lerman discussed a comparison by William and Joan McCord between Wiltwyck School, a private training school, and a state training school. These researchers claimed that Wiltwyck was considerably more successful than the other institution in that it showed complete success in 43 percent of the cases and partial success in 28 percent of the instances, for a total of 71 percent of the cases. The figures on success for the state school were 48 percent complete success and 5 percent partial success, or a total of 53 percent. But in both schools those youngsters who were recorded as partial successes had been in court for law violations following release from incarceration. The critic of this study might suggest that these youths would be more properly classified as failures, rather than as successes. In that event, it could hardly be contended that the private institution was more successful than the public one.

When we discuss the available evidence on correctional outcomes in the pages to follow, we will need to raise the question of the logical and methodological adequacy of the research studies which produced this material. Most of these investigations are centered on training schools, rather than on probation agencies and kindred structures. Unfortunately, few data are at hand concerning the success or failure rates of probation organizations. Several time-and-motion studies of probation do show that probation agents are overburdened with huge caseloads (Hengerer, 1954; Diana, 1955). Inferentially at least, these investigations suggest that probation agencies are not directly responsible for either the successful or unsuccessful cases they produce, for the correctional agents have not devoted much time to them. In one study dealing with the effectiveness of juvenile probation, Frank Scarpitti and Richard Stephenson (1968) studied the results of probation, nonresidential group interaction programs, and institutional commitment on male delinquents in Essex County, New Jersey. They found that the probation agency received the least delinquent, "easier" cases. In addition, a significant number of probationers were "in-program failures" who were sent back to court before completing their program. The boys who did not complete their probation program were more delinquent and less tractable than those who finished the probation period. In this sense they resembled the youths who were in the other programs. Among those boys who completed one or another program (probation, nonresidential treatment, institutionalization), the probationers had the highest postrelease success rate. What all of this adds up to is a picture of probation working with youths with relatively favorable social backgrounds and short delinquency histories. The high success rate for these boys is probably an indicator that they were "self-correctors" who needed minimal treatment, and not that probation per se is responsible for their favorable behavior.

CORRECTIONAL TREATMENT AND THE IMPACT OF TRAINING SCHOOLS

The Rehabilitative Ideal: Growth and Decline

During the first half of the twentieth century, liberal viewpoints and criminological thought both argued that punitive approaches to adult and juvenile offenders ought to be jettisoned, to be replaced by treatment or rehabilitative programs that would endeavor to change lawbreakers into law-abiding citizens or that would strive to reduce various criminogenic social conditions in the community (cf. Gibbons, 1965). The rise of the juvenile court, along with treatment efforts in probation settings or juvenile institutions, was part of a more general and pervasive social movement in the direction of rehabilitation of offenders.

Although it is easy enough to show that the rehabilitative ideal was more often given lip service than it was fully implemented in the various states, the fact remains that until the 1960s therapeutic intervention into the lives of adult or juvenile lawbreakers was widely regarded as the most meaningful and worthwhile correctional strategy. In the name of treatment, individual counseling, group programs, behavior modification efforts, and myriad other forms of correctional-therapeutic handling were directed at offenders.

However, marked pessimism about correctional treatment has become apparent during the past two decades. There is a good deal of evidence that has now accumulated regarding the negligible impact of therapeutic intervention, and in particular, efforts directed at adult offenders have failed to turn up findings that show that treatment has been more effective than traditional modes of custodial handling and the like.

One pessimistic evaluation of correctional treatment endeavors was presented by Walter Bailey (1966), who examined 100 studies of correctional outcome published between 1940 and 1960. He noted that many of those research investigations had failed to turn up evidence in support of treatment, while those studies that did report positive findings concerning therapeutic intervention were flawed in one way or another. Thus much doubt was cast upon the validity of those reports.

Another of these negative assessments of correctional treatment was made by James Robison and Gerald Smith (1971), who examined about a dozen experimental projects that had been conducted in California. They utilized the studies in order to gauge the extent to which different posttreatment outcomes could be produced by sentencing persons to probation rather than imprisoning them, by varying the intensity of probation or parole supervision, or by placing persons on parole as contrasted to discharging them outright from institutions. They claimed that, rather than being the result of treatment, the evidence indicated that any variations in outcomes observed for these different dispositions were attributable to differences among offenders processed by different agencies.

The most comprehensive of these surveys of the results of treatment was conducted by Douglas Lipton, Robert Martinson, and Judith Wilks (1975). They examined 231 treatment projects that had been conducted between 1945 and 1967. The major conclusion from the large-scale review of studies was that (Martinson, 1974: 25) *"with few and isolated exceptions, the rehabilitative efforts that have been reported so far have had no appreciable effect on recidivism"* (emphasis in the original). A similar conclusion was offered by David Greenberg (1977), based on his examination of a large body of treatment evaluation studies.

These surveys, all turning up negative findings concerning correctional intervention, have sent many of the supporters of the rehabilitative ideal reeling. However, some have discounted these negative results and have argued for the continuation of treatment, invoking a medical metaphor in support of their position. They have argued that the negligible impact of therapeutic intervention to date has been due to insufficiently implemented programs; thus it has been claimed that the treatment that has been administered has not been lengthy or intensive enough. Other supporters of therapeutic programs have claimed that few positive results of treatment have turned up to date because particular kinds of intervention have often been directed at inappropriate offender cases. According to this line of argument, some lawbreakers would profit from intensive therapy while others need some kind of group handling. Conversely, intensive treatment is an inappropriate and ineffective recommendation for certain kinds of lawbreakers. This position argues for "different strokes for different folks," that is, for particular kinds of treatment directed at specific kinds of offenders.

The supporters of continued correctional treatment include Ted Palmer (1975), who has argued that the Lipton, Martinson, and Wilks report on the ineffectiveness of correctional treatment actually contained some supporting evidence for the argument that certain specific tactics of treatment produce significant posttreatment effects. Similarly, Charles Shireman, Katherine Mann, Charles Larsen, and Thomas Young (1972) reviewed a dozen studies of treatment within correctional institutions and concluded that certain kinds of therapy may result in significant posttreatment results. Foɪ example, they argued that milieu therapy seems effective with certain kinds of offenders, while certain forms of psychiatric therapy are effective with other offenders.

Marquerite Q. Warren (1976) has been one of the most insistent advocates of treatment of juvenile offenders. She has put forth a detailed and explicit version of the "different-strokes-for-different-folks" thesis, centered around the I-Levels (Interpersonal Maturity Levels) theory which was discussed at length in Chapter 10. In her view, treatment of youthful lawbreakers ought to involve particular kinds of intervention applied to those cases for which they are relevant. Also, treatment workers who are most skilled at particular kinds of treatment, such as psychiatric counseling or group therapy, would be matched with appropriate cases. Although these recommendations seem plausible, the I-Levels scheme has been shown to be an inadequate foundation upon which to erect a program of differential treatment of offenders.

The commentary to this point about the rise and decline of the rehabilitative ideal has been relatively general and not focused specifically on juvenile corrections. Let us turn to the juvenile training school and the evidence that has accumulated about the therapeutic effectiveness of these places.

The Impact of Training Schools

What impact does the training school experience have on the youth who is processed through it? Certainly juvenile institutions are not warm, friendly places in which wards are surrounded by therapeutic influences. Instead, even the best seem to be schools in which few offenders look forward to residing. The preceding accounts of these harsh organizations could easily lead to the hypothesis that their effects are harmful on delinquents, driving them further into deviance as a consequence of the bitterness and hostility they develop out of institutional experience. Yet the training school may have only a benign effect on offenders. Perhaps they enter these places with a bleak outlook on life and antisocial attitudes, but these perspectives may not worsen as a result of incarceration. Accordingly, we need to examine the evidence that can be brought to bear upon the question of training school impact.

What if we should find statistics which show that most wards released from training schools became reinvolved in misconduct? Would this demonstrate that these institutions are directly responsible for recidivism? Not necessarily, for it is possible that the juveniles who are paroled from training schools would continue in criminality even if they had been dealt with in some form of community treatment. In other words, parole failures may be attributable to characteristics and experiences which wards bring with them to the training school, rather than to the effects of the institution itself.

Unfortunately, the kind of evidence which is required in order to probe this issue in depth is not available in quantity. However, one bit of data can be found in the Community Treatment Project in California (Palmer, 1974). In that experimental effort, conducted in Sacramento, Stockton, and San Francisco, youths who would normally have been sent to Youth Authority training schools were instead dealt with in the community. Two kinds of intervention were involved; in one, differential treatment units consisting of a supervisor, treatment agents, and a work supervisor counseled wards who had been sorted into diagnostic types. Guided group interaction units administered group treatment to offenders in the second kind of intervention. Youths in the community treatment experimental groups were matched with control group subjects who had been institutionalized. In the manner of conventional experimental design, wards were randomly assigned either to community treatment or to a training school.

The findings on this project initially seemed to indicate that community treatment is more effective than institutionalization or, stated differently, that training schools are harmful to many wards. Experimental subjects from Stockton and Sacramento who had been exposed to parole for 15 months showed a parole violation rate of 29 percent, while the control group cases had a violation rate of 48 percent.

However, we should not be too quick to accept the community treatment results as an indictment of training schools. Lerman (1968: 57-58) has observed that the parole violation figures suggest that the experimental subjects were less delinquent in postrelease behavior than the controls (institutionalized wards). But in fact, the community-treated youths had committed an average of 2.81 offenses in the parole period as compared to an average of 1.61 for the control subjects. He indicated that the parole officers of the experimental cases were more likely to know about delinquencies on the part of their parolees than were the agents of the controls, so that the total incidence of postrelease misconduct was probably similar for the two groups.

While the agents observed more lawbreaking on the part of the experimental parolees than the control cases, they took action more frequently against the control subjects. When the parole offenses of the subjects are classified in terms of seriousness, interesting results turn up. The percentage of offenders who had their paroles revoked for offenses of low or medium seriousness was considerably higher for the control subjects than the experimentals, so that only in the case of parolees committing high-seriousness acts did the parole agents revoke similar proportions of them. Lerman (1968: 58) concluded:

> Instead of the misleading conclusion derived from using only parole violation differences, it appears that the potential rates of failure of the two programs are similar (at this point in time). The behavioral outputs of the experimentals and controls are probably the same; however, the experimentals' parole agents notice more of this behavior and therefore give the impression that the experimentals are more delinquent. But even though the behavior of the experimentals attracts more notice, it is not evaluated in the same way as the behavior of the controls. This important study may have exercised excellent control over the random selection of boys; unfortunately, the ideology of treating boys in the community spilled over into the postexperimental phase. The experimental and control groups appear to differ in the behavior of the parole agents with respect to the revocation of parole—not in the delinquent behavior of the boys.

These conclusions on community treatment are not to be taken as an argument for the incarceration of juveniles in training schools. To argue that institutions may be benign in effect is not to recommend them. Our suspicion is that these places do not usually contribute much to rehabilitation, so that there is a sense of irrelevancy to them. But we ought to be cautious about indicting them for parole failures in the absence of evidence which shows them to be at fault.

One other observation from the Community Treatment Project is in order. In that experiment, 75 percent of all wards processed through state reception centers met the eligibility criteria for inclusion in the community project, even though many were not assigned to it. Thus training school commitment may be employed too often as a disposition made of offenders.

Let us turn to the matter of training school outcomes. What does the evidence show regarding postrelease behavior of parolees from different training schools? What data are at hand concerning social-psychological dimensions of the training school experience as it impinges upon wards?

Parole Violations

Although nationwide statistics on parole violations by those youths released from training schools are not at hand, several reports are available concerning parole violation behavior of wards released from California state training schools. In one of these, Robert Beverly and Evelyn Guttmann (1962) dealt with the parole performance of wards paroled between 1956 and 1960 during the first 15 months of release from institutions. Parole violation rates varied quite markedly from one institution to another. The investigators contended that these parole violation differences were due to (a) selection factors at commitment which send the least tractable persons to the high violation rate institutions, and (b) variations in training school influences upon wards.

What happens to paroled wards over a longer period of time? Do they eventually withdraw from delinquency and then stay out of trouble permanently? Apparently not, judging from a California study by Carolyn Jamison, Bertram Johnson, and Evelyn Guttmann (1966). In this research, 4000 delinquent wards discharged from the Youth Authority in 1953 and 1958 were examined. Less than 20 percent of the female wards acquired any sort of criminal record in the five-year follow-up period after discharge, so that young women most commonly became "successes." Quite different paths were followed by boys. About 22 percent of the male wards had been discharged from Youth Authority custody as a result of being sent to prison. Another 22 percent were sent to prison within five years after discharge, while another 26 percent received one or more nonprison sentences (fines, jail, and/or probation). Thus only 30 percent of the boys managed to remain free from detected criminality.

Training schools do not seem to be directly responsible for the production of the careers of failure and ruined lives reflected in these dismal figures. Some complex concatenation of factors involving social liabilities stemming from faulty social experiences within the family and community, along with negative effects of correctional handling at earlier stages of the offender's delinquent career, probably lie behind them. By the time these lawbreakers get to training schools, their social opportunities to disengage themselves from misconduct have become severely constricted.

Social-psychological Effects of Training Schools

A group of studies of training school experiences seems to bear out this argument about their effects on youths. Martha Baum and Stanton Wheeler (1968) investigated youths committed for the first time to a Boston Reception Center, in which youths normally stay for six to eight weeks prior to being sent to a regular institution. They interviewed 100 boys who had been in the center for two weeks.

Baum and Wheeler found that most of the youngsters did not have a clear idea of the center and its operations before being admitted there. Most were shocked and upset when informed by the court that they were going to be committed to the center. Most of the delinquents arrived with negative opinions of the staff members and of the other boys in the institution. Baum and Wheeler concluded that most of the delinquents perceived the center as a deprivational experience and expected to receive punishment there, rather than treatment.

Although the center wards brought some negative attitudes about the place with them, more positive sentiments developed on their part. Most of the youths saw their commitment to the place as a fair decision. Over 80 percent of the boys acknowledged that they were mainly to blame for their present predicament. Most of the youngsters continued to have strong, positive feelings about their families and about their eventual return to the parental situation. While most of the youths had developed more negative views of the center after having been there for several weeks and complained about the dull routine, bland food, and so on, their opinions of staff members had become more positive. Most of the boys thought their stay at the center would help them, although many of them were uncertain as to precisely how it would affect them. Parenthetically, most of those who thought the center would help them took a short-run deterrent view of the place, holding that it would "teach me a lesson."

Thomas Eynon and Jon Simpson (1965) conducted research on inmate perceptions in Boy's Industrial School, Lancaster, Ohio, and two open camps operated by the school. The training school had an average daily population in 1960 to 1961 of 887 boys, while the camps averaged sixty-five boys. In Lancaster, 485 first-admission wards were given a detailed multifaceted questionnaire at the point of admission and just before release. The results of this study indicated that the camp boys developed feelings of adjustment to the camp social structure, but the training school wards were more bewildered by life there. The reason for this difference can be found in the gross disparity in size of these places. The most significant finding was that both the training school boys and camp wards developed more positive attitudes, value orientations, and social outlooks during their stay in the institutions. Both groups of boys saw themselves as delinquents at intake and this self-perception did not change over the institutional stay. The camp boys thought they received some benefit from the experience, while the training school youths said they got less than they anticipated from their stay. In response to the question of whether they would want a friend who was in trouble to be sent to the institution, 31 percent of the Lancaster boys and 87 percent of the camp inmates responded affirmatively. Also of some major significance, the boys most often chose cottage supervisors or work supervisors as the persons they knew best, with whom they would share good news, and so on.

Some evidence on the social-psychological effects of training schools is also found in the study of David Street, Robert Vinter, and Charles Perrow (1966), who conducted a comparative investigation dealing with six public and private institutions which ranged in size from 35 to 400 boys. Part of that research dealt with staff-inmate relationships in these schools while another part concerned inmate perspectives. The researchers reported that wards had the most positive perspectives in the treatment-oriented institutions, but the wards of these schools also saw the staff members as unfair and given to playing favorites. The investigators also indicated that the perspectives of boys in custodially oriented schools deteriorated somewhat further over the period of incarceration. In the treatment-oriented plants, group behavior and inmate leadership were structured around more positive attitudes than was true of custodial schools. The boys in the custodial schools were concerned about demonstrating overt behavioral conformity, while the wards in treatment-focused institutions showed more internalized concerns.

The Fricot Ranch study in California also provided information on attitudinal changes on the part of wards in institutions (Jesness, 1965). Part of that experimental study involved psychological measures of various kinds administered to the subjects. The differences between the treatment subjects in the special program and the control wards in the regular Fricot Ranch program were not great, but apparently in the latter the offenders learned impulse control and repression, while in the experimental milieu programs greater self-awareness, spontaneity, and internal anxiety were produced. More important, both the treatment and control subjects seemed to get no worse in psychological adjustment over their stay in the school.

Correctional Treatment and the Suppression Effect

To this point, we have spoken principally of recidivism and nonrecidivism as the measuring rods for correctional effectiveness. In other words, probation, institutional treatment, and other intervention efforts are judged to be effective insofar as the persons who receive these dispositions refrain from further lawbreaking. However, while the recidivism criterion of program impact is the one most often utilized, there are other standards by which program impact might be assessed. In particular, Charles Murray and Louis Cox (1979) have argued that a more appropriate or realistic criterion for judging the effectiveness of programs would be the extent to which they suppress lawbreaking following the intervention period. Suppression refers to reduction in the rate of offending by an individual following intervention, as contrasted to complete cessation of misconduct by that person.

Flowing from this line of argument, a quasi-experimental study was conducted in Illinois between 1974 and 1976 (Murray and Cox, 1979; Lundman,

TABLE 12-1   Suppression Effect of UDIS and Department of Corrections (Training School) Placement

| | NUMBER OF OFFENDERS | MEAN NUMBER OF ARRESTS | | | SUPPRESSION EFFECT (PERCENT REDUCTION IN ANNUAL ARRESTS) |
		BEFORE PLACEMENT	AFTER PLACEMENT	DIFFERENCE	
UDIS					
Nonresidential services	156	5.7	2.7	–3.0	–53%
Residential services	40	5.5	2.2	–3.3	–60
Wilderness programs	14	7.6	4.0	–3.6	–47
Out-of-town camp	45	7.1	2.1	–5.0	–70
Intensive	11	7.7	1.4	–6.3	–82
Department of Corrections	317	6.3	2.0	–4.3	–68
Totals	583	6.2	2.3	–3.9	–63

Source: Charles A. Murray and Louis A. Cox, Jr., in "UDIS: Less Drastic Alternatives", p. 118 in *Beyond Probation: Juvenile Corrections and the Chronic Delinquency.* Copyright © by Sage Publications, Inc. Reprinted by permission.

1984) which examined the postintervention lawbreaking patterns of over 300 youths who had been sent to two state training schools, along with the records of 266 relatively comparable youngsters who had been sentenced to one of several less drastic placement alternatives than training schools. This latter group was handled through a federally funded Unified Delinquency Intervention Services (UDIS) program which was intended to get youths out of training schools. The researchers gathered records of misconduct on the part of the juveniles for the year following treatment.

The suppression effects of various programs are shown in Table 12-1 (Murray and Cox, 1979: 118). As can be seen from that table, *all* the intervention tactics that were studied in this research appeared to bring about sizable suppression results. These data suggest that the picture of correctional failure may not be quite as dismal as first impressions indicate.

EFFORTS TO IMPROVE CORRECTIONAL TREATMENT

Correctional administrators and criminological theorists have frequently given their attention to attempts to increase the positive impact of such correctional experiences as training school incarceration upon delinquent wards. We have noted some of these innovations in rehabilitation in the preceding pages. At this point, let us examine additional research and experimentation which have made an effort to maximize the impact of regular correctional programs, particularly in training schools.

Psychiatric Treatment

One of the most enduring notions in the field of delinquency correction is that offenders can be led to improved behavior through psychiatric intervention which alters the psychological tensions from which their behavior is presumed to be a result. An early effort to deal intensively with delinquents through psychiatric therapy has been reported by LaMay Adamson and H. Warren Dunham (1956). They examined the history of the Wayne County (Detroit) Clinic for Child Study in Michigan. From 1924 to 1948, the clinic staff was heavily augmented with additional psychiatric professionals; thus its effects upon wards should have become more prominent if psychotherapy is effective. But follow-up study showed almost no reduction in the proportions of treated youths who got into further trouble. In 1930, 45 percent of the boys were later arrested by the police, as contrasted to 39 percent of those who had been in the clinic in 1948. Adamson and Dunham concluded that the therapy apparently failed because it probably was inappropriate for the working-class delinquents to whom it was applied.

More recently, Guttmann (1963) has presented findings from a short-term psychiatric treatment experiment in California at Fred C. Nelles School and at Preston School of Industry. In both these institutions, boys were placed in a psychiatric treatment unit in which they received psychotherapy from a psychiatrist, a psychiatric social worker, and psychologists. The parole violation rate of the youths who received psychiatric treatment was compared to that for other control boys who had been processed through the regular school program. The results indicated that the Nelles psychiatrically treated boys had a lower violation rate than did the controls, while the wards treated at Preston did poorer on parole than the control youths. These different effects were probably the result of several factors. For one, the Preston boys were older than the Nelles subjects and they also differed in terms of certain psychological characteristics. In addition, the organizational climate in which psychiatric treatment was pursued differed in the two schools. In Nelles School, the psychiatric unit was new, had high staff morale, and enjoyed other favorable conditions, while at Preston, the unit was older and was the focus of staff hostility from nonclinic personnel. Consequently, the psychiatrically treated boys at Preston may have received invidious handling from staff members which offset any gains from the special therapy.

Treatment Through Social Influences

Alteration of the social relations and attitudes of delinquents has been attempted in a number of ways, including street worker programs which try to get deviant groups to develop new social norms. In institutions this endeavor has often taken the form of group therapy, in which the treatment goal is to get group members to adopt new values and to put pressure upon each other to show allegiance to these new standards. The problem with this sort of activity is that the group members are usually under counter pressures from other inmates in the training school to renounce the values being promulgated within therapy groups. In addition, the conditions of institutional life make it difficult to reward offenders in any meaningful way for any positive psychological or behavioral changes. The realization of these milieu obstacles to group treatment has led to the hypothesis that meaningful therapeutic intervention can best be conducted in the organization or institution structured so as to constitute a therapeutic milieu. In this kind of training school or other treatment site, all of the living experiences undergone by the subjects would be designed to pressure them toward allegiance to prosocial norms and behavior.

Probably the most famous effort to contrive a therapeutic milieu in an institution was the Highfields Project in New Jersey (McCorkle, Elias, and Bixby, 1958). In that experiment, the delinquent subjects were placed in a small institution, formerly the mansion of Charles Lindbergh, which held about two dozen boys. The wards were given a treatment diet of "guided group interaction" (group therapy) in the evenings and, in addition, they were given opportunities to work for pay at a nearby mental institution. They were not compelled to work, as they might have been in a conventional training school, and they could be fired if they did not perform adequately. The architects of the program viewed the delinquent boys as normal youngsters with antisocial attitudes and self-images. The boys tended to denigrate the importance of conventional work careers and regarded other conforming behavior patterns with scorn. This entire program of guided group interaction, along with the related work experiences and peer interaction, was directed toward pressuring the delinquents into new perspectives and improved work habits.

Several lines of evidence seem at first glance to confirm the value of the Highfields program. As a part of the research program associated with that institution, a projective personality test was given to Highfields boys and to inmates of Annandale Reformatory, a conventional state institution, both at the time of admission and at a later point in their school stay. The test results indicated that the reformatory boys moved toward bleaker, darker outlooks on life during their stay there and may have become resigned to further deviation as a life career; the Highfields youths showed movement in an opposite direction.

Lloyd McCorkle, Albert Elias, and F. Lovell Bixby (1958) also compared the parole success of Highfields boys with that of a group of Annandale inmates who had been incarcerated prior to the opening of Highfields but who were thought to be similar to the youngsters sent to the latter place. The reformatory inmates showed a failure rate of 33 percent in the first year upon release, compared to a figure of only 18 percent for Highfields parolees. In a second evaluation of Highfields, H. Ashley Weeks (1963) compared a sample of Annandale parolees with released wards from Highfields. He found that 47 percent of the former and 63 percent of the latter remained in the community and free from criminality for at least one year. Little difference was found in parole failure for white boys in the two places, but black boys from Highfields had a success rate of 60 percent, compared to 33 percent for Annandale black parolees.

These parole statistics seem to show Highfields to be significantly more effective than the conventional reformatory. However, Lerman (1968) reanalyzed Weeks's data, showing them to be less convincing as a demonstration of the effectiveness of Highfields. Lerman indicated that 18 percent of the Highfields subjects did not complete treatment, having been returned to court as unsuitable for the program. Very few Annandale subjects failed to complete a stay there. When the Highfields boys who did not complete the program were included as program failures, the success rates for the two institutions turned out to be quite similar.

Parenthetically, Lerman pointed out that the luxury of being able to reject potential wards for treatment is mainly enjoyed by private agencies, and that caution is therefore in order in evaluating claims they might advance about their rehabilitative efficacy.

The Fricot Ranch study was also an effort at milieu treatment (Jesness, 1965). The conventional, harmful training school milieu against which the experiment was directed is described in the following excerpt from the study report (Jesness, 1965: 4):

> When admitted to an institution for delinquents, boys bring with them delinquent values, a hostile attitude toward authority, and a rejection of conventional goals. The normal tendency of young boys in institutions is to cluster into informal groups, erect subtle barriers toward administrative efforts to reach them, and to maintain value systems at odds with the rehabilitative aims of the school. New boys coming into the school program participate in these natural groups and are apt to undergo an experience which tends to reinforce their delinquent value system. While they may conform outwardly to the school program, no basic modification of delinquent attitudinal patterns takes place. When released, they once again seek associations and engage in behavior congenial to their delinquent character and values.

In order to try to overcome this system which emphasizes control of boys and outward conformity on their part, a group of wards was placed in a twenty-boy experimental lodge, in contrast to the regular fifty-boy living units. The experimental subjects experienced intensified staff-ward contacts and other therapeutic experiences designed to pressure them toward prosocial values.

The results of this experiment initially seemed favorable to intensified milieu treatment. The parole violation rate for boys who had been released for one year was 32 percent for the experimentals and 48 percent for the controls. However, the violation rates for youths who had been released from the school for two years were nearly the same, while 80 percent of the wards in the treated and control groups who had been released three years earlier subsequently became reinvolved in lawbreaking. In short, the Fricot project seemed to retard the speed at which parolees become reinvolved in violations, but it did not significantly reduce the number who eventually get into further trouble. However, even this finding is suspect, for Lerman (1968) has observed that the control subjects were less frequently white youths and more often from poor homes than the experimental youths.

SUMMARY

After some observations about the flow of cases through the juvenile correctional machinery, we took up that brand of thinking in the area of deviant behavior which is usually identified as labeling theory—that perspective which maintains that when offenders are singled out by the police, courts, probation officers, institutions, and

other labelers of deviance, they become stigmatized or subject to other social liabilities which markedly reduce their ability to withdraw from misconduct. We have
attempted to marshal the available evidence on this view, but good data on the effects of the early stages of apprehension and disposition of offenders are lacking.

Much of this chapter centered around the training school, its social structure,
and its effects upon wards who pass through it. Available data point to the benign
impact of the institution, rather than to any directly harmful consequences upon
delinquents. In short, the training school appears to be a satisfactory warehouse for
the storage of delinquents if the community demands that they be isolated for
some time period, but it ought not to be supposed that the institution is a positive
influence.

The following generalizations can be made from the information in this
chapter:

1. The various segments of the correctional apparatus such as police bureaus,
   juvenile courts, probation agencies, and other organizations may have direct
   effects upon delinquent careers. However, little research has been conducted
   concerning the impact of these structures upon delinquency. This subject
   represents one about which investigation is sorely needed.

2. Training schools in the United States vary in terms of size, institutional aims,
   and other conditions, but all appear to be principally structured around the
   goal of control of wards. Even in treatment-oriented training schools the major focus of attention is on conformity, prevention of escapes, and ends of
   that kind.

3. Training schools do not usually succeed in restraining wards from further lawbreaking, for parole violation rates from these places are quite high. Half to
   over three-fourths of first admissions to juvenile institutions apparently become reinvolved in delinquent conduct, although considerably fewer of them
   continue into adult criminality.

4. Training schools apparently have benign effects upon wards processed through
   them; although "reformation" does not usually occur, neither does the institution directly contribute to recidivism. Most training school wards emerge
   from these places with no more criminal skills or more serious antisocial attitudes than when they entered.

An unequivocal answer to the question of whether the training school can be
converted into a therapeutic milieu is premature, but the studies considered here do
not lend much encouragement to those who would remake the training school into
a therapeutic clinic. Perhaps it is time to look for innovative alternatives to institutionalization, in which few if any offenders would be sent to training schools
These matters will be examined in Chapter 13.

REFERENCES

ADAMSON, LA MAY and DUNHAM, H. WARREN (1956). "Clinical Treatment of Male Delinquents: A Case Study in Effort and Result." *American Sociological Review* 21 (June):
312-30.

BARKER, GORDON H. and ADAMS, W. THOMAS (1959). "The Social Structure of a Correctional Institution." *Journal of Criminal Law, Criminology and Police Science* 49 (January–February): 417–22.

BAILEY, WALTER C. (1966). "An Evaluation of 100 Studies of Correctional Outcome." *Journal of Criminal Law, Criminology and Police Science* 57 (June): 153–60.

BAUM, MARTHA and WHEELER, STANTON (1968). "Becoming an Inmate," pp. 153–85. In Stanton Wheeler, ed. *Controlling Delinquents.* New York: Wiley.

BECKER, HOWARD S. (1963). *Outsiders.* New York: Free Press.

BEVERLY, ROBERT F. and GUTTMANN, EVELYN S. (1962). *An Analysis of Parole Performance by Institution of Release, 1956-60.* Sacramento: Department of the Youth Authority.

CARTER, BARBARA (1973). "Reform School Families." *Society* 2 (December): 36–43.

DEUTSCH, ALBERT (1949). "A Journalist's Impressions of State Training Schools." *Focus* 28 (March): 33–40.

DIANA, LEWIS (1955). "Is Casework in Probation Necessary?" *Focus* 34 (January): 1–8.

EYNON, THOMAS G. and SIMPSON, JON E. (1965). "The Boy's Perception of Himself in a State Training School for Delinquents." *Social Service Review* 39 (March): 31–37.

FISHER, SETHARD (1961). "Social Organization in a Correctional Institution." *Pacific Sociological Review* 4 (Fall): 87–93.

FLANAGAN, TIMOTHY J. and McCLOUD, MAUREEN (1983). *Sourcebook of Criminal Justice Statistics, 1982.* Washington, D.C.: U.S. Department of Justice.

GIALLOMBARDO, ROSE (1974). *The Social World of Imprisoned Girls.* New York: Wiley.

GIBBONS, DON C. (1965). *Changing the Lawbreaker.* Englewood Cliffs, N.J.: Prentice-Hall.

GIBBONS, DON C. (1979). *The Criminological Enterprise.* Englewood Cliffs, N.J.: Prentice-Hall.

GIBBONS, DON C. and JONES, JOSEPH F. (1975). *The Study of Deviance.* Englewood Cliffs, N.J.: Prentice-Hall.

GREENBERG, DAVID E. (1977). "The Correctional Effects of Corrections," pp. 111–48. In David F. Greenberg, ed. *Corrections and Punishment.* Beverly Hills, Cal.: Sage.

GUTTMANN, EVELYN S. (1963). *Effects of Short-term Psychiatric Treatment on Boys in Two California Youth Authority Institutions.* Sacramento: Department of the Youth Authority.

HALLECK, SEYMOUR and HERSKO, MARVIN (1962). "Homosexual Behavior in a Correctional Institution for Adolescent Girls." *American Journal of Orthopsychiatry* 32 (October): 911–17.

HENGERER, GERTRUDE M. (1954). "Organizing Probation Services," pp. 45–59. In National Probation and Parole Association, *National Probation and Parole Association Yearbook, 1953.* New York: National Probation and Parole Association.

JAMISON, CAROLYN B., JOHNSON, BERTRAM M., and GUTTMANN, EVELYN S. (1966). *An Analysis of Post-discharge Criminal Behavior.* Sacramento: Department of the Youth Authority.

JESNESS, CARL F. (1965). *The Fricot Ranch Study.* Sacramento: Department of the Youth Authority.

KRISBERG, BARRY and SCHWARTZ, IRA (1983). "Rethinking Juvenile Justice." *Crime and Delinquency* 29 (July): 333–64.

LERMAN, PAUL (1968). "Evaluative Studies of Institutions for Delinquents: Implications for Research and Social Policy." *Social Work* 13 (July): 55–64.

LIPTON, DOUGLAS, MARTINSON, ROBERT, and WILKS, JUDITH (1975). *The Effectiveness of Correctional Treatment—A Survey of Treatment Evaluation Studies.* Springfield, Mass.: Praeger.

LUNDMAN, RICHARD J. (1984). *Prevention and Control of Juvenile Delinquency.* New York: Oxford University Press.

MAHONEY, ANN RANKIN (1974). "The Effect of Labeling Upon Youths in the Juvenile Justice System: A Review of the Evidence." *Law and Society Review* 8 (Summer): 583–614.

MARTINSON, ROBERT (1974). "What Works? Questions and Answers About Prison Reform." *The Public Interest* 35 (Spring): 22-54.

McCORKLE, LLOYD W., ELIAS, ALBERT, and BIXBY, F. LOVELL (1958). *The Highfields Story.* New York: Holt, Rinehart and Winston.

MURRAY, CHARLES A. and COX, LOUIS A., JR. (1979). *Beyond Probation: Juvenile Corrections and the Chronic Delinquency.* Beverly Hills, Cal.: Sage.

OHLIN, LLOYD E. (1958). "The Reduction of Role-conflict in Institutional Staff." *Children* 4 (March–April): 65-69.

OHLIN, LLOYD E. and LAWRENCE, WILLIAM C. (1959). "Social Interaction Among Clients as a Treatment Problem." *Social Work* 4 (April): 3-13.

PALMER, TED (1974). "The Youth Authority's Community Treatment Project." *Federal Probation* 38 (March): 3-14.

PALMER, TED (1975). "Martinson Revisited." *Journal of Research in Crime and Delinquency* 12 (July): 133-52.

POLSKY, HOWARD (1962). *Cottage Six.* New York: Russell Sage.

ROBISON, JAMES and SMITH, GERALD (1971). "The Effectiveness of Correctional Programs." *Crime and Delinquency* 17 (January): 67-80.

ROGERS, KRISTINE OLSON (1972). " 'For Her Own Protection. . .': Conditions of Incarceration for Female Juvenile Offenders in the State of Connecticut." *Law and Society Review* 7 (Winter): 223-46.

SCARPITTI, FRANK R. and STEPHENSON, RICHARD M. (1968). "A Study of Probation Effectiveness." *Journal of Criminal Law, Criminology and Police Science* 59 (September): 361-69.

SHIREMAN, CHARLES H., MANN, KATHERINE BAIRD, LARSEN, CHARLES, and YOUNG, THOMAS (1972). "Findings from Experiments in Treatment in the Correctional Setting." *Social Service Review.* 46 (March): 38-59.

STREET, DAVID, VINTER, ROBERT D., and PERROW, CHARLES (1966). *Organization for Treatment.* New York: Free Press.

TANNENBAUM, FRANK (1938). *Crime and the Community.* New York: Ginn.

TOPPING, RUTH (1943). "Treatment of the Pseudo-social Boy." *American Journal of Orthopsychiatry* 13 (April): 353-60.

VINTER, ROBERT D., DOWNS, GEORGE, and HALL, JOHN (1975). *Juvenile Corrections in the States: Residential Programs and Deinstitutionalization.* Ann Arbor: National Assessment of Juvenile Corrections, University of Michigan.

VINTER, ROBERT D., NEWCOMB, THEODORE M. and KISH, RHEA, eds. (1976). *Time Out: A National Survey of Juvenile Correctional Programs.* Ann Arbor: National Assessment of Juvenile Corrections, University of Michigan.

WARREN, MARGUERITE Q. (1976). "Intervention with Juvenile Delinquents," pp. 176-204. In Margaret K. Rosenheim, ed. *Pursuing Justice for the Child.* Chicago: University of Chicago Press.

WEBER, GEORGE H. (1957). "Conflicts Between Professional and Nonprofessional Personnel in Institutional Delinquency Treatment." *Journal of Criminal Law, Criminology and Police Science* 48 (May–June): 26-43.

WEBER, GEORGE H. (1961). "Emotional and Defensive Reactions of Cottage Parents," pp. 189-228. In Donald R. Cressey, ed. *The Prison.* New York: Holt, Rinehart and Winston.

WEEKS, H. ASHLEY (1963). *Youthful Offenders at Highfields.* Ann Arbor: University of Michigan Press.

WELLFORD, CHARLES (1975). "Labeling Theory and Criminology: An Assessment." *Social Problems* 22 (February): 332-45.

ZALD, MAYER N. (1962). "Power Balance and Staff Conflict in Correctional Institutions." *Administrative Science Quarterly* 7 (June): 22-49.

chapter 13

ALTERNATIVES
TO INCARCERATION

INTRODUCTION

If we were to identify some of the major themes of this book presented in the chapters so far, they would include the following propositions and contentions. Chapter 1 noted that the traditional view of delinquency held by lay persons, and found in delinquency books as well, has been that juvenile lawbreakers are distinctly different from nondelinquents. This portrayal of the real world divides it up into "good boys" and "bad boys," along with "good girls" and "bad girls." Then, too, older perspectives on juvenile misconduct assumed that correctional intervention into the lives of delinquents is needed in order to change them into nondelinquents. Third, lay persons and sociologists alike tended to assume that correctional treatment of delinquents is a goal that is within our grasp. Findings on existing programs showing that correctional intervention often failed to alter the behavior of lawbreakers was not taken as evidence that juvenile correctional treatment is an illusory goal. Instead these data were interpreted as indicating only that more money must be pumped into therapeutic endeavors, better trained workers must be hired, and other improvements in correctional treatment are in order. Finally, older orientations to the delinquency problem rarely involved much concern about the rights of juveniles who were drawn into the correctional machinery. Correctional treatment was thought of as benevolent, benign, and beneficial in its impact upon youths, hence there was nothing from which juveniles need be protected.

The sociological orientations to delinquency that have grown up in the past decade or so contrast markedly to the older notions. As we saw in Chapter 3, the available evidence indicates that the delinquency-nondelinquency dichotomy is false and that most juveniles, particularly in American society, are involved in some degree of youthful misconduct. We noted that the "delinquency problem" in one community or another is comprised not only of the misbehavior of juveniles, but also of the social reactions of police, schools, and other community agencies toward youngsters. That is, delinquency rates based on police arrests or juvenile court referrals often tell us a good deal about the responses of these organizations and relatively little about the actual extent of youthful misconduct in the community. The police in some areas frequently report most of the juveniles they encounter to the court, while in other areas the police deal with most lawbreakers informally, without court referral. Accordingly, delinquency rates based on juvenile court referrals cannot be taken as some kind of stable index which reveals the true extent of youthful lawbreaking.

Another facet of newer perspectives on delinquency revolves around the question of due process protection for juveniles. As we saw in Chapter 2, a number of lawyers, sociologists, and others voiced gnawing suspicions for some years that many youths were in danger of being harmed in one way or another by the well-intentioned but overzealous actions of juvenile courts, in which youngsters had been placed on informal probation without benefit of a court hearing, or in which other questionable actions had been taken against them. These concerns, and the agitation for due process protections which accompanied them, ultimately led to the Supreme Court decisions, including *Kent, Gault,* and *Winship,* that extended due process guarantees to juveniles before the court.

Still another aspect of newer views on delinquency has to do with the conclusion that traditional correctional approaches have failed to rehabilitate offenders and divert them from lawbreaking careers. Indeed, many would now argue that correctional efforts often drive delinquents further into involvement in misconduct, so that these efforts are actually deleterious in their impact on offenders. Also, in this emerging orientation to juvenile treatment, program failure is attributed to more fundamental problems than those of inadequate financing or ill-trained personnel. Some critics hold that correctional intervention often fails because the psychogenic causal theories on which much of it is based are erroneous, while others pessimistically point to a host of organizational and structural problems that get in the way of successful correctional treatment.

Two implications flow from this pessimistic evaluation of traditional correctional intervention activities. One of these is that we need to explore a host of innovative tactics such as community-based treatment, small therapeutic milieu institutions, and parallel stratagems that represent a break with those proven failures that have formed the basis of correctional efforts in the past. A second widely advocated proposal is that we should endeavor to shrink back on the population of youthful offenders that is sent through the juvenile justice machinery. This argument suggests that petty delinquents, in particular, ought to be ignored or diverted out of the court apparatus into private agencies, youth services bureaus, or some other alternative to the official system.

Edwin M. Schur's (1973) writings illustrate this latter recommendation. His survey of reactions to delinquency indicated that we have gone from heavy emphasis upon psychogenic images of delinquents and individual treatment of offenders to a variety of sociologically informed efforts at liberal reform, often taking the form of attempts at community change or creation of new economic opportunities for deviant youths. Schur found much to criticize in these tactics and argued that most of them tend to stigmatize delinquents and drive them further into careers in lawbreaking. After concluding this pessimistic assessment, he (Schur, 1973: 155) offered the following recommendation: "Thus, the basic injunction for public policy becomes: *leave kids alone whenever possible*" (emphasis in the original). The trouble with such a recommendation is that it is relatively useless until we spell out those circumstances and conditions in which it is both possible and desirable to ignore youthful deviant acts. Schur's analysis is not very helpful in this regard.

Chapter 13 is devoted to an overview of these newer proposals for youth diversion activities, innovative alternatives to institutionalization of delinquents, and preventive endeavors.

CORRECTIONAL REFORM: SOME CAUTIONARY REMARKS

It would be well to begin the discussion of correctional change and correctional reform proposals with a few words of warning. For one thing, it is by no means clear that new programs are always better than those they are designed to replace—correctional change cannot always be equated with correctional progress. Additionally, there is a wealth of evidence indicating that correctional reform movements have often languished at the proposal stage; thus many of them have only been minimally implemented, if at all. Finally, we can find an abundance of cases in which well-intentioned correctional reforms have resulted in unanticipated and undesirable consequences. One would be ill-advised to uncritically embrace every plausible suggestion for change in the juvenile justice system that is encountered.

Consider one dramatic proposal urging new approaches to treatment of juvenile offenders: the "shock" program portrayed on the 1979 television program, "Scared Straight," which reported on a program in a New Jersey prison in which allegedly hard-core juvenile offenders were confronted by inmates who cursed and shouted at them, telling them of the sexual assaults, beatings, and other fearful and dismal experiences awaiting them in prison if they persisted in delinquent activity (Lundman, 1984: 136–55). According to the television account, this prison encounter experience between convicts and delinquents had worked wonders, showing a success rate in which 80 to 90 percent of the 10,000 juveniles who had gone through it refrained from further lawbreaking. In the period immediately following the presentation of this television program, large numbers of citizens, celebrities, police officials, and other individuals rushed to urge that similar efforts be undertaken in their own communities or states.

In our view, there are compelling arguments against adoption of correctional endeavors such as the "Scared Straight" program illustrated, even if they produce results claimed for them. There are serious moral questions that need to be raised about activities that expose juveniles to the harsh verbal abuse and other experiences that are involved in correctional programs of this kind. However, the evidence indicates that this is another in a long list of panaceas that have come and gone from the correctional scene. A follow-up study (Finckenauer, 1982: 135) showed that about 59 percent of the youngsters who had been through the program had not been charged with new offenses in the six months following their participation, but 89 percent of the control group of youths who had not been in the program had remained free from delinquency during the same period! These results suggest that the program not only failed to achieve the results proclaimed for it, it may even have been harmful to a sizable number of youthful offenders. The "Scared Straight" episode is an example of an altogether too common phenomenon in the United States, in which a panacea for crime or delinquency is enthusiastically accepted, followed later by disillusioning evidence showing that the supposed miracle cure for lawbreaking is worthless.

Justine Wise Polier, a former Family Court judge, has offered some incisive observations about the problems, pitfalls, and unanticipated consequences that often crop up in juvenile reform ventures (Polier, 1979). Although she acknowledged the validity of the criticisms that have been directed at the juvenile court and practices that have existed in the past, she also warned against the hasty, unthinking acceptance of innovations that might result in the abandonment of valuable existing programs and the adoption of new ones which contain gaps and omissions (also see Rosenheim, 1976).

One example offered by Polier of a questionable reform centers around the movement toward "purchase of service" arrangements, in which juvenile courts have contracted with private agencies for various educational and treatment services for court wards. The logic of this development is that private agencies are less stigmatizing and that private organizations can do a better job of correctional intervention than can the coercive machinery of the court. But, Polier noted that (1979: 221):

> Juvenile courts have been justly criticized for discriminatory dispositions that disproportionately place white children in private residential treatment centers and nonwhite children in training schools. Yet the prescriptions which support purchase of services fail to challenge pervasive racial and religious discrimination in the private sector that determines which children will be accepted or rejected for service. Current prescriptions for reform fail to recognize that diversion from the court will not end such discriminatory selection of children. As overt discrimination is replaced by covert action, including the concealed use of quotas, new and more effective prescriptions are required.

Polier pointed out another problem with the purchase of services arrangement, namely that this practice often lacks accountability in that little or no attention is paid to the quality of the services provided to the offender, because private agencies are not subject to the same administrative scrutiny as are state-administered ones.

Another questionable reform, according to Polier, concerns certain developments in the direction of due process for children. She did not quarrel with Supreme Court decisions such as *Gault* or *Winship* which extended due process protections to juveniles, but she did warn against the potentially harmful consequences to offenders of proposals, offered in the name of uncovering injustice and discrimination, to open juvenile hearings to the public and the media.

Polier also suggested that the movement toward diversion of youngsters out of the justice system could result in a number of negative, unanticipated consequences. For one, she pointed out that (Polier, 1979: 236): "Those intent on reform could not have foreseen the present tendency to label status offenders as 'good' youths and the delinquents as 'bad' youths, incapable of rehabilitation and not entitled to services. Yet that is how the prescription of reform is being increasingly used." The danger against which Polier warned is that a double standard of juvenile justice may grow up, in which first offenders and other petty cases are virtually ignored, at the same time as other juveniles will come to be regarded as "bad" and beyond redemption, so that they then are shunted off to harsh and punitive programs.

Polier's warning about a double standard of juvenile justice is not simply idle speculation. The American Bar Association and the Institute for Judicial Administration have developed a set of model standards for juvenile justice systems which recommend that some youngsters be diverted away from the scrutiny of the system at the same time that determinant sentences designed for punitive purposes be established for certain classes of juvenile offenders. Moreover, these recommendations which seemingly point in different directions have been implemented in some states. For example, Florida, Pennsylvania, Iowa, and Washington have revised their state laws so that status offenders can only be brought under juvenile court jurisdiction as dependent or neglected cases. The majority of states have enacted legislation which forbids incarceration of status offenders in training schools.

These moves in the direction of reduced court intervention have accompanied legislative actions in opposite directions in some states, in which determinant and harsher sentences have been stipulated for delinquents judged to be serious offenders. In particular, the Juvenile Justice Act, passed in Washington State in 1977, explicitly defined punishment of offenders and protection of the general public as major aims of the juvenile justice system in that state. Moreover, in Washington, a relatively fixed set of punishments has been enacted into law. Adjudicated delinquents are sorted out as minor, medium, or serious offenders on the basis of age and prior delinquent record. The juvenile justice system act requires that nearly all serious delinquents be sent to training schools with the length of stay in the institution being determined largely by statute. Middle and minor offenders also receive sentences of fines or are required to perform community services that are spelled out in the juvenile justice act. All of this is a marked departure from the treatment-oriented juvenile court and institutions operating with only very broad limitations on their powers and decisions (Rubin, 1979; Serrill, 1979).

ALTERNATIVES TO COURT REFERRAL AND COURT ACTION

In one important sense, the strategy of responding to delinquency by tactics of "benign neglect," in which little or nothing is done to offenders, is very old and honorable. We have already seen in Chapter 5 that the police dispose of a large share of the cases that come to their attention by giving verbal admonitions to the youths and then dismissing them, rather than by sending them on to juvenile court. A study by Carter (1968) of two adjacent California metropolitan area communities is a specific illustration of police policies of long standing. Absorption of arrested youths into the community without court intervention was commonplace in the two middle income communities he studied. Further, he recommended that absorption be adopted as a police stratagem in other cities and neighborhoods as well.

What distinguishes the newer proposals regarding diversion of delinquents out of the official justice machinery is that these have been informed by detailed theories regarding youthful misconduct. In addition, the recommendations concerning diversion tactics would have us adopt more consistent policies and decisions about these matters than has been the case in the past, in which police dispositions varied from one community to another and in which little explicit discussion of informal disposition of cases by the police took place.

DIVERSION FROM THE JUVENILE COURT AND COMMUNITY TREATMENT

Diversion in Theory and Practice

A plethora of ideas and themes revolving around the notion of diversion has sprung up in the United States in the past two or three decades. Judicious nonintervention, benign neglect, decriminalization, diversion, release on own recognizance, and other notions are all elements of a central theme of reducing the number of offenders in the criminal and/or juvenile justice systems (Lundman, 1984: 79-104). Additionally, a heterogeneous collection of programs has grown up, all identified as diversion efforts. No wonder, then, that there is currently much confusion about diversion as a correctional strategy (Carter and Klein, 1976; Cressey and McDermott, 1974).

Lemert (1971) has provided one detailed exposition of the case for diversion of youths from juvenile court handling. He argued that a number of grave inadequacies plague juvenile courts and prevent them from rendering the kind of therapeutic intervention envisioned by early architects of the court. For one, he noted the *failure to differentiate*, by which he meant that many juvenile tribunals have failed to become juvenile courts in more than name alone. Many are staffed with untrained judges, insufficient probation officers, inadequate clinical personnel, and so on. Lemert also drew attention to the problem of *overburden*; courts are deluged with far more cases than they can handle. Lemert also scored courts for their *bureaucratic* features, claiming that many of them are caught up in routinization of services, a "people-changing" orientation to wards that processes cases in insensitive ways. Finally, he argued that juvenile courts are faced with *overreach of the law* because they deal with petty offenders and violators of status offense provisions who could be better handled outside the court.

Lemert recommended that large numbers of juveniles be diverted out of the juvenile court, in part because of the already mentioned inadequacies and short-comings of the court. But he also suggested restraints in the use of juvenile tribunals because of the suspicion that these agencies may have harmful effects upon youthful offenders, driving them further into lawbreaking instead of out of it. On this point, he observed that (Lemert, 1971: 8-9):

> A final way of perceiving the juvenile court illuminates the way in which it designates deviance, shapes its expression, and helps to perpetuate it in its secondary form. It does so by redefining normal problems of children and youth as special problems requiring legal action and restraining controls. In a real sense it "causes" delinquency by processing cases of children and youth whose problems might be ignored, normalized in their original settings, or dealt with as family, educational, or welfare problems.

The thrust of this argument is that courts inadvertently stigmatize many of the youngsters that are referred there for relatively petty and innocuous acts of delinquency and who might best be ignored or handled outside the court. This stigmatization experience then makes it increasingly more difficult for the offenders to withdraw from deviance. Accordingly, Lemert recommended that some juveniles and their delinquent activities ought to be ignored by the court or, in his terms, be subjected to "judicious nonintervention." Others should be diverted to other agencies instead of being referred to court. Further, Lemert suggested that decisions to ignore, divert, or refer juveniles ought to be based on assessments of their *conduct* and its *manifest consequences* to them and to others, rather than upon such elusive criteria as "treatment needs," degree of psychological pathology, and the like. In short, he argued that the juvenile court should restrict its business to dealing with offenders who engage in serious acts of lawbreaking.

Diversion to What?

There is an appealing simplicity to suggestions that we ought to engage in "judicious nonintervention" and "benign neglect," or that we should leave children alone whenever possible. Similarly, if the critics are correct in their negative diagnoses of the ills of the juvenile court, surely a reasonable policy would be one of diverting youths away from that defective machinery. However, we must then almost immediately face the next question, to wit: To what shall we divert juvenile offenders? Where shall we send them as alternatives to court referral, if it appears that they need some aid or intervention? Many offenders who do not appear to be suitable subjects for court referral still do strike many persons as in need of some kind of action and cannot simply be ignored.

Lemert (1971: 19-34) spoke to this question in his analysis of alternatives to court referral. He examined various possibilities of turning youthful deviants over to the schools, welfare agencies, law enforcement organizations, or community organizations. However, his assessment of the potentialities of these alternative forms of action was generally pessimistic. For example, he observed that the proposal that community agencies somehow ought to involve themselves in greater cooperation and coordination of efforts tends to be a fairly vague or unworkable answer to the question of alternative structures to which to send juveniles.

The perspective on delinquency out of which diversion recommendations flow stresses the episodic and transitory nature of much youthful misconduct. This viewpoint also argues that most juvenile offenders are normal youngsters who are not in need of some kind of clinical intervention. To many diversion theorists, this theoretical foundation implies that juveniles should be diverted to programs that "normalize" their delinquent acts (Rosenheim, 1976). *Problemization*, which involves an individualized approach to locate the sources of delinquency in personal inadequacies of the offender, would be replaced by different assumptions and tactics. Such programs of normalization would adopt a stance toward the misbehaving youth in which his or her lawbreaking would be viewed not as some symptom of personal pathology, but rather as low-level misconduct which is transient and can be remedied through some kind of aid and assistance delivered by the agency.

The normalization recommendations of Rosenheim have much in common with the youth development proposals of Kenneth Polk and Solomon Kobrin (1972). Rosenheim argued that diverted youths should be provided with positive life experiences directed at opening up legitimate roles for them in American society. Diversion programs should work toward enhancing positive self-images on the part of juveniles. Polk and Kobrin outlined four basic components of a legitimate identity: (1) a sense of competence, (2) a sense of usefulness, (3) a sense of belonging, and (4) a sense of power or potency. They also enumerated five conditions that must be met by any program that purports to provide access to legitimacy (Polk and Kobrin, 1972: 21-22):

> First, such access starts from the assumption that young people, including the troublesome, have positive resources to contribute to the community. This assumption is quite different than the classical rehabilitation programs, which begin with the premise that the youth has a problem which must be identified and corrected.
>
> Second, the program proceeds immediately to place the young person in an active role where something valuable is contributed, rather than in a passive role where some service is provided.

Third, it is located within a legitimate institution, i.e., the school, a crucial factor in the formation of legitimate identities.

Fourth, the experience can be organized quite easily so that a mix of "good" and "bad" youth is possible.

Fifth, the activity constitutes diversion, both in the sense that it is not connected with the court process and in that legal coercion is not present, i.e., the program is purely voluntary.

Programs of the kind suggested by Polk and Kobrin have rarely been put into action, and certainly not in full-blown form. Instead, diversion efforts have most frequently been a continuation of the individualized-clinical approach. Let us examine some of the diversion variants and kindred efforts.

Diversion and Youth Services Bureaus

The forerunner to diversion programs was the youth services bureau, originally suggested in The President's Commission on Law Enforcement and Administration of Justice (1976) recommendations. After reviewing evidence on the juvenile court and its shortcomings, the commission argued for a reduced role for the court and suggested the creation of youth services bureaus.

The youth services bureau concept was far from clear and unambiguous. For one thing, the recommendation that community services be coordinated by the bureau assumed that there is a wealth of services to be coordinated when, in fact, the lack of such agencies and services has been an impediment to successful juvenile court work.

A number of authorities have taken note of defects in the youth services bureau concept (Seymour, 1972; Polk, 1971). For example, Polk noted that the original concept in the commission report was relatively vague in nature. He observed that what emerged was a variety of structures all calling themselves youth services bureaus. Some engaged in community organization activities; some stressed community organization coupled with caseworker services to juveniles; still others emphasized group work techniques with street gangs; and a fourth pattern centered around the coordination of existing welfare agencies in the community.

One body of information regarding youth services bureaus in operation was reported by Elaine Duxbury (1971), concerning nine experimental bureaus that were established in California communities in 1969. Each of these bureaus had a managing board appointed by the county delinquency prevention committee. The intervention activities provided by the nine bureaus centered around individual and family counseling.

Duxbury indicated that the bureaus provided services to over 1800 youngsters during a nine-month period in 1970. However, the most significant finding was that (Duxbury, 1971: i): "Although it was anticipated that the bulk of referrals would be from law enforcement and probation, only about one-third of the youth served have been from these sources." Not all of the bureaus received the same proportion of cases from the police, for in one of them over three-fourths originated with the police, while in another less than 5 percent of the cases came from the police. Even so, in all but one bureau, one-third or less of the referrals were from law enforcement agencies. Instead of being an alternative to the court to which court referrals were sent, thereby reducing the population of officially processed youths, the youth services bureaus dealt primarily with a separate group of young-sters. The net result is that the bureaus generated a larger group of juveniles coming to the attention of the official agencies than if they had not existed—the reverse of what these structures were envisioned as accomplishing!

In a later report of these same bureaus, Duxbury (1972) asserted that while it was anticipated that they would center their efforts upon diversion of cases from the court and upon coordination of existing community resources, the nine bureaus varied quite markedly in the extent to which they actually accomplished these goals. During an eighteen-month period in 1970-1971, they dealt with 4000 new cases, with more than 900 of them coming from law enforcement agencies. In some instances, the proportion of police agency referrals increased over this time period, but in others police referrals became a small portion of the caseload over the study period. Moreover, the bureaus received most of their referrals from parents or from youths seeking services on their own, even though these agencies were intended to siphon off police and court referrals and reduce the population of juveniles sub-jected to official intervention.

Nejelski (1976) reported statistics from a national survey in which over 60 percent of the directors of youth services bureaus defined diversion as the primary objective of their agencies. Nonetheless, only 25 percent of the youngsters in those programs were "in immediate jeopardy of the juvenile justice system," which appar-ently meant that they would have been subject to court intervention had they not been sent to a youth services bureau. On the basis of these findings, Nejelski (1976: 98) concluded that "youth services bureaus may be following the established pat-tern of service agencies which, suffering from the battle fatigue of dealing with the hard-to-treat recidivists they were set up to help, increasingly turn their attention to more malleable children whose only offense is an administrative determination of predelinquency."

Varieties of Diversion Programs

Although federal funding of youth services bureaus has been discontinued, agencies of this general form continue to exist in many communities, forming part of the system of diversion programs. However, the theme of diversion has spawned a host of other diversion efforts as well.

One well-publicized diversion venture was found in the Sacramento County 601 Diversion Project which dealt with court referrals for violations of section 601 of the California Welfare and Institutions Code (Baron, Feeney, and Thornton, 1973; Lundman, 1984: 84-92). This part of the code defines a collection of status offenses for which youngsters can be referred to court. In practice, this provision is most commonly used in cases of runaways, truants, and children said to be beyond parental control.

The Sacramento County Project provided short-term family crisis intervention services to a randomly assigned sample of youths and their parents after the youngsters had come to court attention, with an eye toward solving the parent-child conflicts that had led to court referral in the first place. These crisis intervention efforts were carried out instead of putting the youth referrals through further court handling. By contrast, another sample of cases was given regular court handling. The results of the experiment showed that in the first nine months of the project over 800 referrals were processed successfully in the crisis intervention program; only eighteen youths (2.2 percent) had petitions filed against them while over 20 percent of the control subjects were held for formal court action. Additionally, a larger proportion of youths who had been subjected to regular court practices became involved in further trouble during a follow-up period than did the wards who had been provided the crisis intervention assistance.

Some would not define the Sacramento project as a diversion program because youngsters were handled by probation officers within the juvenile court structure rather than being sent to some organization outside the official justice system. However, a large number of programs that have been identified as diversion efforts are similar to this one, for they have been inaugurated and operated by the police or by court workers.

Enthusiasm for the Sacramento project must be tempered in the light of the relatively narrow eligibility limits imposed on it. Out-of-county and out-of-state juveniles were not included, nor were juveniles with another case pending in court, youths already on probation, and certain other cases. In all, about 40 percent of all 601 referrals were judged by the program administrators to be ineligible for diversion.

A good deal of evidence on existing diversion programs can be found in a study of seventy-four programs in California conducted by the California Youth Authority (Palmer, Bohnstedt, and Lewis, 1978). That research found that 51 percent of the divertees in these programs had been sent there by the police or probation departments. Presumably, had diversion agencies not existed, these youngsters would have been directed into the juvenile justice machinery. However, 49 percent of the diversion cases were youths who had not been processed by the police or courts; instead, they had been referred by parents, schools, or were self-referrals.

These figures showing a large number of divertees who were not, in fact, diverted from justice system processing bear out the fears of some commentators who have suggested that diversion may serve to "widen the nets" rather than to reduce the number of youngsters who are singled out for attention. Many have drawn attention to the possibility that diversion may come to be used most often as an alternative disposition for youths who would normally be ignored entirely by the justice system in the absence of a diversion program, with few youngsters who would normally be processed through the justice machinery being diverted.

This California study found that family counseling was the form of intervention to which most divertees were exposed, for three-fourths of the diversion programs centered around family therapy. Individual and group counseling were other frequently encountered forms of diversion programming. In short, most of the programs were patterned after the individualization-clinical model rather than on a youth development-youth advocacy format.

In a subsequent analysis of the results produced by a sample of fifteen programs out of the total group of seventy-four, Palmer and Lewis (1980) found that although recidivism was lower on the part of diverted youths than was true of those who had not been diverted, no single program type or program setting was optimal for all diversion-appropriate cases. In short, they recommended a diversified set of diversion strategies involving "different strokes for different folks."

Malcolm Klein (1979) has conducted a searching examination of diversion and deinstitutionalization programs that have been launched in the United States. Deinstitutionalization is taken up later in this chapter. Klein argued that the evidence indicates that neither of these reform movements has been adequately implemented. His discussion enumerated five major impediments or shortcomings of existing programs.

According to Klein, these reform efforts have rarely been based upon program models or theoretical justifications that have been developed from the knowledge about delinquency. Instead, most have grown up in an *ad hoc* fashion, rather than being informed by social science findings concerning the nature and etiology of youthful lawbreaking.

Klein also drew attention to the fact that diversion and deinstitutionalization programs have often been centered on inappropriate clients. The California survey of diversion efforts in that state provided evidence on that point. After reviewing a large number of programs, Klein (1979: 165-66) concluded that "the bulk of 'diversion clients' are young people who are normally counseled and released by the police, if indeed they have any dealings with the police."

A third shortcoming of these reform ventures is that most of them have provided insufficient and/or inappropriate services to the youngsters who have been processed in them. Klein's review indicated that in the vast majority of these endeavors, clients received few if any services from the agencies. Also, the evidence indicated that the majority of these programs represent the continuation of the individualization-problemization tradition of social service delivery. Klein also noted that much professional resistance to these reforms has been encountered, with the result that many of the programs that have been launched have been sabotaged in one way or another by justice system employees. Finally, many of these reform ventures have been located in inappropriate settings, as for example when diversion efforts are located in a juvenile hall or police station.

Klein's assessment of the diversion and deinstitutionalization reform movements was a pessimistic one. He argued that experiences to date indicate that many of these programs have failed as reforms. Many of them appear to have led to "alternative encapsulation," in which juveniles are merely shifted from one controlling agency to another, rather than being moved away from surveillance and justice system supervision. In addition, diversion programs in particular have often resulted in "widening of the nets," with large numbers of juveniles who would have been ignored in times past being drawn into some part of the justice machinery.

The Impact of Diversion

What can be said about the effectiveness or ineffectiveness of diversion? Is it the case that some kinds of diversion programs work with certain kinds of offenders while others do not? What do the results show regarding the impact of these programs upon offenders? We have already taken note of the findings from the Sacramento 601 project and some other diversion efforts in California. The California survey of diversion programs (Palmer, Bohnstedt, and Lewis, 1978) indicated that 25 percent of the divertees and 31 percent of a comparison group were rearrested during a six-month follow-up period, a statistically significant but relatively slight difference in favor of diversion. Most of the positive impact of diversion was achieved by only three projects which provided more intensive services than did the others.

Gibbons and Blake (1976) examined nine diversion programs for which some kind of outcome evidence was available. They concluded that there was insufficient evidence in the nine studies for one to have much confidence in diversion arguments and contentions.

On the positive side, Feldman, Caplinger, and Wodarski (1983) have presented a detailed body of evidence concerning an experimental treatment project, carried on at a Jewish community center facility in the St. Louis suburbs. This project was focused upon "antisocial" youngsters, that is, juveniles who were involved in a variety of kinds of disruptive or annoying behavior, not all of which would qualify as delinquent conduct. Also, these antisocial youths were referred to the project from a variety of sources, including schools, the court, and other agencies. However, most appeared to be youngsters who would normally be brought under court control; thus the project can be considered a diversion effort.

In this project, some boys with records of antisocial conduct were placed in groups composed largely of nondelinquent peers, while other antisocial youngsters were assigned to groups made up of other misbehavers. A third collection of youngsters without records of antisocial conduct was used as a comparison or control group. The central aim of the project was to discover whether (Feldman, Caplinger, and Wodarski, 1983: 7) "the bad apple spoils the good ones or, conversely, do the latter exert a beneficial influence on the former?" Also, it was designed to find out whether experienced social group workers would have greater impact upon groups than would workers who are relatively inexperienced.

About 18 percent of the subjects who originally entered the program dropped out of it in the first two weeks, while another 18 percent of the enrollees did not continue in the program beyond the initial eight-week baseline period. Experienced group workers managed to bring about behavioral changes on the part of the youths in their groups, while the inexperienced workers failed to achieve these results. Variations in group work techniques were not related to behavioral change, nor did variations in group composition make much difference in program outcomes. Finally, although many of the boys who were treated in groups did seem to be less involved in antisocial conduct at the end of the project period, no evidence was presented showing that *delinquent behavior* was reduced.

Advocates of diversion of youths into community-based programs would do well to take note of the review of a large number of these endeavors that has been carried out by William Wright and Michael Dixon (1977). They reviewed several thousand reports on programs that had been conducted between 1965 and 1974, but only ninety-six of these contained empirical evidence on the impact of these ventures. These ranged over a variety of activities: juvenile court efforts, volunteer programs, individual and group counseling, social casework, streetworker programs, community area projects, educational and vocational programs, and a number of others as well. Wright and Dixon indicated that positive outcomes were recorded for some of these programs, while others produced negative outcomes or no impact. However, virtually all of the research evaluations of these projects were methodologically flawed, so that they contain little or no persuasive support for any form of community treatment.

Mixed reports on diversion continue to appear. Pogebrin, Poole, and Regoli (1984) have discussed a diversion project in Colorado which involved comparisons between an experimental group of diverted youths and a control group who received regular juvenile justice system handling. The diversion program administered individual, parental, and/or family counseling to the diversion cases. According to Pogebrin, Poole, and Regoli, the recidivism rates for the diverted cases were lower than those for the control cases.

On the other hand, Rojek and Erickson (1981-82) examined a diversion program for status offenders in Arizona and came to pessimistic conclusions about it. There was much conceptual and operational ambiguity in the program, and also, one of the key assumptions on which it was based was in error, namely, the belief that status offenders move on to engage in serious crimes if their delinquent tendencies are not "nipped in the bud" at an early stage. Most important, Rojek and Erickson reported that the utilization of community-based programs in place of the juvenile court produced a good deal of competition among agencies for clients and also that juveniles were retained for excessive lengths of time in these programs. Rojek and Erickson were unable to find much evidence indicating that these programs provided attitudinal or behavioral change on the part of divertees. They concluded that (Rojek and Erickson, 1981-82: 263):

> It is becoming increasingly clear that diversion is a fad which serves multiple and conflicting goals. An unintended consequence of the labeling school's attack on the juvenile court has been the inference that the community is the basic resource for rehabilitation and delinquency prevention. Community-based treatment is presumed to be more efficacious than court-based treatment. However ... the concept of community has been poorly opera-

tionalized, particularly in terms useful for public policy. The diversion ideology emphasizes the return of an offender to the community without careful consideration as to what capacity the community has for rehabilitating the offender. Indeed, there is some evidence suggesting that diversion of a youthful offender to a community agency may have negative consequences. Preliminary evidence from this study indicates that some community agencies were less tolerant and more punitive than the juvenile court itself. It is not inconceivable that adolescents need to be protected or diverted *from* some community-based strategies that may be more stigmatizing or punitive than the formal agencies of social control. Diverting a delinquent to the community may in some instances constitute a form of incarceration. (Emphasis in the original.)

It will probably be some time before this controversy over diversion and its effects has run its course. One indication that the argument is likely to rage on can be found in a pair of recent papers by Binder and Geis (1984) and Kenneth Polk (1984). Binder and Geis have argued that sociologists have been too quick to dismiss diversion as a failed experiment in correctional intervention and have ignored positive evidence indicating that diversion works. According to Binder and Geis, this premature rejection of diversion can be explained in terms of the disciplinary narrowness of sociologists, their distrust of the police, and their overidentification with underdogs, in this case, delinquents. Polk has responded directly to these allegations, in the main by reviewing much of the same empirical evidence that we have considered in this chapter. Polk's (1984: 648) assessment of that evidence is that it indicates that diversion has often failed to achieve the goal of getting juveniles out of the juvenile justice machinery, and instead, has expanded the size of the juvenile justice system and the behavior that comes under its control. While in our opinion Polk emerged as the clear winner in this quarrel, it is likely that others will be persuaded of the Binder and Geis thesis.

DEINSTITUTIONALIZATION: EMPTYING TRAINING SCHOOLS

We have already examined some programs that have been tried out in the United States as alternatives to sending delinquents off to state training schools. For example, Chapter 12 commented upon milieu treatment in Highfields, a small residential facility in New Jersey that was developed as an alternative to the large state reformatory to which serious delinquents were conventionally sent. Let us take a look at some more recent efforts in this same general direction (Empey, 1967).

The Provo and Silverlake Experiments

The Provo project was an experimental endeavor carried out in Provo, Utah (Empey and Erickson, 1972). The central theory on which the program was based held that court-processed serious delinquents are usually from lower-income homes, are characterized by failure in school and in work roles, and join delinquent groups in order to attain social, emotional, and economic goals not otherwise available to them. Although the architects of this experiment conceded that the home life of youths may also have had something to do with their drift into misbehavior, the designers of the project were principally concerned about altering the current identifications and involvement of offenders with other antisocial group members. Empey (1967: 38) has summarized the theoretical foundations of this project:

> Postulates for intervention, therefore, suggested that a program should try: (1) to make the delinquent group the target of change—that is, attempt to change shared standards, points of view, rewards, and punishments; (2) to give the delinquent group a stake in what happens to its members by permitting participation with staff in solving problems, exerting controls, and making basic decisions; and (3) to open up conventional opportunities to delinquents in the school, the world of work, and other conventional institutions.

The program activities involved in the Provo experiment included gainful employment of youths in the community, attendance at school, and participation in daily group meetings built around the tactics of guided group interaction. These efforts were conducted in the community, so that the Provo subjects lived at home while participating in the program.

The Provo project design involved the experimental group of cases who received the special intervention, a control group of cases who were placed on probation in the community, and another control group of training school wards.

Unfortunately, the results from this project did not provide much basis for exuberant optimism about programs of this kind. The data on program impact showed that the experimental subjects were more frequently recorded as successes than were probationers who were similar to the experimental cases but who had been under supervision prior to the experiment. More specifically, approximately half of the preexperiment probationers avoided being rearrested in the first six months after release from probation, while 73 percent of the cases initially assigned to the Provo experiment and 84 percent of those who completed the program remained free from subsequent arrests. However, the control group probationers who were on probation at the time of the Provo project showed the same success rate of 73 percent as did the cases assigned to the experimental treatment! When dropouts from the Provo experiment are counted as program failures, the success rate of probation was as high as that for the experiment.

The probationers and experimental cases did show a higher rate of postrelease success when compared to wards who had been released from training schools. However, this comparison is contaminated in that the incarcerated youths probably were not entirely comparable to those youngsters who were on probation or in the project. The incarcerated controls came from the entire state of Utah, including Salt Lake City, while the experimental group contained only juveniles from the much smaller community of Provo.

A second experimental venture that was closely related to the Provo project was the Silverlake experiment, conducted in Los Angeles by La Mar Empey and

Steven Lubeck (1971). This project dealt with boys who were under the control of Boy's Republic, a private training school in that city. The offenders in this experiment were repeaters over the age of fifteen. Some of them were assigned randomly to a special community-based treatment program, while others were subjected to the regular regimen of institutional care in Boy's Republic.

The experimental program in this case involved assignment of youths to a small residential facility which held no more than twenty juveniles at a time. The experimental cases attended daily group meetings in the group home, attended a local high school during the week, and went to their own homes on weekends. The underlying theory that informed this experiment paralleled that of the Provo project; delinquency is a response to strains emanating from the failure of juveniles to achieve success in the schools and other conventional institutions in the community.

Again, as in the case of the Provo venture, the findings relative to program success or failure did not show the experimental strategy to be superior to more traditional approaches. To the contrary, somewhat larger numbers of experimental subjects either became reinvolved in lawbreaking or were runaways from the program than was the case with the control subjects. Althought the experimental program failed to show positive results, it ought to be noted that this was a very careful, detailed, and sophisticated study. As a consequence, Empey and Lubeck were able to pinpoint some of the reasons for the ineffectiveness of the experimental program. They maintain that the Silverlake experiment was not intensive enough to overcome the problems of family disorganization, school failure, and defective work skills characteristic of both experimental and control subjects.

Deinstitutionalization

During the late 1960s and early 1970s in the United States, widespread reductions in institutional populations, both in adult prisons and in training schools took place. For example, in California, early plans to build more maximum security institutions were being abandoned and prisons such as San Quentin had their inmate numbers sharply curtailed.

This decarceration trend for adult prisons began to be reversed in 1973, with the result that prison populations burgeoned in the past decade. However, the reduction of numbers of incarcerated juveniles has continued. At the same time, it would be well to note that Krisberg, Litsky, and Schwartz (1984) have drawn attention to gross regional variations in incarceration practices. Their examination of data from the fifty states uncovered large disparities in admission rates, average length of incarceration, and confinement in adult institutions across the states. Also, the individual states vary markedly in expenditures per child, conditions of confinement, and extent of chronic overcrowding. On this same point, Krisberg and Schwartz (1983) have indicated that most of the decrease in the population of institutionalized offenders between 1974 and 1979 was due to the reduction of involvement of status offenders within the juvenile justice system. The primary consequence of removing status offenders from official handling was the large decline of female admissions to public corrections facilities, with male admissions remaining stable or actually increasing between 1974 and 1979.

The most dramatic case of deinstitutionalization to date took place in Massachusetts, where the entire system of state custodial institutions for delinquents was abandoned. Lloyd E. Ohlin, Robert B. Coates, and Alden D. Miller (1974) have presented a case history analysis of this series of events in that state (also see Ohlin, Miller, and Coates, 1977; Coates, Miller, and Ohlin, 1978). In the period prior to closure of the institutions there were ten state custodial facilities for juveniles in Massachusetts. These institutions had failure rates of between 40 and 70 percent, measured in terms of recidivism. They also indicated that Massachusetts moved in three stages to deinstitutionalization, from emergence of concern for correctional change, to efforts to reform institutional treatment, and finally to community treatment in place of institutionalization of delinquents.

The reform of this state system of juvenile corrections began in the period from 1965 to 1968, in which six major critical studies of the system were produced, each one indicting it for major defects of one kind or another. In 1969, Governor Sargent appointed a new director of the Division of Youth Services, Dr. Jerome Miller. Miller's initial efforts centered around the introduction of reforms into existing institutions, so that he had such practices as shaving the heads of wards discontinued. More important, he also endeavored to restructure the training schools in the direction of making them into therapeutic communities, much in the fashion of some of the experiments such as the Fricot Ranch project that we examined in Chapter 12. Director Miller also instituted other reforms such as establishment of coeducational programs in some training schools, development of community involvement in training school programs, and reduction of the average length of stay in the institutions from about eight months to three months. However, the chronicle of developments for this program indicates that these reform efforts were plagued by inadequate financing and other impediments of that sort. Finally, the director's steps toward institutional reform were also vigorously and bitterly resisted by many of the staff members in the institutions. As a consequence, the director ultimately became disillusioned about the prospects for reforming institutions in the direction of therapeutic communities.

Director Miller's disenchangement with institutional reform ultimately led to drastic moves toward deinstitutionalization. Three of the major training schools in the state were completely closed in 1971-1972 by means of a swift and fascinating "kidnapping" of the wards by college student volunteers who spirited them away from the training schools to alternative placements such as foster homes and group homes.

All of the long-term custodial institutions in this state were eventually shut down, and were replaced by community treatment centers, forestry camps, foster homes and group homes, and an array of other community-based services operated on a regional basis, rather than under central state control.

Much of the significance of the Massachusetts experience is captured in the summary statement of Ohlin, Coates, and Miller (1974: iii) in which they alleged that:

> The Massachusetts Department of Youth Services has undertaken a major pioneering step in correctional reform. It has demonstrated that radical changes in the official ideology, policies, and programs of treatment for delinquent youth can be achieved in a short period of time. Evidence thus far indicates that youth perceive the new system as more helpful and staff more responsive. There is widespread agreement that it encourages more humane treatment of youth and offers staff more resources for integrating youth into their home communities. Whether in the long run these new policies and programs will result in better protection for troubled youth is still to be determined.

The California Community Treatment Project

We have already taken note of some aspects of the Community Treatment Project in California. Chapter 10 included a detailed discussion of Interpersonal Maturity Levels theory which provided much of the theoretical base for the experiment. Chapter 12 examined some of the results from the experiment, noting that the parole violation rate for experimental cases was lower than for the control subjects who had been sent to training schools. However, we also saw that these differential results in favor of community treatment appear to reveal more about the behavior and predispositions of the parole agents than they do about the paroled wards.

Additional information on the Community Treatment Project is contained in a summary of that project by Ted Palmer (1974). Part I of that project was conducted from 1961 to 1969, involving offenders committed to the California Youth Authority for the first time, while Part II of the project was conducted in the period after 1969.

During the lifetime of Part I of the project, 686 experimental subjects were released directly from the reception center to parole, while 326 control wards were randomly assigned to training schools. The experimental wards were then assigned to caseloads holding no more than a dozen male or female parolees, where they were subjected to "differential treatment" based upon their I-Levels classification. The differential treatment tactics matched certain types of wards with types of treatment agents thought to be particularly skilled in dealing with those youngsters. Some of the experimental subjects received individual or group-centered therapy, others were placed in foster homes or group homes, while still others received a special school program carried on in the Community Treatment Project community center.

Clearly, this was a complex, large-scale, sophisticated experimental venture. Not surprisingly, the results were similarly complex. The reports on this program indicated that wards diagnosed as neurotic seemed to receive the most benefit from the community project, while power-oriented or passive subjects gained less from participation in it. The general results for the two groups of experimental and control wards indicated that 44 percent of the community-treated and 63 percent of the training school subjects became recidivists in a 24-month follow-up period. That is, fewer of the community-treated wards became reinvolved in delinquency during the two years after participating in the experimental treatment. Similarly, 50 percent of the control subjects and 69 percent of the community-treated wards received a favorable discharge from the California Youth Authority within five years after having been released to the community on parole. On the other hand, the favorably discharged community subjects averaged 1.67 convictions for new offenses in the four-year period after being released from the Youth Authority, in contrast to a rate of 1.42 convictions for the control subjects. Hence the posttreatment results were not entirely clear-cut. Also, the reader should keep in mind the point noted in Chapter 12, to the effect that the more impressive parole period behavior for the community cases was in part the result of more lenient decisions on the part of their parole agents in instances where they observed their clients in delinquent acts.

One major development occurred in the community treatment program which was not anticipated in the original research-experimental design. As originally conceived, the experimental program would provide intensive treatment to youngsters in the community. Presumably, most of them would reside with their parents and be subjected to supervision and intervention experiences in their home communities. However, Lerman (1975) has dissected the research reports which flowed out of this project and has pointed to the widespread use of detention as a "treatment" stratagem in the program. He indicated that about 90 percent of the youths in the community program were detained away from their homes at least once during their parole period. By contrast, relatively few juveniles received intensive treatment of any kind. Temporary detention of cases in detention centers or the California Youth Authority reception center clinic was employed so frequently that Lerman (1975: 41) concluded that, on the basis of the evidence, "the primary program element actually experienced by CTP wards was short-term confinement and not intensive-treatment services." In this instance, deprivation of liberty came to be redefined through semantic wizardry as a therapeutic measure!

One other observation well worth noting has to do with the costs of community treatment. In many cases, advocates of community-based corrections seem to be persuaded more by the potential for cutting costs in these endeavors than by the therapeutic rationale behind them. The expectation is that we can obtain more treatment for less money through community efforts. But in the case of this project, the cost per offender in the experimental program actually exceeded the average cost of maintaining a ward in a state training school!

Part II of this project, inaugurated in 1969, involved initial assignment of certain wards to training school, followed by treatment in the community. The argument in this portion of the project was that direct release into the community was appropriate for some cases and inappropriate for others. Accordingly, four experimental groups were created: (1) delinquents thought to need institutionalization and who were sent to a training school; (2) youths thought to need institutionalization but who were released to the community; (3) delinquents thought to not require a stay in a training school but who were placed in one; and (4) youths thought to not require commitment and who were not committed. The results indicated that youths in category 2 did poorer on parole than those in category 1, who appeared to require an initial period of incarceration and who received it. The two groups who appear to not require institutionalization apparently behaved relatively similarly on parole.

Summary

Most of the material that we have examined regarding programs of reducing institutional populations or of closing down custodial facilities fails to offer convincing proof that the alternatives to incarceration are markedly more effective than the policies they replace. On the other hand, these programs work at least as well as institutionalization. Then, too, in the usual case, community treatment is probably less costly than is training school commitment. The California Community Treatment Project was relatively costly, but this experiment involved a level of treatment intervention, including small caseloads, that was more intensive than is true of most community treatment ventures. In summary, these findings indicate that there is little to be said for incarcerating juveniles in custodial facilities but much to be said for community handling of offenders.

DELINQUENCY PREVENTION

Delinquency prevention is a massive topic—to do full justice to it an entire book ought to be devoted to the subject. All manner of stratagems have been suggested to prevent juvenile misconduct, with specific suggestions being based on markedly different theoretical premises. As a result, the question of delinquency prevention is complex, confusing, and multifaceted (Stratton and Terry, 1968; Amos and Wellford, 1967; MacIver, 1966; Lundman, 1984).

Our commentary on delinquency prevention in this chapter will be cursory and incomplete. For example, the subsequent discussion will not deal in detail with the matter of prediction of predelinquents, as advocated by Sheldon and Eleanor Glueck (1950) among others. Those investigators argued that available techniques will allow prediction of likely delinquents among children as young as six or three years of age. Further, they contended that intervention efforts ought to be undertaken with children at this early age in order to divert them from law-breaking paths.

These contentions of the Gluecks are preposterous, given the facts about delinquency that have been reported in previous chapters of this book. We have seen that delinquency is a matter of degree; most youngsters engage in some amount of it during the adolescent years. Then, too, much delinquency arises out of situational pressures and forces of that kind, rather than being the consequence of such predictors as family disorganization in the early life experiences of the child. We have seen that much juvenile misconduct is fleeting or transitory in character, so that there would appear to be less urgency to intervention actions than suggested by the Gluecks. For these and other reasons, proposals to engage in early detection and intervention activities fly in the face of common sense. Finally, critics of these predictive ventures have demonstrated quite conclusively that prognostic techniques are extremely crude and imprecise and markedly overpredict delinquency proneness in the case of youngsters who will probably will grow up to be relatively nondelinquent (Toby, 1968).

Forms of Delinquency Prevention

Although the specific features of delinquency prevention efforts vary from one program to another, it is possible to sort these endeavors out into a small number of general types. For example, Helen Witmer and Edith Tufts (1954) analyzed a number of prevention programs undertaken some years ago. They indicated that a number of preventive ventures have centered around improving social environments, either through bringing about alterations in the organization of neighborhoods and social areas or through provision of expanded recreational opportunities. A second general grouping of projects has been educational or therapeutic in character, in which the "target" of prevention consists of predelinquent individuals or small groups, rather than neighborhoods. Preventive social work assistance, street gang work, and child guidance clinics are all examples of this second direction.

Prevention Through Environmental Change

The focus of attention in programs of environmental change is usually more upon *rate-producing* factors in criminality than upon alteration in the attitudes and behavior of specific deviants or upon eradication of the forces impelling them to deviation. Environmental programs frequently center around such things as improvements in community social organization and do not directly involve lawbreakers in a first-hand effort to change them.

One famous and pioneering example of environmental change which was structured to achieve both preventive and therapeutic ends was the Chicago Area Project (Witmer and Tufts, 1954; Kobrin, 1959; Finestone, 1976; Sorrentino, 1977). This project had the dual objectives of preventing delinquency and crime in certain Chicago neighborhoods and also of rehabilitating parolees in these areas. One summary of the goals and assumptions of the Chicago Area Project is the following (Witmer and Tufts, 1954: 11):

> The Chicago Area Project operates on the assumption that much of the delinquency of slum areas is to be attributed to lack of neighborhood cohesiveness and to the consequent lack of concern on the part of many residents about

the welfare of children. The project strives to counteract this situation through encouraging local self-help enterprises through which a sense of neighborliness and mutual responsibility will develop. It is expected that delinquency will decline as youngsters become better integrated into community life and thereby influenced by the values of conventional society rather than those of the underworld.

The underlying theory involved in the Chicago Area Project was that delinquent and criminal values arise from lack of means or lack of access to success goals, predominantly monetary ones, experienced by the majority of persons in lower-class underprivileged slum areas. As a consequence of this frustration, the attachment to conventional norms by some persons is eroded away. Some of these individuals begin to utilize deviant and illegal techniques to attain success goals. At the same time, a general situation of personal isolation exists in these areas in which people refrain from meddling in the affairs of others. The result is a community lacking in social cohesion and embodying conflicts of values, and in which criminal and noncriminal norms exist in the same area, so that tolerance of deviant behavior is widespread. Symbiotic connections between carriers of criminal culture and ostensible nondeviants are commonplace, such as the links between junk dealers and predatory delinquents or among police officers, "policy" gambling figures, and "respectable" citizens.

Proceeding upon this version of slum "disorganization" theory, the Chicago Area Project viewed the key to prevention as self-help activities on the part of noncriminal citizens in slum areas. High-status residents were encouraged to utilize their leadership potential in the program, for only in this way could a sense of neighborhood cohesiveness develop. As a corollary of this approach, outside leadership of community efforts was kept to a minimum. The core of this self-help effort was the neighborhood center, a recreational and educational facility staffed mainly by community residents. However, the Area Project involved a number of other related activities such as discussion groups on child problems. In summary, the Chicago Area Project strived to develop an "antidelinquency society" in slum areas so that pressures toward delinquent and criminal conduct would be reduced in those areas. Moreover, a recent, detailed examination of the project (Schlossman, Zellman, Shavelson, Sedlak, and Cobb, 1984) indicated that it achieved considerable success in organizing local communities and reducing delinquency.

Another example of environmental change is found in the Midcity Project, a delinquency control venture carried on in a lower-class district of Boston between 1954 and 1957 (Miller, 1962). It proceeded upon a sophisticated and complex theoretical rationale, so that in this case the project provides an excellent example of the direction in which treatment ventures might move.

The several kinds of activities constituting the Midcity undertaking all flowed out of a "total community" philosophy regarding control and inhibition of illegal actions among juveniles in working-class urban neighborhoods. The central thesis on which this project was based was that delinquent behavior is generated, encouraged, and facilitated by a number of structural features of the community, rather than primarily by personality disturbances among adolescents. These premises led to action programs directed at the community, family units, and delinquent gangs. These three societal units were regarded as importantly involved in the genesis and stimulation of delinquent actions by juveniles.

The community segment of this program involved two major parts. Attempts were made to "beef up" community citizens' groups so that they might be able to take more effective action against local difficulties of one sort or another. In addition, efforts were made to obtain improved cooperation among various professional agencies in the community having dealings with adolescents, such as churches, schools, and police and probation departments. The intention of these several lines of work was to bring together a number of formerly separate, diffuse, and overlapping services so that their efforts might lead to maximum results.

In the area of family services, the project directed attention toward "chronic problem" families in the area. That is, a number of families with long records of involvement with different social agencies were given intensive doses of psychiatric social work intended to make them less dependent upon agencies for assistance in problem solving.

The major effort of this project centered around delinquent gangs and involved the detached-worker stratagem that was employed in many American cities in the 1950s and 1960s. This part of the project was particularly well-developed, for all the workers were professional persons with degrees in social work. Each agent handled only a single group and therefore was able to engage in intensive interaction with his gang. Finally, each worker had psychiatric consultation available to him, so that he was armed with more methods than usual among detached workers.

The Midcity Project was a demonstration effort, planned to operate for a specific, limited time period and to serve as an illustration of the efficacy of the "total community" approach. Unfortunately, the project failed to achieve a significant reduction in delinquency. The impact of the undertaking was measured in three different but related ways. Trends in disapproved forms of customary behavior, such as certain sexual activity patterns, were studied, as were trends in illegal behavior and court appearance rates for the delinquent gang members included in the project. When evaluated in these terms, the project appeared not to have achieved any significant reduction in delinquency.

In his discussion of this project, Miller pointed out that some parts of the Midcity Project were more completely "tested" than were others, in that some of the segments were developed to a greater extent. The negative impact findings apply most emphatically to the citizens' council operation and to the streetworker activities, for these were the most highly developed. Miller also noted that the project did accomplish certain important results even though it failed to achieve delinquency reduction. For one, the establishment of the project had a calming effect upon the community, which had been fearful and excited about a presumed wave of delinquent behavior. In addition, neighborhood social organization was left in a more highly developed state than when the project began, so that the area was better prepared to deal with community problems, including delinquency, in the future.

A third case of environmental change efforts is the Mobilization for Youth project (1961) in New York City, which was developed from a theoretical base of opportunity theory as articulated by Cloward and Ohlin (1960). This project was an exceedingly ambitious and multidimensional one involving thirty separate "action" programs in the four major areas of work, education, community, and group service.

One of the dominant orienting themes of Mobilization for Youth was that lower-class youngsters must be provided with genuine opportunities to behave in nondeviant ways if they are to be prevented from engaging in delinquent behavior. Mobilization for Youth was also predicated upon the assumption that local residents must be implicated in delinquency prevention. Effective control of delinquent behavior cannot take place solely through the operation of programs imposed upon the community from the outside. In short, the view was that an organized, anticriminal community must be developed in order to create pressures toward nondelinquent juvenile behavior.

Mobilization for Youth was constituted of a number of specific programs of action in the areas of work, education, community, and group services, carried on in a section of New York City's Lower East Side. One of the major parts of the total program concerned "the world of work," in which an "Urban Youth Service Corps" provided paid employment for several hundred unemployed, out-of-school youths. The participants were employed in neighborhood conservation endeavors and a number of other kinds of work activities. This youth corps was intended to create work skills and pro-work attitudes on the part of boys who were initially almost unemployable because of their lack of skills and attitudes. Also in the work segment, a "Youth Jobs Center" acted as a coordinated agency which attempted to find permanent employment for boys who had completed a work experience in the Urban Youth Service Corps.

Mobilization for Youth also involved many activities in education including teacher visitation programs and a laboratory school to demonstrate effective methods of teaching lower-income students. Another educational project was called the "Homework Helper" program, in which academically successful lower-class high school students were hired to tutor elementary school students.

The community part of the Mobilization for Youth project involved efforts to strengthen a preexisting community organization, the Lower East Side Neighborhoods Association. Various specific tactics were also employed to create social organizations among formerly unaffiliated, isolated community residents. In the same way, indigenous operations such as store-front churches, not usually a part of neighborhood organization efforts, were drawn into collaborative area development efforts.

Another feature of Mobilization for Youth concerned assistance of various kinds to "problem" families in the project area. Local "helping stations" called "Neighborhood Service Centers" were established in four Lower East Side areas. These were created to help families obtain social services, redress housing complaints, and so forth.

Finally, the group service section of the Mobilization for Youth project was involved in supplementing services to delinquent gangs that were formerly provided in the New York City Youth Board. Thus detached-worker activities were part of the total program, although not operated specifically by Mobilization for Youth. Another group effort centered around three "coffee shops" which were cultural centers set up in store fronts to serve as more desirable substitutes for conventional neighborhood hangouts. Finally, relatively young children in the project area were drawn into an "Adventure Corps" which was designed to provide appealing non-delinquent activities and experiences for delinquency-prone youngsters.

The Mobilization for Youth program was imaginative as well as theoretically sophisticated. As such, it provided a model for community-level prevention activities. At the same time, it should be noted that the effectiveness of such multi-faceted efforts is very difficult to evaluate (cf. Brager and Purcell, 1967). Given the many different components that are included, it becomes very difficult to untangle the specific contribution, if any, that each part makes to delinquency prevention.

Prevention Through the Schools

The proposal that schools be given an expanded role in curbing delinquency has probably been the most frequently voiced suggestion for prevention of youthful misconduct. However, the various programs and suggestions that have grown up have been based on two divergent sets of premises. One batch of proposals assumes that American schools are viable and healthy institutions but are called upon to deal with a group of unruly, predelinquent youths. Accordingly, in this "rotten kids" view, schools are asked to use their positive resources in the effort to curb the delinquent tendencies of aberrant, nonconformist youths. In the second grouping of preventive proposals involving schools, the schools themselves are seen as fundamentally implicated in delinquency because of various shortcomings and inadequacies within the American educational institution. It follows from these "rotten schools" premises that the target of change ought to be schools and their programs, more than unruly, recalcitrant youths. Let us examine some of these child-centered proposals first, after which our attention will center upon proposals to remake the schools into agencies that are less harmful to youths.

One child-centered venture in the schools was conducted in Columbus, Ohio, involving 1000 sixth graders who were rated by their teachers as delinquents or potential delinquents (Reckless and Dinitz, 1972). One portion of this group was assigned to self-contained seventh-grade classes staffed by special teachers, while the other subgroup was placed in regular classes. The objective of the special experimental treatment was to change the negative self-images of the predicted predelinquents and thereby bring about reduced delinquency rates. However, the follow-up data from the experiment indicated that it had failed to effect the hoped-for alterations.

A large and somewhat parallel venture was conducted in Kansas City, Missouri by Winston M. Ahlstrom and Robert J. Havighurst (1971). In this case, youths regarded as potential delinquents were given a program featuring work experience along with a modified academic program designed to reduce delinquent tendencies on the part of the youngsters. The study began in 1961 and continued to 1969. The study design involved 13- to 14-year-old boys from all inner-city schools in that community. The boys who received the experimental treatment were placed in special classrooms and also participated in supervised work experiences, while the control cases received the regular school program. The results from this project offer little encouragement to those who would use the schools in these ways. Ahlstrom and Havighurst (1971: 5) indicated: "The findings, reported in detail in this book, indicate that only about 1/4th of the boys profited from the work-study program." Regarding the overall impact of the program, Ahlstrom and Havighurst (1971: 2) concluded: "By 1969 it was apparent that all these efforts and expenditures of money had remarkably little effect."

Another of these educational failures took place in Washington, D.C. and involved school dropouts (Jeffery and Jeffery, 1969). It unsuccessfully endeavored to prepare them to pass the high school equivalency test, get a meaningful job, and earn a legitimate living. Still another of these educational-work experience projects (similarly a failure) has been reported by James C. Hackler (1966). His project took place in Seattle in four inner-city, low-income housing areas. The study involved four experimental groups who received some form of work experience and/or remedial education, along with a control group that was involved in a regular school program. The experimental subjects did not differ significantly from the control cases in involvement in delinquency, following participation in the experiment.

There are numerous explanations for the failure of these educational ventures to curb delinquency. One account would have it that most of these activities have not continued for a long enough period to achieve lasting effects on potential delinquents. But another viewpoint argues that the target of intervention efforts is incorrect—that the focus of change ought to be upon schools. This line of reasoning contends that American schools are inadequate and delinquency producing (Polk and Schafer, 1972).

Consider the detailed set of recommendations by Polk and Schafer for basic reforms in the structure of American education, reforms that would be designed to achieve a number of ends including delinquency reduction. Among other things, they argued that available local and federal school funds must be employed toward making a number of changes in school organization in order to increase the educational life-chances of high delinquency-risk groups of students. These modifications would center around such things as expansion of preschool programs in low-income areas, innovations in instructional methods and teaching practices, retraining of teachers, increasing the rewards to teachers for working in low-income area schools, and creating diversity among student groups. They also suggested that schools need to work diligently toward providing better linkages between the secondary school curriculum and the changing world of work, particularly for those pupils who are not likely to go on to college. Students must be assisted toward making intelligent career choices in the direction of jobs that will offer them a sense of meaningful participation in adult life. Polk and Schafer argued that schools must develop means for recapturing, reequipping, recommitting, and reintegrating students who fall behind in school or who engage in deviant behavior. It will not do for schools to cleanse themselves of difficult students by kicking them out of the school, thereby foreclosing on their possibilities of attaining challenging adult work careers.

There was nothing markedly novel in these suggestions and recommendations by Polk and Schafer; instead, these are eminently sensible implications for reform that can be drawn from the large literature that has accumulated in recent years documenting the inadequacies of modern urban schools. But their recommendations represent a large order indeed. Unfortunately, it is difficult to discern many steps taking place currently in American education in the direction suggested by Polk and Schafer.

SUMMARY

This chapter has examined some of the newer approaches to delinquency that have developed in recent years, including moves toward diversion of youths out of the juvenile justice system, community treatment, and preventive efforts. The material considered here adds up to the following conclusions:

1. Juvenile courts and juvenile institutions have failed to be markedly effective in drawing delinquents out of further involvement in lawbreaking, hence diversion of youths from the official juvenile justice system appears to have much to recommend it. At the same time, meaningful alternatives to the court must be devised to provide services to juveniles who are in need of them.

2. Alternatives to institutionalization have been devised, including small, specialized, community-based residential facilities, as well as intensified counseling and probation programs. Although these programs appear to achieve results comparable to those of training schools, it has yet to be demonstrated that these alternatives are markedly more successful than training schools. However, most of these programs are less expensive than institutionalization, which is a strong argument in their favor.

3. Large-scale delinquency prevention efforts directed at fairly massive kinds of environmental change have been conducted in some number in the United States. Although some of the evidence on the impact of such programs is negative, the results, if any, of most of these ventures are unclear. In considerable part, these programs have been so complex and multifaceted as to defy evaluation.

4. Programs centered about changing the behavior of "predelinquents" through special school and work experiences have failed to show any positive results.

REFERENCES

AHLSTROM, WINSTON M. and HAVIGHURST, ROBERT J. (1971). *400 Losers*. San Francisco: Jossey-Bass.
AMOS, WILLIAM E. and WELLFORD, CHARLES F., eds. (1967). *Delinquency Prevention*. Englewood Cliffs, N. J.: Prentice-Hall.

BARON, ROGER, FEENEY, FLOYD, and THORNTON, WILLIAM (1973). "Preventing Delinquency Through Diversion: The Sacramento 601 Diversion Project." *Federal Probation* 37 (March): 13-18.
BINDER, ARNOLD and GEIS, GILBERT (1972). *Youth Services Bureaus in California: Progress Report Number 3.* Sacramento: Department of the Youth Authority.
BINDER, ARNOLD and GEIS, GILBERT (1984). "*Ad Populum* Argumentation in Criminology: Juvenile Diversion as Rhetoric." *Crime and Delinquency* 30 (October): 624-47.
BRAGER, GEORGE A. and PURCELL, FRANCIS P., eds. (1967). *Community Action Against Poverty.* New Haven: College and Universities Press.
CARTER, ROBERT M. (1968). *Middle-class Delinquency: An Experiment in Community Control.* Berkeley: School of Criminology, University of California.
CARTER, ROBERT M. and KLEIN, MALCOLM W., eds. (1976). *Back on the Streets.* Englewood Cliffs, N. J.: Prentice-Hall.
CLOWARD, RICHARD A. and OHLIN, LLOYD E. (1960). *Delinquency and Opportunity.* New York: Free Press.
COATES, ROBERT B., MILLER, ALDEN D., and OHLIN, LLOYD E. (1978). *Diversity in a Youth Correction System: Handling Delinquents in Massachusetts.* Cambridge: Ballinger.
CRESSEY, DONALD R. and McDERMOTT, ROBERT A. (1974). *Diversion from the Juvenile Justice System.* Washington, D.C.: U.S. Government Printing Office.
DUXBURY, ELAINE B. (1970). *Youth Services Bureaus in California: A Progress Report.* Sacramento: Department of the Youth Authority.
EMPEY, LA MAR T. (1967). *Alternatives to Incarceration.* Washington, D.C.: U.S. Department of Health, Education, and Welfare.
EMPEY, LA MAR T. and ERICKSON, MAYNARD L. (1972). *The Provo Experiment: Impact and Death of an Innovation.* Lexington, Mass.: Lexington.
EMPEY, LA MAR T. and LUBECK, STEVEN G. (1971). *The Silverlake Experiment.* Chicago: Aldine.
FELDMAN, RONALD A., CAPLINGER, TIMOTHY E., and WODARSKI, JOHN S. (1983). *The St. Louis Conundrum.* Englewood Cliffs, N. J.: Prentice-Hall.
FINCKENAUER, JAMES O. (1982). *Scared Straight! and the Panacea Phenomenon.* Englewood Cliffs, N. J.: Prentice-Hall.
FINESTONE, HAROLD (1976). *Victims of Change.* Westport, Conn.: Greenwood.
GIBBONS, DON C. and BLAKE, GERALD F., JR. (1976). "Evaluating the Impact of Juvenile Diversion Programs." *Crime and Delinquency* 22 (October): 411-20.
GLUECK, SHELDON and GLUECK, ELEANOR (1950). *Unraveling Juvenile Delinquency.* Cambridge: Harvard University Press.
HACKLER, JAMES C. (1966). "Boys, Blisters, and Behavior–The Impact of a Work Program in an Urban Central Area." *Journal of Research in Crime and Delinquency* 3 (July): 155-64.
JEFFERY, C. R. and JEFFERY, I. A. (1969). "Dropouts and Delinquents: An Experimental Program in Behavior Change." *Education and Urban Society* 1 (1969): 325-36.
KLEIN, MALCOLM W. (1979). "Deinstitutionalization and Diversion of Juvenile Offenders: A Litany of Impediments," pp. 145-201. In Norval Morris and Michael Tonry, eds. *Crime and Justice, 1978.* Chicago: University of Chicago Press.
KOBRIN, SOLOMON (1959). "The Chicago Area Project–A Twenty-Five-Year Assessment." *Annals of the American Academy of Political and Social Science* 322 (March): 19-29.
KRISBERG, BARRY, LITSKY, PAUL, and SCHWARTZ, IRA (1984). "Youth in Confinement: Justice by Geography." *Journal of Research in Crime and Delinquency* 21 (May): 153-81.
KRISBERG, BARRY and SCHWARTZ, IRA (1983). "Rethinking Juvenile Justice." *Crime and Delinquency* 29 (July): 333-64.
LEMERT, EDWIN M. (1971). *Instead of Court: Diversion in Juvenile Justice.* Rockville, Md. National Institute of Mental Health.
LERMAN, PAUL (1975). *Community Treatment and Social Control.* Chicago: University of Chicago Press.
LUNDMAN, RICHARD J. (1984). *Prevention and Control of Juvenile Delinquency.* New York: Oxford University Press.
MacIVER, ROBERT (1966). *The Prevention and Control of Delinquency.* New York: Atherton.
MILLER, WALTER B. (1962). "The Impact of a 'Total Community' Delinquency Control Project." *Social Problems* 10 (Fall): 168-91.

NEJELSKI, PAUL (1976). "Diversion: Unleashing the Hound of Heaven?" pp. 94-118. In Margaret K. Rosenheim, ed. *Pursuing Justice for the Child*. Chicago: University of Chicago Press.

OHLIN, LLOYD E., COATES, ROBERT B., and MILLER, ALDEN D. (1974). "Radical Correctional Reform: A Case Study of the Massachusetts Youth Correctional System." *Harvard Educational Review* 44 (February): 74-111.

OHLIN, LLOYD E., MILLER, ALDEN D., and COATES, ROBERT B. (1977). *Juvenile Correctional Reform in Massachusetts*. Washington, D.C.: U.S. Government Printing Office.

PALMER, TED (1974). "The Youth Authority's Community Treatment Project." *Federal Probation* 38 (March): 3-14.

PALMER, TED, BOHNSTEDT, MARVIN, and LEWIS, ROY (1978). *The Evaluation of Juvenile Diversion Programs: Final Report*. Sacramento: Department of the Youth Authority.

PALMER, TED and LEWIS, ROY (1980). "A Differentiated Approach to Juvenile Diversion." *Journal of Research in Crime and Delinquency* 17 (July): 209-29.

POGEBRIN, MARK R., POOLE, ERIC D., and REGOLI, ROBERT M. (1984). "Constructing and Implementing a Model Juvenile Diversion Program." *Youth and Society* 15 (March): 305-24.

POLIER, JUSTINE WISE (1979). "Prescription for Reform: Doing What We Set Out to Do?" Pp. 212-44 in La Mar T. Empey, ed. *Juvenile Justice: The Progressive Legacy and Current Reforms*. Charlottesville, Va.: University Press of Virginia.

POLK, KENNETH (1971). "Delinquency Prevention and the Youth Services Bureau." *Criminal Law Bulletin* 7 (July-August): 490-511.

POLK, KENNETH (1984). "Juvenile Diversion: A Look at the Record." *Crime and Delinquency* 30 (October): 648-59.

POLK, KENNETH and KOBRIN, SOLOMON (1972). *Delinquency Prevention Through Youth Development*. Washington, D.C.: U.S. Department of Health, Education, and Welfare.

POLK, KENNETH and SCHAFER, WALTER E., eds. (1972). *Schools and Delinquency*. Englewood Cliffs, N. J.: Prentice-Hall.

RECKLESS, WALTER C. and DINITZ, SIMON (1972). *The Prevention of Juvenile Delinquency: An Experiment*. Columbus: Ohio University Press.

ROJEK, DEAN G. and ERICKSON, MAYNARD L. (1981-82). "Reforming the Juvenile Justice System: The Diversion of Status Offenders." *Law and Society Review* 16 (2): 241-64.

ROSENHEIM, MARGARET K. (1976). "Notes on Helping Juvenile Nuisances," pp. 43-66. In Rosenheim, ed. *Pursuing Justice for the Child*. Chicago: University of Chicago Press.

RUBIN, H. TED (1979). "Retain the Juvenile Court? Legislative Developments, Reform Directions, and the Call for Abolition." *Crime and Delinquency* 25 (July): 271-98.

SCHLOSSMAN, STEVEN, ZELLMAN, GAIL, SHAVELSON, RICHARD, SEDLAK, MICHAEL, and COBB, JANE (1984). *Delinquency Prevention in South Chicago: A Fifty-year Assessment of the Chicago Area Project*. Santa Monica: Rand.

SCHUR, EDWIN M. (1973). *Radical Nonintervention*. Englewood Cliffs, N. J.: Prentice-Hall.

SERRILL, MICHAEL S. (1979). "Police Write a New Law on Juvenile Crime." *Police Magazine* 2 (September): 47-52.

SEYMOUR, J. A. (1972). "Youth Services Bureaus." *Law and Society Review* 7 (Winter): 247-72.

SORRENTINO, ANTHONY (1977). *Organizing Against Crime*. New York: Human Sciences Press.

STRATTON, JOHN R. and TERRY, ROBERT M., eds. (1968). *Prevention of Delinquency*. New York: Macmillan.

THE PRESIDENT'S COMMISSION ON LAW ENFORCEMENT AND ADMINISTRATION OF JUSTICE (1967). *The Challenge of Crime in a Free Society*. Washington, D.C.: Government Printing Office.

TOBY, JACKSON (1968). "An Evaluation of Early Identification and Intensive Treatment Programs for Predelinquents," pp. 99-116. In John R. Stratton and Robert M. Terry, eds. *Prevention of Delinquency*. New York: Macmillan.

WITMER, HELEN L. and TUFTS, EDITH (1954). *The Effectiveness of Delinquency Prevention Programs*. Washington, D.C.: U.S. Department of Health, Education, and Welfare.

WRIGHT, WILLIAM E. and DIXON, MICHAEL C. (1977). "Community Prevention and Treatment of Juvenile Delinquency: A Review of Evaluation Studies." *Journal of Research in Crime and Delinquency* 14 (January): 35-67.

chapter 14 _____

THE STUDY
OF DELINQUENCY:
MAJOR CONCLUSIONS

INTRODUCTION

The preceding thirteen chapters of this book dealt with a large quantity of descriptive material, delinquency theories, and research evidence on juvenile lawbreaking. But this text was designed to be more than simply a compendium of information on youthful deviance. Over forty propositions or generalizations were sprinkled throughout the preceding chapters, involving some major conclusions that can be inductively drawn out of the existing delinquency literature. Some of these generalizations are broad, others are specific, and all of them are stated in relatively imprecise terms. Similarly, some of these conclusions are supported by a large measure of empirical data, while the empirical accuracy of others is less clear. However, we would argue that these propositions are about as precise as is warranted by the delinquency data at hand. These broad conclusions can be taken as organizing hypotheses or contentions which might be subjected to more detailed study in delinquency investigations in the future.

These generalizations can be brought together in a single package in the form of a propositional inventory about delinquency. The most general propositions have been listed first, and under them are arranged the more specific contentions which they summarize. The first Arabic number in parentheses following each generalization refers to the chapter in which it originally appeared; the second Arabic number designates the order in which it was originally presented.

PROPOSITIONAL INVENTORY ON DELINQUENCY

The Extent and Patterning of Delinquency

American delinquency statutes empower juvenile courts to intervene in cases in which youngsters are involved in violations of criminal statutes. But in addition juvenile court laws specify that youths can be made wards of the court and dealt with as delinquents if they are involved in various status offenses enumerated under omnibus clauses of these statutes. The behavioral categories identified in status provisions are extremely general and ambiguous ones, e.g., ungovernability, waywardness, or immorality. In effect, these laws put nearly all youths "at risk" of being dealt with as delinquents, for they could be interpreted broadly so as to sweep nearly all juveniles into the courts. (2-1)

Behavior which violates delinquency statutes is commonplace; nearly all youngsters engage in at least some delinquent behavior during their juvenile careers. At the same time, marked variations occur among offenders in the extent and seriousness of their involvement in lawbreaking. Some juvenile delinquents engage in repetitive, serious forms of misconduct, while others are implicated only in relatively innocuous kinds of misbehavior. (1-1)

> Less than 5 percent of the juveniles in this nation are actually referred to juvenile courts in any single year, although a larger portion of the youth population comes to court attention sometime during the adolescent years. Only about one-half of these referrals are regarded by court officials as serious enough to warrant the filing of a petition and a court hearing; the other half are dealt with informally. (3-1)
>
> Police agencies come into contact with almost twice the number of children known to the court. In general, they refer the serious cases to juvenile courts, while disposing of the less serious offenders informally, within the department, by admonitions and warnings. (3-2)
>
> A fairly large number of offenders is dealt with by public and private social agencies in the community, but many of the individuals they process are also known to the juvenile court. The majority of the cases known to agencies but which are unknown to the court are relatively petty ones. (3-3)
>
> Large numbers of youths at all social class levels and in all kinds of communities engage in acts of misconduct and lawbreaking which remain hidden or undetected. In this sense, nearly all juveniles are delinquent in some degree. However, many of the deviant acts of hidden delinquents are the kinds which would often be handled informally or ignored if reported to the juvenile court. (3-4)
>
> Not all of the hidden delinquency in the United States is petty and inconsequential. An indeterminate but important number of serious delinquencies is enacted by juveniles who manage to stay out of the hands of the police or courts. (3-5)
>
> There is no significant social class patterning to petty misconduct, that is, juveniles at all social class levels are about equally involved in minor acts of lawbreaking. Additionally, involvement in petty delinquency is often limited to a few episodes of misconduct. However, those youths who engage in serious, repetitive forms of juvenile misconduct are most frequently from

lower-income backgrounds; thus serious delinquency is related to social class position. (4-1)

Juvenile misbehavior is more common among boys than among girls, but lawbreaking is considerably more frequent among females than is indicated in police arrest data or juvenile court statistics. Involvement in delinquency on the part of juvenile females has apparently increased somewhat in the past decade or so. Although females are less often involved in misbehavior than boys, both groups tend to engage in a varied, diversified collection of delinquent acts, rather than in specialized forms of lawbreaking. (4-2)

Females who become the subject of attention by the police or juvenile courts are often charged with sexual delinquency or with activities which adults in the community suspect are indicators of incipient sexual promiscuity. Police arrest data and juvenile court statistics both underestimate the extent of delinquent involvement among young females and apparently convey a distorted picture of the nature of female lawbreaking. (4-3)

Juvenile misconduct is a phenomenon made up of a number of points along a behavioral continuum: one-time offenders, petty offense recidivists, serious offense recidivists, career offenders, and "ultra-hard core offenders." (4-4)

Although a considerable number of youthful offenders are individuals who get into the hands of the police or appear in juvenile courts solely on status offense charges, many of the persons who are at one time or another charged with status offenses also engage in acts of delinquency that involve violations of the criminal law. (4-5)

Violent offenders are infrequently encountered, even among delinquents who have come to the attention of the police or the juvenile court. Also, juvenile violence often occurs in the course of another crime such as robbery, rather than in the form of random outbursts of aggression by "young monsters." (4-6)

Although delinquents are found throughout neighborhoods and communities in American society, organized group patterns of subcultural lawbreaking tend to be concentrated in urban working-class neighborhoods. (8-1)

The most common form of subcultural misconduct is the "parent subcultural" pattern of delinquency characterized by behavioral versatility rather than specialization. (8-4)

Although the United States apparently has the highest delinquency rate of all nations of the world, juvenile misconduct has increased markedly in many other nations since World War II. The most pronounced increases in delinquency rates have been in European countries. Although the reasons for the upsurge of juvenile lawbreaking are numerous and complex, they center around recent industrialization, the growing complexity of societies and the breakdown of the old social order, and the increasing affluence of European countries. (11-1)

In a number of ways, delinquency in England is similar to juvenile lawbreaking in the United States; males are much more frequently involved in misconduct than are females, juvenile lawbreaking occurs in loosely structured gangs, and it is most common in deteriorated, working-class neighborhoods similar to American "delinquency areas." Juvenile delinquency has apparently increased markedly in England since World War II. Juvenile offenders in that country are frequently drawn from the group of alienated, uncommitted, working-class youths who are involved in the pursuit of short-run, hedonistic pleasures. Most of them do not show a marked sense of status frustration. (11-2)

Police and Court Handling of Delinquency

Those offenders who get into the hands of the police and are processed through the juvenile justice system tend to be the more career-oriented delinquents who are involved in serious misconduct. However, the factors which enter into police apprehension, court referral, and other decisions are several; therefore the offender's prospects of becoming identified as a juvenile delinquent are partially dependent upon characteristics of police officers, police departments, court personnel, and community influences. (1-2)

Police officers deal with large numbers of juveniles, most of whom they handle informally without court referral. The decision to take a youngster to the court is often in part a legalistic one. Those offenders who have been engaged in serious or repetitive acts of lawbreaking are most likely to be turned over to the court. (5-1)

Police dispositions are related to demographic characteristics of offenders; thus males, blacks, lower-income youths, and older boys are most frequently dealt with formally by court referral. These demographic characteristics enter into dispositions in part because males, older boys, blacks, and lower income youngsters appear to be disproportionately involved in serious, repetitive delinquencies. However, some studies have indicated that the police behave differentially toward blacks, sending more of them to juvenile court than they do white youths involved in comparable offenses. (5-2)

Police perspectives which hold that some groups, such as ghetto blacks or other lower-class minorities, are particularly criminalistic probably lead to differential attention directed at them. Serious offenses by members of these groups then have a higher likelihood of being observed by the police and being acted upon. If so, the higher official crime and delinquency rates of these groups may be partially the product of police sentiments, rather than a reflection solely of basic differentials in involvement in crime. (5-3)

In those instances of less serious delinquency, police officers often base their disposition decisions upon the demeanor of the offender. Youths who affect particular clothing styles or who are defiant and hostile tend to be referred more often than polite and contrite youngsters. It is probably also true that demeanor bears some relationship to seriousness of offense; those youths who have engaged in the most innocuous offenses are also most deferential toward policemen. This may explain why police dispositions show a general association with seriousness of misconduct. (5-4)

Police departments show variations in organizational structure over time. Differences in organizational makeup between police agencies also exist. Accordingly, police dispositions of offenders, including juveniles, are far from uniform throughout the country. (5-5)

Youths who have been involved in offenses which arouse members of the community, who commit law violations which result in sizable financial suffering to the victims, and who are repeaters, most often receive official and relatively punitive dispositions from the court, including being placed on the transmission belt to the training school. Ethnic characteristics, sex, age, and other demographic variables seem to be related to dispositions through their interconnection with offense variations, although there is also some indication that court decisions sometimes reflect discrimination against blacks and youths from lower socioeconomic backgrounds. (5-6)

Other factors play a part in probation dispositions. In some agencies probation officers are attuned to the personality characteristics of wards and their decisions are based in part on this consideration. It also appears that ethnic factors are more directly involved in dispositions in some cases; therefore on occasion minority group members are dealt with more severely than comparable white youths. (5-7)

Contrary to fairly widely held beliefs that women of all ages receive preferential treatment in the juvenile and adult justice systems, the evidence points to discriminatory decision making against juvenile females, at least in a number of juvenile courts. (5-8)

Delinquency Causation

Most juvenile offenders are relatively normal youths in terms of personality structure in that they do not exhibit aberrant motives, deep-seated psychological tensions, or other marks of personality disturbance. Officially processed delinquents often do show hostile attitudes, defiance of authority, and characteristics of that kind. However, these are not personality dimensions which are indicative of psychological maladjustment. In addition, some of these personality characteristics may be the product or result of correctional handling. At the same time, some youthful lawbreakers do show atypical personality patterns to which their delinquency may be a response. (1-3)

Delinquency laws forbid a wide range of conduct, so that there are a number of behavioral patterns within the offender population. (1-4)

The specific causal process that leads to one particular kind of delinquent behavior involves a number of etiological variables and may differ from that which produces another delinquent pattern. In this sense, delinquent behavior is the product of multiple causation. At the same time, it is possible to identify the different etiological processes which are involved in various forms of delinquency. (1-5)

Delinquent behavior is learned behavior, acquired in the processes of socialization. Accordingly, the primary causes of juvenile misconduct are not to be found in biological factors (even though biological variables may play an indirect role in juvenile lawbreaking). (1-6)

The learning of delinquent patterns is maximized in a criminalistic society such as the United States. Much delinquent behavior in the competitive, materialistic American society is societally generated and takes the form of direct and indirect assaults upon property. (1-7)

Some delinquent patterns are mainly the consequence of social class variations in socialization and life experiences, along with other social-structural variables. In particular, situations in which legitimate avenues to the attainment of common American goals and values are blocked are importantly involved in certain forms of crime and delinquency. Those members of disadvantaged social groups and social strata may be relatively commonly involved in deviant behavior which is a response to their social and economic deprivation (1-8)

Some delinquent patterns are produced by familial and other socialization experiences which are not class-linked or class-specific. Among these are parental rejection and deviant sexual socialization. These kinds of experiences occur at all social class levels. (1-9)

> Neighborhoods in which gang delinquency is common share a number of eco-logical characteristics, including a high proportion of economically disadvan-taged residents, but economic disadvantage alone does not appear to account for high rates of subcultural delinquency. Rather, poverty and low income are most likely to result in gang delinquency if those conditions are accompanied by low social integration. (8-2)
>
> Strain, as measured by perceptions that occupational and other long-term opportunities are limited, does not appear to be an important factor in pro-ducing delinquent conduct. However, the perception of limited opportunities relative to the more immediate concerns of adolescents is related to delin-quent behavior. (8-3)
>
> Rates of delinquent behavior across neighborhoods and communities re-flect, in part, the degree to which the social institutions in them are effective in fostering social integration of residents into the fabric of community life. In turn, a lack of social integration or social disorganization often reflects the economic and social disadvantages faced by residents in low-income areas, but it may also be a result of other social-structural factors such as residential mobility, ethnic or religious composition of the neighborhood, or the density of the population living in the community. (7-1)
>
> The social institutions that serve as the primary socializing agents in society, particularly the family and the school, are important influences in fostering bonds between individuals and conventional society and thus in reducing the probability of delinquent behavior. The role of the school is particularly crucial since this is the arena in which adolescents spend a good deal of their time. (7-2)
>
> Although social bond and its constituent elements are related to the proba-bility of delinquent behavior, other factors must also be taken into account to adequately explain delinquent conduct. For one, those youths who show low levels of social bonding are also more likely to associate with others who have committed delinquent acts. In turn, association with delinquent others is strongly related to delinquent behavior, with the result that elements of the social bond are related both directly and indirectly to delinquent behavior. (7-3)
>
> Adolescents who have associated with peers who have committed delin-quent acts are more likely to engage in delinquent behavior than those who have not had such associations. There is some evidence to suggest that the association occurs prior to the delinquent behavior, although this has not been firmly established. (9-1)
>
> Definitions favorable to the violation of the law are related both to having delinquent associations and committing delinquent behavior. There is some uncertainty as to whether definitions favorable to the violation of law act as an intervening influence between delinquent associations and delinquent behavior. (9-2)
>
> The process identified by social learning theory may explain how associat-ing with delinquent others increases the probability of delinquent behavior among adolescents. (9-3)
>
> A model hypothesizing that social bonding variables increase the prob-ability of associating with delinquent others, which in turn increases the probability of delinquent behavior, has been shown to be the most tenable explanation of delinquent conduct. (9-4)

Offenders who are engaged in bizarre forms of misconduct and/or who exhibit pathological patterns of personality structure are relatively uncommon among the total population of juvenile offenders and are even relatively infrequently encountered within the group of officially handled lawbreakers. "Behavior problem" kinds of delinquency include firesetting and deviant sex behavior, but the most common form of behavior problem lawbreaking is individualistic aggression. In turn, aggressive behavior comes in various gradations, so that unsocialized aggressive offenders are markedly deviant individuals, while other delinquents exhibit aggression and personality problems of a milder form. (10-1)

Overly aggressive offenders are the product of situations of parental rejection, with the most severe forms of aggression stemming from conditions of early and marked rejection and the milder patterns from less marked instances of parental rejection. (10-2)

The Impact of Correctional Experiences Upon Offenders

The defining agencies (police, probation services, courts, and so forth) play a part both in the definition of deviants and in the continuation of deviant activities. The result of apprehension and treatment may be quite contrary to the expected result. In other words, although one official function of correctional agencies and processes is the reformation of the offender, the actual outcome may often be the isolation of the person, reinforcement of deviant patterns and rejection of society by the offender, the final result being nonreformation. (1-10)

The various segments of the correctional apparatus such as police bureaus, juvenile courts, probation agencies, and other organizations may have direct effects upon delinquent careers. However, little research has been conducted concerning the impact of these structures upon delinquency. This subject represents one about which investigation is sorely needed. (12-1)

Training schools in the United States vary in terms of size, institutional aims, and other conditions, but all appear to be principally structured around the goal of control of wards. Even in treatment-oriented training schools the major focus of attention is upon conformity, prevention of escapes, and ends of that kind. (12-2)

Training schools do not usually succeed in restraining wards from further lawbreaking, for parole violation rates from these places are quite high. Half to over three-fourths of first admissions to juvenile institutions apparently become reinvolved in delinquent conduct, although considerably fewer of them continue into adult criminality. (12-3)

Training schools apparently have benign effects upon wards processed through them; although "reformation" does not usually occur, neither does the institution directly contribute to recidivism. Most training school wards emerge from these places with no more criminal skills or more serious antisocial attitudes than when they entered. (12-4)

Diversion, Community Treatment, and Prevention of Delinquency

Juvenile courts and juvenile institutions have failed to be markedly effective in drawing delinquents out of further involvement in lawbreaking; hence diversion of youths from the official juvenile justice system appears to have much to recommend it. At the same time, meaningful alternatives to the court must be devised to provide services to juveniles who are in need of them. (13-1)

Alternatives to institutionalization have been devised, including small, specialized, community-based residential facilities, as well as intensified counseling and probation programs. Although these programs appear to achieve results comparable to those of training schools, it has yet to be demonstrated that these alternatives are markedly more successful than training schools. However, most of these programs are less expensive than institutionalization, which is a strong argument in their favor. (13-2)

Large-scale delinquency prevention efforts directed at fairly massive kinds of environmental change have been conducted in some number in the United States. Although some of the evidence on the impact of such programs is negative, the results, if any, of most of these ventures are unclear. In considerable part, these programs have been so complex and multifaceted as to defy evaluation. (13-3)

Programs centered about changing the behavior of "predelinquents" through special school and work experiences have failed to show any positive results. (13-4)

SUMMARY

These claims stand as a body of contentions which are supported by some empirical evidence, but which need further research scrutiny. Hopefully, this explication of the major threads in the sociological perspective on delinquency will stimulate and guide future work. Let us also hope that books such as this will lead to greater concentration on theoretically informed research and less on the sort of mindless, eclectic "fast gathering" which has plagued the field of delinquency study in the past.

INDEX

A

Abbott, Daniel J., 194, 204, 209
Adams, Larry D., 130, 132
Adams, Reed, 164, 167
Adams, Stuart N., 182, 192
Adams, W. Thomas, 220, 237
Adamson, La May, 233, 236
Aday, David P., Jr., 31
Adler, Freda, 70, 71, 81
Ageton, Suzanne S., 58, 59, 62, 68, 81, 152, 166, 168
Aggressive delinquents, 187-90
Ahlstrom, Winston M., 264, 265, 266
Ahrenfeldt, R. H., 195, 209
Aichhorn, August, 12, 13, 174, 191
Akers, Ronald L., 114, 117, 161, 162, 163, 164, 165, 167, 168, 169
Amos, William E., 259, 266
Andrews, Kenneth H., 161, 162, 168
Approaches to delinquency, 10-12
Aries, Phillipe, 4, 13
Arnold, William R., 98, 103
Austin, James, 16, 25, 35, 84, 85, 87, 92, 104
Austin, Roy L., 182, 191
Axelrad, Sidney, 18, 103

B

Bailey, Walter C., 225, 237
Bandura, Albert, 163, 168, 188, 189, 191
Barker, Gordon H., 207, 209, 220, 237
Baron, Roger, 248, 267

Bates, P. B., 133
Bates, Ronald, 86, 104
Bates, William, 122, 132
Baum, Martha, 230, 237
Baur, E. Jackson, 197, 198, 209
Bauzer, Riva, 89, 95, 104
Becker, Howard S., 215, 237
Beker, Jerome, 181, 191
Bendix, Reinhard, 152
Bentler, Peter M., 128, 132, 162
Berger, M., 186, 192
Beverly, Robert F., 229, 237
Binder, Arnold, 253, 267
Biological theories, 11-12, 171-74
Bixby, F. Lovell, 234, 238
Black, Donald J., 87, 89, 90, 103
Blake, Gerald F., Jr., 251, 267
Body types and delinquency, 171-72
Bohnstedt, Marvin, 249, 251, 268
Bond theory, 126-29
Bordua, David J., 86, 93, 95, 103, 105, 122, 132, 139, 141, 151, 157, 168
Boyer, Paul, 4, 13
Brager, George A., 264, 267
Braithwaite, John, 67, 69, 81
Briar, Scott, 93, 94, 104
Brim, Orville G., Jr., 133
Bronner, Augusta F., 175, 192
Buffalo, M. D., 128, 132
Burgess, Ernest W., 114, 118, 121, 133
Burgess, Robert L., 162, 164, 165, 168
Bursik, Robert J., Jr., 75, 81
Burt, Cyril, 175, 192
Butler, Edgar W., 182, 192